To Steve,

with Best wishes

from

Dave Wallace

16/01/2012

US and THEM

MANCHESTER CITY versus...
EVERY OTHER CLUB from 1891/92 until 2010/11

David Wallace

King of the Kippax
25 Holdenbrook Close
Leigh, Lancs, WN7 2HL
Tel: 01942 515739
Email: dw001e8104@blueyonder.co.uk

A CIP catalogue record is available for this book from the British Library

ISBN: **978-0-9557056-1-8**

Book Designed by Andy Searle

Printed in Great Britain by Anthony Rowe Ltd

CONTENTS

ACKNOWLEDGEMENTS

Thanks to all contributors as profiled, John Leigh, and mainly Steve Worthington for proof reading plus Nigel Gregory and Ged Isaacs for some friendly game results and information.

To Sue, for all the help and support plus the brilliant profiles of the contributors. To Andy Searle for putting up with the many changes and additions, and to Gary James for providing the foreword. To Manchester City for driving me mad these last fifty odd years, and making it difficult to write about a club with "no history!"

Plus, of course, the trusty index finger of my right hand used to type the majority of this book!

I won't mention all the rock stars and groups who've inspired me over the years (Worthy was stopped from naming <u>every</u> member of <u>every</u> band who inspired him in his book *Over the Blue Moon!*) but I will say that, inevitably, *The Moody Blues* are my favourite group of all time.

Dedications are to Sue and all the family, Marnie, Danny, Kaye, Alex (who are those blokes on the front cover dad?), grandkids Heather, Joe, Ellie, Becky and our latest little star Isaac.

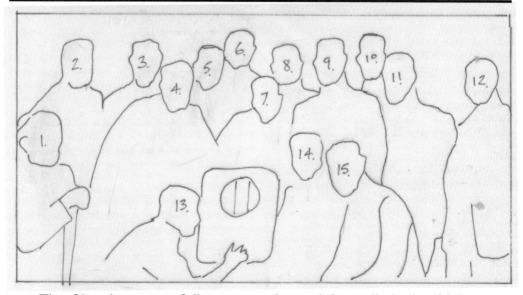

The City players, as follows, crowd round the radio in the thirties:
1. Sam Cowan 2. Billy Dale 3. Fred Tilson 4. Bobby Marshall 5. Alec Herd 6. Frank Swift 7. Eric Brook 8. Alec Bell (trainer) 9. Laurie Barnett 10. Matt Busby 11. Ernie Toseland 12. AEB Alexander (vice-chairman) 13. Jackie Bray 14. Sid Cann 15. Jim McLuckie

FOREWORD

"US and THEM" says it all really. This is a well thought-out and detailed analysis of City – "US" – and the Club's opponents – "THEM" - from the beginning of the Football League to the present day. It has been expertly written and wonderfully illustrated by Dave and Sue Wallace. Together the Wallaces have been well-known figures around the Club for many years, and since the 1980s they have been at the forefront of City's fanzine culture and fan-related initiatives.

It is often overlooked today but other than attendance at games or buying souvenirs, fans had very little opportunity to express their feelings about the Club or football in general in the early 80s, and there were certainly no outlets for fans to talk about their memories, support, and so on. Then the fanzines arrived with Dave Wallace contributing to the first City 'zine Blue Print before setting up "King Of The Kippax" – the only City fanzine still going strong today.

Once the fanzines were produced supporters could talk of their journeys to games, highs and lows of support, memorable matches, infamous defeats, supporter behaviour, ground facilities and so much more. On a personal level, the arrival of the fanzines marked the recognition that many of my own experiences and views were shared by others. I realised I wasn't the only one frustrated when the train to Barnsley was delayed, causing us to miss most of the first half, because the train in front had hit a horse somewhere near Stalybridge.

Nowadays, the City match programme, website, MANC magazine, Sky TV and the press have taken a more fan-centric approach with their style and content, and that is an interesting development, however it still doesn't achieve what supporter produced publications can. This is why I continue to be a passionate supporter of fanzines and why I believe we should all be thankful for Dave and Sue's on-going commitment to the Blue cause.

Despite around 23 years dedication to "King of the Kippax" Dave and Sue continue to give fans the opportunity to express their views.They provide an outlet that I believe we will always need. There have been plenty of times they could have walked away, or said "enough is enough", but like thousands of passionate Blues they have remained committed.

This brings me on to "US and THEM." For me this book is a wonderful addition to my City bookshelves. There have been many, many City books in recent years. Several have covered the same or similar topics, but "US and THEM" is different. It tells the story of City through the Club's opponents and therefore paints a picture that a chronological history or traditional biographical book cannot.

It has been written in a style that allows the reader to delve in. Pick a team, any team, and you'll immediately find a potted history of fixtures between the two sides and, in many cases, supporter memories of a game or games. This is an approach I really like.

When I was given a proof copy I immediately found myself scanning the chapter "H is for Halifax." As well as the facts of meetings between the two, I enjoyed reading Rob H's story of police searches and McVities digestives at the Shay, then I moved on to Simon C's story of going to Huddersfield in the 80s. These both brought back great – and not so great – memories of my own excursions to these grounds. I then leapt forward to read the section on Stoke City – my first away ground (Trevor Francis' debut in 1981) – and, well, let's be honest from then on I kept flicking backwards and forwards around the grounds from Bradford to Bilbao, Mansfield to Milan... One of my aims was to see how many memories coincided with mine, but another was to simply relive games and feelings from years gone by.

Inevitably, fans of all ages will find something to interest them in this book. Of course everyone says that when a book is produced, but for me this is especially true for this one. Obviously, anyone who lived through the nineties, the Swales years or the fifties and sixties will recognise the stories, but any newer fan (and let's be honest, City are bound to be gaining support at the moment) will get a feeling for what the Club is all about and how the game has developed from this book.

I love first hand accounts of experiences and so the supporter memories included in this book add a great deal and help to paint a picture for fans who, for whatever reason, could not attend those games. Steve P's memory of going to Vienna in 1970 is one of great interest to me. I was only two years old when that game was played and I remain envious of anyone who actually managed to travel – in difficult circumstances back then of course – across Europe to attend our first European final.

Within this book Dave has included some great memories from fans of all ages. It is a testimony to him and his quest to produce this book that there are so many of them and such a wide variety of experiences. At times this includes activities such as hooliganism. People often try to forget supporter violence these days and I'm sure most officials would love to wipe all memory of it from our consciousness. However, it was an important part of the game for many years and did impact on many aspects of the sport.

This is a very interesting book which helps to capture moments and memories from City's history that may otherwise disappear. It approaches its subject well. I first started writing on the Blues back in 1987, around the same time as the City fanzines first appeared. As I said earlier, there was very little to read on the Club back then – one of the main reasons I picked up my pen. All these years later there are plenty of opportunities to read about City, but there still remains significant gaps in Blues literature. This book fills one of those gaps, and does so with the usual level of detail, entertainment and passion that we have all come to expect from Dave Wallace.

I'm sure that in the months and years to come most of us will pick this book up to read about the Club's latest opponents, or an unfamiliar team that hits the headlines, or check whether our latest victory in the Manchester derby really is the record for that fixture, and so on.

Thanks Dave for taking the time and effort to create this encyclopedia of City and their opponents. Your efforts are appreciated and the book fully reflects your commitment.

Gary James

www.facebook.com/garyjames4

INTRODUCTION

FOR THE LAST 29 years I've had a little pocket-sized companion. I've lost countless wallets, credit cards, mobile phones, whatever, and survived their loss, but my little companion's presence has been as vital as breathing. It's nicknamed 'The Oracle', as it tells me everything I need to know about Manchester City's match results on a club by club basis. The little book has been amended, updated, admired, argued over and has always been there like a wise and truthful old friend.

I cleverly obtained an A5 hardback book from the stationery department at work to utilise in an attempt to complete this very exercise. It was 1982, Trevor Francis had left, and it was the start of a traumatic season in City's history, although for the first half of the campaign we were going well. We won our first three games, away at Norwich, and home to Stoke, as the new main stand roof was unveiled; then Watford and the unforgettable Bobby McDonald stand-in goalkeeper display.

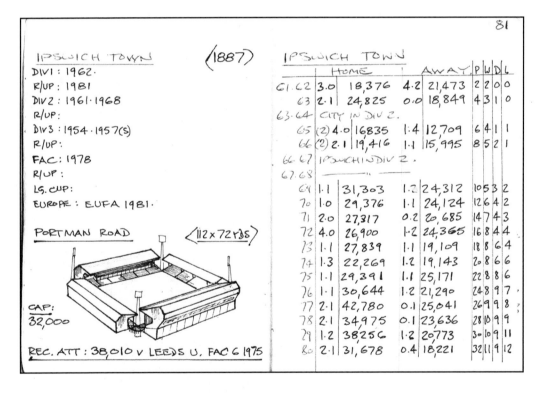

I was always fascinated by how City fared against other teams, but back in the fifties, sixties, and seventies there wasn't much information available, apart from what could be gleaned from City's programmes of the time. I therefore embarked on a mission to complete City's results against the opposition, initially for my own information.

We were still second in November when I contacted Bill Miles, City's curator, who kindly arranged for me to come into the club, where he would allow me to browse through the official season by season record books with all the dates, fixtures, results, scorers etc. It was December 1982 and I was really looking forward to the visit as a 38-year old overgrown schoolboy with a responsible job and three kids. The day dawned and I couldn't believe it as I looked out of the bedroom window to find that heavy snow had fallen. I couldn't bear the thought of cancelling the appointment, so I made the treacherous journey to Moss Side from my home in Astley. I eventually made it and Bill showed me into a cold room off the hallowed corridors where, on a table, he had put out the record books and I began my search for the vital information.

I was pleased to be able to copy out the scores and attendances missing from my little book. Wins I coloured in blue, draws yellow and losses red for easy scan and identification, whilst the pitches on the ground diagrams were, of course, coloured green.

I was joined in my lonesome quest by a student who was a QPR fan doing a similar exercise, for some reason. I recall coming across the 1950/51 City results v QPR, a 5-2 win at home and 2-1 away, which I shouted across to him indicating what a responsible and mature person I can be at times. (Not)

I'd only reached halfway through when Bill asked me to leave, saying I could return later when more time was available.

Fair enough. I did some updating, and arranged with Bill to return to complete the exercise. By this time, in January, City were still doing OK in the League, having beaten Norwich 4-1 at home and drawn 1-1 at Villa. It was January 31st 1983 though and we'd just gone out of the Cup at Brighton 0-4. Bill spotted John Bond in the corridor and shouted over to him, "How you doing John?" "Fine, Bill" he replied. Then Bill turned to me, exclaiming, "He's a great lad, John." I thought no more about it but knew that City fans were currently disgruntled with Bond, irritated by his country bumpkin attitude, general demeanour, and rumours of his affair with a lottery lady at the club.

I completed my task and returned to work elated, where I was greeted by colleagues with the words "John Bond's resigned". "Getaway," I said, "I've just seen him at the club and all seemed fine." But it was true. I was astounded, but not particularly surprised. "Too good to go down" he said on the radio later, but you just knew what was going to happen. Despite a commendable draw at Spurs on the following Saturday (where we always did well in those days) under caretaker manager John Benson, City won only three of the remaining sixteen games, West Brom away 2-0, West Ham home 2-0 and Brighton away 1-0, the penultimate game of the season. No need for me to recount what happened in the last home game of the season v Luton.

I then had a whole new division of teams to record, but City only had one new opponent to face, Cambridge United, although we did also play Torquay for the first time in the League Cup.

So I continually updated 'The Oracle' and thought no more about it, though I was once urged to publish. Its finest moment came when I was on board a plane on the 28th May 1984, flight LH 282, Frankfurt to Turin on business, and the Feyenoord team was also on board, including Johan Cruyff and Ruud Gullitt, who wasn't well known then. One of those occasions when the thought occurred that "Hey, I don't mind if this plane crashes as I'm in good company, and it'd look good on the headstone, and what an epitaph!" Anyway Johan, the great man, had a good peruse of 'The Oracle' and was impressed enough to sign his autograph. He also allowed one of my colleagues to take his photograph on the tarmac after we landed, with me in the background. Sadly, I didn't show up on the photo as my colleague had forgotten to apply the flash!

"I had twenty English pounds at the start of the World Cup in 1974 on Holland to win it," I told him. "I lost more" he said. The Oracle is now a little worse for wear but has been invaluable in the compilation of information for this book.

Fast forward to 2003 when I suggested to author and City fan Ian Penney, after an interview in the fanzine, that a book of City v the rest could prove a winner, then the format could be used for every other club in the country if necessary. Ian put it to a well known soccer book publisher in Derby, who rejected the idea out of hand, but, strangely recently, came up with a similar idea in the *Head To Head* series of books on this very subject (but no City book yet). Perhaps it hasn't proved a winner after all, although much of this book differs in content to those of that series.

So here we are at last with City v the rest. Where to start? The title – *Us and Them* is a well used phrase and is, of course, a Pink Floyd track off the phenomenal album *Dark Side Of The Moon*. There's a photo of the Floyd boys in Nick Mason's book *Inside Out* in Manchester Square, outside the old EMI building, in London, with the Wallace Collection plaque in the background. Spooky, and surely an inspirational omen?

The book begins when City entered the Alliance (League, not Building Society!) back in 1891/92, which seemed like a good idea, but I've commenced records from when City entered the Second Division in 1892.

What's included? There's background on each club we've played competitively. It's compiled in alphabetical order but some foreign clubs have letters in front of their names, like AC Milan or AC Omonia, which I've put under M and O etc., though AFC Bournemouth stay under A (we've a big B chapter!). Also, we've not played teams yet with the initials X and Z!

The different eras have been split; prior to and post World War Two up to the Premiership years, and then the Premiership years themselves up to the end of the 2010/11 season with a summary of results.

FA Cup, League and other Cup competitions, Texaco, Anglo-Italian, Full Members etc. are included. Where significant, or at random, games, scorers, attendances, players debuts and last appearances have been covered. Friendly games have also been listed, but this has been difficult, particularly after the mid 90s as only the scores for first team games seem to be available, but I've left the others in, to an extent.

Wartime games are excluded and also Lancashire and Manchester Senior Cup results as these were mainly, certainly post war, reserve team fixtures.

As always, memories play tricks and mistakes are bound to occur, so the usual cop out is to say "if you spot any get in touch", you never know there might be an update/reprint one day!

Ground diagrams are also included, only the ones where we've played, generally shown when I thought that the grounds had most character, e.g. Molineux in the fifties, or were easier to draw, with, I must admit, a little bit of licence here and there. Grounds with running tracks were a pain and those around the turn of the 20th century were usually little more than the pitch, with, maybe a rickety stand here and there, so have been omitted. A few pictures, photos, favourite programme covers, and cartoons are included here and there to break up the text where space permitted. Some connections are not exhaustive.

Personally, my initial support followed a similar path to fanatics of a similar age, I would imagine. Fired up by the Cup Finals of the mid-fifties, I attended a few games in 1955/56, a few more in 1956/57, then managed all the homes and plenty of aways from 1957/58 to the 1961/62 season. After that I played soccer at local level on Saturdays (Ringlow Park FC, shown in 1966 in the red and black striped shirts two seasons before City adopted them. I'm the goalie) and Sundays (for Caybank, the works team), so my support was limited to mid-week and season start and end matches. Marriage in 1967 and moving to Sheffield, where I played in goal for Darnall Horticultural Club, also restricted

my City support. I was, however, gradually becoming disillusioned with my playing career, generally performed on muddy pitches on top of cold, bleak, wild, rainy and windy Yorkshire and Derbyshire hills. I therefore attended a fair number of games in the 1967/68 season, the pull of City being unsurprisingly strong that year! We travelled over the Pennines in the ice and snow in the Hillman Imp (this model being mercilessly and unforgivably criticised in AC/DC's singer Brian Johnson's *Rockers and Rollers* book) with the head gasket blowing and the front end knocking, dodging sheep on the A57. Sue, my wife, attended her first game that season v Everton at Maine Road, though she generally went shopping when I attended matches in Nottingham and Leeds etc. The kids started to arrive after the 1969 Cup Final, and by the time we'd moved to Doncaster, then later to Hull, after a short stint for me in Canada, we were five strong and I went to as many matches as I could. So I've probably had different experiences than most City fans, being a bit of a loner owing to being, for a while, an 'out of towner'.

The call came though, in 1979, when I was successful with a job application and we moved back to Manchester and Astley. Alex William (no 's' geddit!), our fourth, then came along (cue the vasectomy!) and we had to move to a bigger house, so we settled in Leigh, Lancashire. This meant I was back in the old routine, attending matches home and away with daughters Marnie, Kaye, son Danny, big brother Frank and later the KOTK crew. I'd left Manchester in 1967 and returned in 1980. What does that tell you?

Hooliganism, therefore, mostly passed me by, though I seem to have been there from the beginning as it started to grow from the late fifties. You know how it was? If you wanted to avoid it a sort of sixth sense was subconsciously and instinctively developed. Travel would be by official coach or rail transport with police escorts to and from the ground. If driving I would identify safe places to park (Millwall especially) and pick safe-looking routes to and from the grounds i.e. no dark and dismal back alleys. Also I wasn't much of a drinker, my diabetes, twenty odd years of driving and pre and post match selling of the fanzine restricted that, so the match experience could be classed as a bit boring!

So this is why I've commandeered City fans to tell us their stories rather than relate too many of my own. There are a few hooligan-type tales, believe what you will, and dates don't always tally, but there are enough books on that subject plus player autobiographies already and so I've tried to capture fans' stories that are quirky, hairy, scary, funny, peculiar or interesting, rather than "we got drunk, watched the match and had a curry", which I think I've managed to do with the help of our contributors. They're all typical City fans (plus one away fan and one player!) with respect for other clubs (well maybe with one or two exceptions!) and have written in their own inimitable fan's style. Sometimes more than one tale for a club was received and has been included. If you're not in here - sorry - as we've been requesting tales for a couple of years now in the fanzine! Where were you?!

Obviously, most of the stories are post World War Two as we're led to believe that nothing much happened prior to that, with fans of opposing clubs having a jolly time with each other. Sam Bartram, Charlton's goalie, however, dispelled this myth somewhat, recalling in his auto-biography that he was once hit on the back of the head with a half house brick whilst keeping goal for Charlton!

Generally, though, City fans were too old to remember in detail or with accuracy what went on, so apologies for that, and the lack of tales of the likes of Gainsborough away in 1898, which are definitely lost in the mists of time! Some of the early and later European tales are repeats from the fanzine, but overall it's generally brand new material.

So here we go with *Us and Them*. "You're not famous anymore" was the chant to us in the lower divisions and "Are you watching Macclesfield?" was our self deprecating chant at Stoke when we went down to the third tier in 1998. "We'll never play you again" was the chant when we dropped down the divisions (reciprocated as we went back up!). We are now an established top four Premiership club after Sheikh Mansour's cash injection. We've won our first major trophy, the FA Cup, in 35 years and are playing the really big guns in the Champions League. Hopefully this book will jog a few memories as we enter our next phase of progress.

**Dave Wallace,
October 2011**.

UPS and DOWNS

Manchester City were formed in 1880/81 as West Gorton St Marks playing friendlies on land close to Clowes Street, moving to Kirkmanshulme Cricket Club in 1880/81, then in 1882/83 playing at Queens Road, Gorton. In 1885 City became Gorton F.C. playing at Pink Bank Lane then as Ardwick F.C in 1888 playing at Hyde Road.

1890/91

Ardwick played their first pre-league FA Cup tie winning 12-0 at home to Liverpool Stanley, then scratched against Halliwell away.

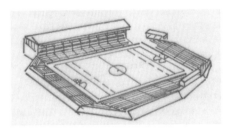

Above: Hyde Road - to the left of the popular side is the Stoneyard Stand, to the right is the Galloway End and the grandstand is opposite.

1891/92 –Alliance League

Ardwick, under manager Lawrence Furness played one season in the Alliance, finishing 12th against: Bootle, Lincoln City, Burton Swifts, Newton Heath, Birmingham St. George, Walsall Town Swifts, Nottingham Forest, The Wednesday, Grimsby Town, Small Heath, Crewe Alexandra, and lost in the FA Cup qualifying round 1-5 to Newton Heath.

A total of 30 friendlies were also played against established League sides and a Canadian eleven.

1892/93 to 1898/99 D2

Ardwick joined the newly formed Football League Second Division along with Small Heath, Grimsby Town, Sheffield United, Darwen, Burton Swifts, Northwich Victoria, Bootle, Lincoln City (City winning 11-3 at home a record in the League), Crewe Alexandra, Burslem Port Vale and Walsall, finishing 5th in their first season, then 13th, 9th, 2nd, (losing to Small Heath and West Bromwich Albion. in the

test matches) 6th, 3rd, and top in 1899, 6 points clear of Glossop N.E.

Josh Parlby become manager in 1893, and there was a change of name in 1894 to Manchester City, and Sam Ormerod became manager in 1895'

Added to the list of opponents were: **1893/94**: Liverpool, Notts County, Middlesbrough Ironopolis, Woolwich Arsenal, Rotherham Town,
1894/95: Bury, Leicester Fosse, Burton Wanderers
1895/96: Loughborough Town, Rotherham United
1896/97: Gainsborough Trinity, Blackpool
1897/98: Luton Town
1898/99: Glossop North End, New Brighton Tower
Additional Cup/Test Match opposition was Fleetwood Rangers, West Manchester, West Bromwich Albion, Preston North End, Wigan County, Bolton Wanderers
(In 1894/95 City failed to enter the FA Cup as an oversight!)

1899/00 to 1901/02 D1

City then spent three seasons in Division One, finishing 7th, 11th and 18th relegated with Small Heath, and with little Cup success.
New opposition was:
1900/01: Sunderland, Nottingham Forest, Everton, The Wednesday, Derby County, Wolverhampton Wanderers, Aston Villa, Stoke City.
1901/02: Bristol City, Manchester United (re-named), Chesterfield, Barnsley, Doncaster Rovers, Stockport County.
No new teams were met in the Cup

1902/03 D2

City bounced straight back up to Division One under new manager Tom Maley finishing in top spot, 3 points ahead of Small Heath with additional opposition: Barnsley, Burslem Port Vale, Burnley, Burton United, but went out of the Cup 1-3 at Preston North End in the first round.

1903/04 to 1908/09 D1

In the first season back in Division One, City finished runners up in the League to The

Wednesday by 3 points, but won the FA Cup 1-0 against Bolton Wanderers beating new opponents Middlesbrough on the way.

In the following season 1905/06 City finished 3rd after a stormy end of season game at Aston Villa, after which allegations of match fixing and financial irregularities were supposedly discovered and leading figures on and off the field were suspended, almost causing the City club to be destroyed.

In 1906/07 Harry Newbould became manager, and Burgess, Meredith, Bannister and Turnbull, were poached by Manchester United. City finished 17th, and lost by a record score of 1-9 at Everton

In 1907/08 City finished third, but in 1908/09 City were relegated along with bottom club Leicester Fosse. There was little success in the Cup other than the win in 1904.

New opponents were: New Brompton, Liverpool, Birmingham City (re-named), Chelsea, Bradford City

1909/10 D2

Again City bounced straight back up finishing top, one point clear of Oldham Athletic. New opponents were Oldham Athletic, Hull City, Fulham, Bradford Park Avenue, Clapton Orient, Leeds City plus Workington, Southampton Town and finally Swindon Town in the Cup.

1910/11 to 1914/15 D1

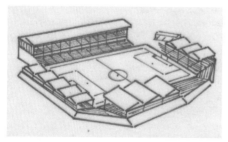

City didn't play any new teams in these seasons, finishing 17th, 15th, 6th, 13th, 5th and the 4th round of the FA Cup was the best achieved. Ernest Mangnall became manager in 1912.

1915/16 to 1919/20 WW1

Wartime competition isn't officially included in the record books, but City played Southport, Southport C. and V. plus Rochdale and Port Vale (re-named) for the first time.

1920/21 to 1925/26 D1

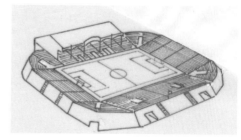

In the next six seasons City finished 2nd, 10th, 8th, 11th, 10th, and 21st being relegated along with Notts. County. The Blues moved to Maine Road in 1923 and reached the semi-final of the FA Cup in 1924 losing 0-2 to Newcastle United, and lost in the final of 1926 to Bolton 0-1, becoming the first team to reach the final and be relegated in the same season. City also posted the record FA Cup win of 11-4 v Crystal Palace! and won a League match by a record 6-1 in a Derby at Old Trafford as well!

David Ashworth became manager in 1924.

New opponents were Leeds United, Leicester City (both re-named) Cardiff City, Darlington, Charlton Athletic, West Ham United., Halifax, Town, Brighton and Hove Albion, and The Corinthians.

1926/27 to 1927/28 D2

Peter Hodge became manager and City finished 3rd as Portsmouth were promoted on goal average (despite City winning their last game 8-0 (Pompey winning 5-1 at home to Preston to clinch it) City made amends the next season by finishing top, 2 points clear of Leeds United, scoring 100 goals.

New opponents were: Portsmouth, Swansea Town, Reading and South Shields.

In the Cup City reached the 3rd and 5th rounds.

1928/29 to 1937/38 D1

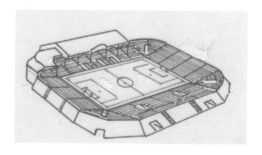

The next seven seasons were City's most successful to date, recording a 10-1 4th rd replay Cup win over Swindon in 1930, reaching the FA Cup semi-final in 1932 losing 0-1 to Arsenal, then the final of 1933 losing 0-3 to Everton but winning it 2-1 in 1934 v Portsmouth. During the Cup run City recorded a provincial record attendance of 84,569 in the 6th round at home to Stoke. The Blues won the League title in 1937, 3 points clear of Charlton, but went down in 1938 with WBA despite scoring 80 goals, more than any other team in the division! City became the only champions to achieve this dubious distinction. Wilf Wild became manager in 1932.

New opponents were: Arsenal, Sheffield Wednesday, Leicester City (all re-named), and Hull City, Millwall, Brentford, Gateshead, Accrington Stanley, and Wrexham, in the Cup.

1938/39 to 1939/40 D2

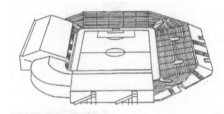

There was no quick return this time for the Blues as City finished 5th, with 49 points, five adrift of the second promotion spot, but still banged in 96 goals, the most in the Division, and went out of the FA Cup in the 4th round. The 1939/40 season was abandoned after just three games after the outbreak of WW2 with City in eleventh place, and all records were expunged.

New opponents were Coventry City, Plymouth Argyle, Norwich City and Tranmere Rovers.

1940/41 to 1945/46 WW2

Again, wartime competition was not officially included in the record books, but City played new opponents New Brighton, and Chester.

The FA Cup was re-introduced in season 1945/46 on a two legged basis and City beat Barrow in the 3rd round but lost to Bradford Park Avenue 5-9 on aggregate after a 2-8 record home defeat in the 4th round.

1946/47 D2

City topped the League in style winning it with 62 points, four ahead of second placed Burnley, but faced only Newport County as new opponents, and lost out at Birmingham 0-5 in the 5th round of the FA Cup. Wilf Wild resigned as manager in November and Sam Cowan took over from December to the end of the season.

1947/48 to 1949/50 D1

On their return City, with new manager Jock Thomson, finished 10th, then 7th and 21st going down with Birmingham City and reached the 5th, 3rd and 3rd rounds in the FA Cup.

No new opponents were faced.

1950/51 D2

No problems bouncing back up at the first attempt again, under new manager Les McDowall, finishing second with 52 points, five behind leaders Preston North End. Only Queens Park Rangers were met as new opponents but City were dumped out of the FA Cup in the third round again, at Birmingham 0-2.

1951/1952 to 1962/63 D1

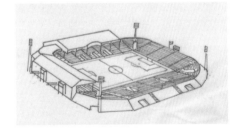

So to City's longest spell in the top flight, to date; twelve seasons finishing 15th, 20th, 17th, 7th, 4th, 18th, 5th, 20th, 15th, 13th. 12th and 21st. City reached the FA Cup Final in 1955, losing to Newcastle 1-3, but won it the following year, beating Birmingham City 3-1. Also beating new opponents Southend United on the way. The League Cup was introduced in 1960, City losing 0-6 to Birmingham in the quarter final of 1962/63 and 2-3 on aggregate to Stoke in the semi-final of 1963/64. Ipswich Town were new League opponents in the 1961/62 season.

1963/64 to 1965/66 D2

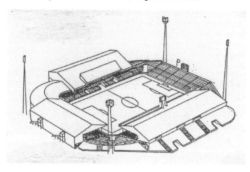

Then followed a couple of dismal seasons finishing 6th and 11th with manager Les McDowall going, and George Poyser taking over. Crowds went down to 8,015 on one occasion. However, Joe Mercer and Malcolm Allison came in and revitalised the club in 1965, taking City up in top spot with 59 points, five clear of second placed Southampton, and reaching the 6th round of the FA Cup, losing out to Everton 0-2 in a second replay.

New opponents were Northampton Town and Scunthorpe United, plus Carlisle United and Mansfield Town in the League Cup.

1966/67 to 1982/83 D1

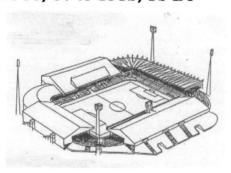

Then followed City's longest time in the First, lasting seventeen seasons and finishing 15th, 1st, 13th, 10th, 11th, 4th, 11th, 14th, 8th, 8th, 2nd, 4th, 15th, 17th, 12th, 10th, and 20th going down with Swansea City (re-named) and Brighton and Hove Albion. City won the League title in 1968, 2 points clear of United, the FA Cup in 1969 beating Leicester 1-0 and the League Cup in 1970 2-1 V West. Brom., and 1976 2-1 v Newcastle, but lost in 1974 1-2 to Wolves. City won the European Cup Winners' Cup in 1970, 2-1 against Gornik Zabrze, but lost 0-2 on aggregate v Chelsea in the semi-final of 1971.

Joe Mercer stepped down in October 1971, Malcolm Allison becoming manager until March 1973 when Johnny Hart took over, and Peter Swales became chairman. Hart was followed by Ron Saunders, Tony Book, Malcolm Allison, John Bond and John Benson.

City reached the League Cup semi-final in 1981 losing to Liverpool 1-2 on aggregate, and also lost the 1981 Centenary Cup Final 2-3 to Spurs in a replay.

New opponents were Southport and York City, in the League Cup plus Wigan Athletic and Oxford United in the FA Cup.

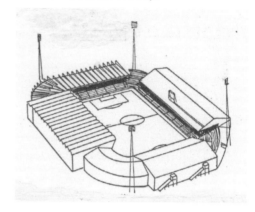

New European opposition was:
1968/69: Fenerbahce
1969/70: Atletico Bilbao, Lierse, AC Coimbra, Schalke 04, Gornik Zabrze
1970/71: Linfield, Honved
1972/73: Valencia
1976/77: Juventus
1977/78: Widzew Lodz
1978/79: Twente Enschede, Standard Liege, AC Milan, Borussia Monchengladbach

1983/84 to 1984/85 D2

It took two seasons for City to return to the First. Under new manager Billy McNeill, the Blues finished 4th then 3rd to go up with Oxford United and Birmingham City, but with little success in the Cup competitiions.

New opponents were Cambridge United in the League, and Torquay United in the League Cup.

1985/86 to 1986/87 D1

City only managed two seasons in the top flight, finishing 16th and 21st going down with Leicester City and Aston Villa, and again with little success

in the either Cup. Jimmy Frizell took over from Billy McNeill (who also took Aston Villa down) in September 1986.
New opponents were Wimbledon and Watford

1987/88 to 1988/89 D2

It took another two seasons for City to pop back up with new manager Mel Machin, finishing 9th and then 2nd going up with Chelsea and Crystal Palace, reaching both Cup quarter finals in 1987/88 losing out to Liverpool 0-4 in the FA Cup and Everton 0-2 in the League Cup. New opponents were A.F.C Bournemouth.

1989/90 to 1995/96 D1/Prem

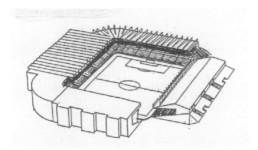

City then had two seasons in Division One finishing in 16th place after Howard Kendall replaced Machin in November 1989, then 5th twice after Peter Reid replaced Kendall in November 1990 and 9th in the newly formed Premiership in 1992/93. Brian Horton replaced Reid in August 1993, City finishing 16th, and then 17th Chairman Peter Swales was ousted by Francis Lee and then Alan Ball replaced Horton in the summer of 1995 with City going down in 18th place with QPR and Bolton Wanderers in 1996.
City lost 2-4 at home to Spurs in the quarter final of the FA Cup in 1992/93, and 0-4 at Palace in the Q/F of the League Cup in 1994/95.
New opponents were Chester City, Bristol Rovers, Barnet and Wycombe all in the League Cup.

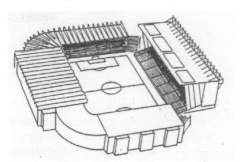

Maine Road in its final state with the North Stand (old Scoreboard) at the top, Main Stand left, Kippax stand right and Patt Lane (umbro) below.

1996/97 to 1997/98 D1

There was to be no quick return, in fact things just got worse for City who struggled, sacking Ball in August 1996, appointing Asa Hartford as caretaker, then Steve Coppell, then Phil Neal as caretaker then Frank Clark in December going on to finish 14th. Under new Chairman David Bernstein, Joe Royle replaced Clark in February 1998 but City finished in 22nd place going down with Stoke and Reading to the Second (old Third) Division. There was no success in the Cups, and no new opponents

1998/99 D2

After a dodgy start, at one point languishing in 12th position, the lowest in the club's history, City scraped back up behind Walsall and Fulham, via the play offs beating new opponents Gillingham (re-named) in the Play-off Final 3-1 on penalties, after the famous 2-2. There was little success in the Cups. Other new opponent was (embarrassingly) Macclesfield Town.

1999/00 D1

Amazingly City came up in second place, two points behind Charlton, with Ipswich 3rd to manage back to back promotions, but with little success in the Cups and no new opponents.

2000/01 Prem

City spent just one season in the Premiership, going down with Coventry City and Bradford City, but lost in the quarter final of the League Cup 1-2 at home to Ipswich a.e.t.

2001/02 D1

Joe Royle was replaced by Kevin Keegan in May 2001 and City bounced back up again finishing in top spot, 10 points ahead of West Brom. and scoring 108 goals but with no success in the Cups, and no new opponents.

2002/03 to date Prem

Consolidation, finishing in 9th, then moving to Eastlands in 2003. Since then so far 16th, 8th, 15th, 14th, 9th, 10th, 5th and 3rd place finishes have been achieved under: Kevin Keegan, Stuart Pearce, Sven Goran Eriksson, Mark Hughes and Roberto Mancini.

FA Cup Quarter finals were lost in 2006 at home to West Ham 1-2, and in 2007 0-2 away at Blackburn.

The League Cup quarter final in 2008 was lost 0-2 at home to Spurs., and the semi-final in 2010, 3-4 on aggregate to United.

City finally won the FA Cup again, beating Stoke City 1-0 in 2011.

The Chairmanship has seen John Wardle, Thaksin Shinawatra, and Sheikh Mansour in control.

New opponents were all European, City qualifying twice for UEFA under the fair play ruling and losing 3-4 on aggregate to Hamburg in the quarter finals in 2009:

2006/07:TNS, Lokeren, Groclin,

2008/09: Streymur, Midjitland, Omonia, Paris St Germain, Santander, FC Copenhagen, Aalborg, Hamburg.

City qulaified on merit in 2010 for the Europa League, and in 2011 for the Champions' League.

2010/11: FC Timisoara, Salzburg, Lech Poznan, Aris Thesalonika, Dynamo Kiev.

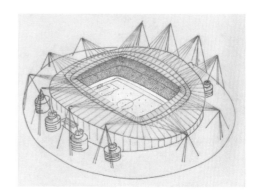

A is for Aalborg

The As take us over to Denmark, Portugal, Greece, Spain, Italy, Lancashire, the South Coast, Scotland, London and Birmingham.

Aalborg BK

A group of pioneering English engineers, who built the Jutland railway system, were responsible for the establishment of Aalborg Boldspilklub in 1885.

Aalborg were twice Cup winners, turned professional in 1987 and won the title three times. Their colours are red and white striped shirts with white shorts.

They failed to progress in the Champions League in 2008 despite beating Celtic on aggregate and drawing 2-2 with United at Old Trafford. In the UEFA Cup they had beaten a weakened Deportivo La Coruna 3-0 at home and 3-1 away, before meeting City in March 2009 in the last 16. City won comfortably at COMS 2-0 but we suffered the fright of our lives in the last few minutes in Aalborg, who notched two late goals, taking the tie to extra time and penalties, won 4-3 by City. Attendance 10,735

Aalborg, situated in the north of Denmark, is north west of Copenhagen. Around 700 City fans, mostly on day trips, were able to spend time in the bars and restaurants of this impressive town. In the stand behind the goal before the game, the locals put on a spectacular display of flag waving, the flags changed from red to white as a giant flag was passed along the home support the length of the stand.

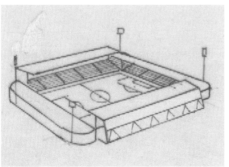

The original ground, the Aalborg Stadium, was built in 1920 and burned down in 1960. Now named The Energi Nord Arena, it has a capacity of 13,800, though limited to only 10,800 for European games.

Friendlies: City did play a team called Aalborg and Aallorg on tour in Denmark in 1949 winning 5-1, though this could have been a different club, maybe from Copenhagen.

Connection: Hans Backe

Academica De Coimbra

Academica were formed in March 1913. They have rarely distinguished themselves in the Liga Sagres, but reached four cup finals. In the first ever Portuguese Cup Final, in 1939 they beat Benfica 4-3. In 1951 they lost 5-1, and in 1969 2-1, both to Benfica. Their best season, prior to playing City, was in 1967 when they came second in their league and were runners up in their cup to Setubal 3-2. Since then they've had little success.

The only meetings of the two teams came in the quarter final of the Cup Winners' Cup in 1970. Prior to facing City, Academica had disposed of Kuopio Palloseura from Finland and the East Germans, Magdeburg.

In the first leg in Northern Portugal, City drew 0-0, a creditable result, in front of 8,000 against a team of supposedly university students and amateur footballers. The ground, since then, (as shown) has been renamed Estadio Cidade de Coimbra, and was redeveloped for the 2004 European Championships, with 50,000 attending the inaugural concert by The Rolling Stones in 2003.

At Maine Road a Tony Towers goal put City through in front of 36,338.

Dave A: 18/3/1970 City 1 AC Coimbra 0

"The first leg had ended in a 0-0 draw so there was everything to play for and much optimism. The first leg in Portugal was played only three

days before City won the League Cup Final at Wembley, beating West Brom 2-1 after extra time. In the earlier rounds of the ECWC that season City had beaten Atletico Bilbao 6-3 and SK Lierse of Belgium 8-0 on aggregate!

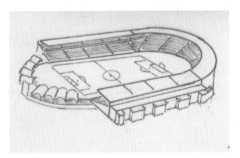

I was living and working in Leeds and learning that I hated Leeds United more than the Rags, and still do. The M62 was being built but wasn't open so we left Leeds as usual about 5pm for the then two hour plus journey for a 7.30pm kick off. We usually got there in time for kick off but it was quite often touch and go. I travelled with my friend Ted Brown, either in my ancient A40 or his Fiat 500. Ted remains a loyal follower.

The team contained most of the usual names of the era but Tony Coleman had moved on and there was no recognised left winger; Mike Summerbee was injured and didn't play so Arthur Mann was at left back with Glyn Pardoe in midfield, George Heslop, Alan Oakes and Tommy Booth all played, with Mike Doyle up front. During the course of the game Tony Towers and Phil Glennon (who you might ask?) came on as subs for George Heslop and Colin Bell.

We had seats in those days in the old Platt Lane stand and met the rest of the family there, including my mother, my sister and her husband and my brother plus a couple of cousins.

It was a damp night with a crowd of 36,338

Academica came and played for a replay from the start, there were no penalty shoot outs in those days. They were well organised, tough if not dirty but very physical and cynical. City attacked throughout the game but just couldn't score. In all honesty I can't remember, or find out from the Internet, whether or not the game went to extra time, but in the very last minute Tony Towers scored a great goal from the edge of the box at the Platt Lane end. We went wild with delight and to my eternal shame I remember finding myself shouting some not very complimentary remarks at the Portuguese.

We usually won at home in those days so the journey back across the Pennines was often a good one. We always stopped for chips in Oldham and were asked without fail in that homely Oldham accent if we wanted "a drop of gravy love?" They were lovely people in the chip shop. I met them about seventeen years later by chance in Huddersfield where they were running a sandwich shop! I recognised them from their accents! We usually got home about 12.30am but later, in the seventies, once the M62 opened we were able to go to my mother's for tea before the match and would get back to Leeds by 11pm ish.

Around that time teenagers, 18+, in the UK were given the vote, Rhodesia, later Zimbabwe, declared UDI and Dana won the Eurovision for Ireland with All Kinds of Everything but City were making their own history and times at Maine Road were exceedingly good."

Accrington Stanley

Accrington FC were founder members of the Football League in 1888, playing at Thorneyholme Road but in 1893 finished above only Newton Heath and rather than be relegated to the new Second Division they chose to resign from the League.

Stanley became founder members of Division Three North in 1921, playing at Peel Park.

Due to financial problems they were unable to complete their Division Four fixtures in 1961/62, resigning in March. Their place was taken by Oxford United the following season. Stanley folded altogether in 1965 but were reborn in 1968.

Now playing at The Crown Ground, they moved up through the pyramid (aided by the transfer sell-ons of Brett Ormerod) and made it to League Two in 2007 taking the place of, ironically.....Oxford United! The TV milk ad 'Accrington Stanley, who are they?' 'Exactly' made them famous.

They finished season 2010/11 in League Two playing in an all red strip.

City played them in a friendly at Hyde Road in 1891/92 drawing 3-3, and then once in a first class fixture in the fourth round of the FA Cup in 1937. City won 2-0 at Maine Road, with goals from Doherty and Tilson, in front of a crowd of 39,135. Further friendlies were played at Accrington in 1990/91 (in support of Manchester's Olympic bid) and 2007/08 with City fielding reserve teams on both occasions.

Ground: Peel Park R/A 17,634 v Blackburn R. Friendly 1954/55, moved to The Crown Ground in 1970, capacity 5,057, including occasionally Jon Anderson, the front man of 70s progressive rock group Yes and who can be heard chanting in a high-pitched voice "C'mon you Stanley/ Accy/Owd reds"! Presumably backed up by David 'Bumble' Lloyd, the cricket commentator.

———≈———

AFC Bournemouth

'The Cherries' were formed in 1899, and joined Division Three in 1923 as Bournemouth and Boscombe Athletic – playing at Dean Court, a lovely setting in King's Park. They changed their name to A.F.C. Bournemouth in 1971, and played some eight games at The Avenue Stadium, home of Dorchester Town FC in 2001, whilst Dean Court was transformed into the Fitness First Stadium.

Generally a lower league team, they had a good cup run in 1957 (I visited the ground whilst on holiday in 1959!) and beat United at home in the 3rd round of 1984. They finished season 2010/11 in League Two, being promoted, playing in red shirts and black shorts.

Post-war: six league meetings with four City wins, and two draws.

City won both games in 1987/88 2-0, and then in 1988/89 won 1-0 at Bournemouth, but only drew 3-3 at Maine Road. This was an incredible game where City went three goals up by half time before conceding two and Blissett striking home a 97th minute penalty to put promotion celebrations on hold, as the relieved news came through that Palace had only drawn at Leicester, meaning that a draw at Bradford City in our last game would clinch a promotion spot.

Next meetings were in the Second (old Third) Division in 1998/99, City winning 2-1 at Maine Road and drawing 0-0 at Dean Court.

John B: 13/2/99 Bournemouth 0 City 0:

Not the obvious choice when compared to the infamous 3-3 draw at Maine Road in the penultimate game of the 1988/89 season, but it's worth a nostalgic glance if only on the grounds that it featured unquestionably one of the worst refereeing performances of modern times.

At Dean Court, it was our misfortune to run into a Mr Brian Coddington of Sheffield, another lower league, dome head, for whom the throwing about of his weight, at the expense of the biggest team he'd been listed to officiate in many a long season, constituted one last chance to go to the show.

The day had actually started well. The weather, given that it was the middle of February, was gloriously warm and bright, and in town that morning, the City captain, Jamie Pollock, had endeared himself to those Blues who had opted to make a weekend-by-the-seaside of it, by grabbing a spotty teenage twerp in a United shirt (a not uncommon sight in Bournemouth) and throwing him unceremoniously into a laurel bush, after he repeatedly tried to spoil a photograph and autograph session. By kick off time, which was delayed by 20 minutes because of the number of people still trying to get in, most City fans were optimistically anticipating a thrilling victory in the South Coast sunshine.

However, a pitch that looked as if it had just hosted a tractor pull, put paid to the thrilling part, and Coddington conspired to ensure that there would be no victory. Seven yellow cards and two reds were brandished in a game with barely a foul worthy of the name, and all to City players, including Pollock who got his marching orders in the 2nd half. The Sheffield official's crowning glory however came 5 minutes from the end. Bournemouth threw over a low corner, and as the 20 year old City keeper Nicky Weaver stooped to collect the ball, he was knocked unconscious courtesy of a wild lunge from the home side's captain, Ian Cox. Incredibly, Mr Coddington waved played on, only then stopping proceedings to tend to the prone and profusely bleeding Weaver, after the ball had been hoofed clear for a throw in. In the understandable uproar that followed, City midfielder 'Super' Kevin Horlock, then became the second Blue of the afternoon to receive his marching orders, because, according to the referee afterwards, he (Horlock) had, and I quote "walked towards me in quite an aggressive manner"!

The toilet brush hurled out of the away end in Mr Coddington's general direction on the final whistle at Dean Court, fell tragically just short.

The last word though went to Jamie Pollock, who counselled sagely that he had "never seen a referee as poor as Coddington. We were playing against 12 men. It was ridiculous. It wasn't a dirty game yet we've had 5 people booked and 2 sent off. The referee was a shambles". No arguments here.

Friendly: 1949 4-2 away

Some connections: Ian Bishop (below), Paul Moulden and managers John Bond, John Benson and Mel Machin.

Ground: Dean Court R/A 28,799 v Man Utd FA Cup 6 1957, (shown 1980s).

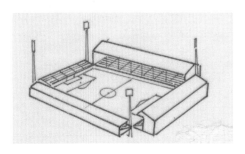

Airdrieonians

'The Diamonds' were formed in 1878, playing at Old Mavisbank until the move to Broomfield Park in 1892. They entered the Scottish League Division Two in 1894 and won the Scottish Cup in 1924.

The teams met in 1971/72 in the Texaco Cup. The first leg was drawn 2-2 at Maine Road, Mellor and Doyle scoring, in front of only 15,033. The second leg resulted in a 2-0 loss, with a crowd of 13,700.

City were heavily criticised in Scotland for playing a virtual reserve team, Corrigan, Book, Booth, Doyle, Summerbee, Bell, Lee, Davies, Mellor and Young being omitted from the team listed in their programme against the part timers. For one City player, Keith Hanvey, this was his one and only first team appearance for City. Were his folks at that match? How did he play? Oh the 'saddo' quiz potential of that question. Name the City first team player who never played in England!

In the next round Airdrie beat Huddersfield Town, then a considerable force, 7-2, then overcame Ballymena United, but lost to Derby County in the Final in January 1972.

They went on to finish fourth bottom of Division One, moved to ground share with Clyde at the Broadfield Stadium, in 1994, folded in 2002, and were replaced in Division Three by Gretna Green. After being reincarnated as Airdrie United, they somehow bought out and closed down Clydebank, replacing them in Division Two in 2002/03 where they finished in 2010/11 playing at the Exelsior Stadium.

Rob. D: 27/9/1971 Airdrie 2 City 0

Ever had that feeling you were the only City fan at an away game? It could have come at an obscure friendly, probably abroad or at Millwall's 2001 League encounter where I did see the odd Blue face on the terraces, ingenuity having beaten the away fans ban. However, a first introduction to this unique experience came at Airdrieonians Broomfield Park on 27th September 1971.

It was barely six years since I'd fallen in love with City, and only a couple of years after falling for Scottish football, a consequence of holidays touring Scotland – the likes of St. Johnstone versus Hibs., Forfar against Albion Rovers – and, primarily by an introduction to the passion and power of Glasgow Rangers largely due to

Rochdale Blues Ian and Alex. Stockport Blue Dave Miller had also placed a piece in City's programme for 'City-Rangers pen pals' and Jim McDowall, the Glaswegian I linked up with has remained a firm friend for well over three decades.

In that Autumn of '71 the prospect of capturing a couple of games on Clydeside was too good to miss as Rangers had a European game at Ibrox the following night. The road north on the day of City's Texaco cup tie was not, unexpectedly, devoid of Blue cars and scarves and I began to feel like a Mancunian emissary taking the sole support, and accent, into the backlands of Lanarkshire.

Finding a wee bed and breakfast – more likely a 'logdin' house' in neighbouring Coatbridge (Albion Rovers territory) I made my way to the ground in good time. The sense of isolation increased but in a challenging way as knowing Scots football crowds, I felt confident enough in any banter. Standing on a crowded open terrace as the teams took to the field, I was aware of the growing growlings of discontent and disappointment as a City team bereft of the stars of the time appeared on the pitch.

What gave me away I'm not sure; maybe body language, a Sassenach shout of encouragement for the Blue boys, or just a desire to 'show a Blue is here' It seemed half of the collective 'old firm' fans in Strathclyde were there to swell the crowd, and a good number, thankfully humourously – rounded on me as to the why and wherefore of City's team selection. I became an unofficial apologist and spokesman for the club, pre-dating Chris Bird, Paul Tyrrell and Garry Cook by so many years that it may well have been a first PR and spin on City's behalf.

As Airdrie took control towards their eventual victory my neighbour's mood mellowed and I sensed, if not a general pity directed my way, the beginnings of a butt of jocularity. My integration approached completion when I gave my indication of the next day's visit to Ibrox. In the social club, after the game I did spy a City 'away face' but it could not detract at all from that isolated, but proudly individualistic feeling of being the one Blue amongst a 13,000 crowd. at Bloomfield Park (as shown)

The following evening, as Rangers overcame Rennes 1-0, in the cavernous terraced rear of the Copland stand I bumped into some of my Broomfield buddies and we were able to make merry about City's lamentable show and my faux-discomfort. Later that season I was at

Barcelona's Nou Camp as 'The Gers' lifted the European Cup Winners' Cup, the one I'd seen City raise in rainy Vienna just two years earlier. Blue halcyon days indeed!

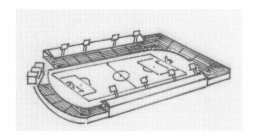

Aris Thessaloniki

Aris, were formed in 1914 by a group of 22 young friends in a coffee bar in the Votsi area. The name Aris is from the God of War, the nickname inspired by the two Balkan wars of 1912/13 when Greece fought against the Ottoman empire.

Aris won 14 titles until 1959 when the united First Division was created. During that time they won three play off titles including their last in 1946 during the Greek civil war.

Aris first achieved European qualification in the 1960's. They won the Greek Cup in 1970, and Wilf McGuinness managed them from 1971 to 1973.

The club declined in the 1980s, hit financial trouble and were relegated briefly in 1997 and 2005. In recent years fortunes improved and they finished as Greek Cup runners up four times and have been handily placed in the League as one of the established big five clubs in Greece.

In the Europa Cup in 2010 they eliminated Jagiellonia Bialystok and Austria Vien in the preliminary stages and in the Group stage beat holders Atletico Madrid, then Rosenburg on aggregate but finished second after losing to Bayer Leverkusen, to face City. In their domestic season they were in 7th place but hadn't lost a European fixture at home in forty years.

They played City in yellow shirts and black shorts.

The teams first met in the Europa League season 2010/11 round of 32. The first leg was drawn 0-0 in Greece in front of 22,000 (811 City fans) and City won the second, comfortably, 3-0 with 2 goals from Dzeko and one from Ya Ya

Toure. Crowd was 36,748 with 3,404 highly-entertaining Aris fans.

The first leg was played in its 'new' ground, named in 1951 after a player, Kleanthis Vikelides, in the Harilaou area of the city. Capacity is 22,800, though a move to a more modern ground soon is imminent.

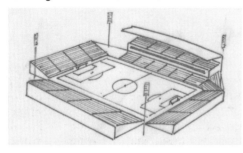

Neil S: 15/2/2011 Aris 0 City 0

The 22:05 from Zurich to Salonika will go down in City supporting folklore. The Sunday evening flight was only half full, but the small percentage of travelling English were more than happy to assist with the emptying of the Free Bar. The travelling time was only just over an hour and it would be an understatement to suggest that it was all getting a bit silly.

Eventually we landed and in contrast to the heavy Police presence in Poznan and Turin, there wasn't even a Passport Control.

I had booked three nights at Hotel Astoria on the day of the draw. The Sunday evening session was merely a dress rehearsal for the Mother of all Benders, the following afternoon. The bar opposite the hotel was owned by a PAOK supporter and it soon transpired that Salonika was no different to Manchester when it came to despising your local rivals. However, unlike Manchester, both Salonika teams originate from the same city.

The hours flew by with the worst busker in musical history and the local television crew all making a guest appearance. The next thing I remember is waking up on my hotel bed fully clothed.

The following day I returned to the last bar I could remember and found everyone in virtually the same position. An Aris supporter appeared on the scene and without prompting he bought us all a drink and offered me a lift to the game.

The scene around the stadium was far friendlier than the television pictures suggested. Indeed the ambience around the home section was not dissimilar to a Rugby game at the Millennium Stadium with a sprinkling of City fans mingling with the locals around dozens of Bars and Fast Food outlets.

Of course it helped that I was with an Aris season ticket holder. He bought me a souvenir from their club shop and uttered the immortal words: "Beware the Greek bearing gifts" Surely Edin Dzeko wasn't a Trojan horse.

He promised to wait for me as I walked around the corner into a convoy of police and drunken City fans chanting "Aris, Aris…who the F*ck are Aris?"

Oh yes, the English sense of humour.

I wasn't frisked and the stewarding was fairly low key. The away end was a Gene Kelly affair, but the biggest problem was the size of the security fences that were last seen in England around the time of City's 4-2 win at the Manor Ground in 1989.

City appeared lethargic and we enjoyed plenty of possession, but the one thing we have got to learn is that brave decisions and substitutions often breed success.

The atmosphere was impressive, but it was only after returning home that I discovered the strength of their home record. City never looked threatened, but similarly, we only created a couple of chances worth noting. The only highlight was the final whistle.

After the game we were kept behind for almost an hour. It was a ridiculous amount of time and if anything, it gave a few Aris fans an opportunity for their two minutes of fame as they waved united scarves and threw bottles of water towards the City enclosure. Predictably, this only increased the irritation of the travelling supporters.

As promised, my Aris companion waited and gave me a lift back to the Astoria. Apparently, Greek fans are sometimes kept in the ground for two hours. All very strange for such a friendly group of people.

PS: Sean Riley had his famous flag, or half of it nicked by local scrotes at the ground, but after pressure from both clubs the flag was returned in a presentation at the return match at COMS, and a new flag was also presented, so all 's well that ends well.

Arsenal

'The Gunners' were formed in 1886, and were elected to Division Two in 1893 as Woolwich Arsenal playing at The Manor Ground in Plumstead before moving across the river to Highbury in 1913, renamed The Arsenal Stadium in the thirties, then onto The Emirates in 2006.

Arsenal were dubiously promoted to the First Division in 1915 though they finished only fifth in the Second Division, leapfrogging Barnsley and Wolves for the 1919/20 season after the First World War, the division being increased from 20 to 22 clubs. Chelsea remained in the First, but just to rub it in Spurs were relegated!

Since then they've never been out of the top flight. They were the dominant team in the thirties under Herbert Chapman, and have regularly won trophies through each of the subsequent decades, only the European Cup eluding them, so far. They finished season 2010/11 in the Premiership playing in red shirts with white sleeves and white shorts.

Pre-war: 64 league meetings with 26 City wins, 10 draws and 28 losses.

In the opening game of season 1906/07 City's revamped team, with five players making their debuts under a new manager Harry Newbould, after the suspensions, faced Woolwich Arsenal at Hyde Road in a heatwave with temperatures of 90 degrees in the shade. Thornley collapsed and went off, as did Grieve. Conlin went off, despite having a hanky on his head, but returned later. Dorsett scored but collapsed, leaving City down to eight men. Kelso went off to leave City 4-1 down with seven men, and finally there were six as Buchan left the field. Referee A J Barker had earlier decided not to abandon the game. Arsenal, being made of sterner stuff, finished the game with 11 men.

Frank Swift commented in his autobiography *From The Goalmouth* that in the thirties City had a plan against them and usually won!

The crowd of 79,491 at the 1935 Maine Road game was the highest in the league until later in the season when 82,905 attended the Chelsea v Arsenal game at The Bridge. This was then topped by the 83,260 at the United v Arsenal game at Maine Road, the crowd probably being swelled by 50,000 City fans supporting Arsenal. The crowd of 84,569 at the City v Stoke Cup game in 1934 has, of course never yet been topped in England or Wales.

Post-war: **D**isastrous (no plan!), 74 league meetings with 14 City wins (last at Highbury in 1975/76, 3-2), 24 draws and 36 defeats. These included a 3-7 away defeat in 1956/57. There was an entertaining game at Highbury in 1961 when City pulled back a 3-goal deficit only to lose 4-5.

The Guvnor: 23/9/1967 Arsenal 1 City 0

Football hooliganism was at its highest then. There were no CCTV or mobile phones, just the Old Bill with truncheons and radios that did not work under metal roofs. When you are seventeen, skinhead with sheepskin, boots and shaved-in partin' and braces, the world's your oyster. We took a few birds, all skins, with us to Arsenal on the train, not the special, but the service that arrived at 10:00 am in the morning at Euston. Millwall were at Euston waiting, but only about twenty of them and they didn't want to know as they went through their barrier to board a train to wherever they were playing. West Ham however did want to know, they had a good sized mob. Off it went in the concourse, fists flew and missiles were thrown. The Old Bill knew it was happening and arrived in their vanloads. We were separated and put on the opposite side of the station, the public being scattered and City's day in London had begun. West Ham were gathered up and kept inside the station as we went through Soho and Carnaby Street mob handed with about sixty of us, a great start to the day. "Let's go robbin' and get some clothes from the shops in London". I got a new sheepskin and some new braces, not a bad mornings work. I gave my old sheepskin to a fella that had only an old Hartington on. He was made up and onwards and upwards we went. We had a few beers and set off on the tube to Arsenal (Highbury) we all knew where we were going, splitting up into little groups and making towards the Northbank. This would be the first time that we would have entered this stand as a mob - a large following of City, and the plan was on. There must have been over four hundred of us in their end and as the old Bill could not get this many out it was game on. As City piled forward on the pitch, we piled down towards the Arsenal bootboys. We pushed them right down to the bottom of their stand and we held the higher ground. Fight after fight broke out but City never ran, although we were pushed by the Old Bill towards the left of the stand and

Arsenal's crew were on the right. We were left in all the game and we won the day with taunts to our opposite numbers of "You'll never take the Kippax". 1-0 to City, but 0-1 on the pitch.

In the Premiership: Equally as bad, in fact worse, 28 meetings, City losing 20, including a painful 4-0 and 5-0 double in 2000/01, drawing five and winning only three.

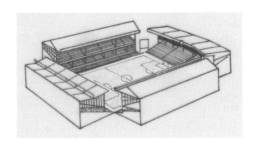

Season	H	A	Pl	W	D	L
Pre 08/09			22	1	3	18
08/09	3-0	0-2	24	2	3	19
09/10	4-2	0-0	26	3	4	19
10/11	0-3	0-0	28	3	5	20

In the FA Cup, meetings in three rounds.
1904 2nd rd: 2-0 away
1932 semi-final at Villa Park 0-1, Arsenal scoring a late goal after being outplayed.
1971 5th rd: 1-2 home

In the League Cup, no joy at all until season 09/10
1977/78 5th rd: 0-0 home, 0-1 away
1985/86 3rd rd: 1-2 home
1986/87 3rd rd ; 1-3 away
1990/91 3rd rd: 1-2 home
2004/05 3rd rd: 1-2 home
2009/10 5th rd: 3-0 home

In the Charity Shield of 1934/35 it was a 0-4 loss at Highbury

Some connections: Joe Mercer, Niall Quinn (right), Paul Dickov, Nicolas Anelka, Brian Kidd, Eddie McGoldrick, Kolo Toure, Emmanuel Adebayor, Tommy Caton, Gael Clichy

Ground: Highbury R/A 73,295 v Sunderland Div 1 1935. (shown 1990's) Emirates Stadium capacity 63,000

Aston Villa

'The Villans' were formed in 1874, and were founder members of the Football League in 1888, playing at Aston Park, then Perry Barr and Wellington Road, before moving to Villa Park in 1897.

Villa were a strong team in the 1890s, winning the title and FA Cups regularly right through to the 1930s. They won the Cup in 1957 for the then record 7th time, but have failed to win it since and dropped down to the old Third Division but came back strongly to win the title in 1981 (with ex City manager Ron Saunders) and the European Cup in 1982, followed by numerous League Cups.

They finished season 2010/11 in the Premier League playing in claret shirts with sky blue sleeves and white shorts.

Pre-war: 58 meetings with 23 City wins, including a 5-0 in 1935/36 at Maine Road, 10 draws and 25 losses, so fairly even.

In the last game of the 1904/05 season City, after a 3-0 win at Wolves, needed to win at Villa and hope Newcastle would drop a point at Middlesbrough to take the title. If Newcastle lost then City could have afforded a draw as City's goal average was marginally better than Everton's, who City had beaten 2-0 in a bad-tempered game the week before.

Villa, the Cup winners, went 3-0 up then City pulled back to 3-2 but in the last half hour fights broke out though no-one was sent off. Tempers continued to fray, even after the final whistle. Turnbull was even pulled into the Villa dressing room and given a beating. The City party were also confronted by an angry mob armed with stones when leaving the ground.

The FA Council, on the 4th August 1905, suspended Turnbull for one month from 1st

September 1905. On statements brought to their attention it was alleged that Meredith had offered a sum of money to a Villa player, even though at that time he declared his innocence (then later admitted it for some reason), and was suspended from taking part in football until 30th April 1906. The referee was also suspended for one month from 1st September 1905, but, surprisingly, no Villa player was punished.

Unfortunately, the matter did not end there, for on the 14th February 1906, the City Directors asked the FA to deal with Meredith on the ground that he had demanded from them not only wages, to which he would have been entitled had he not been under suspension, but wages at the rate of £6 per week (which was above the maximum wage) and bonuses which the club had agreed and promised to pay to him. Commissioners appointed by the FA, during their investigations, obtained such evidence as to the conduct of the club that they decided to widen the scope of the inquiry and examine the system of management since 1902. As a result of the Commissioners' report, the Council of the FA, on the 31st May 1906 decided that Mr. W. Forrest, the former Chairman, and Mr. T.E. Maley, the Secretary and Manager of City, should not be allowed to act again in any capacity in connection with football under the jurisdiction of the Football Association.

Two other Directors, Allison and Davies, were suspended until the 30th April 1907, and the other directors, who pleaded ignorance or inattention to their duties, were ordered to resign.

Seventeen players were suspended until 1st January 1907, ordered to pay fines ranging from £25 to £100 each and were barred for ever playing again for Manchester City. The club was fined £250.

The punishment was extremely harsh, and with the loss of the management and so many players, City's first great team, which included the whole of the 1904 FA Cup winners, was destroyed.

Once the ban was lifted Burgess, Turnbull, Meredith, and Bannister joined United and helped them become successful for the first, and only, time pre-war.

Strangely, without Meredith, City made a decent fist of 1905/06 season but tailed off and finished fifth. The club, however, were devastated by the suspensions for the 1906/07 season, though City did win the 'grudge match' 4-2 against Villa at home in October 1906.

Post-war: 58 meetings with 18 City wins, 20 draws and 20 losses. In the 1958 end of season game at Maine Road Jackie Sewell scored the 100th goal against City.

In the 1962 game at Villa, City were leading 1-0 when the game was abandoned after 48 minutes. The pools panel voted it as a City win, but Villa won the rearranged fixture 3-1 in May which helped seal City's relegation.

City wins included the 5-1 at Villa Park in 1990/91, revenge for the 1-5 in 1960/61. The 2-1 win there in 1990 virtually ensured City's safety in Division One but the game was marred by poll tax protesters infiltrating the City support in the televised game.

John B: 20/4/1991 Villa 1 City 5

Bogey teams – everyone's got them, City's bête noir right now is Everton and there's seldom any logic involved.

Happily though, from a reverse perspective, there are teams out there, who for whatever reason, seem congenitally incapable of beating God's Own Manchester City, one of which is dear old Aston Villa. Of the 20 odd times I've seen us play the Villa, home and away, since the early 1980s, not once have we lost.

For the particular game selected, a midweeker close to the end of the 1990/91 season, victory was perhaps not wholly unexpected. The Villans, under the guidance of Dr Josef Venglos, ended the season in a disappointing 17th, whilst from our point of view, Peter Reid's thirst for 60 yard passes and general GBH of the football, was not yet at the point where it would destroy the fine passing side he inherited from Howard Kendall five months earlier, and consequently we went on to finish 5th.

However, the margin of City's superiority on the night was something that could not have been predicted, and it owed almost all to David White's finest hour. David White was Blue to his core, a 6ft 1" powerhouse of a winger, who had come up through the youth team, and whilst perhaps not the most technically gifted of players, he possessed phenomenal pace and was, by and large, an unerring finisher.

Opening the scoring after just five minutes, following a slick one two with the mighty Quinn, he then doubled the City lead with a well taken lob, before streaking clear of an offside trap just after the break. The excited "go on's" from the City faithful behind the goal being attacked ringing in his ears, he set up Mark Brennan for the third.

Villa then pulled one back, David Platt converting a harshly awarded penalty for handball against Steve Redmond. Whitey then resumed centre stage again, curling a beauty in off the far post to make it four, and then, as the rain started to come down hard, catching Nigel Spink unawares at his near post by cutting in from the left flank and letting go a 20 yard scudder.

During a 3 year purple patch from 1990 to 1992, David White scored 50 top flight goals for City, no mean feat for a wide man without a single, solitary trick in his armory, and all the more impressive for the fact that he pinged them in not just against the makeweight sides in the division but against all comers, United, Liverpool, Arsenal and Chelsea included.

In the Premiership 26 meetings with 12 City wins, including the 1-0 at Villa Park in 1996 when it looked like we'd escape relegation, followed by the Maine Road celebratory Oasis concert, 9 draws and 5 losses

Season	H	A	Pl	W	D	L
Pre-08/09			22	10	8	4
08/09	2-0	2-4	24	11	8	5
09/10	3-1	1-1	26	12	9	5
10/11	4-0	0-1	28	13	9	6

In the FA Cup, meetings in eight rounds:
1900 1st rd: 1-1 away, replay 1-3 home
1910 3rd rd 2-1 away
1915 2nd rd 1-0 home
1934 semi-final at Huddersfield 6-1
1936 6TH rd 2-3 away
1995 4TH rd 1-0 home

2006 5th rd 1-1 away, replay 2-1 home
2011 5th rd 3-0 home

The 1934 semi-final was played at Huddersfield in front of 45,473. Villa were favourites for the Cup but City produced one of their finest ever Cup efforts. Ernie Toseland put the Blues ahead after 4 minutes, then in a remarkable spell in the first half City scored three in four minutes to go 4-0 up at half time, though Frank Swift had to make a couple of fine saves. By the 72nd minute City were leading 6-0, Freddie Tilson having bagged four and Alex Herd the other though Villa grabbed a late consolation through Astley.

In the League Cup, meetings in three rounds:
1976/77: 2nd rd 0-3 away
1983/84: 3rd rd 0-3 away
2000/01: 3rd rd 1-0 away

In the Charity Shield of 1972, City won 1-0 at Villa Park, when the Cup winners and League champions couldn't be bothered. Was it the worst front cover of a programme of all time? This was a shame because Villa often produced superb programme front covers.

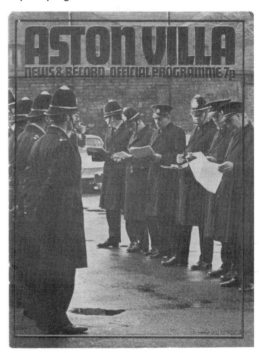

Friendlies: 1907/08 2-2 away

Some connections: Richard Dunne, Gareth Barry, Darius Vassell, James Milner, Stephen Ireland, Frank Carrodus,, Ken McNaught, Martin O'Neill, Managers Ron Saunders and Billy McNeill

Ground: Villa Park R/A 76,588 v Derby, F. A Cup 6 1946. Current capacity: 42,584 (shown 2010)

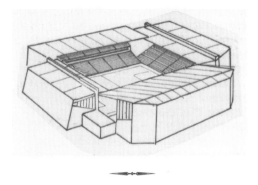

Atletico Bilbao

British miners and foundry workers arriving in the 1890's astonished the locals with their footballing antics and, together with returning Spanish students from the UK, prompted Bilbao, the oldest club in Spain nicknamed Los Leonos being formed in 1888. They had maintained First Division status since the formation of the League in 1928 winning the title six times and the cup 21 times, and once beat Barcelona 12-1 in 1930/31, by the time they played City. The team was made up entirely of Basques and played in red and white striped shirts and black shorts adopted from Southampton.

They had played at Maine Road previously when they lost to United 3-0 in the European Cup of 1956/57. After the end of the Franco regime in 1975 they changed their name back to Athletic Bilbao.

The teams first met in the 16th finals of the European Cup Winners' Cup in season 1969/70.

In the first leg over in the Basque country City earned a 3-3 draw, in front of 45,000 and in the return leg won convincingly 3-0 in front of a crowd of 49,665, but with nothing like the hype that United received with that similar score in 1957. Since those City games they've won La Liga and the Cup a couple of times, plus were UEFA Cup runners up in 1976/77.

Steve P: 17/9/1969 A. Bilbao 3 City 3

After beating Spurs 3-0 in London , as a railway employee it was free travel to Bilbao for me, overnight to Paris, and Spanish border by Monday night.

I found a Youth hostel which had now become a hotel and the owner sent me to a new hotel for the night. Spanish railway route to Bilbao goes the long way round so I hitched the eighty miles from the border. It took five hours to get half way so I took the local train for the rest of the way.

I then found a boarding house and booked beds for my railway colleagues who were coming the next day. No tickets yet, only a letter from City saying that I could get them at the ground before the match. This was in the days before we'd exported hooliganism.

I wandered down to the San Mames (shown 1980s, named after a child Martyr), Bilbao's stadium, and interrupted manager Ronnie Allen's press conference asking "excuse me, where do I get tickets for the match" and I was then sent to the City team's hotel, where I obtained three tickets. Rumour had it that it was there, pre-match, that Joe Corrigan punched a bloke with one criticism too many (and this was before his howler against West Ham!). I spent the night at the hotel and three more BR workers arrived without tickets. I tried the team's hotel but they were out for the day, so an hour before the match we were still trying to get tickets. I brandished my letter on MCFC paper and the Spanish official got excited and sent me down a tunnel underneath the stand. They opened the door for me and I was in City's dressing room. I'd got my red and black striped shirt on and the Official thought I was one of the players who'd got lost in the crowd…. despite the glasses I was wearing!

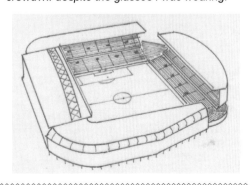

Malcolm Allison wasn't fooled though, he knew I wasn't the sub, as I explained why I was in the dressing room thirty minutes before the kick off! "Any tickets, lads?" he asked. With half a dozen comps in hand I beat a hasty retreat. Three spare tickets were given to Spanish urchins

The tickets weren't together but the Spanish were friendly, sharing half-time wine from Porro. Bilbao went two up after eleven minutes but a Neil Young special brightened half-time even before the wine. The guy with Porro was still friendly, even after Bilbao lost a 3-1 lead to Tommy Booth and a late own goal. "Manchester City" he says "bueno equipo mas poco duro" City, I thought, duro? Neil Young and Ian Bowyer? You should see Nobby Stiles, duro as nails and twice as daft.

The journey home was not helped by an allergic reaction to something in the Paella. But if this was Europe then I was all for it. We sealed the tie with a 3-0 home win, Oakes, Bell, Bowyer. Next round we drew Lierse SK. Who? Where? Belgium. Blowed if I was going to learn Flemish; I hadn't even learned how to spit!

Friendlies:

Aberdare Athletic 1902/03 a 1-0
Admira Vienna 1933/34 a 5-3
Ayr United 1902/03 a 2-1, 1934/35 a 4-1.
Altrincham 1904/05 a 1-3, 1905/06 a 2-3, 1911/12 a 1-0, 1966/67 a 4-0 1971/72 a 1-0, 1979/80 a 0-2, 1992/93 a (John King T/M), 1997/98 a, 1998/99 a res, 1998/99 a, 1999/2000 a res, 2000/01 a res
F.K Austria Vienna 1933/34 h 3-0, 1934/35 a 3-4
F.K Admira Wacker 1933/34 a 5-3
Aarhus a 1937/38 11- 1
Admira Vienna 1953/54 h 3-2
Army X1 a 53/54 5-5, 57/58 a 3-1
Aberdeen 1954/55 h 4-3, 1966/67 a 1-2, 1973/74 a 1-0
Alemannia Aachan 1954/55 a 2-4
Atlanta Chiefs 1967/68 a 2-3,1-2
Ajax 1968/69 h 3-0, 1969/70 a 3-3
All Stars X1 1974/75 h 4-6, (Tony Book T/M) 4-4 (Ken Barnes T/M)
Anderlecht 1970/71 a 0-1
Australian X1 1970/71 h 2-0,1984/85 h 1-3

Armenia Bielfield 1971/72 a 0-1
All Stars XI 1973/74 a 4-2
Ashton United 1974/75 a 8-1 2000/01 a
Atletico Madrid 1976/77 a 0-2, 1994/95 a 1-1
A.Z 67 Alkmaar 1978/79 a 1-5
A.C.Roma 1978/79 a 2-2, 1979/80 (N.York) 3-2
Aveliono 1978/79 a 2-0
A.E.K. Athens1982/83 a 0-1
Aarau1986/87 a 1-1
Al Ahly FC 1986/87 a 3-1
Aaribem 1986/87
Al Nasr F.C. 1986/871-1
Askim I.F. 1989/90 a 2-1
Avondale Select X1 1990/91
Ards 1993/94 a 5-1
F.C. Antwerp a 1993/94 0-2
Agovvapeldoorna 1993/94 a 2-0
Atherton Coll 1994/95 a 6-1
Atherton LR 1994/95 a 1-1
Athlone Town 1995/96 a, 1996/97 3-1 a
Anglesey 1996/97 a

B is for Barnet

THE B's take us down south over to Yorkshire, up to the North West, down to the Midlands, to Lancashire to Italy, Germany, Yorkshire, and the South West.

Barnet

'The Bees' were formed in 1888 but disbanded in 1901. Alston Works FC were then formed who changed their name to Barnet Alston FC in 1906, and in 1912 combined with the Avenue to become Barnet and Alston FC, then in 1919 plain Barnet FC They played at Queens Road, Totteridge Lane and in 1907 moved to Underhill.

As a non-league club they won the FA Amateur Cup in 1946 and were promoted to Division Four in 1991, with infamous cockney spiv and ticket tout Stan Flashman as chairman

They finished season 2010/11 in League Two but were relegated playing in amber and black striped shirts and black shorts.

The only meeting of the teams was in the 1994 League Cup second round over two legs. City lost the first leg 1-0 on a rainy night at Underhill which had a bad tempered finish with Tony Coton kicking the ball at City fans behind the goal, who were dishing out the abuse at City's failure to recover from going behind after 28 seconds. It was remedies though in the second leg when a 4-1 Maine Road win was recorded.

Ground: Underhill (shown 1994), R/A 11,026 v Wycombe W. FA Amateur Cup 4th rd 1951/52.

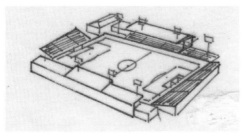

Barnsley

'The Tykes, Reds, or Colliers' were formed in 1887 by the Rev T. T. Preedy, curate of Barnsley St. Peter's, the name being dropped in 1897 a year before they entered the Second Division.

They moved into Oakwell in 1888, and as a Second Division club were runners up in the FA Cup Final in 1910 to Newcastle, drawing the first game 1-1 but losing 2-1 in the replay. Two years later, and still in the same division, they went on to win the FA Cup, beating WBA 1-0 with a goal in the last minute of extra time in another replayed game, the first game finishing 0-0. Generally a lower division club, they came up from the Fourth Division and eventually made the Premiership for a season in 1997/98, and knocked United out of the FA Cup. In season 2007/08 they reached the semi-final of the FA Cup, winning at Liverpool and beating Chelsea on the way before losing out to Cardiff City.

They finished season 2010/11 in the Championship playing in red shirts with white shorts.

Pre-war: 10 league meetings with 5 City wins including a 5-0 in 1898/99 and a 7-3 in 1927/28, both at home, and 5 losses.

Post-war: 18 league meetings with 8 City wins 5 draws and 5 defeats.

In 1946/47, City won both games on the way to promotion, 5-1 at Maine Road and 2-0 at Barnsley. There were two league meetings in 1950/51 with City winning 6-0 at Maine Road and drawing 1-1 at Oakwell, on the way to promotion. This was followed by eight league meetings in the 80's, City winning two drawing four and losing two. The City special train, having hit a horse on the track, arrived late for one of these away games and City supporters on the open Kop were treated to the amusing sight of Blues running down the hill to the ground. The 2-1 win in September 1988 saw the launch of the City fanzine *King of the Kippax*, Trevor Morley scoring the winning *Brazilian-like* goal.

Then there were a further six meetings, City winning three and losing three, as Barnsley did the double and went on to promotion in 1996/97 with Blues fans singing "we'd rather be in Barnsley than Barbados" referring to the absent Chairman Francis Lee. But in 1999/2000 it was City's turn to gain promotion, though there were half time disturbances in the City end at Barnsley when they ran out of pies! In 2002, City's 5-1 Maine Road win sealed promotion with two games remaining, which were both won!

C. Savage: 6/4/2002 City 5 Barnsley 1

Wolves' loss at Millwall the day before, following our victory at Molyneux during the week, had ensured that we would be playing in the Premiership in 2002/3 so this was a chance to celebrate with the pressure more or less off, against a team battling against relegation. A win would guarantee us the title as well so plenty to play for.

I was offered the chance of a corporate jolly, thanks to one of our suppliers at the time, who was none other than Harry Dowd's son, Alex. We turned up early and had some lunch in the box, which was in the Platt Lane stand and Alex was telling us about his dad. Amazingly, Harry treated football as just a job, something he was good at. He had no real interest in the game at all and before games Joe Mercer would give the team talk. "Now Harry" Joe would say "we're playing Arsenal today and they wear red shirts with white sleeves."

As anyone who has done the corporate thing will know, there are betting slips on the tables and someone comes round to collect them. I don't usually bet but decided to splash out this time, as all my colleagues were doing so. I fancied a good result for us so split the bet between a 3-1, 4-1 and 5-1 scoreline to City.

The game kicked off and, with Ali Benarbia pulling the strings, City went into a 2 goal lead with the little genius setting up Huckerby in the 11th and 36th minutes. Barnsley had few chances but converted one just before the break and at half-time I'm one more City goal away from being in the money. That duly came from Jon Macken in the 53rd minutes, followed by Huckerby's third and our fourth in the 62nd minute. Macken then got the fifth goal with just over 20 minutes to go. City were rampant and the chances of it staying 5-1 looked remote. My colleagues were increasingly amused by my howls of anguish as one chance after another looked like it was heading for the net yet somehow stayed out. The minutes ticked agonisingly away and with each, frequent, City attack my potential winnings seemed about to vanish in front of my eyes.

However, the whistle finally went without further score, City had won the Championship and I'd won a fair bit of money. The crowd stayed long after the game to celebrate and all in all it had been a good day out. After the game however, among all the euphoria, Keegan chose to launch an emotional attack on the FA for not allowing him to appoint Arthur Cox as his assistant when he was England manager. Stuart Pearce also announced his intention to retire from playing at the same time. Everything looked rosy in the garden with our next season in the Premiership also being our final season at Maine Road but, City being City, less than 12 months later we were to be in boardroom turmoil again.

Neil S: 31/7/2008 City 2 Streymur 0

When I first visited Oakwell I was wearing my school uniform and Phil Boyer was leading the City attack. Twenty eight years and five relegations later, my dreams of City invincibility had long since faded.

I've seen Barnsley score in the first minute and equalize in the last minute. I've witnessed police brutality and the home mascot provoking the away fans. I've even queued up for the toilets next to Charlie Williams. Win, lose or draw, there's always a clown with a drum.

How ironic that as Bojinov approached full fitness, our first home fixture should clash with a Bon Jovi concert at Eastlands. At least Bon Jovi lasted ninety minutes.

To avoid the inevitable traffic jams on Snake Pass, we meandered towards Buxton and Sheffield. The Sat Nav sounded totally bewildered and after surveying the thunderous South Yorkshire skyline I found myself asking the same question.

Most of the pubs were closed and the town centre was deserted. It would be an understatement to suggest that the locals lacked enthusiasm for the Manchester City roadshow.

The sum total of the Barnsley effort amounted to Wonderwall and a couple of City flags draped over the seats near the corner flags in the opposite stand. A coachload of screaming Streymur schoolkids was hardly the missing ingredient as City kicked off to a backdrop of midsummer apathy.

Overall the match was too lively for a Testimonial, but lacked the intensity of the Premier League. We could have won 10-0 and it would still have been boring.

City never looked in danger, but the match

was a perfect advertisement for the cricket season. Meanwhile, Sods' Law had dictated that the clown with the drum was sat two rows in front of me. We drove home in silence all secretly praying for a future that didn't involve City playing in July.

In The FA Cup, meetings in two rounds:
1948 3rd rd 2-1 home 1993 5th rd 2-0 home

In the League Cup, meetings in two rounds:
1981/82 4th rd 0-1 away
2004/05 2nd rd 7-1 home

Friendlies: 1949/50 a 0-0, 1996/97 a (Gary Fleming T/M) 2-2, 2009/10 a 1-1.

Some connections: Mick McCarthy, Fred Tilson, Eric Brook, Gary Fleming

F. TILSON

E. F. BROOK (MANCHESTER CITY)

Ground: Oakwell (shown 2000's*) R/A 40,255 v Stoke FA Cup 5 1936

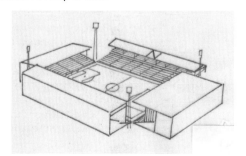

Barrow

'The Ziggers, then the Bluebirds' were formed in 1901 and played at The Strawberry, Ainslie Street, and Little Park before moving to Holker Street (R/A 16,874) a former rubbish tip, in 1909. They were founder members of Division Three in 1921, and were successfully re-elected no less than ten times before failing in 1972, to be replaced by Hereford United.

They finished season 2010/11 in the Blue Square Premier playing in blue/white shirts with Blue shorts.

The teams have met just the once, in the FA Cup third round of 1946, when for the only time, each round was played on a two-legged basis, City winning 6-2 in the first leg at Maine Road and drawing 2-2 in the second at Holker Street.

Friendlies: 1982/83 a 2-2, 1991/92 a 3-1, 1993/94 (Colin Cowperthwaite T/M), 1993/94 (Billy McAdams T/M) a 0-0

Connection: Billy McAdams

Ground: Holker Street (shown 1940's) capacity now 4,256

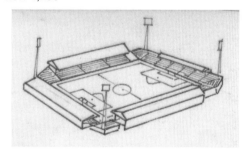

Birmingham City

'The Blues' were formed in 1875 when cricketing enthusiasts and members of Trinity Church Bordesley then formed the Small Heath Alliance football club which played on waste ground near Arthur Street, at Ladypool Road. They moved on to Muntz Street in 1877 then as Birmingham to St. Andrews in 1906, adding City to their name in 1945.

The club was a founder member of Division Two in 1892, and after promotion in 1893 were mainly a First Division club. They were, losing FA Cup finalists in 1931 and 1956, won the

League Cup in 1963, and were losing finalists in the Inter Cities Fairs Cup in 1960 and 1961. They then spent time in the Second Division, spent seven seasons in the First and then yo-yoed, even having a stint in the old Third Division before eventually making it back to the Premiership. Ups and downs since then and they finished season 2010/11 in the Premiership , winning the League Cup but being relegated playing in dark blue shirts and white shorts.

Pre-war: 58 league meetings with 25 City wins 8 draws and 25 losses.

First meetings were in the Second Division in 1892/93 but in 1893/94 the Brummies (as Small Heath) registered a 10-2 win at St. Andrews which for some reason isn't recorded as City's biggest ever defeat (possibly as City were still named Ardwick!?), City's goalie went missing for part of the time, and it was the most goals City have conceded! This came two days after City's 0-5 loss at Notts County and seven days before the 0-6 loss at Lincoln. In season 1895/96 City finished second in the Second Division and played Test matches against West Brom (bottom of Division One) and Small Heath (2nd bottom of Division One, respectively) to determine who played in Division One the next season. After drawing at home with Albion (when the club put prices up, and fans stayed away in protest) then losing 1-6 away, City beat Small Heath 3-0 at home but lost 0-8 away to remain in Division Two, WBA stayed up, Liverpool were promoted as Champions of Division Two and Test match winners and Small Heath were relegated. The 1898/99 season was the first to feature automatic promotion which City achieved, clinching it with a 2-0 home win over Small Heath, with two games remaining which were also both won.

Out of the last fourteen games in the 1930s City lost only once, v Brum and the final game of 1936/37 season, a 2-2 draw was City's 22nd league game without defeat.

Post-war: 62 league meetings with 30 City wins 11 draws and 21 defeats.

Each team generally won their home games. The game at Maine Road on February 15th 1958, City's first home game after the Munich Air disaster, was abandoned after 40 minutes due to a waterlogged pitch with the scores at 1-1. Season 1958/59 saw strange Christmas results. City lost 1-6 away on Boxing Day with

four own goals being amongst the six, and the following day a confident Birmingham team were sent home from Maine Road with a 4-1 defeat!

The 1961/62 home game saw City's youngest ever player, Glyn Pardoe, make his debut at the tender age of 15 years 314 days. It was a 1-4 defeat and Glyn was later converted from centre forward to full back.

After the humiliating League Cup exit in 1962/63 City managed a couple of doubles in the late seventies. In 1980 Birmingham had a rare win at City, 1-0, which was John Bond's first game in charge as manager.

The teams were neck and neck for promotion in 1984/85 and in April, a 0-0 draw at St Andrews seemingly put City on course though there were a few stumbles before third place was clinched.

In the Premiership:

Season	H	A	Pl	W	D	L
Pre-07/08			8	5	1	2
07/08	1-0	1-3	10	6	1	3
09/10	5-1	1-1	12	7	2	3
10/11	1-1	2-2	14	7	4	3

Birmingham have also featured in three FA Cup semi-final replays at Maine Road. First was in 1946 when they lost 4-0 to Derby County, in front of 80,480, a record mid week attendance on a club ground. Next was in 1951 when they lost to Blackpool 2-1 and then in 1975 they also lost, surprisingly to Second Division Fulham.

Neil S: 11/12/1989 B'ham 0 City 2

According to Wikipedia the Birmingham Zulu Warriors acquired their nickname from a specific chant against Manchester City in 1982. I don't remember the occasion, but I'm sure most City supporters can recall a game when the Battle of Isandlwana has been restaged at St Andrews.

If there was a Champions League for misery, Manchester City would be perennial semi-finalists alongside Atletico Madrid (until the 2009/10 season's Europa Cup triumph) and Espanyol. Birmingham City would win the competition every year. They're probably my second favourite club, but any outfit that considers Manchester City as a bogey team, can't be taken too seriously.

Their fans are vocal and often frightening, but there's an admirable sense of stoicism as they sing "Keep right on to the end of the road" during their frequent moments of adversity. The Blues will never attract glory hunters.

When City travelled to Birmingham in 1989 the similarities were painfully obvious. Both clubs resembled a financial shambles as United and Aston Villa began to emerge as powerful contenders in the top division.

On the pitch, the teams were heading in opposite directions. City were heavily reliant on the youthful promise of the Class of '86, but in the immortal words of the Birmingham skipper, Vince Overson:"This club isn't a sleeping giant; it's comatose"

We sat in the Main Stand and I remember this game for three reasons:

First, the game kicked off to a backdrop of total anarchy as the home fans demonstrated against the Board. Their actions were obviously premeditated and at one point they were smashing into the executive boxes. Even the stewards applauded.

Secondly, Neil McNab scored from a long shot just outside the penaly area that curved so viciously in the swirling wind it hit the inside of the side netting. To put it bluntly, the goal didn't belong in the Second Division.

Thirdly, as the game drifted towards a comfortable City victory, the atmosphere reverted to something resembling a Christmas Truce.

One of the pleasing aspects of supporting Manchester City is that we rarely kick anyone when they're on their knees. Birmingham were suffering and as the City supporters chanted "Sack the Board", there was an audible roar of approval from the Tilton Road End.

Back and forth, the newly found mutual respect continued.

"You're the pride of Manchester"
"You're the pride of Birmingham"

In the middle of a particularly bleak and depressing period for English football, two sets of football fans had found common ground. By the time of our next meeting the roles had reversed.

In the FA Cup, meetings in eight rounds, plus a Final.
1899 1st rd 2-3 away
1913 1sr rd 4-0 home
1927 3rd rd 1-4 away
1929 3rd rd 1-3 away
1947 5th rd 0-5 away
1951 3rd rd 0-2 away
1955 6th rd 1-0 away
1956 final 3-1
2001 3rd rd 3-2 home

Roy Paul lifts the FA Cup after defeating Birmingham City 3-1 in 1956

There were some stirring cup battles, including a 0-5 loss in 1947 and a sixth round tie at St Andrews in 1955 when City exorcised their bogey by winning 1-0. This was followed by the 1956 Cup Final, when City's patched up team beat the 'Iron Men of the Midlands' and red hot favourites 3-1 with Bert Trautmann playing the last part of the game with a broken neck. Hayes, Johnstone and Dyson netting our goals

In the League Cup, meetings in two rounds, City losing away in the fifth round of 1962/63 0-6, but winning 6-0 at home in the third round of 2001/02.

Some connections: Roy Warhurst, Alex Harley (30 goals in a relegations season), Robert Hopkins, Joe Hart, Trevor Francis, and managers John Bond and Howard Kendall

Friendlies: 1969/70 (Ron Wylie T/M), 3-2 at St Andrews.

City lost the 1924 semi-final 0-2 to Newcastle at St Andrews in front of a crowd of 50,039

Ground: St. Andrews (shown 2010) R/A: 66,844 v Everton FA Cup 5th rd in 1939.

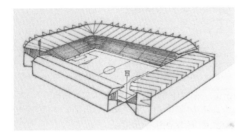

Blackburn Rovers

'T'Rovers were formed in 1875 when a group of public school old boys started playing at Leamington Road, moving to Ewood Park in 1899. Leading light was John Lewis (founder of the Lancashire FA, later a double Cup Final referee, and vice-president of the FA and Football League) who formed the club.

They were founder members of the Football League winning the title in 1912 and 1914 and the Cup five times before the turn of the century and once since in 1928.

They were invariably a First Division club but post war spent many seasons in the Second and even the Third Division, until, after winning the Full Members Cup in 1987, Jack Walker's cash catapulted them into the 20th century. They won the Premiership in 1995, and the League Cup in 2002. Maggie Thatcher was (in)famously an Honorary President.

They finished season 2010/11 in the Premiership playing in blue and white halved shirts and white shorts.

Pre-war: 60 league meetings with 21 City wins 18 draws and 21 losses.

The teams first met in season 1899/00 and despite a 4-1 win at Ewood Park in 1902, City drew their last match at home to Stoke and took the drop, Stoke staying up! Results were then mixed right up to the war period, ending up 'even stevens', with a few FA Cup encounters too, but without a City win at Ewood after the 1-0 in 1930/31.

Post-war: 24 league meetings, with 10 City wins, 0 draws and 14 losses

The Ewood bogey continued post war ending briefly with the 4-1 fifth round FA Cup win in 1969, and again in 1985 on manager Billy McNeill's birthday when the 2-1 win on an icy pitch put City on top of the Second Division, albeit briefly. City's 0-4 loss on 15th April 1989 (with left footed Ged Taggart playing at right back) was also the tragic day of the Hillsborough disaster

Promotion was gained in the last match of 2000, with a 4-1 win after Rovers had gone ahead and hit the woodwork on four occasions. Goater, Dailly og, Dickov and Kennedy scoring the City goals.

Brian D: 15/4/1989 Rovers 4 City 0

A top of the table clash, well almost. With Chelsea running away with Division Two it seemed that City, in second place, or Blackburn would go up with them. Having taken nine points out of the previous twelve we were going great guns, and the whole of our ticket allocation was snapped up. This gave us one whole end and half of one side, constituting about 7,000 of the just under 17,000 attending. (Don't let anybody EVER tell you that money doesn't bring success - this was Rovers' biggest crowd of the season by far - their home support at the time was in the region of 8,000 for a normal game, the archetypal "Sh*t Ground, No Fans!" Of course, all that changed when Uncle Jack came along with his millions.....) We were in the terracing at the side, packed in, shoulder to shoulder. On my way to the toilet before the match started, I noticed that the seated area behind us was built on tiered wooden beams - underneath these were piles of rubbish. Had we learned nothing from the Bradford City fire? The sun was shining, promotion was within our grasp and everybody was in confident mood. Of course, we got slaughtered. I exaggerate not when I tell you the 0-4 scoreline flattered us. They hit the woodwork, they had it cleared off the line and they missed shots when it was easier to score. What was novel at the time was that the Riverside Terrace fans, opposite us, still followed the tradition of moving from one end of the ground to the other, depending on which goal they were playing towards. They particularly relished being at our end as they could enjoy our discomfort. Our response? - we burst into a triumphant rendition of "Are You Watching Liverpool?" Well, what could you do? It was just one of those days.

About ten minutes from the end of the game came the following announcement:

"Our thanks to all City fans for your magnificent support. Just to remind you, the gates at your end of the ground will remain shut for a few minutes to allow the home support to clear, then you will be given a police escort back to your transport - safe journey home"

This announcement was repeated five minutes and two minutes from time. On the final whistle the announcement was made again as we all trudged towards the gates only to find them open! 7000 of us spilled onto the streets to find an escort of ONE mounted policeman to lead us *"back to our transport"* even though this included coaches, cars and presumably, the train!

Now in life in general, and sky blue life in particular, events occur from time to time which put things into perspective. We were not too chuffed at the afternoon's proceedings and faced a long, disgruntled trip home. Is there anything worse? Well, yes, actually, as we found when we switched on the car radio to hear the news that the FA Cup semi-final between Liverpool and Nottingham Forest that afternoon had been abandoned....

In the Premiership: In 1994/95 with City struggling, and Rovers riding high, we gained a magnificent 3-2 win which looked like handing the title to United. Happily Rovers pulled their form round to clinch it, though they lost their last game at Liverpool whilst United failed to win at West Ham. In 2003/04 another 3-2 away win saw City briefly top the table in September less than five years after losing at York City who, by that time, had been relegated from the Football League.

Season	H	A	Pl	W	D	L
Pre 08/09			20	3	7	10
08/09	3-1	2-2	22	4	8	10
09/10	4-1	2-0	24	6	8	10
10/11	1-1	1-0	26	7	9	10

In the FA Cup, meetings in five rounds:
1907 1st rd 2-2 away, 0-1 home
1914 3rd rd 2-1 away
1934 3rd rd 3-1 home
1969 5th rd 4-1 away (much postponed)
2007 6th rd 0-2 away

Blackburn lost the 1958 semi-final 2-1 at Maine Road to Bolton.

In the League Cup, just the one meeting in the fourth round of 2001/02, which Second Division City lost 0-2.

In the Simod Cup first round of 1988/89 City lost 3-2 at Blackburn.

In the Anglo-Scottish Cup City lost 0-1 away in 1975/76

Some connections: Colin Hendry (below), Nicky Reid, Peter Dobing, Johnny Williamson, manager Howard Kendall

Friendlies: 1891/92 h 1-1, 1900/01 h 1-2, 1939/40 a 2-1, 1976/77 a (Mick Heaton and Andy Burgin Benefit match) 1-2, 1990/91 a (Noel Brotherston T/M) 2-0.

Ground: Ewood Park (shown 2010) , R/A 61,783 v Bolton FA Cup 6th round in 1929

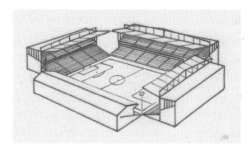

Blackpool

'The Seasiders' - Blackpool St Johns, were formed in the summer of 1887 in a meeting of St. John's School old boys in the Stanley Arms Hotel. They previously played at Raikes Hall from 1888, and had a brief spell at The Athletic Grounds in Stanley Park. They merged with South Shore FC who had previously played at Cow Gap Lane, in 1899 and moved to Bloomfield Road.

Blackpool were elected to Division Two in 1896, failed to achieve re-election in 1899, were re-elected in 1900, and stayed in Division Two until 1930. After a few years back in Division Two they were promoted to Division One in 1937 and stayed there for thirty years, reaching FA Cup finals in 1948 and 1951 and winning it in 1953 when they were a prominent First Division team. After relegation in 1967 their fortunes dipped and they dropped down to Division Four before climbing all the way back up to the Premiership. They finished season 2010/11, playing in Tangerine shirts and white shorts, in the Premiership but being relegated.

Pre-war: 20 league meetings with 10 City wins, 6 draws and 4 losses.

First meeting was in Division Two in 1896/97 and City had the upper hand in the pre-war meetings including a 7-1 win in 1931/32, and 5-1 in the following season, both at Maine Road. Ironically Blackpool's 4-2 win at City in 1930/31 and their late equaliser in the 2-2 last match of the season at Bloomfield Road helped them to stay up by a single point. (a similar situation to that of 1960/61 the game being drawn after City were three up at half time) However City failed to win any of the last five meetings before the war at the seaside.

Post-war: 36 league meetings with 12 City wins, 12 draws and 12 losses. A 5-0 home win was recorded in 1952/53 a couple of weeks before their Cup Final appearance, but Blackpool won 6-1 at Maine Road in 1955 the week before our Wembley final. In 1960 Bert made his 400th appearance for City at Maine Road in the 2-3 defeat at Maine Road, a record later surpassed by Alan Oakes. He also appeared for the Football League v The Irish League at Bloomfield Road in 1960/61

At the start of the 1998/99 season a crowd of 32,134 turned up to watch City beat 'Pool 3-0, at Maine Road our first game in the third tier.

Roger R: 3/8/1974 Blackpool 1 City 1 Team: Corrigan, Barrett, Donachie, Doyle, Booth, Oakes, Summerbee, Bell, Lee, Marsh, Tueart. This was a Texaco Cup match (one of three games in a pre-season "mini tournament").

I can still remember this day when City were playing Blackpool at Bloomfield Road – it was a really hot, sunny, early August day and my late Dad was driving (as he always did, even driving us all the way down to Chelsea for the European Cup Winners' Cup Semi Final first leg match in 1970 in an old beaten up Cortina. He drove us back again after the match in thick fog for most of the way. He was a real star!) Anyway, Dad was driving us to Blackpool for this Texaco Cup match. We had left fairly early as we usually went for fish and chips on the sea front, and even though it was a red hot day we weren't going to change the habit of a lifetime! As we were driving along, in front of us was none other than the familiar sight of a Finglands coach, and yes, it WAS the first team coach! Needless to say I suddenly became the "big kid" that exists in all of us and we spent most of the way there zigzagging past the coach and then letting it go past us hoping that we might catch a glimpse of the City players! The game itself ended up being a useful pre-season "work-out" with Dennis Tueart scoring City's goal in a 1-1 draw.

In the Premiership just the two meetings, a 3-2 win away and 1-0 at home in season 2010/11

In the FA Cup, meetings in four rounds:
1956 3rd rd: 1-1 abandoned (fog),
2-1 replay home
1966 3rd rd 1-1 away 3-1 home
1984 3rd rd 1-2 away
1988 4th rd 1-1 away, 2-1 home

Blackpool have also featured in an FA Cup semi final replay at Maine Road in 1950/51 winning 2-1 v Birmingham.

In the League Cup, meetings in six rounds:
1962/63 2nd rd: 0-0 home, 3-3 away, 4-2 home
1967/68 3rd rd 1-1 home, 2-1 away
1968/69 2nd rd 0-1 away
1978/79 3rd rd 1-1 away, 3-0 home
1984/85 2nd rd 1st leg 4-2 home,
2nd leg 3-1 away
1997/98 1st rd 1st leg 0-1 away,
2nd leg 1-0 home lost 2-4 on pens

Anglo-Scottish Cup 1975/76 a 0-1

Texaco Cup 1974/75 a 1-1

Friendlies: 1891/92 H 4-0, 1892/93 H 2-7, A 1-6, 1896/97 A 1-2, H 1-2, 1935/36 A 4-1, 1936/37 A 0-1, 1939/40H 5-3, A 3-0, 1941/42 A 3-1, 1963/64 A 1-4, 1973/74 A 0-0 Walter Jackson (Bobby Charlton X1), 1983/84 A 1-3, 199/98 A

Some connections: Northern Irishman Peter Doherty, possibly City's greatest ever player, signed in 1936, for £10,000, helped win the title in 1937, but moved on to Derby County in the war years. Paul Stewart, Roy Gratrix, Ken McNaught, Tommy Browell,

FOOTBALL · P. J. DOHERTY. BLACKPOOL

Ground: Bloomfield Road (shown 1958) R/A 38,098 V Woves D1 1955. or 39,118 v Man U. D1 1932

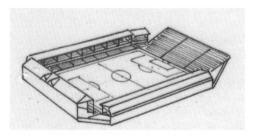

Bologna

'The Rossoblu (red-blues) Felsinei' were formed in 1909 as AGC Bologna. Their colours, red and blue stripes, were thought to have been adopted from those of Crystal Palace. Seven times Champions, and Italian Cup winners in 1969/70 and 1973/74). They played at The Stadio Littoriale from 1927, which was re-named Stadio Communale after the war, and then the Stadio Dall'Ara in 1983.Capacity 38,000.

The teams met in the Anglo-Italian League Cup Winners' Cup in September 1970. Bologna won the first leg 1-0 at home (28,000) and drew the second 2-2 at Maine Road, Heslop and Lee scoring in front of 25,843. In the programme Derek Potter of the Daily Express thought that major English clubs rushing towards paying £200,000 for a player were committing financial suicide!.

They've had little success since the 70's, winning only the Intertoto Cup in 1998.

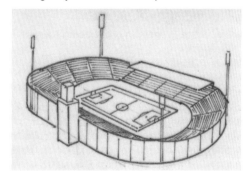

Bolton Wanderers

The Trotters' were formed in 1874 by the boys of the Christ Church Sunday School, but broke away to form Bolton Wanderers when too many rules were laid down regarding usage of Church premises in 1877. They played at Park Recreation Ground, and then Cockle's Field before moving to Burnden Park in 1895, and then the Reebok Stadium in 1997.

They were founder members of the Football League in 1888, and spent most of their time in Division One, winning the FA Cup in 1923, 1926, 1929 and 1958.

However after relegation in 1964, they went down to the Third, came back up to the First in the seventies, but sank down to the Fourth before bouncing back up to The Premiership in 2001, where they've stayed since and finished season 2010/11 playing in white shirts and navy blue shorts.

Pre-war: 48 league meetings with 17 City wins, 16 draws and 15 defeats.

From 1900/01 until 1937/38 it was even stevens, each team generally winning their home games with City registering Bolton's heaviest defeat, 7-0, at Maine Road in 1935/36, when Fred Swift kept goal for Bolton, and brother Frank kept a clean sheet for City.

Post-war: 42 league meetings with 16 City wins, 6 draws and 20 defeats.

Again, each team generally won their home games. New signing Bobby Johnstone made his debut in the 4-2 home win in 1955, immediately winning over the doubters.

Ted K: 3/9/1958 Bolton 4 City 1

I was in my second year at Old Moat Secondary School in Withington. It was a day I'll never forget, City were playing away at Burnden Park. Two weeks previously we had travelled to Burnley to witness a 4-3 victory after being 3-0 down at half time, so we were expecting a similar game that night, but unfortunately it didn't turn out that way. In those days all the newsagents had a billboard outside their shops advertising forthcoming football trips and on this particular occasion we were picked up around 5-30 pm outside Clough's Newsagents on Princess Parade in Fallowfield for the short journey to Bolton. Having finished school at 4pm I rushed home, had a quick tea, wash, and change of clothes and made my way to Cloughies shop "over the bridge" as we called it, because it was over a railway line.

The game was our fourth of the new season and we had drawn 3-3 with Bill Ridding's team at Maine Road the week before, (August 27th) in a 6-30pm kick off! We went into this match on four points (in those days it was only two points for a win), in front of a massive crowd of almost 40,000. Bolton were FA Cup holders, with the likes of Nat Lofthouse, Tommy Banks, Dougie Holden, Ralph Gubbins, Eddie Hopkinson etc. We had our usual team from the late fifties, and to be honest, were a club in decline at the time, fighting against relegation most seasons, but generally succeeding. This night the Trotters were in fine form, bombarding Trautmann's goal

and Dave Ewing was given a torrid time by Dennis Stevens and Nat Lofthouse up front. A steam train used to stop at a signal behind the open end, and even the train driver was applauding his team from his cab. He must have paid the signal man to do that! With the score at 0-0 Ray Parry shot from an oblique angle; Trautmann had his near post covered but the ball found a 'hole' in the side netting and a goal was given. What an injustice, and Bert raced to the half way dragged the referee, Arthur Ellis, back to point out the damage to his side netting. Arthur, wasn't having any of it though, and the goal stood. As a consequence our team lost their discipline and ended up losing the game 4-1 with Joe Hayes scoring a consolation goal with the score at 4-0.

Before catching our coach back home we had pie, chips, and peas from a chip shop across the road and they tasted better than the defeat. Following that infamous game City went another six games without a win. We always maintain they were happy days and I suppose they were but our rollercoaster syndrome was in evidence fifty years ago. Would we change it? NO WAY that's what MCFC are all about

Roger R: 10/4/1965 Bolton 4 City 0
Team Dowd, Bacuzzi, Gomersall, Kennedy, Wood, Cheetham, Connor, Crossan, Ogden, Oakes, Young. Second Division

I was only eight and the ground seemed absolutely huge! My dad and I were sitting at the back of one of the big stands – at what seemed to be "eye level" with the railway line that ran at the back of the terracing behind the goal at one end. City were absolutely annihilated 4-0, and we did well to get 0. Messrs Davies, Hill and Lee played a major part in this Trotters victory, and all of the trio later went on to play for City. This was one of those rare occasions when my Dad saw fit to take me to an away match, and it was possibly the biggest disappointment for an eight year old, although it didn't take much longer for me to get used to seeing City being absolutely stuffed on a more regular basis, especially away from home!

In the **Premiership:** City included a 6-2 home win in 2003/04, though SWP was sent off.

Season	H	A	Pl	W	D	L
Pre 08/09			14	6	3	5
08/09	1-0	0-2	16	7	3	6
09/10	2-0	3-3	18	8	4	6
10/11	1-0	2-0	20	10	4	6

In the FA Cup, meetings in six rounds plus two finals:
1898 2nd rd 0-1 away
1904 Final 1-0, at Crystal Palace.
1905 2nd rd 1-2 home
1922 2nd rd 3-1 away
1926 Final 0-1 at Wembley – City being relegated one week later!
1933 5th rd 4-2 away
1937 5th rd 5-0 away
1947 4th rd 3-3 away, rp1-0 home

Bolton have won two FA Cup semi-finals at Maine Road, 4-3 v Everton in 1953, and 2-1 v Blackburn in 1958.

In the League Cup, just three meetings:
1966/67 2nd rd 3-1 home
1971/72 3rd rd 0-3 away, First Division table toppers City losing out to Third Division Bolton by a Gary Lee hat-trick
2007/08 1-0 away

Friendlies: 1891/92 H 0-3, 1892/93 H 3-0, 1893/94 H 0-5, 1894/95 H 2-3, 1900/01 A 0-2, 1902/03 H 3-1, 1924/25 A 0-3, 1939/40 A 2-2, 1955/67 13th August not played 15th August 0-0, 1989/90 A (Nat Lofthouse T/M) 2-0, 1990/91 (Freddie Hill T/M) 1-2 1992/93 (Frank Worthington T/M) 2-4

Some connections: Francis Lee, Wyn Davies, Freddie Hill, Billy McAdams, Nicolas Anelka, Peter Reid, Martin Petrov.....

Ground: Burnden Park (shown 1950's), R/A 69,912 V City FA Cup 5th round 1933, moved to The Reebok in 1997, capacity 28,723

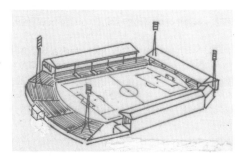

Bootle

'The Boot Boys' (possible nickname?) were formed in 1880, as Bootle St. John's F.C, by The Reverend Alfred Keely, and played in blue and white striped shirts and navy shorts.. They moved to the cricket ground on Hawthorne Road in 1884 and in 1889 they recorded an estimated record crowd of 20,000 in a friendly v Everton. They were founder members of Division Two in 1892, but despite a decent season finishing eighth they resigned owing to financial problems, their place being taken by.......Liverpool!

City, played them in the first game in the Alliance in 1891, then on the 3rd September 1892, won 7-0 which was Ardwick's first game in Division Two, even though the Blues first penalty was saved by the Bootle keeper. City lost the return 3-5.

New club, Bootle Athletic formed in 1948, folded in 1953/54, then a new Bootle FC emerged and finished season 2010/11 in the North West Counties League Premier Division.

Borussia Monchengladbach

Founded in May 1900 the result of an amalgamation of two local youth teams from this small textile town in the Ruhr. They languished in the regional leagues until 1960 when they became surprise winners of the German Cup, though a few months later they lost 11-0 to Glasgow Rangers in the first round of the European Cup Winners' Cup. Their turning point came in 1964 when they appointed Hennes Weisweller as coach who immediately put his theories on open attacking football into operation. With Gunter Netzer and Bertie Vogts in their squad they won the Bundesliga in 1970 and 1971. They were Champions again in 1975, 76 and 77 under new coach Udo Lattek. They also won the 1975 UEFA Cup, and in 1977 were runners up in the European Cup when their striker, Alan Simonsen was voted European Player Of the Year. Season 2010/11 saw them lose several first team players and struggling in The Bundesliga.

In 1978 they entered the UEFA Cup and by March 1979 they had progressed to the quarter finals after defeating Sturm Graz (Austria),

Benfica (Portugal), and Slask Wroclaw (Poland) and were drawn to play City at Maine Road in the first leg - a 1-1 draw in front of 39,005, with Mick Channon scoring for City.

Steve M: 7/3/1979 City 1 Borussia M 1

Three of us set off from leafy Tunbridge Wells after a gruelling morning's work calculating insurance policy surrender values. A train into Charing Cross with the first bevvy of the day, then underground to Euston for the train to Piccadilly. Armed with ample cans, we chatted excitedly about the forthcoming evening's game and the impact which the recently-returned Big Mal would have had on Booky's team selection. Would we really risk giving 18 year-old Nicky Reid his debut in such a big game?

Arriving in Manchester around 4.30, it was straight onto the 76 bus to Maine Road, getting off a stop early so as to avail ourselves of the delights of the Manchester Programme shop on Upper Lloyd Street. Now a full six months into my first job, I was feeling relatively flush and bought a huge wad of City programmes, including some real rarities. Next stop Roy Clarke's Social Club, for a few pre-match pints before heading off, somewhat unsteadily, to the turnstiles. The combination of the cold March air with alcoholic overindulgence had inevitable consequences, although we didn't help ourselves by standing in Windy Corner! Head spinning and brain focussed primarily on trying to stay upright, the one thing I do remember was suddenly realising that I was no longer in possession of my programmes – still, no worries, there'd be plenty of time for a couple more beers in the Social Club after the game and no doubt someone would have found them and put them behind the bar.

The game passed by in a blur, the only time I've been drunk at a match and unable to remember anything about it. How I wish I'd done it far more often over the subsequent 30 years! After the 1-1 draw it was back to the Social Club for a couple more pints before heading back to Piccadilly for the London sleeper. But, alas, without programmes. They weren't where I left them before the game and no-one had handed them in. Surely a fellow City fan wouldn't have nicked them? Must've been the bloody Germans. A lesson learned? I wish!!

We were desperate for a few hours' kip on the way back to London, but any hopes were scuppered when we were joined in our compartment by three Norwegian Blues, still full of enthusiasm after their own expedition and eager to lap up as much City knowledge as they could. They were also well equipped with booze and, however much you've had, you never turn down free drink, do you? They'd created a splendid tribute to Asa Hartford, which I've never heard anywhere else but also never forgotten. "Asa Hartford, Asa Asa Hartford, playing in the midfield, playing like a king" to the tune of "It's a Heartache" by the grotesquely misnamed "Bonnie" Tyler. It must have received literally hundreds of airings throughout the early hours, along with the full back-catalogue of more familiar chants. Sleep was not on the agenda.

Anyway, we arrived back at Euston about 6am, in that no-man's land between drunk and hungover, and eventually got to Tunbridge Wells by 7.30, allowing a couple of hours' kip before scraping into the office just before the 10am deadline under the "flexitime" system. We were met with disdain by our colleagues, unable to comprehend the concept of a 19-hour round-trip just to watch a football match, especially when none of us could remember anything about the game! "Christ, you'd be able to see the away leg in less time than that!" was the general sentiment. Sadly, that was out of our price range.

In the return leg it was a 3-1 loss for the Blues, with Kaziu Deyna scoring the goal in front of 30,000.

This was City's last European game until season 2003/04. B/M went on to win the UEFA Cup but have only won a single German Cup since.

Roger R: 20/3/1979 BM 3 City 1
**Borussia Monchengladbach...20.3.1979
Team: Corrigan, Donachie, Power, Reid, Watson, Booth, Channon, Viljoen, Kidd, Hartford, Barnes**

I can still remember – somehow – ending up in the Holiday Inn in Monchengladbach and seeing some of the City players as they relaxed prior to the match. Asa Hartford even came up to me and had a chat! I was there for the day and walked around the town prior to the match….and I can recall thinking to myself where is all the graffiti? It must have been at that time the cleanest town I had ever seen – not a trace of graffiti or rubbish anywhere, and I even bought for myself some German underwear – a sort of cross between boxers and pants, bought deliberately on the basis that I would be the only guy in Manchester wearing German underwear! Anyway, when it was time to walk up to the ground – with about four hundred other City fans, my first sight of the stadium was a bit of a let down as the stand only looked to be as big as the main stand at Stockport County. When we got inside we discovered that the pitch was actually well below ground level – and the stand we'd seen and indeed the stadium itself - was actually huge. Memorably the City fans – surrounded by 30,000 Germans – started singing "Two World Wars and one World Cup " – and you could have heard a pin drop at the time, completely non PC of course., but very funny looking back on it (not at the time!) You can always rely on City fans to show a sense of humour whatever the occasion! The match itself – City played youngster Nicky Reid and "surrendered" 1-3, despite Tony Henry hitting their post just before their goal, costing us the tie 2-4 on aggregate. It was actually the start of the decline under Malcolm Allison but we didn't realize it at the time! If only we had known what was to follow!

Bernd S: 20/3/1979 BM 3 City 1

I don't remember much of the actual game. Only that it had been a sell-out and that City fans started a riot in the South stand before the kick off. This was soon sorted out by the wooden batons of the MP from their HQ located nearby. Borussia deserved to win the game on the night, but City surely had the nicer strip of all sky blue, while Borussia wore their traditional all white. Sadly the next 30 years would become a more or less lean spell for both clubs. Since that night I've become a bit of a City supporter.

Ground. They often switched games to Dusseldorf but, by 1978, had upgraded The Bockelburgstadion by building a new main stand and improving the three open sides of terracing taking the capacity up to 36,800

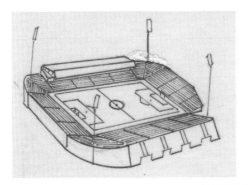

Connections: Michael Frontzech

Bradford City

'The Bantams' came about after Manningham RFC gave up rugby in 1903 and formed Bradford City, continuing to play at Valley Parade and were immediately accepted into the Second Division. Pre-war they were a First Division club for many seasons and actually won the Cup in 1911 beating Newcastle United 1-0 in a replay at Old Trafford after a 0-0 draw at Crystal Palace. They did have a number of seasons in the lower divisions, and their darkest day was on May 11th 1985 when, after clinching promotion from the Third Division, they played at home to Lincoln City and the main stand burned down killing 56 people and seriously injuring 200. City beat Charlton 5-1 to go up that day. They subsequently battled their way up to the Premiership in 1998 for two seasons, going down with City in 2001. Since then they've dropped down and finished season 2010/11 in League Two wearing claret and amber striped shirts with black shorts.

Pre-war: 20 league meetings with 10 City wins, 2 draws and 8 defeats between 1909 until 1927, all but two in the First Division. The most significant game was the 8-0 win on the last day of the 1926/27 season at Maine Road when City thought they'd secured promotion to the First for sure. Portsmouth, however, kicked off fifteen minutes later and beat Preston 5-1 at home to clinch second place on goal average - City 108/61 (1.770) Portsmouth 87/49 (1.775). If it had been goal difference in those days it would have gone in City's favour (47 to 38). One more goal would have done it for City. Bradford, however were already relegated.

Post-war: 10 league meetings with 7 City wins, 2 draws and 1 defeat.
The 4-2 win at table-topping Bradford in season 1987/88 was our first in 35 away games and a seemingly interminable 21 months. Paul Lake swallowed his tongue in the return game in April 1988, from which, thankfully, he made a full recovery, game finishing at 2-2. The 1-1 draw in the last game of 1988/89 season at

Bradford saw Trevor Morley's late goal clinch promotion in second place. The 2-1 defeat, Shaun Goater's debut in 1997/98, contributed to City's relegation (as did Bradford's last home game capitulation to Port Vale).

John B: 13/5/1989 Bradford 1 City 1

If Manchester City were an Everest expedition, it goes without saying they would eschew the thermal undergarments, ice axes and oxygen cylinders on offer, in favour of attempting the climb carrying an umbrella, and wearing a tweed jacket and loafers whilst smoking a pipe. I took the train for the trip over the Pennines on a gloriously sunny day, and assumed my place on the cramped terrace behind the goal that City would defend in the first half, inflatable banana at the ready. The Hillsborough tragedy had only occurred some four weeks earlier, so the sloping cages were still in place, with nasty looking spiked balls affixed to the top bar like some murderous abacus, only painted bright red and yellow so you could reflect on how pretty they looked as you bled to death.

On the field, we started slowly, too slowly, and on the quarter hour a blocked shot rebounded to the never to be heard of again, Mark Ellis, who swept a daisy cutter past Paul Cooper. The mood darkened further with the news that Palace had taken the lead against already relegated Birmingham, and as half time came with no sign of an improvement in City's performance, so the frustration gave way to anger. Former manager John Bond, giving an interview in the tunnel next to the away end, the unlikely target for an outpouring of venom that pretty much soured his relationship with the club for good.

Clearly, there was plenty of invective to be had in the dressing room as well, and whatever the normally unassuming Mel Machin – later to be famously sacked by Peter Swales for not having enough charisma – had to say, had an immediate impact on the pitch, as City were galvanised after the break. Wave after blue wave of attacks crashed down on the Bradford goal, but the equaliser stubbornly refused to come. And worse still, Crystal Palace had scored a second, and a third, and a fourth - the stress finally proving too much for one denim clad Blue, who raced out of the stand and onto the pitch, where he then ran from one City player to the next to tell them that Palace were 4 up and that we had to score or they

would go up instead of us (a tale eloquently recalled by Paul Lake in the 'End of an Era' DVD years later. "We know mate", said Lakey, "we know!").

In the end then, salvation finally came as late as the 87th minute. Paul Cooper caught a free kick at the far end of the ground and threw it out quickly to Nigel Gleghorn, who in turn swept it straight on to Paul Moulden out on the left wing. Moulden slipped the ball forward into the inside left channel, whereupon the human express train that was David White raced away into the Bradford penalty area with it. On his right peg, Whitey was a deadly finisher, but Jackson the centre half had sufficient pace in the chase to force the City winger wide onto his left foot, and as this particular instrument had previous for being about as much use as an aromatherapist in a military field hospital, behind the goal we mentally braced ourselves to receive a shank in the face. Ah, we of little faith. Wavy Davey's low ball across the six yard box was sweet and true, and Trevor Morley slid in to steer the ball into the far corner of the net. The City end went mental, and for once, barring an extremely risky back header from Andy Hinchcliffe, we held on in relative comfort.

When the final whistle blew, and Blues poured onto the pitch out of the main stand and the home end, the stewards did the sensible thing and opened the gates in the cages to allow us all out onto the field of play. My final memory was of being part of a large group that triumphantly shouldered a near naked Ian Brightwell (he got well and truly stripped by souvenir hunting fans) round and round the ground long after the other players had made it to the sanctuary of the dressing room, and of a British Rail train back to Manchester that rocked with joy. City were back in the big time and the Maine Road massacre lay just around the corner!

In the Premiership just the two meetings in 2000/01 with City winning 2-0 at home and drawing 2-2 away as both teams took the drop.

It wasn't until season 1997/98 that the teams met in the **FA Cup**, with City winning the third round tie at Maine Road 2-0.

No League Cup meetings

Some connections: Sam Barkas, Sam Cowan

Ground: Valley Parade (shown 2000's) R/A 39,146 v Burnley FA Cup 4 1911.

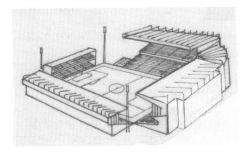

Friendlies: 1972/73 A 5-0, 1999/2000 a *, 2006/07 A 1-0

Bradford Park Avenue

'The Avenue, BPA, The Stans' were formed in 1907 when they moved into Park Avenue. They were elected into Division Two in 1908, spent some seasons in Division One, dropped down the divisions, but after successfully gaining re-election from 1967 for three seasons failed in 1970, and were replaced by Cambridge United.

Then followed years of struggle, lower league football, ground sharing but they re-emerged in the 1990's and finished season 2010/11 in the Evo-Stik Northern Premier Division playing in green and white broad striped shirts and white shorts.

Pre-war:10 league meetings with 5 City wins, and 5 defeats between 1910 and 1939. City had a 5-1 win in 1938/39 at Maine Road. In 1915, City ended the season with a 1-3 loss at Bradford, the third consecutive loss, leaving the Blues in fifth place three points behind champions Everton. In 1921 Tommy Browell scored his 30th goal of the season, in City's 1-0 win, making him the first City player to reach that total.

Post-war: Two league meetings in 1946/47, 7-2 at Maine Road, some consolation for the 1946 Cup defeat, and 1-1 away

In the FA Cup there was a remarkable 4th round meeting in season 1945/46 of the two Second Division teams. Cup games were played over two legs that season and in the first leg City won at Bradford 3-1 but lost the second leg 8-2 at Maine Road, City's record home defeat.

Here's how it went: City, standing up to the heavy going better than Bradford, playing consistently accurate football deserved their 3-1 win to gain a comfortable position for facing the second leg (!!). Gibbons and Shackleton starred for Bradford but City took the lead through Smith in the 37th minute. Gibbons equalised 3 minutes later with a brilliant header. Swift made wonderful saves to keep the score at 1-1. After the interval City wore Bradford down and scored two goals within a minute after half an hour through Herd and Smith. 25,014 was the crowd.

However..... Appalling weather affected the Wednesday Maine Road crowd, only 15,026 turning up for the *formality* of the second leg. Bradford travelled by road and were met with blizzard conditions, almost causing them to turn back and surrender the tie. They arrived at the ground only 15 minutes before kick off.

The programme advised that "unless something extraordinary happens this afternoon, City should be in the hat for the fifth round draw. ...and "we wish you luck Bradford but we fear the worst" Doh!

City set a cracking pace but Gibbons, Bradford's amateur centre forward was again causing problems. Bradford went ahead in the 21st and 23rd minutes to wipe out City's first leg lead, but Constantine pulled one back for City in the 36th minute. The Blues were blitzed in the second half even though Swift made saves, and centre half Cardwell was injured mid way through the half, going on the wing. Goals came from Knott (Gibbons in some reports) in the 48th, Gibbons in the 56th and 64th minute, Knott in the 65th, Smith for City in the 78th, a Farrell penalty in the 85th and Dix made it eight in the 87th. Futture West Ham and England manager Ron Greenwood played in both games for Bradford PA.

Further consolation was gained by the 5-2 FA Cup win in the third round at Bradford in season 1953/54.

The teams have never met in the **League Cup.**

Some connections: Charlie Pringle, Joe Fagan, Derek Kevan and manager Tom Maley

Friendlies: 1995/96 a

Ground: Park Avenue (shown 1950s) R/A 34,429 v Leeds 1931

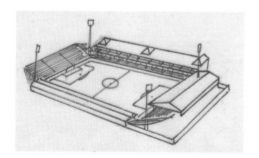

Brentford

'The Bees' were formed in 1889 playing at Clifden Road, Benns Fields, Shotters Fields, Cross Road, Boston Park, moving to Griffin Park (previously an orchard), in 1904, and were founder members of Division Three in 1920. They finished season 2010/11 in League One playing in red and white striped shirts and red shorts.

Pre-war: 6 league meetings with 3 City wins, 1 draw, and 2 defeats, all between 1936/37 and 1938/39 when Brentford were in the First Division. City's three wins included a fine 6-2 at Griffin Park in 1936/37 (the home game was abandoned at 0-0 after 40 minutes, later won 2-1 by City) helping the Blues to the title, but Brentford's double in 1938/39 aided City's relegation.

Post-war: Two league meetings in the 1950/51 season, City winning 4-0 at Maine Road but losing 0-2 at Brentford as the Blues headed for Second Division promotion.

In the FA Cup, meetings in three rounds:
1932 4th rd 6-1 home
1989 4th rd 1-3 away, leaving the Blues to concentrate on promotion (that old chestnut!)
1997 3rd rd 1-0 away, City fans arriving at the rescheduled evening game to find it was postponed again, due to a frosty pitch and when it was finally played, a Nicky Summerbee goal put the Blues through to the next round, giving new manager Frank Clark another good result.

Neil S: 28/1/1989 Brentford 3 City 1

For me, the FA Cup defeat at Brentford had an ironic twist. This was the season when the football world were rebelling against the dreaded ID scheme proposed by Thatcher and Moynihan. An album was produced and a host of various artists, including Half Man Half Biscuit *and* I, Ludicrous *donated songs to the cause.*

Around the same period, the Sunday Express Colour Supplement featured an article on the inflatable craze that was sweeping through the Football League.

Both the article and the album cover included photographs from the City end at Griffin Park. A sea of balloons, bananas and smiling faces all waiting for their heroes to enter the field of play.

Only one person looked miserable. Yours truly was never a great fan of blind optimism.

I knew that City were doomed after reading that the Brentford centre forward was a season ticket holder at Maine Road. As sure as night follows day, Gary Bissett was going to have the game of his life.

Brentford raced into an early 2-0 lead, but Gleghorn, reduced the arrears at the start of the second half. There was also a serious crowd disturbance after an incident involving Andy Dibble and a time-wasting opponent. In true City style we went out in disgrace.

Eight Months later, City returned to Griffin Park for the first leg of a League Cup encounter. City won the tie, but the context of the result was more important than the first leg defeat.

After staying at friend and Whaley Bridge

legend John Atkins' house in Epsom, I remained in London for Stockport's game at Loftus Road the following evening. Firstly, I caught the train from Epsom to Euston. Upon arrival at Euston, I was recognised by a gang of United supporters travelling to Portsmouth. At first the banter was light hearted, but when their numbers swelled I was fighting a losing battle. United had just bought "a galaxy of quality players'"and the following Saturday they were due to play at Maine Road. "It's going to be a f*cking massacre" threatened the Ashley Grimes lookalike.

If only I'd known…

In the League Cup in 1989/90 the clubs met in the second round over two legs. On the Saturday City had lost 1-0 at Wimbledon, then faced another London trip on the following Wednesday. It was too much for British Rail as the train was delayed just outside the Capital waiting for a relief driver. Some Blues, headed up the tracks to make their own way to the ground, the rest arriving at half time. David Oldfield scored a late goal to give City a lifeline for the second leg, but things didn't look good for Saturday's match v United. As it happened the Blues won that one 5-1, and went on to beat Brentford 4-1 in the second leg.

Some connections: Stan Bowles, manager Uwe Rösler

Ground: Griffin Park (Shown 1990s) R/A 39,626 v Preston FA Cup 6 1938

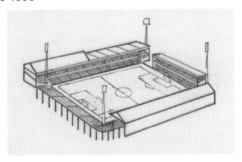

Brighton and Hove Albion

Brighton United were formed in 1897, and played at the County Ground before folding in 1900. They reformed as Brighton and Hove Rangers, playing at Withdean, but folded again in June 1901, when Brighton and Hove United were formed. They then became Brighton and Hove Albion, 'The Seagulls', and moved from the County Ground to the Goldstone Road in 1904 when Hove F.C moved out. They were founder members of Division Three in 1920, eventually making it to the First Division in 1979 and the Cup Final in 1983, which they lost in a replay to United. The first game finishing 2-2, when in the dying minutes the commentator exclaimed excitedly "And Smith must score" but future Blue Gordon missed a sitter.

They moved out of The Goldstone in 1997 to share The Priestfield Stadium with Gillingham, then went back to the temporary home of the Withdean Stadium in 1999 whilst dropping back down the divisions, but a new stadium is currently being built to open for the 2011/12 season.

Brighton finished season 2010/11 in League One playing in blue and white striped shirts with white shorts and were promoted to the Championship.

Post-war:14 league meetings with 7 City wins, including the penultimate game of 1982/83 season at Brighton when Kevin Reeves' goal, put Brighton down and looked to have helped save City from relegation. However, the home loss to Luton Town the following week, put City down. There were 4 draws and 3 defeats.

Dave A: 1/4/1989 Brighton 2 City 1

April 1989, rather than drive all the way to the south coast again which had bad vibes, the plan was to drive to Manchester, to meet up with my mother, and catch the 'special' train from Piccadilly (or was it still London Road?) with a few hundred other April Fools. I think the train set off about at 8am but I can't be sure. We arrived in time to have a quick look at the sea and then found our way to the Goldstone Ground.

It was a dump, the only word for it, and high perimeter fences made viewing difficult. The team was interesting, Paul Cooper, ex Ipswich, playing his first game instead of the injured Andy Dibble, Ian Brightwell, Hinchcliffe, Lake, Gary Megson (really!),Redmond, White, Moulden,

Oldfield, Ian Scott, on debut in place of Neil McNab and Trevor Morley. Nigel Gleghorn, who is now an excellent pundit and wasn't a bad goalkeeper either, and Gerry Taggart were the subs. It was a young team with the majority having progressed from the FA Youth Cup Final winning side of 1985/86. In that Final we beat the Rags 3-1 on aggregate. You have to mention that whenever you can!

But with McNab and Bryan Gayle missing, and an average age of about 21, the team lacked experience and it showed. We went one up but then fell away rather worryingly and lost 2-1 to a poor Brighton side. We were 'herded' to the station by the police, as was the fashion in those days, but it was a long, quiet, sombre journey back to Manchester with real concerns about the visit to Shrewsbury the following Wednesday night. Inevitably, I suppose, City beat Shrewsbury 1-0 on the Wednesday night. I went to the game from Leeds, via Manchester to pick mother up, along the old Chester Road to Whitchurch and down the A49.

Trevor Morley scored the goal. Mel Machin, only nine months away from being sacked, picked a defensive line up with Gayle and Taggart both playing and Nigel Gleghorn added to the midfield. We played for a point, hoping for a break and we got one for a change! We won again on the following Saturday and a modicum of optimism returned but it was shortlived... see the report of the Oxford away game which was played just three weeks later!

In the FA Cup, meetings in two rounds:
1924, 3rd rd 5-1 against Third Division Brighton at the Goldstone 5-1.

1983 4th rd 0-4 at the Goldstone, after which manager John Bond was (allegedly) verbally abused by City fans on the way home, and resigned/was pushed in the following week, with John Benson taking over temporarily.

At that point City were * in the table but only won another three games to take the drop.

In the League Cup, Premiership City went down to lowly Brighton in the second round in 2008 going 1-0 up, conceded a late goal, drew 2-2 in extra time and lost on penalties. The game was played at The Withdean Stadium.'

Some connections: Gordon Smith, Mike Robinson, Neil McNab, Joe Corrigan (below), Brian Horton

Ground: The Godstone Ground (shown 1980's) R/A 36,747 v Fulham D2 1958/59 until 1997, when they ground shared with Gillingham until the move to The Withdean Stadium, capacity 7,000, in 1999, finally moving to the Amex Comminity Stadium in 2011.

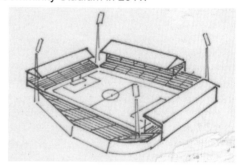

Bristol City

'Bristol South End were formed in 1894, playing at St John's Lane. They turned professional in 1897 and became Bristol City, 'The Robins'. In 1901 they merged with Bedminster another leading Bristol club, and moved into Ashton Gate, a former Bedminster ground in 1904.

They were elected to Division Two in 1901 and pre-war played in Division One for a short period, finishing as runners up in 1907 and reached the Cup Final in 1909, where they lost to United 1-0 at Crystal Palace. (Ex Blue Sandy Turnbull scoring the goal)

After climbing up from the Fourth Division, they reached Division One again in 1976, staying for four seasons, and finished season 2010/11 in

The Championship playing in red shirts and white shorts.

Pre-war: 12 league meetings with 2 City wins, one of which was a 5-1 at Hyde Road in 1908/09, but City lost the last game of the season 0-1 away to go down on goal average. There were 2 draws and 8 defeats, including all 6 games in Bristol,

Post war: 10 league meetings with 4 City wins, all at Maine Road, 4 draws and 2 defeats, and still no wins in Bristol. On February 5th 1966 City drew 1-1 in Bristol, the first time City were featured on MOTD.

Roger R: 19/2/1977: B. City 1 City 0
Team: Corrigan, Clements, Donachie, Doyle, Watson, Power, Owen, Kidd, Royle, Hartford, Tueart.
League Division One.

This was a memorable occasion for me as myself and a pal drove to the match in my first ever car, an old white mini (registration OLG 913H!) It was the first time that I had ever travelled any distance with all the responsibility of getting us there and back in one piece. The initial part of the journey was incident-free but, as we neared the old Tom Wood Services on the M5, the darned car started overheating (literally "boiling over!") My first thought was that we wouldn't get to the match at all, but a fantastic AA man came to our help at the services and suggested simply taking out the thermostat from inside the radiator unit and that did the trick. Then I "put my foot down" on the accelerator and we got there just in time, despite parking what seemed like miles away from Ashton Gate and "legging it" to get there just before kick-off. After all that City were beaten by a well drilled Bristol side 1-0. It was my first visit to Ashton Gate and I can remember the noise of the home fans too. It's a shame that Bristol City haven't really had any success since they are "a big club", a term City fans know so well.

The two Cities have never met in the **FA Cup**

In the League Cup the Blues won 2-1 in the second round in 2007 at Ashton Gate finally nailing the bogey down there, though they had a last minute goal disallowed.

Friendlies: 1974/75 A 2-2, 1999/2000 A 0-1

Some connections: Gerry Gow, Joe Royle, Shaun Goater, David James

GERRY GOW

Ground: Ashton Gate (Shown 2007) R/A 43,335 v Preston FA Cup 5 1935

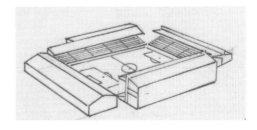

Bristol Rovers

Formed in 1883 as 'The Black Arabs' as they wore black shirts. They became Eastville Rovers in 1897, but quickly changed their name to Bristol Rovers, and nicknamed 'The Pirates' or more recently 'The Gas'. They were founder members of Division Three in 1920, hovering between the divisions, and recorded their most famous cup victory in 1956 4-0 over the famous Busby Babes. This was because, and I quote, "most of those United players hadn't played in the FA Cup before!" In 1980 the South Stand at Eastville burned down (Bristol City fans still suspected), forcing a five game move to Ashton Gate), then after a stint back at Eastville, they moved to Bath City's Twerton Park in 1986, and then to Bristol RUFC's Memorial Ground in 1996.

They finished season 2010/11 in League One being relegated, playing in blue and white quartered shirts, and white shorts.

Post war just the two meetings in the Second (old Third) Division in 1998/99. There was a 0-0 home draw, and at the Memorial Ground, City went two up in the penultimate game of the season, only to be pegged back to 2-2. On the same day Walsall took second place, leaving City to face the play-offs, and Bristol City were relegated from the First Division, much to Rovers' fans delight.

John I: 1/5/1999: B.Rovers 2 City 2
The away game at Bristol Rovers fell into the 'must-see' category, as we'd previously been to see City play at Rovers' former home, Twerton Park. Now resident at The Memorial Ground, the biggest problem was tickets. This was the last season of presenting your away match stubs as evidence of loyalty, and you needed 17, so we were OK! The game was scheduled for a Saturday evening on the first of May, and with the play-offs looking a probability, the season still had a real buzz about it. I still reckon that the hardcore City fans rate the 1998/99 season as one of the best ever, as we toured plenty of new grounds. After checking into a swanky City-centre hotel we had a few cold ones and then jumped a cab to the ground. Once in the picturesque ground, others in the 1100 strong City-contingent told how they'd been drinking nearby, in a packed pub with Rovers' fans, when the place was attacked by rival Bristol City fans – their team had been relegated in a 3pm kick-off fixture.

Our game was pretty entertaining with 'The Goat' and Terry Cooke putting us 2-0 up, but Rovers came back well to grab a late 2-2 draw (a Desmond - Tutu!).

Back in the city centre later on we had a few more beers and a curry, then turned in, only to be woken at 3 am by a (seemingly genuine) fire alarm sounding! Surreal. Out of the back of the hotel, down the metal stairs, and onto the street below, with other half dressed guests. It wasn't a dream, but the end of that same month was; then it was City's turn to recover from a two-goal deficit in that never-to- be- forgotten thriller at Wembley.

In the League Cup The teams met in the second round of 1992/93, City drawing the first leg 0-0 at Maine Road, and winning the second 2-1 in extra time at Twerton Park, with Rick Holden scoring an over celebrated winning goal.

Some connections: Keith Curle, David Wiffil

Friendlies: 1905/06 a 5-3

Ground: Eastville R/A 38,472 v Preston FA Cup 4 1960; Twerton Park R/A 9,464 v Liverpool FA Cup 4 1992; The Memorial Ground (shown 1999)) capacity 12,000

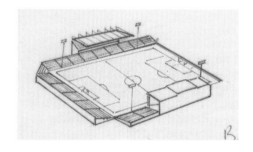

Burnley
'The Clarets' were formed in 1881 from the defunct Burnley Rovers Rugby club. They played at Calder Vale and moved to Turf Moor in 1882. They were founder members of the Football League in 1888 and usually a First Division club, winning the title in 1921 and 1960 plus the FA Cup in 1914. By the late seventies, when the abolition of the maximum wage finally caught up with them, they sank down the divisions, and almost out of the League in 1987. They made The Premiership in 2009/10 but were relegated and finished 2010/11 in the Championship wearing claret and blue shirts with white shorts.

Pre-war: 32 league meetings with 15 City wins including a 6-0 in 1902/03 at Hyde Road, and an 8-3 at Maine Road in 1925/26 (City lost the following game 8-3 at Sheffield United!). 7 games were drawn, and 10 lost.

City's 3-0 win at an overcrowded (estimated 55,000) Hyde Road in 1920/21, when a gate was smashed down and fans were sitting on the roofs of stands, marked the end of Burnley's record unbeaten run of 30 games. Burnley eventually took the title with City runners up. In 1929 Tommy Johnson netted his 32nd goal of the season, creating a new record and went on to finish the season with 38, an all time record.

Post-war: 52 league meetings with 20 City wins, including a 7-0 at Maine Road in 1968/69, a 4-3 at Turf Moor in 1958/59 after being 3 down at half time, and a 6-0 there in 1998/99, 15 draws and 17 defeats, including the final game of 1959/60 season when a crowd of 65,981 witnessed a 2-1 Burnley win who took the title ahead of Wolves. At a packed Maine Road the only place to be was in the corner between the Kippax and the Platt Lane stand where there was always plenty of room no matter how big the gate (pre-segregation)

Brian D: 25/11/1967; City 4 Burnley 2
2/3/1968 : Burnley 0 City 1

My first ever City game was the home match v Burnley in November 1967, so it was with not a little personal reminiscence that I welcomed their recent promotion. Fitting too, was that my first away match also involved Burnley, later that same season. With apologies to younger readers, this was the season when City were chasing the league title and we were fourth in the table in March when this particular fixture was played.

I went to the match with a Burnley supporting friend and was given a lift there by his Uncle and Auntie. They were all Clarets, so I was the only Blue in the car. City were going great guns and there was lots of City traffic on the roads north that Saturday. The full significance of this didn't hit me until we entered the ground. Immediately on passing through the turnstile we were met with the sight of a fleeing Burnley fan being hunted down by 2 City fans who gave him a kicking and stole his scarf. In those days nearly everybody wore a football scarf and there was this practice of taking them from rival fans. The theory was if you defeated an enemy you took his scarf, in the manner of a Comanche taking a scalp from a vanquished foe. (That was the theory anyway - in practice, I suspect many of them were simply snatched when the wearer wasn't looking or taken by gangs from individuals - "Give us yer scarf!") I can remember seeing lads on the Kippax with four or five different scarves hanging from belt loops, epaulettes and wrists.

Of course, at 13 years old I understood that these things happened but this was the first time I had witnessed it up close, only a few feet away. I reckon that almost half the people in Turf Moor were Blues as City completely took over the Long Side and the Open End and certainly many a Burnley fan was relieved of their scarf that day, one way or another. I actually witnessed City fans selling some back to young Clarets later in the afternoon.

The match was quite a tight affair. Burnley had been one of the leading teams in the early 60s and still boasted a number of international players at this time - Ralph Coates, an England International who later played for Spurs, Andy Lochead, an old fashioned rough and tumble centre forward and Scottish international and Willie Morgan, a young Scottish winger. The encounter was settled by a Francis Lee goal and at the final whistle you could sense the belief growing in the City crowd as this was our fifth game undefeated, having won 3 and drawn one of our previous 4 matches. The Long Side had become a second Kippax and in one mass Blues moved across it like an army, towards the open end, the exits and home.

There is an interesting post-script to this story. Some years later, when at college, I became good mates with a City fan called Danny Stoddard. When discussing previous matches – as you do – he said that he had also been at that match. Such was its importance, he told me that at the age of 14 he had cycled (Yes, CYCLED!!) from Burnage to Burnley and back again on the day of the game! He recounted how he had become a mini celebrity along the way as City traffic passed him going up hill, only for him to pass them going down hill as they were caught in the long lines of slowly moving coaches and cars, a process repeated over and over as the old mill town grew nearer. Now that's commitment! Danny is a season ticket holder to this day.

In the Premiership, just the two games with a 3-3 draw at COMS and a 6-1 win at Turf Moor. City were 5-0 up at half time, a record for the Premiership, and, but for persistent rain in the second half which threatened but luckily didn't cause the game to be abandoned, City could have finished with a higher margin than six.

In the FA Cup, meetings in three rounds:
1931 3rd rd 0-3 away
1933 6th rd 1-0 away
1991 3rd rd 1-0 away

In the League Cup, just the one meeting over two legs in the first round of 1999/2000 , City winning the first leg 5-0 at Maine Road, and the second 1-0 in front of only 3,667 at Turf Moor.

In the Charity Shield in season 1972/73, City lost 0-1 at Maine Road.

Some connections: Mike Summerbee, manager John Bond, Kevin Reeves, Dennis Tueart

Friendlies: 1894/95 h 0-1, 1897/98 a 2-2, 1898/99 h 2-2, 1939/40 a 2-2, h 3-1; 1962/63 in Dublin1-1, 1971/72 a (P) 1981/82 a 3-3 (Alan Stephenson testimonial) 1995/96 a 1-2, 1997/98 a 3-0, 2000/01 a 1-2.

Ground: Turf Moor, (Shown 2010) R/A 54,755, two new stands built in the 60's, and two in the 90's.

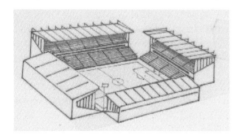

Burton Swifts

'Swifts' were a founder member of Division Two in 1892 having moved into Peel Croft in 1890. They amalgamated with Burton Wanderers to become Burton United in 1901. City played the Swifts 14 times between 1892/93 and 1898/99 seasons, all in Division Two, winning 6, including a 9-0 at Hyde Road in 1897/98 season, drawing 4, losing 4.

Burton United

Were formed in 1901 on the amalgamation of Burton Swifts and Burton Wanderers. They played at Peel Croft, but failed to gain re-election in 1907 and folded in 1910. City played them just twice in the Second Division in season 1902/03 winning the games 2-0 at home and 5-0 away.

Burton Wanderers

Were elected to Division Two in 1894 playing at Derby Turn, meaning the town had two Football League teams for a short time. They vacated Derby Turn and amalgamated with Burton Swifts in 1897 after failing to gain re-election, to become Burton United. City played the Wanderers six times between 1894/95 and 1896/97 season, all in Division Two, winning just the once, drawing 3, and losing twice including 0-8 away in 1894/95.

Bury

'The Shakers' were formed in 1885 when Bury Wesleyans and Bury Unitarians merged to form Bury FC playing at Gigg Lane (R/A 35,000). They were elected into the Second Division in 1894, winning promotion and played their very first game against newly named Manchester City, winning 4-2 at Gigg Lane.

They were a First Division club for many seasons pre-war, winning the FA Cup in 1900 beating Southampton 4-0, and then by the record score of 6-0 over Derby in 1903. Post war they've hovered between the Second, Third and Fourth divisions and reached the Football League Cup semi-final in 1963 losing to Birmingham 4-3 on aggregate.

They finished season 2010/11 in League Two and were promoted, reverting back to original colours of light and dark blue half shirts with blue shorts as opposed to the more traditional white shirts with royal blue shorts.

Pre-War: 32 league meetings 30 of which were in the First Division, with 17 City wins, 7 draws and 8 defeats.

There were some remarkable score-lines including a 6-1 City home win in 1908/09, a 5-1 City win at Hyde Road with its three new stands in 1910, 5-6 loss at Bury in 1925/26 and a 6-4 Maine Road win in 1928/29.

Post war: 12 league meetings with 4 City wins, 5 draws and 3 defeats. In the February 1964 game which finished 1-1, Colin Bell scored his first goal at Maine Road (for Bury), then goalkeeper Harry Dowd equalised after injuring his shoulder and played upfront, Matt Gray taking over the 'keeper's jumper. The 0-1 home City loss in February 1998 sparked the sacking of manager Frank Clark and resignation of Chairman Francis Lee. An angry fan ran onto the pitch and threw his season ticket down. This was returned to him later, in the post, by a member of the groundstaff, who didn't see why he shouldn't have to suffer "like the rest of us".

In the FA Cup, meetings, in three rounds:
1932 6th rd 4-3 away 1938 4th rd 3-1 away
1963 4th rd 1-0 home

In the League Cup there have been two meetings. First Division City losing 0-2 in 1972/73 to Fourth Division Bury at Gigg Lane when Malcolm Allison, allegedly worse for wear, couldn't take the team talk. Then in the first round of 1985/86 City won both legs 2-1, the first played at Old Trafford to accommodate the crowd of 11,377.

Tony P: 3/10/1972 Bury 2 City 0

I was just sixteen years old and working as an apprentice hairdresser in Manchester. My boss, Frank who lived in Bury bought tickets and drove me in his car. In the Bury side at that time, was none other than former Blue George Heslop who by now was well into the twilight years of his career. George, also sported what I thought was one of the best comb-over you could wish to see; although it turns out he was actually wearing a wig. A crowd of 16,614 attended the game and the ground came as a culture shock, being the first I'd visited outside the First Division, but it was not as big a shock as I was given by the end of the game. Manchester City FC, with its star names, Summerbee, Bell, Lee and Marsh were totally humiliated by a George Heslop inspired Fourth Division outfit. So desperate were we that with City 0-2 down and ten minutes remaining, City fans tried to have the game abandoned by running on the pitch and refusing to move. Sadly, it didn't work. City's list of humiliations to lower league clubs has grown quite considerably since 1980, and these days it's not as shocking as it once was. We are always reminded of the Halifax and Shrewsbury defeats from the days before these results became a regular occurrence, but I'm surprised that the Bury game is

never mentioned, not that I'm proud of it. My nightmare wasn't yet over though. I had, for some reason, assumed that Frank would take me home or at least back into Manchester. Instead, he dropped me off at Bolton Street station in Bury at 9.30pm and said that there'd be a train in the next half an hour which would take me to Manchester Victoria. Making my way home didn't worry me, after all, I'd made it to three away games the previous season. The trouble was, I only had 30p (6 shillings in real money) left and I doubted that it would be enough to pay my train fare to Victoria and bus fare from Manchester to Chorlton. It didn't seem an adult thing to start crying and asking for my mum, so I waved him goodbye and stood in the cold, dark, deserted station. The train never came and so I caught a bus to Manchester and walked from the city centre to Brooks Bar and walked home from there, arriving back at around midnight.

Friendlies: 1939/40 a 4-2, 1953/54 a 1-3, 1961/62 a 2-1 and 4-0 , 1967/68 h 4-2, 1968/69 a 5-4 (B. Turner T/M) 1970/71 a 5-4, 1972/73 a 2-0, 1975/76 a (Paul Aimson T/M) 1984/85 a 2-0,1989/90 a , 1999/2000 a, 1-2, 2002/03 a, 2004/05 a 0-0.

Some connections: Colin Bell, Bobby Owen, George Heslop

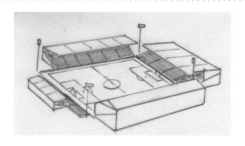

Ground: Gigg Lane (Shown 2000's) R/A 35,000 V Bolton F.A Cup 3 1960. It was covered on all four sides in 1946 for 35,000 as the programme cover shows

Friendlies:

Belfast and District 1901/02 a 3-1
FCBasel 1934/35 a 5-1
Barcelona 1951/52 a 1-5, 1956/57 a 2-3, 1974/75 a 2-3, 1986/87 a 1-1, 2002/03 h 2-1 2009/10 a 1-0 (Jean Gramper trophy)
Bayern Munich 1953/54 a 3-3
Borussia Dortmund 1956/57 a 1-4, 1967/68 h 4-0, a 1-2 (USA) 2010/11 a 1-3
Blackpool Wren Rovers 1991/92 a 0-2
Bath City 1956/57 a (Tony Gough T/M) 1968/69 a 5-5,, 1966/67 a 5-0, 1980/81 a 3-2
Best all X1 a Doncaster 1970/71
Bangor 1974/75 a 6-2
K Beerschot VAV 1979/80 a 1-0
FCBrugge 1979/80 a 2-3
SC Braga 1980/81 a 3-1
NAC Breda 1980/81a 3-2
Bideford 1980/81 a 5-0, 1981/82 a 4-1
SK Beveren 1980/81 a 0-4
Bordeaux 1981/82 a 2-2
Burtrask 1990/91 a 6-0
Buxton 1990/91 a
E Borel 1990/91 a 3-1
VFL Bochum 1982/83 a 3-1, 1991/92 a (in Germany) 1-1
Bohemians 1991/92 a 1-0
Bamber Bridge 1991/92 a
Brescia 1992/93 a 1-2
Bodo Glimt a 1993/94

C is for Cambridge

THE C's take us down to Cambridge, South Wales, Carlisle, London, Cheshire, Derbyshire, Colchester, Denmark and Coventry......

———◆———

Cambridge United

The 'U's' were formed in 1919 as Abbey United, playing at The Celery Trenches until moving to the Abbey Stadium in 1933. They turned professional in 1949, becoming Cambridge United, and were elected to Division Four in 1970, replacing Bradford Park Avenue. They reached the Second Division in 1978 but sank down the leagues eventually going down into the Conference in 2005

They finished season 2010/11 in the Blue Square Premier League playing in amber shirts with black shorts.

City met them twice in the Second Division in 1983/84 season, drawing 0-0 away on Mick McCarthy's debut and winning 5-0 at home.

Dave W: 17/12/1983 Cambridge 0 City 0

It was a cold December day, we were bussed from the station, and they halted the traffic for us, giving us that feeling of power, and we had to walk the final bit through a soggy park. The heating on the train didn't work on the way home and on discussing the game we commented on how their players were built like brick shithouses and how we didn't have any. We all agreed and after a pause someone, Stuart I think said, "no, but we've got a lot of shithouses!" and you had to laugh. City won 5-0 at Maine Road in the last game of that season as they went down to the Third Division and City finished fourth below Chelsea, Newcastle and Wednesday.

Andrew H: 17/12/1983 Cambridge 0 City 0

For those City fans like me who were teenagers in the 1970's, this season was the first time ever we had followed the Sky Blues outside the top flight of English football. If ever there was a reality check that City were at least temporarily out of the big time, this was it, an away trip to Cambridge for the first ever competitive match between the two teams, and still one of only two that City have played against Cambridge United.

I was working in London at the time, and travelled to Cambridge by train from Liverpool Street. It was the last Saturday before Christmas, and a horrible day weather-wise, with steady rain which lasted most of the day and left me soaked and freezing cold.

I remember being struck vividly by the surreal and incongruous atmosphere of the day. There were bicycles throughout the city, and I spent the morning visiting many of the town's historic University buildings. Enjoyable and interesting though this was, it just seemed very strange and unreal to think that this was the place where Manchester City were going to be playing later that day.

If ever the title "Stadium" was an inappropriate one, this was it. The ground was tiny and I stood with City's characteristically large and loyal away following on a small but homely uncovered terrace. The crowd was just 5,204, unbelievably small for a City league match in those days, but to put that in perspective, this was 2,200 more than had watched Cambridge United's last home match against Fulham two weeks earlier.

They had done remarkably well to hold on to Second Division status for six seasons, but poor form and declining attendances had led to their sacking of manager John Docherty in the week leading up to the match.

The Cambridge squad included David Moyes amongst its ranks, and in a hard fought goalless draw, City's star man on his debut was Mick McCarthy, who had been signed by Manager Billy McNeill and went on to win the Player of the Year award that season, despite not making his debut until this game just before Christmas.

"Cambridge, Cambridge, ra ra ra!!" was the mocking chant of the City supporters for their posh opponents during the match, and at the end of the game, City fans were escorted through open fields and allotments onto a double decker bus which took us free of charge back to the railway station. It wasn't my most memorable day as a City supporter, but it sticks

in the memory as a very different day, and all these years on, City have never played at the Abbey Stadium in a competitive match since.

Some Connections: Danny Granville, and Bill Leivers (below) was once their manager and piloted them into the Football League.

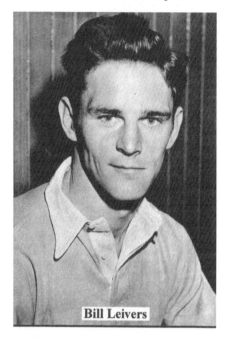

Bill Leivers

Ground: The Abbey Stadium (shown 1983) R/A 14,000 v Chelsea friendly 1970

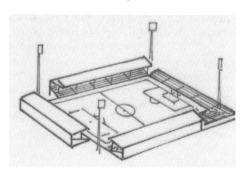

Cardiff City

'The Bluebirds' were formed in 1899 from the Riverside cricket club. Cardiff became a City in 1905 and in 1908 the club were allowed to call themselves Cardiff City.

They moved into Ninian Park, often a Welsh International venue, in 1910 after turning professional and were elected into Division Two in 1920. Promoted in 1921, they were First Division runners up in 1924, FA Cup runners up in 1925 and winners in 1927, the Arsenal goalie's shiny, slippy shirt being cited as the reason the ball was fumbled into the net, but were relegated in 1929. They have never quite reached those heights again, having ups and downs eventually to the Fourth Division and almost back, but reached the Cup Final in 2008 only to lose to Portsmouth. They moved to The Cardiff City stadium in 2009 and finished season 2010/11 in the Championship, wearing blue shirts and white shorts.

Pre–war: 12 league meetings in the twenties in the First Division, with 6 City wins, including a 5-1 in 1922/23 at Hyde Road, 5 draws and 1 loss

Cardiff were quite a team then, but only got the better of City once.

Post-war: 26 league meetings, with 10 City wins, 10 draws and 6 losses including a 0-6 in 1952/53 season at Cardiff. In season 65/66 Cardiff won 4-3 at home, Matt Gray being our first goalscoring substitute; they were one of only five teams to beat City that season.

In the FA Cup, meetings in five rounds:
1924 4th rd 0-0 home (76,166 then record crowd) , replay 1-0 away
1961 3rd rd 1-1 away, replay 0-0 home, 2nd replay 2-0 at Highbury
1967 4th rd 1-1 away, replay 3-1 home
1982 3rd rd 3-1 home
1994 4th rd 0-1 away

Dave W: 7/1/1961 Cardiff 1 City 1

In the third round in 1960/61 at Cardiff, the 25,640 crowd gave the home side terrific vocal support. The Welsh fella behind me said that "on form there's only one team that will win the cup this year" That meant Spurs would get the double, unheard of at the time, they would have been the first team since Preston in 1889 to do it. "Yes but they won't" I said, but they did! It was a 1-1 draw and a 0-0 in the replay at City, then the Blues won 2-0 at neutral Highbury on a Monday night where City had narrowly lost 4-5 the previous Saturday to get the majority of the 24,168 mainly Arsenal fans on our side. City were victors twice in the cup games of 1967 and 1982, the latter when their fans chanted "what a waste of money" at Trevor Francis and we chanted back "at least we've got the money" which of course we hadn't! The final meeting to date was in the fourth round in 1994 at lowly Second Division Cardiff which by then was an intimidating venue, fans enacting the strange Arabic custom of slapping themselves on the head, but without the blades, obviously. The players had to leave their coach and walk the last few hundred yards to the dressing rooms and stories abound about batterings from both sets of fans, depending on who you talk to. City lost 0-1 after having what looked like a perfectly good goal disallowed, and Keith Curle missed a penalty. The gloom was only lifted by the announcement that Swales had finally been ousted by Francis Lee as Chairman, and things could only get better, couldn't they?

Neil S: 29/1/1994 Cardiff 1 City 0

Every once in a while, the football experience can take you away from your comfort zone. Your sense of destiny is hijacked by the fear of the unknown.

I expected trouble at Ninian Park. I always expect trouble at Ninian Park. Cardiff City thrive on xenophobia.

Bizarrely, there's only one other Welsh team in the Football League and Cardiff hate them as well.

One of the abiding memories from Italia 90 is the image of Frank Rikaard spitting into Rudi Völler's face/hair. It was a disgusting moment that outraged FIFA and the Football Community.

Four years later, a Cardiff City supporter gobbed in my face outside Ninian Park. His mates laughed and the nearby policeman pretended that he hadn't noticed. In the words of Joe Royle, I must have missed a rule change.

I'd been to Cardiff ten years previously. The ground hadn't changed and neither had their attitude to black players. Replace Tony Cunningham with Terry Phelan and wait for the spite and bile to pour from the home terraces.

The atmosphere was a lesson in hatred. City are no shrinking violets, but you could almost taste the poison in the anti-English songs and chants. It was as if Heysel and Hillsborough had never happened. The terraces reeked of stale piss.

Blake scored a spectacular winner and as the fat lady cleared her throat and aimed a gobful of phlegm at the away fans, City contrived to miss a last minute penalty.

A horrible day and a horrible result.

Some connections: Roy Clarke, Andy Dibble, Dave Bennett, Ron Healey.

ROY CLARKE

Friendlies: 1998/99 h 0-0

Ground: Ninian Park (shown 1990's) R/A 61,566 Wales v England 1961 then The Cardiff City Stadium capacity 26,828

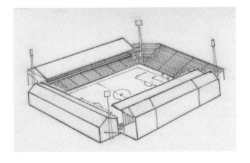

Carlisle United

'The Cumbrians' or 'The Blues' were formed in 1903 when Shaddongate United and Carlisle Red Rose amalgamated. They moved from Devonshire Park to Brunton Park in 1909, and were elected to Division Three North in 1928 replacing Durham City. They were the first club outside London to erect floodlights in 1952. They yo-yo'd between divisions regularly despite having Bill Shankly as manager for a spell, and actually made the First Division in 1974/75, but dropped out of the League in 2004, bouncing back in 2005 under manager and ex Blue Paul Simpson.

They finished season 2010/11 in League One playing in dark blue shirts and white shorts.

Post–war: 8 meetings between 1965/66 and 1984/85 seasons, with 3 City wins, 2 draws and 3 losses, one being a 1-2 Maine Road defeat in that 1974/75 season.

Dave W: 19/3/1975 City 1 Carlisle 2
19/2/1985 City 1 Carlisle 3

This was even more humiliating as I took along my brother–in–law, Irving, a life long supporter of little Carlisle, and they followed that up with a 3-1 Maine Road win in 1984/85. So no bragging rights there then. The other loss was 0-2 up there, one of the coldest I've ever been at any match, in November 1984. City fans gave want away Tommy Caton some stick, singin in high-pitched voices, 'I want to play for England', then gave some to Tommy Craig as he took a corner from which, naturally, they scored. Jim Tolmie missed a penalty after being psyched out by future (brief) Blue goalie Dave McKellar.

Neil S: 19/11/1983 Carlisle 2 City 0

In 1983, a day trip to Carlisle was the perfect advert for binge drinking. Alan Kelsall had family connections with a pub in Penrith and the minibus left Whaley Bridge in plenty of time for an epic session.

At the time, I'd never been further north than Blackpool. I remember appreciating the Cumbrian mountains for the first time as we sped up the M6. I was still young and naïve and totally confident of a City victory.

Penrith had reached the FA Cup first round and the town was packed with boisterous Hull City supporters. We responded with the City version of the KC and the Sunshine Band classic.

Brunton Park was bleak and desolate. We

queued in a muddy field and there was an icy breeze drifting across the open terrace. Wembley '81 was already a distant memory.

As I walked through the turnstile I was handed a sinister leaflet. City were due at Stamford Bridge the following weekend and the information outlined the meeting place for the hooligan express. This was the time of the Casual movement and most hooligans preferred golfing jumpers to club colours.

The standard was poor and the facilities worse. Tolmie missed a penalty and Nicky Reid was sent off for violent conduct. City lost 2-0 and I missed both goals whilst queuing in the toilets.

We repeated the journey for the goalless draw at the start of the following season. Penrith must be regretting the day that Manchester City got promoted.

In the League Cup, meetings in three rounds:
1963/64 2nd rd 2-0 home
1970/71 2nd rd 1-2 away
1973/74 3rd rd 1-0 away

Some connections: Paul Simpson (right), Stanley Bowles, Ian Bishop, Dave McKellar

Friendlies: 1985/86 in the Isle Of Man 3-0, 1988/89 a 4-1, 1991/92 a 3-1

Ground: Brunton Park R/A 27,500 v Birmingham FA Cup 3 1957 and v Middlesbrough FA Cup 5 1970

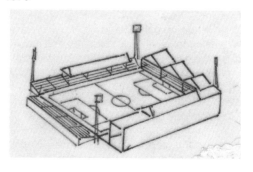

Charlton Athletic

'The Addicks' or 'Valiants' were formed in 1905 by a group of 14 and 15 year old youths. They played at Siemen's Meadow, Woolwich Common, Pound Park and Horn Lane before settling into The Valley in 1923, but even then moving out for six months to Catford (The Mount) in 1924. Financial problems forced them to ground share at Selhurst Park and Upton Park between 1985 and 1991 before they returned to The Valley in 1992, after a tremendous political campaign.

They were elected to the newly formed Division Three South in 1921, made it to Division One in 1936, finished runners up to City in 1936/37, were runners up in the Cup in 1946, winners in 1947, then nothing. After flirtations with the Premiership they finished season 201011 in League One, playing in red shirts and white shorts.

Pre-war there were only four league meetings, City winning one (5-3) at Maine Road in 1937/38, and the other three were drawn.

Post-war: 38 league meetings with 15 City wins 6 draws and 17 losses

Odd, with Millwall just down the road, that Charlton has usually been a friendly place for visiting City fans, where the Blues have recorded some decent wins.

Over the years there have been a few big scores too. City losing 1-5 at home in 1954/55, and Bert Trautmann was sent off when the referee awarded a penalty at 1-4, which Bert disputed vociferously. This was compounded by him telling the ref. he was Stanley Mathews and there was a further incident in the tunnel with the ref. after the game, leading to a two match suspension for our German keeper.

City fans had a fruitless journey to The Valley in 1966, the game on April 9th being a late postponement. By the time the game was played on Friday May 13th, promotion and top spot had already been clinched so the 3-2 win was just icing on the cake. Not quite so in 1985 when a number of teams could've been promoted on the last day of the season, Portsmouth, in fact, finishing on level points with City, who destroyed Charlton 5-1 at Maine Road to take third place behind Birmingham and Oxford. That hot sunny day was marred only by the news of the Bradford fire, and a Birmingham fan being killed at the

home game with Leeds when a wall collapsed. Worse was to follow a couple of days later with the Heysel disaster, marking an all time low in off the field football happenings.

There was also a 0-5 reversal at Selhurst Park in 1986/87.

In the Premiership there's been 12 meetings.

Season	H	A	Pl	W	D	L
Pre 06/07			10	4	3	3
06/07	0-0	0-1	12	4	4	4

Just the one **FA Cup** meeting, in the first round of 1922/23, First Division City losing 1-2 at home to Third Division Charlton.

No **League Cup** meetings

Some connections: Nicky Weaver, Jim Melrose, Paul Hince.

Ground: The Valley R/A 75,031 v Villa FA Cup 5 1938. Rumour has it that the ground was never filled, and a larger attendance could have been recorded at the 1960's 'Who' concert.

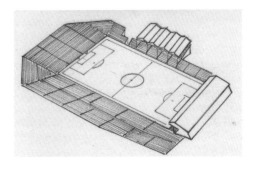

Chelsea

'The Pensioners', or latterly 'The Blues' were formed in 1905, moving into Stamford Bridge, which needed a tenant, only after Fulham had rejected the idea, and gained immediate admission to the increased Second Division.

In season 1914/15 they lost 0-3 in the Cup Final to Sheffield United at Old Trafford and also finished second bottom of the First Division, but as the division was increased to 22 clubs after the First World War, they remained in Division

One. Success didn't come until 1954/55 when they won the title, then the League Cup in 1965, FA Cup in 1970, and European Cup Winners' Cup in 1971. Their next success was the Full Members Cup in 1986, then the FA Cup was won in 1997, followed by continued success in the Harding then Abramovich eras.

They finished season 2010/11 in the Premiership, in their all blue strip.

Pre-war: 40 league meetings with 15 City wins, 11 draws and 14 defeats.
Generally each team won their home games and lost away, with no big scores recorded.

Post-war: 64 league meetings with 22 City wins 21 draws and 21 losses,

In season 1952/53 the teams played out a relegation battle at the Bridge in the last game of the campaign. Chelsea won 3-1 to reach 35 points the same as City, who were already safe, and both teams stayed up by one point, Stoke and Derby taking the drop. Two years later City were in the Cup Final and Chelsea were Champions! Five goals were registered at home by the Blues in three consecutive seasons, 1956/57, '57/58 and '58/59. Rodney Marsh made his debut at Maine Road in season 1971/72 boosting the crowd up to 53,322, after which the 'in the bag' title was lost. The 6-2 Maine Road win in 1977/78 marked the end of City's post war home dominance over Chelsea, City winning only one more game (2-1 in 1990/91) before the Premiership when results went from bad to worse, until recently. January 1979 marked the disastrous return of Malcolm Alison. The 1983/84 Second Division Maine Road game was played on a Friday night for Channel 4, which City lost 0-2, Chelsea gaining promotion as Champions and it was the first Second Division game shown on TV. In March 1990 Niall Quinn scored on his home debut in a 1-1 draw, helping the Blues to stay up that season and going on to have a fine career at City.

In the Premiership there's been 28 meetings. The 2-2 home draw in 1993/94 saw the 'Kippax last stand' (it was opened in 1957 v Chelsea) before the terrace was replaced with a three tier seated job. It was never the same afterwards.

City had not scored a goal in the seven meetings at The Bridge before banging in 4 in 2009/10, and a 0-5 defeat in 2002/03 and a 0-6 in 2007/08 have also been suffered.

Season	H	A	Pl	W	D	L
Pre 08/09			22	2	4	16
08/09	1-3	0-1	24	2	4	18
09/10	2-1	4-2	26	4	4	18
10/11	1-0	0-2	28	5	4	19

In the FA Cup, meetings in three rounds:
1915 3rd rd 0-1 home
1948 4th rd 2-0 home
1971 4th rd 3-0 away

In the League Cup meetings in two rounds:
1984/85 rd 4 1-4 away
1993/94 rd 3 1-0 home.
City beat Norwich 6-1 in a second round replay at The Bridge in 1975.

Biggest games between the teams were the **European Cup Winners' Cup** semi-finals of 1970/71 season, when a much depleted City team lost both legs 0-1, and Chelsea went on to win the Final against Real Madrid.

Off the field battles between supporters are legendary, and in the 1971 semi-final at Maine Road City's Kippax voluntarily evacuated to the newly opened North Stand, after which Chelsea claimed they'd 'taken the terrace'

In the 1985/86 Full Members Cup Final City lost 4-5, at Wembley and in the **Simod Cup** City lost 0-2 at home in 1986/87.

The 1986 final was a strange affair when Chelsea fans infiltrated the City areas without much success, and City pulled back from 1-5 down to 4-5 in the last few minutes and had a goal disallowed. Chelsea hooligans trailed City supporters' coaches after the game firing bricks, wooden spurs and smoke bombs into them.

The Guv: 14/4/1971 Chelsea 1 City 0

It was a Wednesday morning in Manchester in 1971. I had just finished a nightshift and decided that I must go to watch City play Chelsea that night in the European Cup Winners' Cup at Stamford Bridge. With no available transport, the only way to get there was to nick a car which I did before contacted a few lads to come with me.

We set off at ten in the morning and got to London at five o clock just in time for the pubs to open. We met up with about thirty lads in the pub opposite Stamford Bridge, I think it was called the Rising Sun.

We were in the pub before the doormen got on duty and we had settled down to await the

Chelsea boot boys coming in. Sure enough at about six o clock in they came in ones and twos. Three of our lads in the far corner were asked to leave because their Manc accents were a bit loud (I was glad really because we would have had our plans spoilt otherwise) At seven up went the cry of Manchester La La La and bottles were hurled from our corner into the centre of the room at the Chelsea scum. A great battle ensued with all the Chelsea lads backing out of their pub. I managed to get their loudest kid in his sheepskin and had him on the floor giving him the kicking of his life. The doormen did not come in and Chelsea had gone and there was lots of blood on the floor of the pub. We had not only smashed their boys we had wrecked their pub as well. The bar was shut and we were pinned inside the pub. The Old Bill arrived but could only keep us inside because the Chelsea lads were now outside in their hundreds waiting for us to come out. The Police restored order outside and then instead of arresting us they arranged an escort to the ground. The skirmish was over and we had won hands down. We now had to put plan B in operation. A few of us had to get away from the police escort going to the ground as we had plans for the Shed. City had never visited the Shed but this was the day that changed. We evaded our escort and met up just inside the Shed turnstiles. There were twenty of us, that was enough for a little sortie. The game started and we were in place. We waited about fifteen minutes, City hit a post and that was time to go up with chants of City, City, City. A ring soon appeared around us and into battle we went, fists and boots were going in all over the place. There were no police because they thought we would not dare go into their end, but we did and took them apart before the Police waded in with numbers and truncheons. Five lads were thrown out, but the Chelsea boys had lots of injuries, Stanley knives and boots were used and a steel bar as well which was found on the terrace afterwards. The rest of us were taken around the pitch to where our fans were in the open end, who gave us a rapturous ovation.

We had faced the Chelsea boys twice within the hour and come out with no serious injuries except those from the Old Bill and recorded two magnificent wins on the fighting front. Chelsea to this day have never done what we did that night and this was the start of going in away ends on a regular basis.

We set off home after the match and we were involved in a car crash, I personally had a finger amputated and leg and arm broken, also ribs cracked and a slice off my head. All the other guys were unhurt because they had been asleep. It was a day to remember and a journey home to forget. After two months of rehabilitation I was ready to carry on my hooligan days. Not very proud of what I did back then but when it was happening we were a force to be reckoned with and in those days we were very proud and never beaten.

Later, along came the gangs with names (Cool Cats, Guvnors, and Young Guvnors). We did not have names but we did have balls of steel and never ran from a fight. We never had the protection of Police or video cameras. Yes protection. We just battled and were never stopped by any large army of Police who surrounded us. We were just a group of lads who took it to our opponents wherever and whenever they wanted it.

Wythenshawe Langley and Moss Side we were and still are, all now in our 50's, still all as one.

CTID. Guvnor now living in Leicester.

Alan Menzies: 23/1/1971 Chelsea 0 City 3

Twelve just men, or was it the dirty dozen, all rabid Blues employed as drivers and guards by Manchester Transport Department set out in a Dormobile from Hyde Road bus depot en route to Stamford Bridge for the fourth round of the FA Cup in 1971.

We set off to join the M1 at Derby and broke down approximately two miles short of the Motorway, oil gushing out of the bonnet. Some dipstick had topped up the oil and forgotten to replace the top!

Plan B came into operation - a hike to the M1 hard shoulder to flag down anything to take us to London. An empty coach drove past, slowed down one hundred yards away and stopped. Salvation was on hand and we sprinted towards our lifesaver who must have thought better of it as he viewed us in full flight and sped away.

We all collapsed in a heap in a mixture of laughter and tears. Half an hour later a driver of a works van took pity on us but was only going to Luton, at thirty mph at that, and when we got there it was too late to get to Chelsea. Luton were playing Newcastle in a friendly so Kenilworh Road it was for the 0-0 bore draw.

One of the lads had a transistor radio and we roared each goal as City tore Chelsea, the Cup holders, apart 3-0.

Some connections: Clive Allen, Terry Phelan, SWPhillips, Nicolas Anelka, Wayne Bridge, Clive Wilson, David Rocastle, Daniel Sturridge

Ground: Stamford Bridge (shown 1990's) R/A 82,905 v Arsenal D1 1935

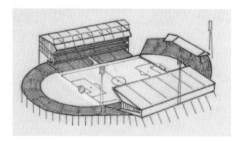

first leg, and 3-0 in the second leg played at neutral Edgeley Park.

Next meeting was in **the FA Cup** 3rd round in 1999/2000, City (Div 1) winning 4-1 over Chester (Div 3) at The Deva Stadium.

Some connections: Cliff Sear, Alan Oakes (below), Roy Cheetham

Chester City

The 'Blues', 'City' or 'Seals' were formed in 1884, though medieval football was supposedly played in the city. Kings School Old Boys amalgamated with Chester Rovers to become Chester F.C. They played at Faulkner Street, Old Showground, Whipcord Lane, moving to Sealand Road in 1906. More recently they shared with Macclesfield Town for a couple of seasons before in 1992 moving into the Deva Stadium.

They were elected to Division Three North in 1931, replacing Nelson, became Chester City in 1983. Always a lower league club, they dropped into the Conference in 2000, came back into the League 2005, then dropped back into the Blue Square Conference before being wound up in February 2010. A new club, Chester FC emerged, who play in the Evo-Stik North Premier league in season 2011/12, wearing blue and white stripe shirts with blue shorts.

The teams didn't meet until 1991/92 in the League Cup second round, City (Div 1) Chester (Div 3) City winning 3-1 at Maine Road in the

Friendlies: 1947/48, 1-0 a, 1968/69 a 4-4, 1971/72 a 4-0, 1983/84, a 1984/85 a 1-2, 1988/89 a 0-1, 1991/92, 2001/02 a, 2002/03 a.

Brian D:

A pre-season friendly, a few years ago. The game had been billed as part of our pre-season build-up and as I now live less than a dozen miles from the Deva Stadium, what better way to spend a free summer Saturday afternoon? I parked in the adjoining trading estate and walked to the ground. It felt a bit like a home game as everyone seemed to be wearing City colours of some description, but as I approached the ground I experienced something I had never encountered before (nor since). There was a picket line of Chester fans pleading with us not to enter the stadium. Apparently they were boycotting the club in protest at the American owner who had, according to them, ruined the team and caused their demise as a Football League club. I must confess to some ignorance of their situation and had a little sympathy (we all know what it's like to have our club ruined by an ego -maniac.......) However, having gone to the trouble of getting there I was not going to be deterred. This was City, virtually on my own doorstep, after-all. "I bet you don't even know it's only your youth team, do you? Half jibed one of the Cestrians. "What?!?" "Yeh, that's what we're up against, they have deliberately not told anyone, just to boost the gate." Oh well, I'm here now, thought I, so in I went. What a tiny ground! Capacity in the region of 4,000, the away end was by far the most full as the picket line had been largely ignored by a few hundred Blues who'd made the trip, but still nowhere near packed. I bumped into someone I had previously worked with who was there with his young son "Colin" (after "The King") and the afternoon passed quite pleasantly.

Chester were clearly trying to physically intimidate our youngsters out on the pitch, but ultimately we ran out comfortable winners. (2-0 if memory serves me well) I have a feeling that Chris Shuker scored one of the goals and was quite impressive generally.

With regard to Chester, they are great rivals with our other local team, Wrexham. My son, in addition to being a Blue, will occasionally go to Wrexham with his mates and he sings one of their jolly football songs, one I haven't heard anywhere else. To the tune of Tom Hark:

> "Your brother's your Dad,
> Your sister's your Mum,
> You're all inbred
> You're Chester Scum!"

Who says the age of poetry is dead?!?

Ground: Sealand Road R/A 20,500 v Chelsea FA Cup 3rd rd replay 1952. Deva Stadium (shown) capacity: 5,328.

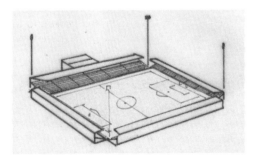

Chesterfield

'The Spireites' were formed in 1866 as the fourth oldest Football League club after Stoke City, Notts County and Nottingham Forest.

They moved into The Recreation Ground at Saltergate permanently in 1877, joined Division Two in 1899, failed to gain re-election in 1909, but joined the newly formed Third Division North in 1921

They won the Anglo-Scottish Cup in 1981 and reached the FA Cup semi-final in 1997 but lost to Middlesbrough, in a replay, after the biggest travesty of justice the competition has ever seen, probably, apart from Brighton in 1983.

They finished season 2010/11 in League Two and were promoted playing in blue shirts and white shorts, having moved to their new ground at the start of the season.

Pre-war: Four meetings, all in the Second Division, City winning all four games,

Post-war: Six meetings with three City wins and three draws, again in the Second Division but twice in the old Third in 1998/99.

In the League Cup it was a 1-0 City win away in the second round of 1977, but in 2006 it was a humiliating 1-2 loss away in the second round.

Geoff L: 20/9/2006 Chesterfield 2 City 1

It was going to be a formality; Division One strugglers against a team with an international strike force of Samaras and Corradi. Being an ex-pat Manc living in Chesterfield, a local night match was a godsend, time for an after-match pint and still be in bed before midnight – perfect.

The omens weren't good though. The City ticket office messed up (incredible but true!) so how to get a ticket. Chesterfield locals had descended from the hills in the hope of seeing quality football... and Reyna. So no tickets from their ticket office available.

(Buying a match ticket at Chesterfield is usually a heart warming, nostalgic experience. You go to the club main entrance; knock on a sliding glass window, a smiling face greets you with "Hallo, duck. Where would you like to sit or stand (!)" whilst showing you a seating plan on which sold seats are crayoned in. You almost expect to be charged half-a crown)

Now the story gets complicated. Daughter had returned to Chesterfield from uni. She'd got a 'yuppie' flat in Chesterfield in a converted factory with boy friend; other yuppie neighbours were a technician with the McClaren F1 team and a Chesterfield player, Alan O'Hare, whose mate was Derek Niven (I think they'd both been transferred from Bolton to Chesterfield). Daughter had started to go to Spireite matches so surely I could scrounge a ticket? No chance; the club had restricted players (free) tickets and most had relatives coming to 'the big match' – their cup final!

Last chance, a former work colleague of my wife was Dave Pugh, an ex Chesterfield and Wales player. Result, Dave got me a ticket in the main stand with Chesterfield 'fans', obviously, (The fan I sat next to was knitting throughout the match – and so was his wife!).

Security at Saltergate is 'relaxed' so when I got into the ground I was able to walk along the touchline and shake hands with Derek Niven (Derek is currently recovering from testicular cancer; don't forget to check 'em out, guys). Daughter was able to let grandson in his Chesterfield kit have his photo taken with Derek. (Obviously, grandson Fenton is a Junior Blue but sponsors Derek's bootlaces; his dad is a Coventry supporter so he has a lifetime of suffering before him!).

Kick-off, with City never really imposing their class (!) but eventually, after 40 mins, the Greek goal machine gave us a lead to take into the interval. A newspaper report said City "…never looked comfortable…" so it was no surprise when Folan equalised on 51 mins, a goal which began his climb to greatness with Wigan and Hull.

In the meantime, I'd got a bit restless sitting amongst the Spireite faithful and not being able to offer my usual advice to the City players, so I had a word with one of the stewards explaining that I was a City fan and was it possible to transfer to the City section. Quite reasonably he said this wasn't allowed but that if I chose to climb over the low barrier when he looked the other way then there would be no problem. Now I could celebrate each time City scored!

On 71 mins, Derek Niven "thundered a spectacular shot from 25 yards into the top corner" prompting manager Pearce to introduce Ireland, Miller and Dickov alongside Corradi and Samaras; shock and awe tactics.

Quote from Niven, now a Chesterfield hero "We sensed they were nervous and took advantage. We pressurised them into making mistakes…". Little did he know that City don't need pressure to make mistakes.

Postscript:-

- Endless grief from the countless thousands of 'lifelong' Chesterfield fans
- Derek's friendship continued to the extent that my grandson was to be a pageboy at his wedding – in a kilt!
- When Chesterfield FC got into trouble because of a dodgy owner (imagine that) I had sent a small donation to their supporters group who were attempting to take over the club. Some time later I received a share certificate for 200 shares in CFC (2001) Ltd
- The match happened on my birthday – cheers, City.

Some connections: Bill Leivers, Keith Marsden.

Ground: Saltergate (shown 2006) R/A 30,968 v Newcastle Div 2 1939. B2net Stadium capacity 10,338

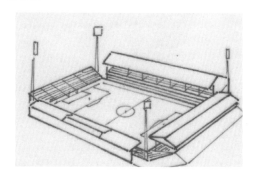

Clapton Orient
See Leyton Orient

Colchester United

The (other) 'U's' were formed in 1937 when Colchester Town turned professional and changed its name to United. They continued to play at Layer Road where Town had played since moving there in 1909.

They were elected to Division Three South in 1950 when it was increased to 24 clubs but were relegated to the Conference in 1989. On regaining their league place they were promoted to Division Three in 1992 replacing Aldershot. They've had various ups and downs, including a famous 3-2 FA Cup win over Leeds in 1971 and finished season 2010/11 back in League Two, playing in blue and white striped shirts with blue shorts, and moved to the New Community Stadium in 2008

City have played them in just two league meetings, winning 2-1 at home and 1-0 away, a first-ever televised Saturday evening K.O. for us in 1999 in the Second Division.

Ground: Layer Road (shown 1990's) R/A 19,072 v Reading FA Cup 1 1948. New Community Stadium Cap: 11,000

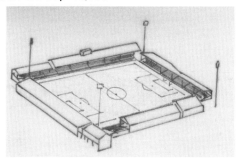

F.C. Copenhagen

Were formed in 1992 as F.C. Copenhagen when the two existing clubs from the city merged - Kjobenhauns BoldKclub (KB) (formed1876), and Boldkaubben (formed (1903)
Since then they'd won the title six times and the cup three times.

In 2008/09 in the UEFA Cup they'd seen off Cliftonville 11-0 on aggregate, beat Lillestrom and F.C. Moscow, lost 1-0 at home to St Etienne, drawn 1-1 with Valencia, 1-1 with Rosenburg, and beaten Club Bruges 1-0 away .

They have a fan club known as FC Kobenhaun (FCKKFC) which has 20,000 members. They have groups known as The Urban Crew, Copenhagen Casuals, and Copenhagen Cooligans, who frequent the C stand lower and the B stand lower known as the atmospheric stand.

European colours were all white for home games and all Mayo Blue for aways though their third kit was all orange.

They averaged over 10,000 for the first time in 1997/98 but reached 23,795 in 2006/07.

Their record attendance was 41, 201 v local suburban rivals Brondby in 2006.

When they played City, after 17 games in their league they were second, two points behind Brondby who had 39 points, and 6 points ahead of 4th place F. C. Midtjylland.

The teams met in February 2009 in the UEFA Cup round 32, playing away in the first leg, which City drew 2-2, and the second leg at COMS was won 2-1.

John L: 19/2/2009 FCK 2 City 0

Having come through the group stages of the UEFA Cup, City were drawn to travel back to Denmark for their Round of 32 tie against FC Copenhagen. Looking to take the aggro out of organising myself for this European trip, I booked the Thomas Cook official flight, hang the expense. (I'd previously messed up my Cyprus flights, booking before the clubs then reversed the fixtures, and only got to Santander via Luton and Reus). Anyway, come the 19th February, I turned up for the early morning trip and joined the throng at the bar enjoying a couple of cold ones.

An unremarkable flight ended with a touchdown in a very snowy Copenhagen, and as our plane taxied in, a massive snowplough carried on clearing the runway – cue a load of clichés about how "Britain grinds to a halt", etc…).

Inside the airport terminal, we were greeted by the Kobenhavns Politi – the Copenhagen police, who greeted us cheerily and handed us an 8-page supporters guide, which provided useful information about public transport, how to get to the ground, and the rules about what they expected in terms of behaviour. My brother-in-law Craig and I had been railroaded into helping deliver a large batch of King of the Kippax magazines to a bar about a mile from the centre of Copenhagen, so once we'd got off the coaches, which parked right outside the famous Tivoli Gardens, our group began walking away from that major tourist attraction, and through the attractive, but quiet town centre.

Pushing open the door to the Bloomsday bar it was no surprise to find it full of Norwegian Blues, and over the next couple of hours we enjoyed relatively cheap food, and very expensive beer. Gradually our contingent grew as John Duffy got in from Stansted, Nigel's son Chris arrived straight from Germany, and Martin made it direct from South Africa.

Naturally, I got chatting to another of Dave's pack-horses, regular KotK contributor Neil Shaw. Coincidentally, it turned out that Neil lived a few miles away from me in Disley, Cheshire, and works in Hazel Grove. The bloody unbelievable coincidence was that, as a manager at a company about 500 yards from where I live, he'd recruited my 17-year old son Alex for some part-time evening work just the previous week! Alex had told me about this top Blue he'd met at work; it must have been strange when his college lesson was interrupted with a …..."guess who I've just met?" text from 1000 miles away….

Deciding (from bitter previous experience) that watching City after severage beverals is not a great idea, a few of us wandered off for a decent meal in the afternoon, and found an excellent steakhouse in an area where most pubs seemed full of City fans. Then it was onto the coaches for the journey to the Parken Stadium, on the northern outskirts of Copenhagen, and one of those grounds which looks ordinary by Premier League standards, but which nonetheless sports a retractable roof, often hosts Denmark international games, and accommodates 38,000 spectators. And FC Kopenhagen are a club with an excellent European pedigree since their formation in 1992. They had relaid their pitch just three days before this fixture, and one of the ends featured a large (Arsenal-style) mural, shielding the fact that a major new stand was in development.

The game itself finished 2-2, with a remarkable goal by Nedum Onouha opening the scoring. It was a rubbish goal, but remarkable only for the fact that he became City's 20th different scorer of the season. If City did goalscoring charts, that season's would have been the biggest…. probably. One City fan immediately launched into a Spiderman impersonation, climbing about eight feet up some netting that didn't seem to be serving any obvious purpose….

Typically, City then looked like they'd achieve the win their play deserved. Steven Ireland put us 2-1 up, but dozy defending once again cost us dearly when an unmarked Vingaard equalised in stoppage time.

So it was off to the airport in a rather deflated, yet still-confident mood, which was dampened further when it took about an hour to de-ice the plane before take-off. Cue one or two more clichés. By the time we found ourselves approaching Manchester Airport, the pilot gave us the news that one of the two runways was closed for maintenance, and the other was ice-bound….

Now the threat of a diversion to East Midlands airport loomed, as we didn't have enough fuel to hang around. Happily, after a couple of circuits, we got permission to land at Manchester, something of a relief. Two weeks later, after a 2-1 win in the home leg, we were safely through to the last 16 of the UEFA Cup.

Previous meetings: City also played in Copenhagen at their old ground but against Gornik Zabrze in the 1971 European Cup Winners' Cup 3rd round replay winning 3-1 with goals from Young, Booth and Lee before 12,100.

Friendlies: Copenhagen X1 in 1937/38 on tour winning 4-1 twice and 8-0 but drawing 3-3 and losing 2-1 in 1948/49.

Some connections: Niclas Jensen, Hans Backe

Ground: The Parken Stadium, also the home of the Danish National team, built in 1992. Current capacity 34,098, which will rise to 38,000 when the new D stand, under construction, is completed.

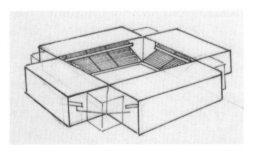

Corinthians

Were formed in 1882 by N. Lane Jackson and played mainly friendly games, indeed having written into their rules that they should not compete for any cups or prizes whatsoever. They notably beat FA Cup holders Blackburn Rovers 8-1 shortly after the 1884 Final, and League Champions Aston Villa. When they relaxed their rules to compete in Cup competitions, they won the 1900 Sheriff of London Shield, and also won 10-1 against the Bury side that had beaten Derby County 6-0 in the 1903 Final.

World wide recognition was achieved with Real Madrid adopting their white shirts, and

Sport Club Corinthians Paulista in Brazil adopting their name. Also in 1904 a Swedish tournament called The Corinthian Bowl was set up in commemoration.

In the same year they inflicted on Manchester United their record defeat of 11-3. After World War 2 they competed in the FA Cup but with little success, and also lost the 1927 Charity Shield to Cardiff City 1-2. In 1939 they amalgamated with the Casuals to become Corinthian Casuals. They moved to King George Field in Tolworth in 1988 and play in the Isthmian League Division One South.

City played them in the third round of the FA Cup in 1926, drawing 3-3, with a late equaliser, before 27,900 at the old Cup Final venue of Crystal Palace, and winning the replay 4-0 at Maine Road in front of 42,303.

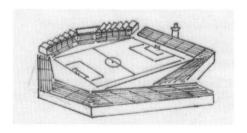

Friendlies: Casuals a 3-2 1897/98, 1899/1900 a 1-1, h 2-2, 1905/06 a 1-4, 1920/21 2-0 h,

Max Woosnam was the City connection

Coventry City

'The (cheeky) Sky Blues' were formed in 1883 by workers at the Singer Cycle factory and changed their name to Coventry City in 1898, playing in blue and white quarters, They played at Binley Road, Stoke Road and moved to Highfield Road in 1899. They were elected to Division Two in 1919.

From being a Fourth Division club in the mid fifties they made it to the First Division in the sixties, changed colours to sky blue, won the FA Cup in 1987, but went down to Division One in 2001 along with two other City's, us and Bradford, and moved to The Ricoh Stadium in 2005.

They finished season 2010/11 in The Championship playing, in sky blue shirts with white shorts (They once played in an horrendous all brown away kit). Ex Blue Ray Ranson is Chairman.

Pre-war the clubs met twice, in Division Two in 1938/39, City winning both games, 3-0 home, 1-0 away..

Post-war: 52 league meetings with 27 City wins, 12 draws and 13 losses.

They were pushing City for promotion in 1965/66, and knocked the Blues out of the League Cup 3-2 away in the third round, but tailed off in the league and were overtaken by Southampton, settling for the title the following season.

City had by far the better of exchanges in the 60's and 70's, best was the 5-1 at home in 1985/86, but it was pretty well level pegging from the 80's onwards. The 1972/73 game at Maine Road was Joe Mercer's return with Coventry and, after a standing ovation, he was well satisfied with the 2-1 Coventry win. In 1993 after a 1-1 Friday night draw at Maine Road, City's new manager was announced as….Brian Horton, which did not go down well with the City faithful, although a few good results initially took off the pressure.

In the Premiership

Season	H	A	Pl	W	D	L
Pre 00/01			8	2	3	3
00/01	1-2	1-1	10	2	4	4

In the FA Cup the teams have met in three rounds:

1982 4th rd 1-3 home
1985 3rd rd 1-2 away
1996 4th rd 2-2 away, replay 2-1 home
Highlight, or otherwise, of the 1985 Cup game at Highfield Road was Second Division City's fans taking exception to the third round 1-2 exit to First Division Coventry and being seated on an open terrace on a frosty January day, as they dismantled the seats in the open end behind the goal (first all seater stadium in 1981) and whizzed them at Coventry's goalie – Ogrizovic. In the 1996 replay at Maine Road the Coventry fans in the North stand invaded the main stand.

In the League Cup, three meetings:
1965/66 3rd rd 2-3 home
1973/74 5th rd 2-2 away, replay 4-2 home
1989/90 4th rd 0-1 home

Roger R: 19/12/1973 Coventry 2 City 2
Team: Macrae, Pardoe, Donachie, Doyle, Booth, Towers, Summerbee, Bell, Marsh, Lee, Leman.
Football League Cup 5th Round.

This game was played on a midweek afternoon and I can still remember it so well. I "skived" off school in order to be able to go but as my Dad was at work I decided to go on one of the City official supporters club coaches – and I ended up travelling to the game on "big Helen" (Turner)'s coach. What a character and massive City fan she was by the way! It turned out to be quite an experience going on her coach, plenty of stories and singing, notwithstanding that everyone, even hard up schoolboys like I was at the time, had to contribute to the coach drivers tip on the return leg of the journey! It was a bit of an unreal experience for me too as we parked in what seemed to be the centre of the city and then walked a hugely long way to the old Highfield Road ground (the game was played at a time when you always expected to be attacked by home fans on the way to or from the match – so the long walk was NOT appreciated at all!)

The match? I remember it so well, was 2-1 to Coventry and we looked like we were going out of the League Cup until pint-sized Dennis Leman rose majestically like the proverbial salmon to all of his 5' 3 " in height and headed the ball past Coventry keeper Bill Glazier to earn City a replay. We went on (famously!) to win that replay at Maine Road, again on a Wednesday afternoon, and again I skived off school to watch the match. City then went all

the way to Wembley where we lost to Wolves despite it being the most one-sided final in the history of the competition!

Some connections: Ray Sambrook, David Bennett, Peter Bodak, Tommy Hutchison, Chairman Ray Ranson

Friendlies: 1948/49 a 1-2, 1957/58 a 1-3, 1965/66 a 2-4, 1979/80 Skol Tournament, Edinburgh 1-3

Ground: Highfield Road (shown 2000's) R/A 51,457 v Wolves D2 1966/67. Ricoh Arena Capacity 32,000

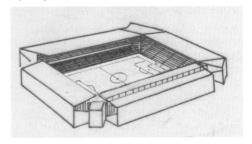

Crewe Alexandra

'The Railwaymen' were formed in 1877 from a cricket team and took the name 'Alexandra' after Princess Alexandra. They played at The Alexandra Recreation Ground before moving to the adjacent Gresty Road (first) in 1896, then Gresty Road (second) in 1906.

They were founder members of Division Two in 1892, after losing in the semi-final of the FA Cup in 1888 to Preston but failed to gain re-election in 1896.

They were elected back into the newly formed Division Three North in 1921, and finished season 2010/11 in League Two playing in red shirts and white shorts

Pre-war: 6 league meetings in Division Two between 1892/93 and 1895/96 seasons, with 5 City wins, 1 draw and 2 losses. In the 1893/94 1-1 draw at Crewe, City played with ten men, after Whittle and a reserve player missed the train!

Post–war: 6 league meetings with 4 City wins, 1 draw and 1 loss.

First post war meetings were in season 1997/98 in the First Division, with City wins including a 4-0 in 1999/2000 and a 5-2 in 01/02.

The original game in December 2000 was postponed due to a frozen pitch, advised as fans were well on the way to the game, and the match was eventually played in March, City winning 3-1, Shaun Goater scoring his 30th goal of the season.

Neil S: 12/3/2002 Crewe 1 City 3

It seems like only yesterday that a football quiz question requested the five League clubs with the letter x featuring in their name. Judging by the fate of the other four (Exeter, Halifax, Oxford and Wrexham), I bet Crewe Alexandra supporters are terrified.

Despite living on the Cheshire border I didn't make it to Crewe until the 2001-2002 season. Indeed, Gresty Road was my last North West venue on the great Manchester City tour of the lower divisions.

It's funny how some games can be grouped together. I was on a supporters coach in Marple when the Stoke game was postponed in 1981. Similarly, we were on the M5 when the referee announced that Home Park was unplayable in 1988. Thirteen years later, I was sat in the Railway Arms when a policewoman entered the premises and announced that the match was postponed.

Nobody took her too seriously. The game was only an hour away and the conditions didn't appear particularly horrendous. Was she a strippogram in disguise?

By the time of the rescheduled game, I was on crutches after breaking my ankle. My mate Bainy worked near Crewe and had managed to obtain tickets for the Main Stand. We arrived in plenty of time and for the second time in my life I was supping in the Railway Arms, three hours before kick off

Alongside Macclesfield, Crewe supporters are probably the friendliest in the Football League. They claim to be the original blue mooners, but I wouldn't have the faintest idea. All I wanted was three points on the march to promotion.

Benarbia netted from long distance and during the half time interval I discovered that having a leg in plaster can sometimes work to your advantage. There wasn't a queue for the disabled toilet and I was given a complimentary programme by a sympathetic steward.

This was the zenith period of the Keegan reign. Travelling to Crewe, expecting to win was a relatively rare experience. Every game was a sheer delight and for that we should be eternally grateful.

There have been no meetings in the **F. A Cup**

In the League Cup just the one meeting in the second round of 2002 City winning 3-2 at home.

Some Connections: Peter Leigh, Dave Ewing, Neil Lennon (below), Stan Bowles

Friendlies: 1966/67 a 4-0, 1968/69 a 5-2 (Peter Leigh T/M), 1984/85 a 5-1

Ground: Gresty Road (shown 2001/02 R/A 20,000 v Spurs FA Cup 4 1960

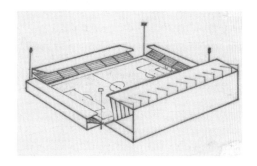

Crystal Palace

Though there was a Palace club in 1861, 'The Eagles' were formed in 1905, played at Crystal Palace, Herne Hill, The Nest, and moved to Selhurst Park in 1924. They were founder members of Division Two in 1920, moved up and down the divisions including stints in all four, were FA Cup runners up in 1990, and won the Zenith Data Systems Cup in 1991.

They finished season 2010/11 in The Championship playing in red and blue striped shirts (thought to have been adopted by Barcelona) and white shorts.

Post–war: 36 league meetings with 16 City wins, 9 draws and 11 losses.

Last game of the season at Maine Road in 1973 saw already relegated Palace win 3-2, giving Malcolm Allison some satisfaction. Then in 1981 it was a 1-1 draw in City's last home game before Wembley, when, again, Palace were already relegated!

There was a ferocious game in 1987/88 when, after going a goal up City lost their composure as Mark Bright broke Eric Nixon's nose and Eric struck out subsequently being sent off, Steve Redmond taking over in goal, as City lost the game 1-3. The following year as the two teams contested second place and automatic promotion City held on to a 1-1 draw at home on May day. Nigel Gleghorn put City one up in the 8th minute then had to go in goal when Dibble went off injured in the 35th minute, doing a sterling job, but was finally beaten in the 75th minute by Ian Wright. In 1992/93 a 0-0 draw at Maine Road with a game remaining virtually cost Palace their Premiership place, going down with 49 points.

Jerry D: 18/12/1965 Palace 0 City 2

Am I right in thinking that children and younger people are oblivious to the extremes of outdoor weather? Is it only when we get older that we become more selective and protective, making sure to take our sun-cream or our waterproofing with us (according to the forecast) or sometimes even cancelling our plans?

I ask this question because I can remember standing with two school friends on the open terrace at Selhurst Park watching City play Crystal Palace in driving rain on a raw and cold December day in 1965.

We must have returned home soaked to the skin and chilled to the marrow. But I cannot recall that any of us felt that we had done anything foolhardy – I don't even think that any of us commented upon the weather or complained at any discomfort.

And yet it must have been bad out there. The 'Sunday Times' wrote:

There was a Dostoyevsky setting of great swirling clouds of cold rain, and a churned-up muddy surface. The last half hour was dismal as the horrible conditions worsened. If anyone had tried to work a horse on such a surface, or stand it on the uncovered terraces, he would have been prosecuted.

Perhaps I was feeling warm inside, enjoying myself as City (wearing an all-maroon strip) coasted to a 2-0 win in that Championship and promotion winning season.

Most excitingly of all, the afternoon brought my first introduction to a new and young City player who would play a massive part in the club's success over the next decade. The 'Daily Telegraph' wrote:

'Mike Doyle, 19, a slender yet robust six-footer, scored both City's goals.

Born in Manchester, Doyle is living proof in a number 4 shirt that the supply of 'cards' has not yet dried up. He loves to communicate his feelings to friend, foe, referee and crowd. Above all, he loves scoring goals.

"He likes going up in attack. We can't stop him," confessed Joe Mercer, City's manager.'

In the Premiership there's been 6 meetings with 2 City wins, 3 draws and 1 loss. In 2004/05 a 2-1 win at Palace did relieve the pressure on Kevin Keegan.

Season	H	A	P	W	D	L
pre 04/05			4	0	3	1
04/05	3-1	2-1	6	2	3	1

In the FA Cup, meetings in three rounds:
1921 1st rd 0-2 away
1926 5th rd 11-4 home
1981 3rd rd 4-0 home
City 11 Palace 4, record Cup victory - City went ahead after 4 minutes with a Billy Austin penalty. Frank Roberts scored in the 12th and 22nd minutes to make it 3-0. Tommy Johnson made it four in the 26th, then Roberts again in the 30th completed his hat- trick. Tommy Browell made it seven with two goals just before the interval, although Callender in the Palace goal was playing well.

Palace pulled one back through Cherrett in the 55th but Browell made it 8-1 in the 58th. then Cherrett again scored to make it 8-2. Clarke scored from a penalty first parried by Goodchild, and McCracken made it 8-4.

Roberts made it nine, then ten in the 75th and 82nd minutes, and Hicks made it eleven just before the end. Despite the scoreline Palace's goalie Callender was carried shoulder high by fans in recognition of some great saves watched by 51, 630.

In the League Cup, just the two meetings, Palace putting paid to our hopes in the quarter final of 1994/95 with a 4-0 win but City winning 2-1 in the third round of 2009/10, both games at Selhurst Park.

Some connections: Manager Malcolm Allison, Derek Jeffries, Steve MacKenzie, Perry Suckling

Friendlies: None

Ground: Selhurst Park (shown 2009/10) R/A 51,482 v Burnley D2 1979

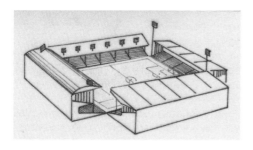

Friendlies:
Chirk 1891/92 a 3-2, 1895/96 h 9-1, 1895/96 1900/01 a 4-0, 1901/02 a 2-1, 1997/98
Canadian X1 1891/92 h 3-1
City combined X1 1894/95 h 2-0
Chirk/Wrexham X1 1909/10 a 4-4
Crook Town 1968/69 a 6-1
Caernarvon X1 1969/70 a 1-1, 1984/85
Chorley 1979/80 0-2 a, 1985/86
Champions X1 h (Roy Clarke T/M)
Cork United 1981/82 a 4-0
F.C Cologne in Spain 1981/82 1-1
Curzon Ashton 1986/87 a 2-1, 1995/96 (K Clements T/M), 1996/97 a 2-1
Cobh Ramblers 1990/91 a ,
Cork City 1990/91 a 1-0, 1991/92 a 1-0, 1995/96 a 7-0,, 1996/97 a 3-1
Cramlington Sunday League 1991/92
Capetown 1992/93 a 1-0
Cremonese 1992/93 a 2-2
Chatsworth Rangers 1992/93 a
Congleton Town 1994/95 a 1-0, 1996/97, 1997/98
Colwyn Bay 1998/99
Carlstad 2007/08 a 4-0
Charleroi 2007/08 a 0-2
Club America 2010/11 a 1-1 (4-1 pens), 2011/12 a 2-0

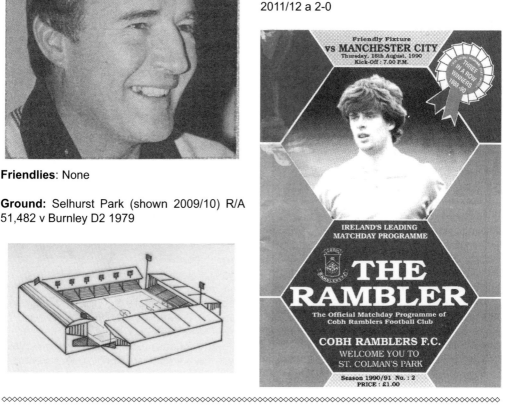

D is for Darlington

The D's take us up to the North East, Lancashire, Derbyshire, Yorkshire and the Ukraine.

———◆———

Darlington

Darlo, 'the Quakers', were formed in 1883 and became founder members of Division Three North in 1921, playing at Feethams. They were eventually relegated to the Conference in 1988 but promoted back to Division Four in 1989.

They moved to the oversized Reynolds Arena in 2003 but went into administration in 2004, though retained their place in Division Four.

They finished season 2010/11 in League Two playing in white shirts and black shorts

Pre-war: The teams met twice in Division Two in season 1926/27, City winning 7-0 at home and drawing 2-2 away.

In the first round of the **FA Cup** in 1922, at Hyde Road, City won 3-1 courtesy of a Tommy Browell hat-trick. Fast forward then to season 1998/99, with City in the Second Division, and a second round FA Cup tie at Feethams, where, after going a goal down and chants of "where's our City gone" from Blues fans, Paul Dickov secured a replay with a late equaliser. Michael Brown notched the winner at Maine Road in front of a paltry 8,595.

Neil S: 4/12/1998 Darlington 1 City 1

Has it really been over a decade? A week might be a long time in politics, but for Manchester City, the 1998-99 season was from a different Universe.

It wasn't a difficult decision. My office Christmas party offered a host of tipsy and attractive teenage girls enjoying a lavish medieval banquet. Meanwhile, a friend had offered a spare ticket for the supporters club coach to Darlington. My head stated the obvious, but my heart chose masochism.

I waited outside the Pineapple Inn in Stockport hoping not to be recognised. The streets were full of freezing Christmas shoppers, totally oblivious to the torment I was about to face. Never mind Cup fever, I was on the verge of catching Cup pneumonia.

The coach arrived at noon and as we skated through North Yorkshire, our steward Alan Potter served Bovril and corned beef sandwiches. In the background Mel Gibson was motivating the Highland hordes before the Battle of Stirling. They can take our lives, but they'll never take our stupidity.

In all honesty, the City support was fairly minimal. The Friday night game was live on Sky anyway, and the only attraction was the opportunity to visit a new ground. The North East Constabulary showed their appreciation by making us wait on the outskirts of Darlington for almost two hours.

As we parked outside the ground we were politely informed:

"The ground is on your right. Anyone who goes left will be arrested"

Welcome to Darlington? You must be f**king joking.

To make a freezing night even colder, Feethams was next to the cricket ground and exposed to the elements. The pitch didn't look playable, but the locals preferred it that way. City were on a hiding to nothing.

One of the great unwritten laws of football is that any player who used to play for Manchester City will always score against us. Gary Bennett was too old for most fans to remember, but there was a sense of inevitability as he opened the scoring. Paul Dickov eventually equalized, but nobody was fooled and the game drifted towards a replay. Wembley and Europe would have to wait for at least another decade.

The coach arrived back in Stockport at midnight. I caught the 192 bus to Hazel Grove and hitch-hiked to Whaley Bridge. Nobody stopped and I collapsed in bed at around 3am. Apparently the Christmas party was great.

Some connections: F.W. Wrightson (1930), Davis Brightwell, Gary Bennett, John Burridge.

Ground : Feethams R/A 21,023 v Bolton Lg Cup 3 1960 (shown), Reynolds Arena/New Stadium/ Williamson Motors Stadium R/A : 11,600 v Kidderminster H. 2003. Capacity: 25,000

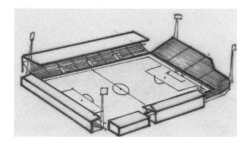

Darwen

Formed in 1875 and were elected into the Football League in 1891 where they remained until failing to gain re-election in 1899 (last game a 1-1 draw with Newton Heath!), playing their games at Barley Bank, part of a cricket pitch which is now covered by housing. They then moved to The Anchor Ground after dropping into the Lancs League/Combination.

In 1893 they beat Notts County 3-2 in a Test Match at Hyde Road in front of 5,000.

'The Salmoners' folded in 2009 and a new club AFC Darwen was formed who finished season 2010/11 in the North West Counties Division One playing in all red.

Pre-war: Twelve league meetings in Division Two between 1803 and 1899, City winning five at home including a 10-0 in 1888/89, losing one, and winning three and losing three away.

Friendlies were played in 1893/94 0-7 h, 2-5 h. then possibly reserve games in 1977/78 a, 1979/80 a, 1989/90 a

Ground: Barley Bank R/A 14,000 Friendly v Blackburn R. 1882. Anchor Ground capacity 4,500

Derby County

'The Rams' were formed in 1884 from the cricket club, and were one of the original twelve members of the Football League in 1888/89 playing at The Racecourse Ground. They moved to the Baseball Ground in 1894 at the instigation of Sir Francis Ley, then to Pride Park in 1998.

Derby were generally a First Division club until the mid fifties, winning the FA Cup in 1946, but then suffered relegations to the Third Division before bouncing back under manager Brian Clough and winning the League at City's expense in 1972. They then won it again in 1975 under Dave MacKay.

Ups and downs since, they finished season 2010/11 in the Championship after just one further season in the Premiership in 2007/08, recording the lowest ever number of points (13-1 v City) in the Premiership.

Pre-war : 44 league meetings with 21 City wins including a 4-0 home win in City's first home game in Division One in 1899, 6-0 home win in 1904/05 and a 6-1 home and 7-1 away win in 1937/38. 9 draws 14 losses.

The 1-4 defeat at Derby on Christmas Day in 1933 marked Frank Swift's debut.

October 1934 saw H.R.H. Duke of York attend the 0-1 City defeat at Maine Road, he later became King George V1.

Post-war: 46 league meetings with 18 wins 10 draws and 18 losses. City won seven of the Maine Road games after the war, but form in Derby was particularly poor losing 0-7 in 1949/50, 0-5 in 1952/53 and 0-6 in 1989/90, and no wins since 1970. In the 1971/72 game which City lost 1-3 at The Baseball Ground Brian Clough was interviewed on MOTD and was asked what he thought of City. "*Manchester City, are a very good team, made today to look a little bit ordinary by Derby County*". In the return game, City's last of the season, at Maine Road, City won 2-0 to go top with 57 points. However as the other teams all had games in hand and were to play each other in some instances, it was a case of waiting to see who would overtake us. As it happened Derby beat Liverpool, Leeds lost at Wolves then Liverpool drew at Arsenal to allow Derby to take top spot and they celebrated on the beach in Spain when they heard the news.

!n 1974 at Maine Road, Barry Davies, commentating on MOTD, came out with the immortal words as Franny Lee scored in their 2-1 win "*Interesting, very interesting*" then "*just look at his face, just look at his face*" Not funny.
The 0-4 loss at Derby in 1977, with Brian Kidd

sent off, virtually put paid to City's title hopes. Joe Corrigan was booked for correctly striding out the twelve yards to re-mark the penalty spot which had disappeared into the mud. In November of that year with the score at 2-1 to Derby, referee Derek Civil blew for full time as Dennis Tueart's header was about to enter the net! Cue Civil War! Derby's 3-1 home win in 1980 in the 41st match couldn't prevent them from being relegated. In 1991 City's 2-1 win in the 35th game aided Derby's relegation.

Bryan D: 4/12/1971 Derby 3 City 1

David Porter, Terry Cocking and I had been going to a few away matches by this stage, being aged 15 and 16 and on this occasion Charlie Mottley attended his first away game. We travelled down by coach. It was quite a walk from the coach park to the ground and en route we met a couple of other City fans who had obviously had a few (by which I mean they were absolutely bladdered!) "C'mon ladsh, into the Pop Shide, all doh City fansull be in der"
  In those days all the away fans were corralled into half the 'Pop Side' of the ground with the local yobbos in the other. Which side were we in? Yes, you've guessed it – but we hadn't! In we went, singing and clapping and found ourselves unwittingly in a six man assault by the whole of the Derby mob. The ensuing exchange lasted a matter of seconds and we beat a hasty retreat, Charlie Mottley suffering a fat lip and chipped tooth on his first away day. This he took full advantage of telling anyone who would listen (and showing those that wouldn't!) at the Motown Club the following night. I'm sure the girls were very impressed!

John B – 20/4/1991 City 2 Derby 1

A game with a real end of season look to it this, but one that by the final whistle had turned into a keenly felt victory because of events that had unfolded during the course of the match. Sporting a full length plaster cast on a broken right leg, I had to be driven to Manchester from Birkenhead for this match by my then girlfriend, and future wife, sitting sideways on the back seat (me, not her) of a beat up Vauxhall Corsa. For similar reasons, I had engineered end of row seats in the Main Stand, so I could sit with the offending limb stuck out in the aisle.
  As far as Derby County were concerned, the relegation trapdoor was wide open and the

slightest nudge would send them through it. City, riding relatively high in the top 6 and on the back of a 5 game unbeaten run, were well equipped then to help the Rams on their way, and quickly established a 2-0 lead, courtesy of the deadly duo of David White and Niall Quinn.

However, just when it looked as if a cricket score might be on the cards, the game turned on its head when the visitors earned, and by earned I mean conned, themselves a penalty. Long before Ruud Van Nistlerooy perfected the art of flicking one leg out sideways in the opposition area to ensure contact with the nearest defender, and then collapsing theatrically to the turf, Dean Saunders was the most prodigious 'winner' of penalties in the top flight, and, around the half hour mark, the Welsh striker chased a ball down the inside left channel, and as the City keeper, Tony Coton, slid out to smother, duly launched himself into a full triple lutz with pike. It was an utterly preposterous dive, but to the astonishment of all present, the referee, white stick in hand, pointed to the spot. Suitably enraged, Coton took off his gloves and hurled them at the hapless official's feet, firing off a simultaneous volley of abuse that saw him red carded into the bargain. With no reserve goalie on the bench, Maine Road seethed as Niall Quinn donned the keeper's jersey. However, what few, if any, of us knew, was that Quinny had been a useful Gaelic footballer in his youth, and for a striker was pretty accomplished between the sticks. Dean Saunders clearly didn't know it either, because preparing to celebrate after having hit what looked a perfect penalty, low into the bottom left hand corner, his face turned to a mask of horror, as the mighty Niall plunged acrobatically to his left to tip it around the post. The delighted roar of approval from the crowd only then increased when from the resultant corner, Quinny swaggered out off his line and plucked the ball from the air aka Gordon Banks.

Derby did eventually pull one goal back, but the 2-1 defeat meant they were relegated, whilst City, reaching the crest of the current wave, recorded a 5th place finish for the second season in a row.

In The Premiership just the two meetings City winning 1-0 at COMS and drawing 1-1 at Derby in 2007/08

In the F.A Cup, meetings in four rounds :
1932 5th rd 3-0 home
1933 SF 3-2 at Huddersfield
1950 3rd rd 3-5 home
1955 3rd rd 3-1 away

In the League Cup of 1998/99 (City in D1) second round it was a 1-1 draw at Pride Park and a 1-0 loss at Maine Road, Paulo Wanchope scoring for Premiership Derby.

Some connections: Paulo Wanchope, Dave Watson, Peter Doherty, manager Nigel Clough, Francis Lee, Mark Lillis

Friendlies were played in 1893/94 h 2-1, and 1957/58 a 5-0

Ground: Baseball Ground (shown 1990's) R/A 41,826 v Spurs D1 1969/70. Pride Park Cap : 33,957

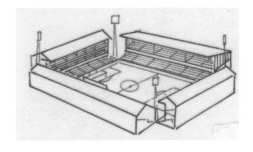

Doncaster Rovers

'Rovers' were formed in 1879 and flitted in and out of the League in the early 1900's, They gained election to Division Three North in 1923 after vacating Intake and Bennetthorpe and moving to Belle Vue.

'Donny' dropped into the Conference but came back in 2003, moved to the Keepmoat Stadium in 2007, after a dodgy arson attempt on the main stand involving their then Chairman, and finished season 2010/11 in the Championship, playing in red and white hooped shirts and white shorts.

Pre-war just the one league meeting in the Second Division in season 1902/03 the Blues winning 4-1 at home and 2-1 at the Intake ground.

Post–war: Two meetings in 1950/51 in the Second Division, City losing 3-4 after being 3

goals up at half time to a Peter Doherty inspired Rovers at Belle Vue, (*very embarrassing to be reminded of when I started work in Doncaster in 1971!*) and drawing 3-3 at Maine Road.

In the League Cup tie of 2005, it was 0-0 at full time, City then took the lead through a Vassell penalty in the fifth minute of extra time, but Doncaster equalised in the 118th minute with a disputed penalty. Nedum Onuoha was wrongly sent off, later rescinded, and they won 3-0 on penalties. Humiliating.

Roger R: 21/9/2005 Doncaster 1 City 1 (0-3 pens)

Team James, Onuoha, Thatcher, Jihai, Dunne, Distin, Ireland, Reyna, Vassell, Sibierski, Hussein subs Croft and Jordan. Football League Cup Second Round.

I was privileged to have been appointed as the youngest Secretary in the Football League when I became Club Secretary at Doncaster Rovers in the summer of 1979 and my fervent wish, every time there was a League Cup or FA Cup draw, was for Rovers to be drawn to play Manchester City . Well I finally got my wish about twenty two years after I had left Doncaster Rovers! The game was played at the old Belle Vue ground (which had seen better days even when I was there so it was certainly in a sorry state at the time of this match!) City strolled around in the first half looking like they were going to murder the Rovers even though we had a much changed side and a young kid of a triallist playing called Hussein (who never appeared again after this match!) Sadly, Rovers had a much better second half and the tie finished 1-1 after a bizarre moment involving their goalkeeper and Iffy Onuoha when he was sent off in spite of the fact that he had clearly been involved in a 50:50 challenge with the Rovers keeper. Sadly the injury to the goalkeeper was serious and the referee chose to send off Nedum even though he had clearly been innocent of any deliberate offence. Anyway, City managed to end the match and extra time all square. Rovers substitute goalkeeper proceeded to pull off several amazing saves to ensure Rovers won the penalty shoot out rather than City. Where was I watching the match? In the old main stand surrounded by Rovers fans and ensuring I did my very best to keep quiet as best I could when City were attacking!

Various friendlies have been played all at Doncaster - 1930/31 3-0, 1971/72 2-0, 1972/73 International X1 for Alick Jeffrey 3-4, 1999/2000 1-1, 2004/05 1-1 and finally 2007/08 the opening of the new Keepmoat Stadium, Sven's first game in charge and a 3-1 win.

Some connections: Peter Doherty, Bill Leivers, Colin Barlow, Tony Coleman (right)

TONY COLEMAN

Ground: Belle Vue (shown 2007) R/A 37,149 v Hull D3N 1948. Keepmoat Stadium, Capacity: 15,231

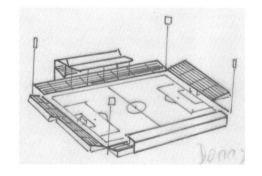

Dynamo Kiev

Dynamo Kiev were formed in 1927, are known as 'The White-Blues', and play in the city which is located in the Ukraine on the banks of the broad river Dniepr.

As members of the Soviet League they won 13 titles 9 Cups and 3 USSR Super Cups. After the collapse of the Soviet Union they became founder members of the Ukrainian Premier League and have won 13 titles and 4 Super Cups.

In Europe they'd won two Cup Winners' Cups and one UEFA Super Cup. In the Champions

Cup they were semi finalists three times and quarter finalists six times. In 1995 however they were expelled from the UEFA champions League for allegedly offering bribes to officials and banned from Europe for two years but this was later reversed.

In the 2009 UEFA Cup they lost 3-2 to Shakhtar Donetsk, their bitter rivals in the semi-final.

They emerged from the 2010 season month winter break 12 points adrift of Shakhtar but much stronger under new manager Yuri Semin and were expected to clinch a Champions League place for the 19th successive year.

In the previous round of the Europa Cup they'd defeated Besiktas 8-1 on aggregate. Their most famous player is Andriy Shevchenko, although Andrei Kanchelskis was once a star

Home colours are all white, and away all blue.

The teams first met in the Europa Cup in March 2011. City lost the first leg in Kiev 2-0, Shevchenko and Gusev doing the damage in front of 16,000 with 536 Blues. Second leg was a 1-0 win with Kolarov scoring but Balotelli being sent off. Crowd was 27,816 with 578 Ukrainians. Kiev went on to lose 1-1 on away goals on aggregate with Braga of Portugal.

The original stadium was built by youth brigades after the Revolution, and opened on 12th August 1923, 13 days before Maine Road. It was then rebuilt to open in 1941, which unfortunately coincided with the day the Germans invaded. Worse still they smashed it up on their retreat in 1943!

After rebuilding, the stadium was renamed in 1962 after Nikita Khrushchev, but in 1964 reverted to its original title of the Ukrainian Republican Central Stadium.

Between 1966 -70 a second tier was added to take the all seated capacity up to 104,000, then 100,164 and it was used every day by the public for fitness classes and leisure. The Central Stadium is one of three, the other two being the centrally located Dynamo Stadium and the Smart Stadium which is a few kilometeres northeast. This is where the infamous 'match of death' took place; the story goes that the Ukrainians beat various German teams after which eight members of the winning team were eventually executed. Bert was obviously not in goal for the Germans, and it is presumed that the film 'Escape to Victory' starring Mike Summerbee, and co. was based on this tragic event.

However, the first leg was played in the 16,900 capacity Lobanovsky Dynamo stadium.

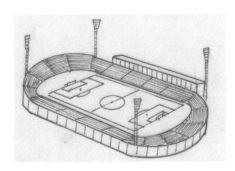

Neil Shaw: 10/3/2011 D.Kiev 2 City 0

The food was crap, but the beer was cheap and the hotel had its own lap dancing bar. Meanwhile our star signing (Balotelli) has developed an allergy to grass.

The Thomas Cook package was more appealing because it arrived the day before the game. The flight took an hour longer than published, and we arrived at our hotel around mid afternoon with a general feeling of nervous anticipation. Kiev was a brand new adventure, but nobody had any currency. We were all in the same boat, but the check-in procedure and currency exchange were relatively painless.

My room was on the fourteenth floor and rather disturbingly the window opened all the way. Health and Safety had obviously bypassed the Ukraine.

The hotel bar served beer at English prices, but it wasn't too difficult to find cheaper bars in the city centre, close to the ground. Eventually we found the appropriately named Mafia restaurant and settled down for a shambolic evening meal with cold food, pink horseradish and appalling service. We successfully negotiated a reduction, but only after slipping into the typical English concept of speaking slower and louder with plenty of hand signals.

By the time we returned to the hotel, the biting wind was drifting across from the River Dnieper. It was only 9pm and the City game wasn't kicking off until an hour later the following evening.

I couldn't be bothered with the lap dancers, but judging by the number of stories at breakfast I was obviously in a small minority.

As per usual the coaches were delayed by a selfish clown who couldn't be arsed getting out of bed for the 12:30 departure. We were

driven to the car park above the ground with a panoramic view of the small stadium and the impressive surroundings.

Friends Dee and Bev suggested a bit of sightseeing and after meandering around St Michael's church the first person we bumped into was Roberto Mancini. It was all a bit strange, but thankfully our esteemed manager wasn't too tired for the obligatory photo. I asked him if he was confident and he replied with a single word:

"Yes"

As we walked towards St Sophia church we bypassed the two coaches carrying Spike's party. Meanwhile, a local spotted my scarf and cheerfully predicted a 2-0 victory for Kiev. The game was rapidly approaching, but there was still time for a few drinks and an evening meal at the traditional Kiev establishment, TGI's.

By the time of the kick off the temperature had dropped considerably. A woman approached us and told us to walk towards a group of policeman outside the ground. We were given an escort, but in all fairness every Kiev supporter was cheerful and friendly. It was the local police that frightened me to death.

In contrast the away contingent was a travelling mass of alcoholic poisoning. Many fans had lost the ability to stand without assistance and in over thirty years of travelling to City games I don't think I've ever witnessed so many supporters vomiting in public. Perhaps it was the strong vodka, but I suspect it was the cheap prices.

For the first eighty minutes there was a father and son combination to my left. The son was in a dreadful state and spent the entire game in a drunken coma. However the second Kiev goal was the catalyst for the father to somersault over the row in front. God knows how he didn't break his neck, but I'm sure he'll see the funny side in years to come.

The ground was a contradiction of classic architecture and portable toilets. Just like Poznan, the catering was a choice of hot coffee or cold coffee.

City were poor, but I thought 2-0 was a little harsh. Hart was at fault for the first goal, but if it wasn't for his last minute save, the tie would have been over.

Remarkably the sprinklers were switched on after the final whistle and there was a genuine moment of hilarity as they drenched the local TV reporters. Both sets of supporters applauded each other and we made our way back to the coaches.

After an hour long coach journey and a four hour flight we eventually landed in Manchester at 5am local time. The players might have been tired, but they didn't have to be in the office by noon.

Friendlies:

Denton 1891/92 3-1h, 2-0 a, 1972/73 Int X1 a
Druids 1888/89 6-1a
Danish X1 - 1909/10 3-2 a, 2-5 a
Duisberg 1936/37 0-0 a
Dundee United 1961/62 1-2 a
Dundee 1965/66 h 1-2, 1985/86 a 2-2, 1-1 in San Jose
Dunfermline 1967/68 1-1,1-1, 0-0, 0-0 (all USA)
Droylsden 1970/71 a, 1972/73a 1979/80 a 1987/88 a, 1994/95 a, 1998/99 a
Djurgaarden 1978/79 a 1-1
Drogheda 1984/85 2-2 a, 1999/2000 a
Dynamo Dresden 1991/92 a 1-2
Derry City 1991/92 2-0 a
Dundalk 1993/94 a 4-1
Droemeda United 2000/01 a 1-0

E is for Everton

The E's take us down the East Lancs Road to Merseyside...

Everton

'The Toffees' were formed in 1878 when St Domingo's Sunday School formed a football club which played in Stanley Park, Priory Road, and Anfield Road. In 1879 they expanded membership and changed their name to Everton playing in black shirts with a white sash and were nicknamed The Black Watch. In 1884 they moved to Anfield but rent increases forced their move to Goodison in 1892 (after winning the title in 1891). Royal Blue was adopted in 1901. In 1888 they were founder members of the Football League where they've stayed for most of their history, regularly winning the FA Cup and League Titles plus the European Cup Winners' Cup in 1985. They finished season 2010/11 in the Premiership, playing in blue shirts and white shorts.

Pre-War: 60 league meetings with City winning 25, drawing 14 and losing 21.

The teams first met in season 1899/1900, and in 1905 City recorded a 2-0 home win over the then league leaders with two games to go. Tom Booth flattened City's Frank Booth in the game, who needed a police escort from the pitch. Tom Booth, the referee and linesman were subsequently suspended for a month. Everton finished 2nd (47 points) and City 3rd with 46, Newcastle taking the title with 48 points. Everton recorded their record win, and City's record defeat in 1906/07 with their 9-1 victory over a much changed City team after players were suspended following the bribes scandal. This game was played just two days after City lost at home to Arsenal 1-4 finishing the match with only six fit players. Everton were five goals up at half time and were seven up before City replied but they finished with a further two goals, Young being the danger man with four. There doesn't seem to be any excuses of injured or exhausted players, City were simply outclassed by the Cup holders, Everton who finished third from top and City fourth from bottom at the end of the season.

In 1923/24 Everton won 6-1 at Goodison but in 1928/29 City recorded a fine double, 5-1 home and 6-2 away. City were late arriving for the latter game, getting changed on the train which was delayed, then taking two taxis to the ground, and the match kicked off four minutes late. It was only 1-1 at half time, but City took control in the second half. Everton also won 9-0 in a 1941 war time game at Goodison, but lost 7-1 at City in 1942.

Post-war: 68 League meetings with City winning 24 drawing 21 and losing 23. In Frank Swift's last game City drew 0-0 at home in 1949 but lost the last game of the season at Goodison which confirmed the drop. There was another fine double for the Blues in 1957/58 City winning 6-2 at Maine Road including Ken Barnes' three penalties, and a 5-2 (after being two goals down) at Goodison. Then, apart from a 0-4 loss at Goodison in 1985/86 scores have been fairly close. City appeared in red and black striped shirts at Goodison in 1968 which enraged some City fans, though these turned out to be lucky colours for City in the following seasons. In October 1971 Malcolm Allison first took control of the team for the visit of Everton in a 1-0 home win.

In The Premiership there have been 28 league meetings, with nine City wins, including a 4-0 in 1994/95, 5-0 in 00/01 and 5-1 in 03/04, four draws and 15 defeats including a 2-5 in 1992/93 at Maine Road, the last match of the season, goalie Martyn Margetson being substituted at half time with City 3-0 down. City's win in 2008/09 was their first at Goodison in eleven visits since 92/93

Season	H	A	Pl	W	D	L
Pre 08/09			22	8	4	10
08/09	0-1	2-1	24	9	4	11
09/10	0-2	0-2	26	9	4	13
10/11	1-2	1-2	28	9	4	15

In the FA Cup, meetings in five rounds between 1933 and 1981, including a semi-final and Final:

1933 Final 0-3 Wembley
1949 3rd rd 0-1 away
1956 6th rd 2-1 home
1962 4th rd 0-2 away
1966 6th rd 0-0 home, replay 0-0 away 2nd replay 0-2 at Molineux
1969 SF 1-0 Villa Park
1981 6th rd: 2-2 away, replay 3-1 home

Four pages of Week-end Entertainment—

MANCHESTER CITY

Mr. A.H.HUGHES
Chairman of Directors
L. LANGFORD
Mr. W. WILD.
Secretary-Manager

S. CANN
W. DALE

M. BUSBY
J. BRAY

S. COWAN

A. HERD
J. McMULLAN

E. TOSELAND
F. TILSON
E. BROOK

R. Marshall is Reserve for Tilson.

—every Saturday in the *News* & *Chronicle*

19

In the 1933 Final Everton were captained by Dixie Dean and had ex Blue Tommy Johnson, the only Everton player with previous Cup final experience, in their team, (he played for City in 1926). Everton went ahead in the 40th minute through Stein. In the 46th minute Langford in City's goal then caught a high cross but Dean's charge caused him to lose the ball which went into the net. Surely a foul? Dunn then added a

third. Players were numbered 1-22, with City's from 12 to 22 and City played in scarlet jerseys and white knickers. Sam Cowan reputedly told the King that City would be back the next year to win the Cup! Which we did!

In the 1956 game there was a crowd of 76,129 with spectators scaling the floodlights and climbing on top of the half time scoreboard. Everton fans wrecked the trains on the way home. Only 15,227 turned up for the league game at Maine Road on the following Wednesday afternoon, a 3-0 City win.

Tommy Booth scored the winner in the 1969 semi-final, despite, he reminds us, a forward line of Bell, Lee, Summerbee, Young!

Sean R: 7/3/1981 Everton 2 City 2 and 11/3/1981 City 3 Everton 1

A titanic battle between two proud clubs located at each end of the East Lancs. Road. My memories of both games are still clear to this day. Having heard the draw at school, and thinking we had it all to do, I made my way to Goodison with a few of my dad's friends. It was my 16th birthday. We very nearly didn't make the journey, as 'Tag' wouldn't get into the car because one of the five in our group was a Red!

Our tickets were in the towering three storey main stand, and the famous old ground (which hasn't changed much since!) was bursting at the seams with just under 53,000 (including 12,000 or so Blues who had made the short journey over to Merseyside) packed inside. We went behind in a frenzied atmosphere, but Gerry Gow got us back into it with a great equaliser, hooking the ball over his shoulder into the roof of the net in front of the Gwladys Street faithful.. I can remember seeing the masses of City fans swaying in the paddocks below, stretching from the half way line, right round to the far side of the Park End. Everton restored their lead however, with future Blue Imre Varadi winning a dubious looking penalty, which was despatched home by locally born (Ashton-U-Lyne) tough guy Trevor Ross. Ratcliffe was sent off for headbutting Tommy Hutch, and nicknamed Lurpak (best butter!). with only a few minutes remaining, and Everton seemingly confident of a place in the semis, City counter attacked, and captain Paul Power was at the end of a move, which saw him lob the ball over the advancing Jim (later Seamus!) McDonagh in the Everton goal. The crowd held its breath, as the ball seemed to take an eternity to drop (which it eventually did!), and bounce (which it did!), fortunately for us, and it bounced underneath the bar and into the empty goal. Pandemonium ensued amongst the sky blue masses, as we secured the replay. Coming out afterwards was like a war zone, running battles between hundreds of fans everywhere you looked. Fortunately I didn't get any bother (mind you I was with some pretty big blokes!).

The next morning it was straight down to Maine Road on two buses, to join a queue, which I believe circled the whole of the ground TWICE!!! to secure a precious ticket for the replay four days later.

And so to the Wednesday night at Maine Road. Stan Gibson worked a miracle on the pitch after incessant rain for three days and it was the last time ever our ground would house an evening crowd in excess of 50,000 to see City playing there (actual attendance 52,532, which was the total capacity). Packed like sardines, the Kippax was just absolutely jammed solid. That night we hailed a new hero, tough tackling no nonsense Scottish full back Bobby MacDonald, who powered in two headers (if my memory serves me correctly!) to more or less kill off the tie. We dominated the match, Paul Power added a third, before Everton scored a token goal late on. The John Bond revolution was in full swing, we just KNEW we were bound for Wembley. Again there were ugly scenes outside the ground, and back into Manchester. The special buses drove us back with all the lights switched off, to make them less of a target for the large gangs of Blues and Scousers armed with bricks. Pretty scary when you think back now, but you wouldn't have missed these games for the world...

In the League Cup, meetings in two rounds:
1969/70 4th rd 2-0 home
1987/88 5th rd 0-2 away

Friendlies: 1891/92 h 1-1,1893/94 h 2-3, 1894/95 h 9-0, 1896/97 h 0-1, 1897/98 a 4-2, 1924/25 Everton/Liverpool X1a 2-3, 1986/87 h 1-4 (P. Power T/M), 1991/92 a 4-1 (A. King T/M), 1999/2000 a 0-1 (Ebrell T/M), 200/01 a 1-3 (Joe Parkinson T/M)

Some connections: Tommy Johnson, George Heslop, Paul Power, Joe Royle, Joleon Lescott, Imre Varadi, Brian Kidd, Asa Hartford, Peter Beagrie, and managers Joe Mercer and Howard Kendall

Everton have been involved in a number of FA Cup semi-Finals and League Cup replays at Maine Road:
1950 Liverpool 2 Everton 0
1953 Bolton 4 Everton 3
1977 Liverpool 2 Everton 2
1977 RP Liverpool 3 Everton 0
and in 1984 Milk Cup Replay :
Liverpool 1 Everton 0

Ground: Goodison Park, (shown 2000's) R/A 78,299 v Liverpool D 1 1948/49

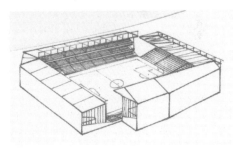

Friendlies:
Esjberg 1937/38 a 2-0, 1948/49 a 4-1
East Fife 1953/54 h 2-1
England X1 1954/55 h 0-0, 2-2 1957/58 a 2-2 1977/78 (M.Doyle testimonial) h 4-3 1981/82 h 1-2 (Bill Taylor testimonial)
SV Eintracht Trier 1954/55 a 5-1
Eintracht Nordern 1955/56 1-1 a
Eintracht Frankfurt X1 1956/57 a 0-2
Eintracht Brunswick 1966/67 a 2-1
VFB Eppingen 1983/84 a 4-2
IF Elfsborg 1984/85 a 1-2
Edmonton Brickers 1985/86 a 3-0
Eastwood Hanley 1987/88 a
Ernest Borel (HK) 1990/91 a 3-1
Emley 1991/92 a

F is for Fenerbahce

THE F's take us over to Istanbul in Turkey and down to London...

Fenerbahce

In 1895 an Englishman, James Lafontaine, who doesn't sound very English, introduced football to Kadikoy but as the Sultan had banned the game, the students who formed Fenerbahce (Lighthouse is the English translation) in the city had to keep their heads down until 1908 when the Sultan was confined to his Palace.

They famously beat a British Army X1 in 1923, and ground shared with Besiktas from 1960 to 1984 whilst their own stadium was being redeveloped.

Fenerbahce wore blue and yellow striped shirts with white shorts, and had won the title eleven times. This was their fifth attempt at the European Cup yet they'd never progressed beyond the first round, and they'd lost their last nine European ties away from home!!

In the first leg at home City's programme cover had changed to that shown from the previous ones that season, an unusual change during a season. Also there was absolutely no mention of the previous friendly game between the teams which City won 5-1 at Maine Road, the second game under the new floodlights, Johnny Hart notching three and Sowdon two, in season 1953/54.

Malcolm Allison had famously predicted that City would scare Europe to death, after the title win at Newcastle, but it was not to be. City drew the first leg at Maine Road 0-0, in front of 38,840 but lost the second leg 2-1 in the National Stadium of Istanbul, crowd was 45,000 officially.

Reporter Peter Gardner (taken from the Juventus programme of September 1976):

City missed chances galore in the first leg and it was thought that in the second leg they'd be too good for the Turks, who would have to come out and play instead of defending. All went well in the first half, the players had silenced an hysterical home crowd, overcome indifferent refereeing, poor pitch and the lighter, softer ball. There was a crowd of over 54,000 in the ground, 10,000 over the official limit. Most of them had been in there since the morning and City went ahead through Tony Coleman in the twelfth minute, latching onto a mistake by the Turkish keeper. Ogun, their terrier-like striker, who didn't play in the first leg, and had been specially imported from his loan spell at Washington Whips in the North American League, had a goal disallowed for offside, and the Turks seemed to lose heart both on and off the field. The second half then looked a formality. However...!

Within sixty seconds Ogun laid on a cross for Abdullah, a second half substitute to score the vital equaliser with his first kick of the game. The Blues were then in for a gigantic battle though still holding the whip hand with the away goal counting double. However, (again), with twelve minutes remaining Ogun shot his team into the lead and City out of the competition, as goalie Mulhearn's 'mare' continued. The headline read "Ogun outguns City"

Fires burned on the terraces and baton swinging riot police had to clear a way through to the dressing room for players of both sides, so excitable were the Turkish fans. It was the most important moment in Turkish football. For City it was one of the worst and forty eight hours after the game when Malcolm finally broke his silence he said it was the biggest disappointment of his whole career.

City had paid for their complacency and naivety in the first leg, missing chances, being kicked up and down, shaking hands with their opponents, but it was a lesson learnt and the Blues went on to win The Cup Winners' Cup the next season.

Friendlies: 1953/54 h 5-1 1993/94 a

Fulham

'The Cottagers' were formed in 1879 as Fulham St Andrew's Church Sunday School F.C. and played at a host of grounds until moving in to Craven Cottage in 1896. They were elected to Division Two in 1907 and have hovered between all four divisions ever since, but were runners up in the Cup in 1975, when they were in the Second Division, to West Ham.

They ground shared at QPR for two seasons 2002 to 2004 whilst the Cottage was being renovated, were losing finalists in the 2010 UEFA Cup Final to Atletico Madrid, and finished season 2010/11 in the Premiership, playing in white shirts, with black shorts.

Pre-war: 8 league meetings with City winning 4, drawing 2, and losing 2, all in the Second Division.

Post-war: 26 League meetings with City winning 13, drawing 4, and losing 9

The Cottage has always been a pleasant place to visit with its idyllic setting by the Thames in the park.

City just have the edge in encounters but there have been good and bad moments both at City and down at Fulham for the Blues. New Years Day 1946 saw the debut of future Liverpool manager Joe Fagan.

City lost the game 0-1, down there in 1949/50, a match which was memorable for a remarkable performance from Bert Trautmann.

Indeed, the Londoners, after initially calling him a Nazi, and giving *Heil Hitler* salutes, gave Bert "one of the greatest ovations he is ever likely to get in his career". The Fulham players sportingly stayed behind to shake hands with him, and backstage after the game, Directors, ground staff and spectators could talk of nothing else" This was a tremendous boost to City's German goalkeeper who was attempting to overcome racist bigotry, particularly in the capital.

In 1961/62 City overcame a three goal deficit to win 4-3 at Fulham, then doubled the Londoners with a 2-1 win at M/Rd and after four games of that campaign were top of the league. By the end of January, however, the Blues were bottom, but escaped relegation that season, putting it off for only a year! Fulham got revenge for a 5-1 drubbing in 1968 with their own 5-1 in 1984 at the Cottage, which included a hat-trick from future Blue Gordon Davies..

Neil S: 17/3/84 Fulham 5 City 1

In all honesty the 1983-84 season remains a drunken blur. Apparently, I missed the Miners strike, but as Frankie collided with Culture Club and Michael Jackson, I was more concerned with the decline of the Parlane-Tolmie Partnership.

Manchester City were paying the price for the financial excesses of the late 1970s. Indeed we didn't fully recover until September 2008. Thirty years of misery, but we loved every minute.

Coincidentally, the Raddy Antic nightmare had completely overshadowed a controversial defeat for Fulham at the Baseball Ground, the same afternoon. Both teams were desperate for victory, but as relegation threatened Derby held on for grim life, the atmosphere began to resemble the 1923 FA Cup Final, with home supporters surrounding the pitch and aiming wild haymakers at anything in a Fulham shirt. The game had also ended prematurely with the referee fearing for his own safety.

Fulham were undoubtedly the finest team in the division, but had failed to seize the moment. City's relegation coupled with the re-emergence of Newcastle, Chelsea and Sheffield Wednesday, merely added to the pressure.

The Fulham side included a youthful Ray Houghton and Paul Parker, together with Tony Gale and the future City enigma Gordon Davies. An early midweek fixture betrayed the gulf in class, but City somehow scrambled a goalless draw. Both teams remained on the fringes of the promotion race until the return match at Craven

Cottage, the following March.

Intriguingly, the fixture clashed with the University Boat Race. None of us were remotely interest in rowing, but there was a sense of history as we set off for London a couple of hours earlier than normal.

I was the youngest of the Whaley Bridge travelling contingent. Allan Kelsall had seen us beat Gornik in Vienna; Mick Chandley was a veteran of Wembley success; Chris Girling was the usual driver with an imaginary attitude towards the concept of sensible drinking. We all shared a passion for Manchester City, but the idea of watching a game sober was completely alien.

The seeds for my downfall were planted at an early stage. The beer was flowing and after ten pints and a dinky pork pie our enthusiasm for the boat race had faded into oblivion. Unbeknown to us, Cambridge had crashed into a bridge and the race had been rescheduled for the following afternoon.

We were sat in the posh seats with the majority of City supporters standing on the far right, next to the Cottage. The home supporters were fairly well mannered by the standards of the mid eighties. The game kicked off in a torrential downpour with Fulham playing from left to right.

Unfortunately, the dinky pork pie was beginning to take its toll. My head was spinning and my stomach was beginning to churn. I made my excuses and made a sharp exit for the nearby toilets underneath the stand. A dark thought suggested that it might be the alcohol.

For the next hour my condition varied between a desire to vomit and a desire to stop vomiting. It would be an understatement to suggest that I was in a terrible state.

I could hear the noise from above, but the alcohol had obviously affected my ability to calculate the score. Surely City couldn't be losing 5-0?

Eventually, I plucked up enough courage to return to my seat. Apparently it was my round, but as Neil McNab smashed a glorious volley into the Fulham goal my worst fears were confirmed. City had already conceded five goals.

The journey home was long and miserable. Fulham were too good and they weren't even in the top five. Dinky pork pies were off the menu.

In the Premiership, 18 meetings and I suppose season 08/09's 3-2 Fulham win after City were coasting at 2-0 could be classed as a payback for the 4-3 in 1961.

Season	H	A	Pl	W	D	L
Pre-08/09			12	4	5	3
08/09	2-3	1-1	14	4	6	4
09/10	2-2	2-1	16	5	7	4
10/11	1-1	4-1	18	6	8	4

In the FA Cup, meetings in two rounds :
1908 3rd rd 1-1 home, replay 1-3
1914 1st rd 2-0 home

In the League Cup the teams have met just the once, in the fourth round of 1967/68 a 2-3 loss at Fulham.

Some connections: Rodney Marsh, Stan Horne, Gordon Davies, Dickson Etuhu and manager Mark Hughes.

In 1974/75 Fulham won a semi-final cup replay at Maine Road, against Birmingham, but went on to lose the Final to West. Ham

Ground: Craven Cottage (shown 2010) R/A 49,335 v Millwall D2 1938/39

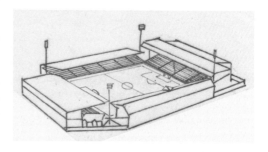

Friendlies:

Fairfield 1892/93 2-1 a, 1893/041-1 a, 1894/95 2-3 h,
Fleetwood R 1894/951-0 h
Fiorentina 1933/34 a 3-3
Frankfurt 1953/542-2 a
Furth Nuremburg 1953/54 2-0 a
Fioriana 1971/72 0-0 a
Fredrikstadt 1978/79 a 5-0
Fleetwood 1981/82 res?
Finn Harps 1984/85a 5-0
Flixton 1988/89 res?
Faaberg 1989/90a/n 0-0
Flint Town 1994/95 a
Feyenoord 1994/95 h 2-4, 2003/04 a 2-1
Falk SK 1994/95 *
Falkirk 1997/98 a 1-1

G is for Gainsborough

THE G's take us over to Lincolnshire, up to the North East, then to Kent, Derbyshire, Poland, Vienna and Copenhagen....

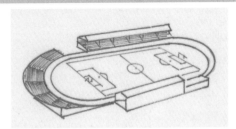

Gainsborough Trinity

'Trinity' were formed in 1872, elected to Division Two in 1896 from the Midland League, replacing one of Burslem Port Vale/Rotherham Town/ Crewe Alexandra, staying for sixteen seasons before failing to gain re-election in 1912.

Games were played at Northolme, which was also a cricket ground, They also played a few matches at The Bowling Green Ground and Sincil Bank (but not v City) when Northolme was needed for cricket matches.

They finished season 2010/11 in the Blue Square North League.

Pre-war: Ten meetings between 1897 and 1910 all in the Second Division. Their first home game was against City, Sept 12th 1896, a 1-1 draw, in front of 2,500. City won all five home games (including a 9-0 at Hyde Road in 1902/03, when the first goal arrived after half an hour!) and two aways with two losses and one draw.

Friendly: City won 2-1 at home in 1891/92.

Gateshead

Were formed in 1930 from the South Shields club and joined Division Three North that season playing at Redheugh Park.

They failed to gain re-election in 1959/60 despite finishing above Oldham and Hartlepool, were replaced by Peterborough, and joined the Northern Counties League but eventually folded prior to the 1973/74 season, after moving to the Gateshead International Stadium. They reformed with slight name changes and are currently in the Unibond Premier.

City played them in the third round of the Cup in 1933 drawing 1-1 away and winning the replay 9-0. Next meeting was in the third round of 1947, City winning 3-0 at Maine Road.

Gillingham

'The Gills' started out following the success of The Royal Engineers of Chatham which prompted other clubs to form including Excelsior, becoming New Brompton in 1893 playing at the Priestfield Stadium. In 1913 there was a name change to Gillingham, who joined the newly formed Division Three in 1920. After flirtations with The Championship they finished season 2010/11 in League One, playing in black and blue striped shirts with black shorts.

Post-war: It wasn't until season 1998/99 in the Second Division, that the teams met in the League. City drew 0-0 at Maine Road but won 2-0 at The Priestfield Stadium in the April, with both teams heading for the play-offs.

The showdown arrived in the Final on a drizzly May 30th day at Wembley in front of 76,935. In a poor game Gillingham went two up with late goals from Asaba and 'big fat Robert Taylor', who was later to join City. As the City fans left in droves, and scarves and programmes rained down from the balcony tier, and when all looked lost Kevin Horlock scored what looked like a consolation goal, but Paul Dickov plundered an equaliser in injury time. Cue hordes of City fans making their way back into the Stadium ("I think City are calling you back in") to watch an uneventful extra time followed by a nail biting penalty shoot out resulting in a 3-1 win. Kevin

Horlock, Terry Cooke and Richard Edghill being the penalty kings, with Nicky Weaver making the crucial saves.

Everyone has a story of that day and David Chidlow produced a nifty A5 booklet 'City 'til I Die' which encapsulated the day perfectly.

John B: 30/5/1999 Gillingham 2 City 2

In the absence of a flying saucer, piloted by Elvis and Lord Lucan, landing in the centre circle at either Maine Road or Priestfield during the course of any other of the clubs' meetings, there is only one game any City, or indeed Gillingham, fan, could possibly select for a venture such as this, and it is of course the 1999 League One Play Off final epic at Wembley Stadium.

To a degree, personalising an account of this momentous day in Manchester City history is a thankless task in so much as the subject has been so comprehensively covered already, and nowhere more eloquently than in Mark Hodkinson's 'Down Among The Dead Men' book. However, so important to both the short and long term future of the club was this one match there was no real way of looking anywhere else!

For the uninitiated (if there are any), City had fallen into the third tier of English football the previous May for the first time in its 105 year existence, and in December 1998 stood at its lowest ever recorded league position of 12th. With the club finances in tatters, the Blues were circling the metaphorical footballing drain, but a post Christmas surge up the table into the play off places had offered a tantalising glimpse of salvation. Passage to the Final itself had of course then been predictably fraught, City gifting opponents Wigan the advantage after just 13 seconds of the first leg of the semi, and then, after equalising to secure a 1-1 draw, scoring early in the 2nd leg to lead 2-1 on aggregate before clinging on for dear life for the win. Gillingham at Wembley

promised no less in the way of tension, and it was testament to the magnitude of the occasion that nearly every City fan that made the trip to London, recognised in advance that they were looking at arguably the most critical 90 minutes in the club's history. If that might sound strange in light of 2 league titles, 4 FA Cups, 2 League Cups and a European Cup Winners' Cup, then Hodkinson summed up the logic eloquently enough, when he opined that:

".....a promotion play off final is more important to a club's well being than a cup final. The latter is a pleasant day out, a celebration regardless of the result. The former is the future of your club condensed into 90 minutes."

That the match unfolded as it did, served only to further accentuate its importance retrospectively. Goalless for 81 minutes, Gillingham then scored twice in quick succession and as the stadium clock ticked over into the 90th minute with only stoppage time to come, City looked doomed at 2-0 down. Four days earlier, United had bagged two goals at the death to snatch an undeserved European Cup victory against Bayern Munich, and it seemed for all the world as if the Gods were mocking the Blue half of Manchester. For many, staring into such an abyss was too much to take. Out of frustration, anger and/or a sense of utter hopelessness, an estimated 5000 of the 40000 faithful present stormed the exits in the aftermath of Fat Bob Taylor's second goal for the Gills. We were dead, buried and Father McKenzie had wiped the dirt from his hands as he walked from the grave. That yours truly was not one of those leaving was in no way due to loyalty. In over a quarter of a century of watching City live, I had never seen us score two goals in injury time, ever (probably the nearest thing I could recall was trailing 1-0 at home to Oxford in the late '80s before Steve Redmond and Trevor Morley turned the game on its head, but even then there had been a good 6 minutes left to play), so the prospect of us doing so at Wembley in front of an 80000 sell out crowd seemed nothing less than a preposterous joke. No, like many I remained seated simply out of sheer energy sapping despondency, and indeed when Kevin Horlock pulled a goal back on the very stroke of normal time, my reaction was one indicative of someone struggling to contain their fury, rather than optimistically anticipating that an equaliser would surely follow.

'Typical City, pull one back, give us all false hope and then fail to deliver.

Not surprisingly though were we roundly acknowledged as the most consistently perverse institution in the football world. Tucked into the corner of the ground on the same side as the dug outs, as Paul Dickov and SuperKev sprinted back to the halfway line with the ball, we could not see the board being held aloft by the 4th official indicating that 5 minutes of injury time lay ahead, and so lived on the agony of our nerves for the duration of that period, one eye never leaving referee Mark Halsey. And so to what still stands head and shoulders above all else as the greatest Manchester City watching moment of my whole life. Any self-respecting Blue can do it in their sleep. Just 49 seconds to go, one last desperate punt of the ball downfield by centre back Gerard Wiekens, a flick on from big Gareth Taylor, the Goat gets on the end of it, tries to shoot, blocked, the ball squirts sideways just inside the box to Dickov, who then pulls back his right foot, a blue and black striped defender slides despairingly across to try and intercept….. and then as the sound of 40000 voices shouting "Go on" fades on 40000 pairs of lips, the ball rockets into the top left hand corner of the Gillingham net. A split second later a thunderous explosion of noise rends the North London air as the City end goes completely and utterly mental, a rucking, pounding, bellowing mass of arms and legs, falling over the low slung Wembley bench seats, banging shins, dropping phones, shedding clothes, getting trampled on, getting back up, falling down again, screaming, hugging, yelling, on and on and on, whilst on the pitch the iconic image of Paul Dickov sliding to his knees, fists clenched, head back roaring at the heavens, is captured for Blue posterity. By the time a semblance of normality descends, the game has both restarted and finished.

The rest of the match is legend. When Robert Taylor had put Gillingham two up, those of their fans who were not day trippers or foreign exchange students, had treated us to a rendition of that most triumphal and goading of terrace anthems "You're not singing anymore". As extra time got underway, they received the gale force version back in their faces. Thirty more minutes of football came and went with no further goals, footballing anti-christ Tony Pulis stood on the touchline with a face like a smacked arse as three of the four Gillingham penalty takers bottled it in the cacophonous din of boos and whistles that accompanied their attempts to score from the spot in the shoot out. City keeper Nicky Weaver set off on his very own personal lap of honour,

Big Andy Morrison, one of the club's finest ever captains, led the team up the famous old steps to collect the trophy, Liam Gallagher pounded on the glass of his executive box in celebration as the PA played 'Roll with it', and the City support, famously buoyed in number by those who had left early and then returned after news of Dicky's equaliser filtered through out in the car parks, bouncing up and down to Status Quo.

Outside afterwards the atmosphere was equally remarkable, but for different reasons. On arriving at the ground, there had been singing and shouting as we had followed Bruce Jones (Les Battersby of Corrie fame) and his entourage up Wembley Way, but now, joining the huge mixed queue of Blues and Gills for the train back into London, not a word was spoken by anyone, every last drop of mental energy and emotion having been spent inside the stadium over the course of the previous two hours. City manager Joe Royle summed it up best when he spoke of a giant hand coming down from the sky to indicate an end to years of suffering.

"That wasn't a game", he said, "It was an event!"

In the FA Cup: The teams met in the second round in 1908, drawing 1-1 at Hyde Road but City winning the replay at Priestfield 2-1.

In the League Cup the teams were drawn together in 2000/01 in the second round. City drew 1-1 at Maine Road and won 4-2 after extra time at the Priestfield.

Some connections: Robert Taylor and Johnny Hannaway

Friendly: In 2000/01 City won at Gillingham 3-0.

Ground: The Priestfield Stadium (shown 1999) R/A 23,002 v QPR FA Cup 3 1948

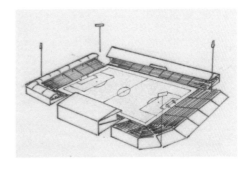

Glossop North End

'The Hillmen' were elected to Division Two in 1898, changed their name to Glossop F.C. in 1899 when promoted to Division One (as the smallest town ever) and eventually played at North Road, part of a cricket ground after moving from various other grounds. Their chairman was Sir Samuel Hill-Wood who later became Arsenal's chairman. They were present until the end of the 1914/15 season when they failed to get re-elected. They changed their name back to North End in 1955 and moved to Surrey Street, and finished season 2010/11 in the North West Counties Football League Premier Division playing in all blue.

Pre-war: Eight meetings between 1898/99 and 1909/10, six in the Second Division and twice in the First Division (1899/1900). City won six, drew one and lost one.

In the FA Cup the teams met in the first round in 1907/08 City drawing 0-0 away but winning 6-0 at home.

Connection: Irvine Thornley, who had a shop in Glossop, found himself financially worse off after signing for City, so City made him additional payments, which led to an FA investigation and prompted the subsequent bribes scabdal in 1904.

Friendlies 1898/99 2-1 h, 0-2 a; 1903/04 1-3 a, 1999/2000 and 2000/01 reserve friendlies.

Ground: North Road R/A 10,736 v Preston FA Cup 2 1914, Surrey Street 1955

Gornik Zabrze

Poland was under German rule before 1945, and Zabrze was known as Hindenburg moving into the Stadion Gornik in 1934. After liberation in 1945 a team called Zjednoczenie Zabrze took up residence and in 1948 joined five other local clubs to form Gornik - Pride of the Polish miners - from the coalfield of Upper Silesia.

They became Poland's most successful and best supported club but with average gates of only 15 to 20,000, and as the stadium capacity was only around 23,000, big games were transferred to the Chorzow Stadion Slaski set on the borders of Katowice and Chorzow.

It was a huge bowl with an athletics track and a capacity of 100,000. By the time they played City they had a decent record in Europe from 1961/62, and were known to Mancunians for being narrowly defeated by United in the third round of the European Cup in 1967/68 2-1 on aggregate. They played in white shirts and white shorts.

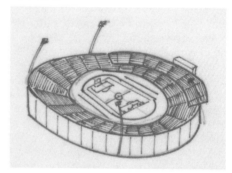

The first meeting with the Polsh Cup winners was in the Final of the European Cup Winners' Cup in 1970 in Vienna.

Steve P (pre Blue Vicar): 29/4/1970 Gornik 1 City 2

I went by train via Paris, Basle and across Switzerland, the only way to go if you like lakes and mountains.

I stayed with missionary friends in Paris and in Basle discovered two other Blues who'd been on the same train since Paris and we commandeered a compartment for the night.

We'd had the same socks on since Manchester, took our shoes off for the night and when the ticket collector came round at daylight he opened the door, took one whiff and said "oh you're from Manchester" and left!

We arrived in Vienna at 9 am on the Tuesday, bought a £2 ticket from the Austrian Football Association, and were told that programmes were also on sale and asked "how many do you want?" I discovered he was giving them away for free, and not feeling too cheeky asked for and got ten. They hadn't printed enough, even for the estimated 4,000 City fans, and they're like gold dust now.

In the bar next to the Austrian FA there were a few City fans already in place. One of them fancied the barmaid, and I translated "why are you so beautiful" for him, but she was unimpressed, both by my translation, and him!

I took in the city sights, including the Blue Danube, which was a rather mucky grey, then went out to the Vienna woods to the Youth hostel where City fans impressed, or otherwise, North American tourists with farting competitions!

Off to the match and the few Polish fans looked wary of chanting City fans. Rain started as we entered the ground and realised that £2 for a good seat in the rain was a waste.

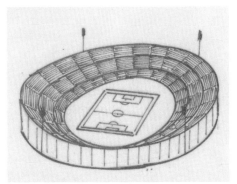

Once Nelly had scored, the heavens opened, but an all-seater stadium with no roof is no joke so the 4,000 or so of us all settled under the canopy of the bar, and some Blues settled in the bar and ignored the match!

Nelly broke away again and was pulled down, Lee Won Pen making it 2-0, and even when Gornik pulled one back there never seemed to be any danger. So we'd got a European trophy at only the second attempt.

After the match we walked back to town through the Prater fun fair and my mates treated me to watch a striptease show which was over in a flash (!) and even my mate poking his banner through the curtains failed to reveal any more.

We ended up in a giant beer tent where the band didn't know any football songs, and my mates then smuggled me into their hotel where there was a spare bed.

Then it was a gentle, happy, beautiful, journey home through the mountains. I even chatted to a girl from Lichtenstein who was surprised that anyone should go halfway across Europe to see a football match (well it wasn't even on telly, the FA Cup Final replay, Leeds v Chelsea at O/T was shown instead)

I decided that being one of the 8,000 v Swindon AND one of the 4,000 v Gornik made me a true Blue.

City became the first team to win a major domestic and European trophy in the same season (Leeds had almost previously done this,

but their European win was carried over into the next season)

City then played Gornik in the quarter final of the same competition the next season, losing 2-0 in Poland. Starman Lubanski put them ahead after thirty five minutes and Wilcek adding a second in front of a fanatical crowd of a reported 100,000. It was described as being played on an ice rink pitch on an emotion charged bleakly-cold evening. This result gave City a formidable task in the second leg but I was there as we won 2-0 at Maine Road, and there again for the 3-1 win in the play off in Copenhagen.

Grimsby Town

'The Mariners', were formed in 1878, as Grimsby Pelham and helped form Division Two along with Ardwick and others. They first played at Abbey Park, moving to Blundell Park in 1899, which is actually located in Cleethorpes.

"Who would want to play in the reserves at Grimsby on a wet Tuesday night?" is the oft quoted lament from a player dropped from any first team. Who ever it was put the *Grim* in Grimsby knew what they were doing but the fish 'n chips there can be quite tasty (except when they leave the skins on the fish).

They consolidated in the First Division during the thirties and their finest achievement was to reach the FA Cup semi-final in 1939 when they lost to Wolves at Old Trafford in front of a record crowd, to this day (2010), of 76,962, so have always been a bigger attraction at O/T than the mighty Man. U. themselves (as we like to keep reminding them!) Indeed in 1930/31 season they ended with a higher average attendance than United, as they continued their spell in the First Division.

They ended season 2010/11 in the Blue Square Conference, playing in black and white striped shirts and black shorts.

Pre-war: Thirty six league meetings with eighteen City wins (including a 7-2 home victory in 1898/99, when Grimsby fielded seven debutants) four draws and fourteen losses, including 0-5's in 1893/94 and 1895/96, both away. March 1928 saw the debut of Eric Brook in a 2-0 home win.

Post-war: Sixteen League meetings, with seven City wins, six draws and three losses.

Two games were in Division One (1947/48) fourteen in Division Two (or Division One), including a 2-2 home draw on the last day of the season in 1951 which clinched promotion with Grimsby already relegated, a 0-4 home loss in 63/64, and a 4-0 home win in 2001/02 when City finally won (at the eleventh attempt in the league) at Grimsby 2-0 with a Huckerby penalty and a last minute Goater effort.

In the FA Cup, three meetings:
1936 5th rd 2-3 away
1959 3rd rd 2-2 away, replay 1-2 home
1966 4th rd 2-0 home

Dave W: 10/1/1959 Grimsby 2 City 2 and 24/1/1959 City 1 Grimsby 2

On Saturday January 10th 1959, we paid 16/6d to go on the special train to New Cleethorpes for the FA Cup third round game; it was cold and the pitch was covered in snow. There was, as always, a big contingent of daft, as ever, City fans in the 14,964 crowd. Grimsby, managed by ex red Allenby Chilton (sent off in the 1955 4th round cup tie at Maine Road, though the City players pleaded with the ref to let him stay on) were fourth from bottom of the Second Division and City nineteenth in Division One, so both teams were low on confidence, probably. Before kick off, some City fans decided to climb over the perimeter fence and we wondered what they were up to, as you just didn't do that. They proceeded to walk round the pitch waving like Royalty, to the Grimsby fans but then had to endure the snowballs raining down on them from the home fans on their uncovered terrace before returning to the sanctuary of the away end. All good clean fun.

The programme cover was in black 'n white and looked as bleak as the day. I still shiver when I look at it. City were soon two goals down on the snowy pitch, Grimsby fans becoming excited at the prospect of knocking a First Division team out of the Cup. "We're not really a First Division team " I said to one (we stayed up by the skin of our teeth at the end of the season) "well we're not really a Second Division team" he said (and indeed Grimsby went down at the end of that season). City drew level with goals from Hayes and Barlow in the second half after Billy McAdams had missed a sitter and we'd had two goals disallowed. So we were confident for the replay.

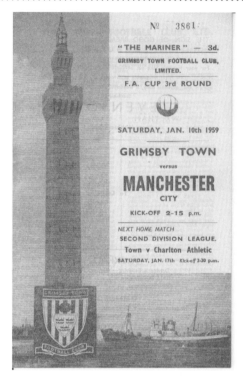

This was postponed a couple of times due to a frozen Maine Road pitch, the braziers not helping, and when eventually played City contrived to lose 2-1 after Bobby Johnstone put us ahead in the first half. Grimsby equalised, then scored the winner from a free kick, despite City battering them all game. For some reason someone got me a ticket at the front in the main stand for this game. I sat with him, and missed being with the scoreboard crowd, blaming that for the defeat.

So we were out of the Cup for the third season running at the first hurdle, and it hurt.

Neil S: 13/4/1985 Grimsby 4 City 1

From Parlane and Simpson to Prior and Huckerby, the fall and rise of Manchester City can be measured in fixtures against Grimsby Town. I attended them all, but despite the relative success, it's the embarrassing defeat in 1985 that I remember with the greatest clarity.

It was a typical Manchester football weekend. Heysel was only a month away, but as United and Liverpool prepared for a particularly spiteful FA Cup Semi-Final, City were engaged in their annual battle against self destruction. After leading the table in March, the team was freefalling out of the promotion reckoning.

I drove to Grimsby in a yellow Fiat 126, which wasn't the trendiest of vehicles, but there wasn't a cat in hells chance of facing a breathyliser. My only travelling companion was an old school friend, Andy Stoneley, from High Lane. We were enthusiastic, but well versed in the 'Cups for Cock Ups' syndrome.

In a lifetime of supporting Manchester City I can only recall two occasions involving sunbathing on a beach, a couple of hours before the kick off. I can't think of any other reason why Grimsby and Omonio Nicosia would be mentioned in the same sentence.

We sampled the obligatory fish and chips before making our way to the ground. The sun was shining and as City prepared to kick towards our end, we enjoyed the last flickering moments of pre-match optimism.

City were hopeless, clueless and spineless. Most footballers enjoy fifteen minutes of fame, but Gary Lund was obviously awarded two bites of the cherry. The Mariners were cruising and by half time we were lucky it was only 2-0.

The stirring half time team talk was about as effective as a chocolate teapot. The farce continued and as Grimsby increased their lead, the atmosphere grew ugly. Earlier in the season Alex Williams had been used as target practice at Highfield Road. This time he shook his head in frustration as the City fans turned on the team.

"CITY ARE SHIT"

"WE'VE COME ALL THIS WAY…WHERE'S YOUR PRIDE?"

Almost unnoticed, Paul Simpson reduced the arrears, but as Lund helped himself to the easiest hat-trick of his life the revival was short lived.

Given the benefit of hindsight and rose tinted spectacles, the defeat at Grimsby was merely a diversion on the road to glorious promotion. Liverpool equalised in the last minute against United and their wonderful supporters bricked the houses on Thornton Road after losing the replay at Maine Road. Four weeks later they played Juventus in the European Cup Final.

Six Years later, City contrived to hit the woodwork four times and lose in the last minute at Meadow Lane in the FA Cup. The scorer was Gary Lund.

In the League Cup it was a 2-0 win in the second round in 1978/79 at Maine Road.

Connection: Bobby Kennedy, who played for City from 1961/62 to 1968/69 and managed Grimsby for a while between 1969 and 1971. You know the story - when City went on tour to America in 1968 there was a curfew on the players and when Senator Bobby Kennedy was shot, Chairman Albert Alexander, on being told, exclaimed, "What was he doing out at that time, he should have been in bed like the rest of the lads." Chairmen eh!

Bobby Kennedy? But which is which?

City also played them in a friendly in 1900/01 losing 0-1 away.

Ground: Blundell Park (shown 2002) R/A 31,657 v Wolves FA Cup 5 1937

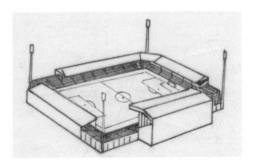

Groclin……

One of the new breed of Polish clubs backed by a wealthy owner and had come to prominence in the past few seasons.

The teams' first and only meetings were in the UEFA Cup second round in 2003/04. They'd won 6-1 on agg to Atlantas in the qualifying round, then 1-0 v Hertha in the first round

Ged I: 6/11/2003 City 1 Groclin 1

Klub Sportowy Groclin Grosdisz Wierlopolski Dyskobolia is not a football club it's a tongue twister. At COMS Nicolas Anelka put City

ahead in the sixth minute, but the anticipated goal avalanche did not happen. In the sixty fifth minute Mila scored with a free kick to give Groclin the draw and a precious away goal. A big disappointment for the crowd of 32,506 including 583 delighted Groclin fans.

Sean R: 29/11/2003 Groclin 0 City 0

Manchester Airport at 5.30am on the day of the game, with everyone dressed as Eskimos. We landed in Poznan two hours later in confident mood, but were surprised to find that there was no ice, snow, or fog, the possibility of which had caused the kick off to be brought forward to 4.15pm, and it was warmer than in the UK!

We were taken by coach to the city of Poznan, similar in size to Manchester, and spent a couple of enjoyable hours there drinking the cheaply priced beer, then journeyed to Grodzisk which took about an hour.

The Cameral stadium lay in the middle of nowhere enabling the new floodlights to be seen for miles around, as the region was very flat. The locals came out to see several coach loads of City fans arriving, and some Blues fans sang songs which weren't very complimentary.

Getting into the ground wasn't comfortable, no turnstiles and fans let in two at a time through steward operated gates, surely breaching every H and S rule in the book? The view from the away terrace was also poor, with a high fence and being quite a distance from the goal.

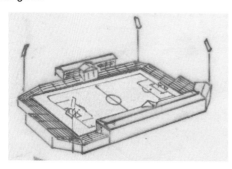

First half was memorable only for slow City build ups, a couple of scares from Groclin, and a bad tackle on SWP which merited a sending off, but their player stayed on.

At half time there were a few unsavoury incidents between fellow City fans. Second half there was not much urgency on the pitch and the game petered out to a 0-0 draw and we were out on the away goals rule.

It was a sombre journey back to the Airport where the team walked past us shame faced and were serenaded with "you're not fit to wear the shirt" etc.

A month ago we'd won at Southampton 2-0 in fine style, to go fifth in the League but it'd all gone pear shaped since then, both in the league, losing at home to Leicester then at Newcastle, both 3-0, and now out of the UEFA cup, to a team of nobodies.

Attendance was around 5,000 with 1,000 Blues.

In 2008 Groclin Dyskobolia merged with Polonia Warszawa and a new Dyskobolia team joined the Polish fourth league.

Friendlies:

Gabon 1986/87
Galway 1995/96 a 3-0
George Robey X1 1904/05 0-3h, 1907/08 4-3h
German X1 1936/37 a 2-3
Glasgow Celtic, 1892/93 0-5 h, 0-1 a 1894/95 0-0h, 1895/96 3-2 h, 1901/02 1-1h, 1902/03 1-0h, 0-0 a, 1953/54 h 1-1, 1970/71a 0-0, 1992/93 (Ireland) 2008/09 1-1 a 2009/10 h 2-1
Glasgow Rangers 1899/1900 0-3 h,1901/02 2-1h1903/04 1-1a, 1934/35 0-1a, 4-2h, 46/47 2-1h, 54/55 4-1a, 55/56 1-2 h, 1981/82 a 0-2 2009/10 a 2-3
Glasgow Rangers/Celtic combined X1 1924/25 2-2 h (Billy Meredith testimonial)
Glentoran 1923/34 h 7-2
Gorton Villa 1891/92 h 1-2, 1892/93 h 1-1
IF Gothenburg 1909/10 3-2 a, 6-0 a1981/82 1-1 a,
Gothenburg combined X1 1937/38 2-2 a
Great Britain X1 1955/56 2-2 h, 1957/58 (Jimmy Meadows testimonial) 2-4 h
SF Grey (Oslo) 3-3 a
Great Harwood 1975/76 2-2 a, 1984/85 a
Grenchen (Switzerland) 1959/60 1-1 h

H is for Halifax

The **H's** take us to Yorkshire, Germany, the North East, Hungary, and Humberside....

Halifax Town

'The Shaymen' were formed in 1911 and were founder members of Division Three North in 1921, playing at The Shay, with one of City's old Hyde Road (modified) stands as their main stand.

After years in the lower leagues they were relegated to the Conference in 1993, but despite brief re-appearances they went bust in 2008 re-formed as FC Halifax and finished season 2010/11 in the Blue Square North Premier Division playing in blue and white striped shirts with blue shorts

In the FA Cup the teams first met in the second round in 1924, drawing 2-2 at Halifax, 0-0 at Maine Road with City winning 3-0 at Old Trafford as the Blues eventually marched on to the semi-final.

Next meeting was the ill fated Cup tie in the third round of 1980, when Fourth Division Town were psyched up by the hypnotist Romark, who Mal (reputedly) later punched, and in atrocious conditions Town scored a late goal to beat First Division City 1-0.

Rob H: 5/1/1980 Halifax 1 City 0

I would be about 18 or 19 and travelled to the game with a group of friends. Hooliganism was at its worst and it was usual to be searched when entering grounds.

Don Barrie (of McIvta fame) was searched last and was wearing a trench coat. A young rookie PC did the honours and felt what he thought was a brick in a pocket. He immediately called his mates who gathered round and then proceeded to empty the contents of Don's pocket, only to find a packet of McVities digestive biscuits. "What are you going to do with these" asked the young constable? "Well, in Manchester, where these come from, we eat them" replied Don!

The result was one red faced young P.C. and several other older coppers pissing themselves with laughter! Mind you, that did turn out to be the highlight of the trip as we all know what happened later!

Revenge eventually arrived in season 1998/99 in the first round of the Cup, when Second Division City won 3-0 at Maine Road over Third Division Town.

Friendlies were played in 1999/2000 a 2-0, 2001/02 a 2-1

Some connections: Freddie Hill, Mark Lillis

Ground: The Shay (shown 1980) R/A 36,885 v Spurs FA Cup 5 1963

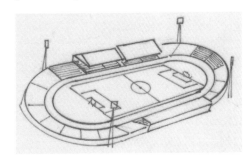

Hamburg S.V.

HSV Hamburg are commonly known as **The Red Shorts.** They were formed in 1887 and history has it that British sailors first introduced football to Hamburg, as they used to have a kick-about at the waterfront whilst waiting for their ships to unload. The present club came into being with the merge of three city teams in 1919, and they are the only team in Germany to boast continual top flight football since the inception of the Bundesliga in 1963. They have a clock on their website which tallies up the time down to the second that they've spent in the Bundesliga! (so that's where United get their ideas from!)

In 1977 Hamburg defeated Anderlecht 2-0 in the final of the European Cup Winners' Cup, and the next ten years provided their most successful period with three Bundesliga titles in 1979, 1982 and 1983.

Hamburg's finest hour arrived in 1983 when a spectacular Felix Magath volley destroyed Juventus and also broke the English monopoly of European Cup success. Hamburg were also the losing finalists against Nottingham Forest in a dreadful 1980 final.

They moved into the Altona Stadium, just outside Hamburg, in 1925. It was renamed Oberliga Nord after the war and then, further to improvements, when Hamburg SV moved in, as the Volksparkstadion – The People's Park Stadium in 1953 and opened with a game v Birmingham. City. Floodlights were first used in a European Cup tie win against Burnley in 1961.

In 2000 they moved to the new Volksparkstadion which in 2001 became the AOL Arena and then the HSH Nordbank Arena in 2007.

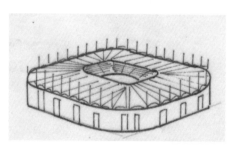

First competitive meetings of the teams was in 2008/09 in the quarter finals of the UEFA Cup. This was to be, as suspected by many Blues, the last European adventure of the campaign. City fans travelled to Germany by land, sea, coach and car, plus there were organised flights with coach transfers. City fans spent a hot day in the pleasant city of Hamburg, congregating in a square off the Reeperbahn singing and drinking. The coach park for the ground was a good twenty minutes away, similar to Schalke, and German efficiency didn't manifest for one coach in particular who missed the park and added an hour or so to the journey.

Hamburg were managed by ex Spurs boss Martin Jol who watched as City took a very early lead, but they came back strongly and won the game 3-1, and it could have been more. It wasn't pleasant listening to the gloating Germans, who thought they had the tie won, on the walk back to the coach park.

City suffered a set back in the second leg at COMS when they conceded an early goal but fought back strongly in front of a vociferous home crowd of 47,009 – prices being slashed - winning the game 2-1 and hitting the post twice. So near yet so far, the story of the last thirty three years, and the final in Istanbul was crossed off the list

Hamburg went on to lose the two-legged semi-final to Werder Bremen winning 1-0 away but losing 3-1 at home. In the final it was Shaktar Domesk who came out on top.

Some connections: Emile Mpenza, Vincent Kompany, George Boateng, and Nigel de Jong. Ironically, considering Kevin Keegan's reputation for disappearing when the going gets tough, *Mighty Mouse* is still revered in Hamburg for his battling qualities and never say die attitude.

Friendlies were played in 1909/10 a 2-0 win though this was against Hamburg Vic? 2002 and 2008 both 1-0 losses away.

Ground: Nordbank Arena capacity 57,274 (50,000 for European games)

Hartlepool United

'The Pool' were formed in 1881 from West Hartlepools, playing at Victoria Park They joined Division Three North in 1921, and were always a lower league side, despite being Brian Clough's first club as manager. They dropped United from their name (and who could blame them?) but added it back in again later!

They finished season 2010/11 in League One playing in blue and white striped shirts.

The one and only meeting was in the FA Cup third round of 1976 when City triumphed 6-0 at Maine Road, the game being infamous for Dennis Tueart's sending off for brealing his mate George Potter's nose with a headbutt.

Ground: Victoria Park R/A17,426 v Man U FA Cup 3 1957

Honved

Post war Honved took over Kispest F.C. whose young players, Puskas and Bozsik in particular were showing promise.

Most young men were drafted into the army which meant that Honved were soon to have the best players in Hungary.

They were Champions four times in six years 1950, 1952, 1954 and 1955 and provided the nucleus of the great 'Magical Magyars' team of the early 50's, Puskas, Czibor, Koscis, Grosics, Lorant who humbled England at Wembley 6-3, and 7-1 in the return in Budapest.

Honved's team were in Spain playing Atletico Bilbao in the European Cup then went on a tour of South America at the time of the 1956 Hungarian uprising. The second leg was played in neutral Brussels and then the players defected to other countries. The team was never to be the same again.

Honved did play in the Cup Winners' Cup in 1964, and 1965 and when they met City this was their fourth European venture, third in the Cup Winners' Cup.

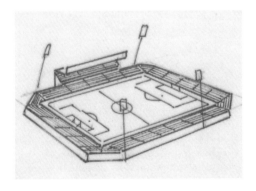

First and only meeting of the teams was in the eighth finals of the Cup Winners' Cup in 1970. First game was a 1-0 win for City in the "untidy Budapest suburb of Kispest" with a Franny Lee goal before 14,000. Second leg a 2-0 (Lee, Bell) City win in front of a Maine Road crowd of 28,770.

Huddersfield Town

'The Terriers' were formed in 1908, by Mr Hilton Crowther, joining the North Eastern League playing at Leeds Road, until the move to The Alfred McAlpine (now The Galpharm) stadium in 1994. They joined Division Two in 1910, going up in 1920 when they were runners up in the FA Cup. They were dominant in the 1920's under Herbert Chapman, winning the title three times, runners up three times, (once in 1934), winning the FA Cup in 1922, runners up twice and were twice FA Cup runners up in the thirties. Since then ups and downs to the Fourth Division, but ended season 2010/11 in League One, playing in blue and white striped shirts and white shorts.

Pre-war: 36 league meetings with 12 City wins, including a 5-1 at M/Rd in 1925/26, 11 draws and 13 defeats. The 2.913 crowd at Huddersfield in April 1931/32 was excessively low for no apparent reason.

In the last game of the season in 1938 Herd hit the bar in the 78th minute, but City lost 1-0, and every one of the other strugglers, Grimsby, Portsmouth, Birmingham and Stoke won, finishing on 38 points, and City, as Champions, despite scoring 80 goals, more than any other team, were relegated on 36 points. Had they won, a superior goal average would have kept them up, but Huddersfield would have been relegated on 37 points.

Post-war: 36 league meetings with 12 City wins, including the 2-0 M/Rd 1965/66 top of the table clash and the 10-1 in 1987/88, 11 draws and 13 defeats including a 1-5 away in 1951/52. The last game of the season, away at Huddersfield, in 1948/49, a 1-0 loss was to be Frank Swift's last game and celebrated by City fans all the way back to Manchester. However, ironically, Frank was called on to play a few more games the following season!

In March 1955, a week before the FA Cup semi-final with Sunderland, Johnny Hart was unfortunate to break his leg. He later recovered to score City's 100th goal of the season at Everton in 1958, and became the manager briefly in 1974.

The 10-1 started tamely enough with Huddersfield going close on two occasions, before City opened the scoring through McNab, and by half time were 4-0 up with further goals from Stewart, Adcock and White. No-one thought

City would get double figures, particularly Malcolm MacDonald Huddersfield's manager, and TV pundit Frank Worthington. However, in the second half Adcock then Stewart then Adcock again completing his hat-trick made it seven. Stewart then completed his hat-trick. Two more goals from White, completed his hat-trick, making it ten but ex Blue Andy May converted a penalty to finish the scoring at 10-1. Crowd was 19,471, making many Blues who missed the game despondent! Serves 'em right.

In the FA Cup, meetings in two rounds. The fourth round in 1926 City winning 4-0 at Maine Road (74,789, when barriers collapsed and spectators were injured) and 1988 third round drawing 2-2 away, drawing again 0-0 at home, winning the replay 3-0 away.

Simon C: 25/1/1988 Huddersfield 0 City 3

Huddersfield in the late eighties was a little bit like, I imagine, big towns in the east of Germany before the wall came down: grey, oppressive, harbouring a horizon of disused chimney stacks and shell-shocked warehouses, dark satanic mills and full of fellas with cauliflower ears, bent noses and eyes slightly too close together. My mate lived in a place called Lockwood, where refugees from a sink estate would have given the place a severe social uplift. I would regularly drink stuff called Hobec (four and out if you were on form, three and idiot behaviour in the street if you weren't) in the local hostelries (The Grubby Mugger and The Asbo Tavern) just to lend myself the courage to stay in the pub all night. I have only been to one place that gave me the heebeejeebies in greater quantity than Huddersfield on one of its wild nights, and that's Halifax. But that's another story and doesn't have a football match attached to it.

As luck would have it on this particularly nasty, wet winter's evening, City were in town for an FA Cup second replay. We had already tonked The Town 10-1 that season, so the locals were reasonably keen to eke out a tiny slice of revenge, one way or another at Leeds Road. What ensued was a typically raw, committed cup tie. Big turn-out, five-or so thousand Blues on the open terrace all trying to keep warm in the driving sleet. Ah, the good old days. After ninety minutes of thud and blunder, it was time to move on to something less likely to give us hypothermia.

Come the walk home, we had to leave the cosy, copper-lined escort to the railway station, in order to make our way back to bedecked Lockwood. Within seconds of doing this we were surrounded by people with scary eyes. They were looking at us suspiciously. Our eyes were normal distance from each other and both looking in the same direction.

Something inside told me that our appearance may have been a slight give away (hour and a half on that terrace in the freezing rain and we looked like one of the bedraggled team members from a very small Belgian village at the end of that water game on It's a Knockout. The one where they had to climb a plastic pyramid covered in axle grease whilst wearing a nine foot dinosaur outfit and holding a fat local lass dressed as Tintin. I could hear Stuart Hall blowing and frothing in my subconscious "Oh, and here come two more City fans!!!")

Our eyes kind of met. The nearest bloke was looking at me and John at the same time and John was five feet to my left. "Leg it" I shouted, but alas too late for John, who got a giant, wet, Yorkshire fist straight on his hooter. There followed a keystone cops chase up the road, with plenty of knuckle draggers giving it legs behind us. I could hear the grunting, but we shook them off and went for a Hobec or two to cool down. We had won 3-0. John had a nose like Joe Bugner. The steam was rising off us. We didn't care. It had been a brilliant night out. We would have similar near death experiences at Molyneux and Vale Park and live to tell the tale. They don't make em like that anymore

In the League Cup just the one meeting, in 1968/69 in the second round first leg 0-0 away, second leg 4-0 home.

Friendlies were played in 1910/11 a 2-3, 1960/61 a 2-5, 2001/02 (Dyson testimonial) a 2-0,

Some connections: Manager Brian Horton, Denis Law, Mark Lillis, Peter Doherty, Andy Morrison

Ground: Leeds Road (shown 1980's)R/A 67,037 v Arsenal FA Cup 6 1932. Galpharm Stadium Capacity: 24,500

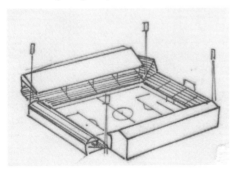

City played in two semi-finals at Leeds Road, winning 3-2 against Derby County in 1933 (51,961) and 6-1 v Aston Villa in 1934 (45,473)

Hull City

The Tigers' were formed in 1904, playing at The Circle, then Hull F. C's Boulevard rugby ground, then Anlaby Road, moving to Boothferry Park in 1946, and then moving yet again to the Kingston Communications Stadium in 2002.

They joined Division Two in 1905, and have hovered between the lower divisions, almost going under at one point, but revived and made the Premiership for the first time in their history via the play offs in 2008, for two seasons but ended season 2010/11 in the Championship, playing in all amber shirts with black shorts.

Pre-war, six League meetings with City winning three drawing two losing one

Post-war, six League meetings with two City wins two draws and two losses, including the first game of the 1988/89 promotion winning season, an outrageous 0-1 loss with five new players, as Frank Newton's banana craze took off.

In the Premiership there's been four meetings, so far, with one win, two draws and one loss. City's 5-1 win at COMS in 2008/09 witnessed the infamous half time 'on the pitch talk' to the Hull players by manager Phil Brown which seemed to work as they drew the second half 1-1 after being 4-0 down.

Season	H	A	Pl	W	D	L
08/09	5-1	2-2	2	1	1	0
09/10	1-1	1-2	4	1	2	1

In the FA Cup, meetings in three rounds:
1930 5th rd 1-2 home
1934 4th rd 2-2 away, replay 4-1 home
1970 3rd rd 1-0 away

In the League Cup it was a 3-0 win away in the third round in 1963/64.

In the Full Members Cup in 1985/86 Northern semi-final first leg it was a 1-2 loss away, and a second leg 2-0 home win.

Neil S: 11/12/1985 City 2 Hull 0

Strictly speaking, the Paul Power free kick at Villa Park wasn't our last appearance in a Cup semi-final (prior to 2011). Dig a little deeper and you'll discover a freezing night at Maine Road in 1986.

From Heysel to Hillsborough, the road to redemption had more potholes than the Kippax Car Park. English football was a social embarrassment.

The football authorities reacted with typical short sighted vision, as a Super Cup was quickly arranged for those clubs affected by the ban from Europe. United played Everton and Norwich, but did anyone really care?

A competition was also organised for the remaining clubs from the top two divisions. City were grouped with Leeds and Sheffield United, and to a backdrop of total apathy, qualified for the later stages.

After thrashing Sunderland on penalties, the only obstacle remaining was Hull City in the Northern Final. Chelsea defeated Oxford in the Southern Final.

Brian Horton was sat in the Hull dug out and City lost the first leg 1-2. In the real world, City were struggling to consolidate in the First Division.

Excluding the attendance for the Wembley final, the crowd for the second leg at Maine Road was the highest in the entire tournament. Alternatively, just over ten thousand braved the elements.

I was sat in the Main Stand with Andy Stoneley. Phillips opened the scoring, but City had been struggling for goals all season. The game was meandering towards stalemate and confusion.

Was there extra time or penalties?

Did away goals count double?

Nobody knew

Nobody cared.

The temperature was dropping as the icy breeze drifted over the Kippax corner. The game was torture and our biggest fear was an extra thirty minutes. In all honesty, a Hull equalizer wouldn't have been a total disaster.

As the minutes ticked towards injury time, City mounted one final attack towards the North Stand. The cross was deflected and Jim Melrose pounced at the far post. The roar of relief was the loudest of the evening.

The players didn't bother with a lap of honour. Most of the crowd were already on the bus.

Some connections: Paddy Fagan, Brian Horton, Don Revie

Friendlies, were played in 1904/05 1-0 home, 0-0 a. 1968/69 (Andy Davidson testimonial) a 0-2, 1972/73 a 1-0 in Sweden, 1985/86 a 1-2, 2004/05 a 4-0.

Ground: Boothferry Park (shown 1980's) R/A 55,019 v Man U. FA Cup 6 1949. Kingston Communications Stadium Cap: 24,504

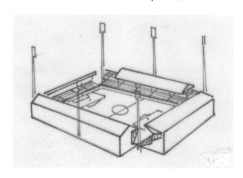

Friendlies:

Heywood Central 1891/92 h 4-0

Hibernians 1898/99 h 1-3, 1951/52 h 1-4, 1955/56 a 1-2, 1957/58 h1-0, a 2-5, 1959/60 h 1-1, 1979/80 a (Skol) 1-1, 1984/85 a 0-0,

Hyde District XI 1903/04 a 0-2

Hearts 1904/05 a 1-2, 1950/51 a 0-1, 1953/54 h 6-3 (1st floodlit game at M/R), 1956/57a 4-3, 1957/58 a 5-3, USA 5-6, 2-5, 7-1, 0-6, 1979/80 a (Skol) 1-1, 1995/96 a 1-5,

Hurst 1916/17 2-2 a,

Hyde United 1968/69 lights a, 1997/98 a 3-1, 1999/2000, 2000/01 & 01 McKenzie, , 2001/02, 2002/03

Hertha BSC a 0-1a, h 1-1 1971/72 a 0-1, 1982/83 a 0-2

Hammarby a 1972/73 3-3 Sweden*

Hamer a 1978/79 7-0

Hollywood Kickers 1985/86 a 3-1

Huelva 1986/87 a 2-2

Hong Kong X1 a 1987/88

IFK Holmsund 1987/88 a 3-2,

Harnosand a 1989/89 a 6-1

Horwich RMI 1989/90, 1991/92 a

Hitachi Omiga/Reysol a1992/93 1-0

Haslimgden RF 1993/94

Halsteren 1993/94

Hall Road Rangers a res F 1994/95

Hednesford Town 1997/98 a*

Harrogate 1997/98

Hucknall Town RF

HFK Sonderjylland 2002/03 a*

I is for Ipswich

Ipswich Town

'Blues' or 'Town' or lately 'The Tractor Boys' were formed in 1878, arriving at Portman Road in 1888 at the East Sussex CCC. The Ipswich Cricket and Athletic Ground company was formed in 1905 providing the club with its own pitch. Town turned professional in 1936 and joined Division Three South in 1938 playing at Portman Road.

Ipswich were promoted in 1957, then to the First Division in 1961, won the League in 1962 but went down two seasons later. They came back up in 1968 won the Cup in 1978, famously beat United 6-0 in 1980, (missing two penalties in the bargain!) and were runners up in the League in 1981. They ended season 2010/11 in The Championship playing in blue shirts and white shorts. Crisis used to be when they ran out of wine in the boardroom but then they got Roy Keane as manager!

Post war, 52 league meetings with 16 City wins 13 draws and 23 defeats.

The League away record is abysmal, City going from 1961/62 until 1994/95 before achieving another win. City doubled Ipswich, the eventual Champions in 1961/62, 3-0 home and 4-2 away.

City's 1-2 loss at Portman Road in April 1972, the penultimate game of the season virtually cost the Blues the title.

One of the most memorable games was at Maine Road in April 1977 when both teams were neck and neck for the title. Dave Watson's thunderous meat-header settled it for City who eventually finished second and Ipswich third.

Dave W: 2/4/1977 City 1 Ipswich 0

I was returning from doing a feasibility study at the Sicilvetro Glass factory in Sicily where the sand they were having delivered was full of stones and had to be screened. "Why don't

you get an alternative supplier" I asked "We did" they replied "but the mafia blew the lorry up en route!" I was picked up at Manchester Airport in the firm's chauffeur driven Mercedes and by my reckoning drove down Princess Parkway and past Maine Road just as Dave's header almost ripped through the back of the net!? We arrived back in Doncaster, where I lived at the time, and I've always been miffed that none of the neighbours saw me arrive home in style!

In November 1982 when City lost 1-0 at Portman Road the Blues were second in the table with 23 points, two behind Liverpool. (Swansea and Brighton went down with the Blues that season and at the time they were both also comfortably placed) but we were eventually relegated.

In January 1994 with City winning 2-0 at Maine Road the match was called off after 39 minutes due to a waterlogged pitch, City won the replayed game 2-1.

City's defeat at Portman Road in May 2001, in the penultimate game of the season, consigned the Blues to Division One, United allowing Derby to win at O/T and thus escape the drop. Ironically Ipswich fans unfurled a banner showing Joe Royle with the caption 'City, the weakest link, goodbye' Royle later became their manager! Always a tedious journey to Ipswich, with little reward, and a town with not much nightlife.

Roger R: 8/10/1988 Ipswich 1 City 0
Team: Dibble, Seagraves, Hinchcliffe, Gayle, Biggins, Redmond, White, Moulden, Morley, McNab, Lake.
Football League Division Two

I was working for "Football in the Community" which was then a newly launched initiative aimed at encouraging youngsters (boys and girls) to start watching football and to help to try and reduce hooliganism at matches. We had been successful in securing some key financial support from a number of agencies including the then Sports Council in order to purchase three brilliant minibuses, so we decided to try them out for the first time by taking a few groups of young people from inner-city Manchester to see City in action at Ipswich. It was the first ever official trip as part of Football in the Community! All I can recall was that the kids themselves were really well behaved considering what was a really long journey there and back. Although the match ended in a 1-0 win for Ipswich, the game was fairly even and City had their share of chances to score too (even though Ipswich were something of a "bogey" side for City at that time!)

In The Premiership there's been eight meetings with four City wins, including a rare 2-1 at Portman Road in 1994/95 season - first in 23 visits! One draw and three defats.

Season	H	A	Pl	W	D	L
Pre 01			6	4	1	1
00/01	2-3	1-2	8	4	1	3

In the FA Cup, meetings in three rounds:
1967 5th rd 1-1 home, replay 3-0 away
1981 semi 1-0 Villa Park
2001/02 4th rd 4-1 away

In the semi-final of 1981 City were very much the underdogs to title chasing Ipswich, and the journey down was marred by the odd coachload of United fans on their way to Coventry displaying Ipswich signs. However City held out for the 90 minutes and eleven minutes into extra time from a free kick just outside the box Steve Mackenzie rolled the ball to Paul Power whose left footed shot curled over future Blue keeper Paul Cooper into the net to set City on the way to the Centenary Cup Final. The journey back up the M6 was a joyous one and the extra time meant that the United cars and coaches encountered on the motorway were subjected to much gloating and taunting by Blues fans. Despite winning their last half dozen or so games of the season United were so bitter at City getting to Wembley, they sacked Dave Sexton, their manager!

In the League Cup the teams have met in three rounds:
1961/62 1st rd 2-4 away
1977/78 4th rd 2-1 away

2000/01 5th rd 1-1 home (abandoned after 23 minutes due to a waterlogged pitch).), 1-2

In the Full Members Cup in 1986/87 round 4 it was a 2-3 loss at Maine Road (11,027)

Some connections – Colin Viljoen, Brian Gayle, Joe Royle, Paul Cooper.

Ground: Portman Road (shown 2000's before the stand behind the goal was completed) R/A 38,010 v Leeds FA Cup 6 1975

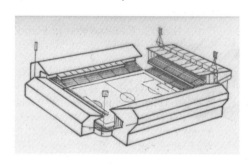

Friendlies:
International XI D Weir testimonial 2-2 h 1891/92
Inter Milan 2010/11 USA 0-3, 2011/12 Dubli 3-0
International X1 1892/93 h 0-5, 1922/23 h 3-1, 1963/64 5-4 h Bert Trautmann testimonial, 4-5 a B and Powell?, 1970/71 a 7-5 R Clayton, 1972/73 at Doncaster Alick Jeffrey 3-4,
Ilford a 3-3 1906/07
Israel Nat X1 1974/75 a 2-0
IFK Gothenburg 1981/82 1-1 a,
IFK Rundvik 1988 10-0
Iceland Nat X1 19081/82 a 2-1
IFC Cologne 1982/83 1-1 a
Int Porto Al 1982/83 1-3 a
If Elfsborg 1984/85 1-2 a
Isle Of Man XI 1989/90 a 8-1, 1994/95 a 4-1
IFK Holmsund 1987/88 a 3-2
IFK Rundvik 1987/88 a 10-0
IFK Kraft 1987/88 a 2-0
Ilkeston 1996/97 a

J/K is for Juventus

Just the one 'J/K' which takes us over the water to Italy, and a **'K'** friendly!

Juventus

'Juve, The Old Lady' or the lesser known 'Fiancée of Italy' was formed in 1897 by students. They adopted their famous black and white striped kit in 1906 when a member returned from England with a Notts. County shirt. They first played at The Velodromo Umberto 1 (named after the late King) but in 1920 moved to their own ground on Corso Marsiglia, in the North of the City, also known as Campo (no connection to the bloke out of Last Of the Summer Wine!) Juventus. 'The Zebras' as they were now sometimes known (any ideas why?) moved to The Stadio Municipale Comunale which 'Benito Mussolini' had built in the run up to the 1934 World Cup, later known as Stadio Comunale.

At the time of playing City Juve had won the Italian title a record sixteen times, were in their 14th consecutive year in Europe but had never won a cup, though this was to be rectified time and again in future years.

Their team included the likes of Dino Zoff, Claudio Gentili, Marco Tardelli, Romeo Benetti, and Roberto Bettega. Recent past names included John Charles, Omar Sivori and Giampiero Boniperti. Gigi Peronace was the famous 'super agent' of the time who arranged transfers between English players and Italian clubs including Juve and Torino etc.

The first meeting of the teams, was in the first round of the UEFA Cup in season 1976/77.

The first leg was at Maine Road, and City won with a Brian Kidd goal.

The second leg was won 2-0 by Juventus, who went on to knock out United in the next round, and subsequently win the Cup..

Charlie H: 29/9/1976 Juve 2 City 0

After a 1-0 win at Maine Road two weeks earlier, this was the first flight ever organised by the Supporters Club Travel club. About 140 people flew out on a day trip to Turin, arriving about lunchtime. There was plenty of time to go round the town sampling the bars and inspecting the red light area etc. There were no signs of any trouble and we had good seats near the Toffs in the covered centre stand at the old Stadio Communale.

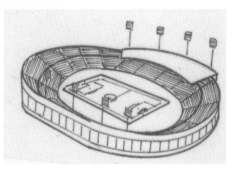

I remember a little dose of Italian anger by the Toffs after a penalty was turned down after Joe Corrigan dived at the feet of an onrushing forward.

Near the end of the 2-0 defeat Joe Royle missed a late chance which would have given us a lucky away goal win. On leaving the stadium waiting for the coaches to take us back to Turin airport there were plenty of Italian 'boys' hanging around, waiting to get at us, but we survived intact. On arrival at the Airport we were treated like terrorists by armed police, the first time I had experienced overseas 'hospitality' reserved for the English – an unhappy finish to the trip.

Roger R adds: 29/9/76 Juve 2 City 0
Team Corrigan, Docherty, Donachie, Doyle, Watson, Booth, Keegan (sub Lester), Kidd, Royle, Hartford, Tueart.
UEFA Cup First Round Second Leg

I recall going to the match on one of the official City trips to Turin on what was (apparently!) a typically grey and rainy Turin day (somebody told me on the day that Turin reminded them of Bolton?!) Anyway the trip seemed to go well and I can remember being on one of the coaches to the ground and seeing, for probably the first time, Italians giving a hand on the arm salute (first time I'd seen that particular gesture but definitely not the last!) We arrived at what was Juventus's old ground only to find out that there was little, if any cover. The stadium was open virtually all the way round so all the City fans (and Juventus fans to be fair) got absolutely soaked! I remember bumping into then City Commercial Manager Phil Critchley near the ground as I was frantically looking for a programme or some sort of souvenir of the match. The best I could do was to buy a local newspaper which I still have, although it is a bit "worse for wear" having got a bit soggy on the day! Anyway, the match itself saw Juventus kick City off the park. The City players all seemed to take the kicking until Mike Lester came on just before the end and he was the only City player who kicked them back (actually he kicked them first!) The City fans watching all enjoyed his cameo performance even though we lost 2-0 to go out of the competition by 2-1 on aggregate. The trip back to the airport went OK but on arrival there was then a long, long wait before we boarded the plane and some City fans managed to tear down a washbasin leaving water flowing everywhere!

Juventus 2010/11

The next time the teams met was in season 2010/11 in the group stage of the Europa Cup.

The first leg was drawn 1-1 at COMS Iaquinta opened the scoring for Juve and Adam Johnson equalised for City. The crowd was 35,212 with 641 Juve. In the second leg Giannetti opened for Juve and Jo equalised for City. The crowd was only 6,992 with 1476 Blues.

This was the final result in the group stage with City on top, Lech Poznan second, Juve who drew all their six games third and Salzburg bottom.

As you'd expect much had happened in the intervening years from 1977 to 2010 for both clubs with Juventus faring much the better despite that dreadful day at Heysel in 1985. They had, however, recently fallen on harder times being involved in match fixing scandals causing two titles to be stripped and relegation to Serie B. They were now back in Serie A, and on the road to recovery with limited success in Europe including an incredible defeat to Fulham last season in the UEFA Cup in 2010.

In 2010 in the Italian league, Buffon, Del Piero, (Noel Gallagher's mate, and big Oasis fan) Chiellini , Aguilani and company were around 5th in the table but only a few points behind

leaders AC Milan. They once, in 1905/06, had a President called Albert Dick, commonly known unfortunately as A. Dick!

They vacated the old Stadio (Municipale 'Benito Mussolini') Communale, built in 1934, original capacity 70,000, and moved to a new stadium, Delle Alpi built for the 1990 World Cup, capacity 60,000 with 55,000 seats. This had now also been vacated as it's been demolished and a new stadium, capacity surprisingly only 41,000 is being built, to be ready in 2011/12.

So the second leg was played back in their temporary home, the old ground, renamed the Stadio Olimpico, sharing with Torino, much to their distaste, where the capacity is reduced to 27,944. Strange for a club boasting the highest level of support in Italy and worldwide.

This was the ground where we played in the first round of the UEFA Cup in 1976/77, only difference being it's now all seated and has a roof.

Dave W: 1984 to 2010

Ah, Turin! I was first there in May 1984, on a business trip, flying to Frankfurt then on to Turin, when the Feyenoord team were on our plane, including Johan Cruyff, and the relatively unknown Ruud Gullitt. They were playing a friendly with Juventus I think.

Almost exactly a year later, on the same project, we had to visit Belgium for expediting purposes. "We could take in the European Cup Final" my colleagues said. I didn't think this would be a good idea, hotels would be full and there'd be loads of soccer fans milling about, probably looking for trouble, so I persuaded them to go the week before. I was then sweating on getting back for City's promotion showdown with Charlton (won 5-1). We asked the locals if they'd be going to the game, and they told us no, as all the tickets for the neutral section next to the Liverpool fans had been snapped up by the large Italian community, the stadium was crumbling, and they thought it could be a hassle.

At night in one of the bars a young local policeman was bigging it up, strutting around with his gun in its holster. He annoyed me. "You'll have your work cut out next week with Italians and scousers" I told him. "No way, we had Everton over here last week just over the border in Holland (they beat Rapid Vienna, who took about 50 fans there, I think, to win the Cup Winners' Cup) and it was no problem."

"Right, if you say so Rambo".

The previous year Liverpool fans had allegedly been bricked, sticked and bottled exiting the Roma stadium after Brucie's wobbly legged show to win the Final but this wasn't reported, certainly not in the national press, as hooliganism was only the 'English disease'

We all know what happened next, but we've never got to the bottom of it. 39 Italian fans tragically died in horrendous circumstances, when charged by Liverpool fans, who were maybe goaded, and a wall collapsed causing the crushing of those fans. The Belgian police were useless.

The TV cameras picked out a spectator coming out of the Juventus end. He was hit on the back of the head by a half brick thrown at him, and then staggered over for safety to the police cordon lined up in front of that end, one of whom battered him mercilessly with his truncheon to add insult to injury (he was, apparently a Scotsman who suffered a fractured skull). Commentator Jimmy Hill told us gravely "that man deserves everything he gets" showing how out of touch with reality Jim was.

The previous weekend we'd had the Bradford fire, and a Birmingham fan was killed when a wall collapsed at St Andrews, in the game v Leeds.

It was a week when everything that was wrong with football did go wrong, and the Football Supporters Association was formed by Rogan Taylor, so that fans could be consulted more. But it was not until Hillsborough that the penny finally dropped with the authorities and the Taylor report (no relation to Rogan) changed things, eventually for the better.

In 2010 Sue and I went on the official trip which flew us over the Alps with breathtaking views and we enjoyed the sights of the beautiful city of Turin with fellow Blue Neil Shaw.

Sean R: 16/12/2010 Juve 1 City 1

Our final game in the Group Stages brought us to an extremely icy cold Northern Italy, with the Grand Old Lady herself already dumped out of the competition courtesy of too many drawn games.

Most of the sight seeing we managed en route from the airport, a few hours being available to find a quiet café bar, where the owner was only too happy to ply us with free food and nibbles to keep the custom. Four euros a beer seemed the going rate, and smuggling supermarket beer in didn't seem appropriate on this occasion…

The poor attendance from Juve wasn't entirely unexpected, but still there was disappointment they had not offered us additional tickets, as there were 21,000 empty seats! The away support we had was at its vociferous best, and the vast array of flags added a splash of colour to a drab stadium.

Ticket supply was short, and never likely to meet the demand, but the evidence of small pockets of Blues around the home section of the stadium did seem to suggest that some Blues had circumnavigated the stringent entry requirements. We were searched three times and had to show our tickets with our names on the back with our passports. Toilets consisted of Portaloos. There was, inevitably a '1985 banner' in the Juve section.

City fans took the opportunity to practice the well rehearsed Poznan shindig, although the frequency of the song that night had more to do with the freezing cold temperatures I suspect.

The 1-1 result enabled us to top the table so it was reasonably satisfying. Our return flight was delayed for a couple of hours whilst they replaced missing nuts and bolts from parts of the aircraft (?!), and a thorough de-icing of the plane was required before we were allowed to take off - with an outside temperature recorded at a withering minus 15 degrees C. Those Blues who had driven in from Milan and other areas were hampered by snow blizzard conditions, resulting in cancelled trains and planes and an extra day or two journey time for most.

Friendlies:

Kaffirs 1899/1900 a 4-3
Kings Lynn 1906/07 a 4-0
Jutland select 1948/49 a 1-2
Japan National XI 1975/76 a , 3-0, 1-0, 1-0, 2-0
Kettering T 1979/80 a 3-1
Kuwait 1981/82 a 1-2
Kelantan State 1984/85 a 3-0
Kefah State 1984/85 a 5-0
Jamaican National team 1997/98 h 0-0
Kilmarnock 1997/98 a 4-0
Kaizer Chiefs 2009/10 a 1-0, 0-1
Kashima Antlers (Shanghai tournament) 2007

L is for Lech Poznan

THE L's take us over to Poland, Yorkshire, the Midlands, London, Lincolnshire, Belfast, Belgium, Liverpool, Loughborough, Bedfordshire...

Lech Poznan

The club is named after Lech, the legendary founder of Poland. Established in 1922, as Lutnia Debiec, it's changed it's name several times, and from 1933 to 1934 has been closely linked to the Polish state railways, hence the nickname The Railwaymen.

They joined the Polish top division in 1948, and their best eras were the early 1980's and early 1990's. They won the Cup in 2009, and the title in 2010, making them Polish League winners six times, the Cup five, and the Super Cup four.

Colours are blue and white stripes with blue shorts or the away change strip is white shirts and blue shorts.

They have a decent pedigree in the three European competitions, first playing in the UEFA Cup in 1978/79 but have never progressed too far in any competition.

Season 2009/10 in the Euro Champs league they won through against Inter Baku but lost 2-0 on aggregate to Sparta Prague to drop into the Europa Cup. They'd drawn 3-3 in Turin with Juventus and went on to win 2-0 at home v Red Bulls, after a poor first half, to top the group.

They have the strongest fan support in Poland but their local rivals are Warta Poznan who play in a different league.

The teams first met in season 2010/11 in the group stage of the Europa League. City won the first leg 3-1 at home with a hat-trick from out of favour striker Adebayor, Tshbamba scoring for Lech. Crowd was 33,388 with 2076 doing the Poznan. In the return leg City went a goal down but equalised through Adebayor (still out of favour) but a late goal from Amboleda put Lech in front. They then scored an injury time third goal by Mozdzen which meant in the event of both teams finishing top or second the teams would be level on the head to head. Crowd was 43,000 with 1327 Blues.

They went on to lose 2-1 on aggregate to Braga in the round of 32.

The second leg was played in the Stadion Lecha, after the move from the Stadion Miejski. It is a modern ground, though with poor away viewing, and regularly holds 45,000

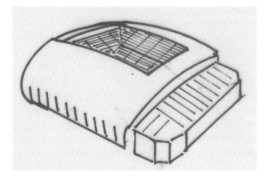

Steve P: 21/10/2010: City 3 Lech P 1
He recalls the most impressive away support ever seen at COMS:

What japes! It was harder to know whether to watch the game or the Poznan fans, whose entertainment value (and ticket money) justified City's decision to get in as many as they could from the ex-pat community here. The club wrote to everyone who'd bought a ticket for City areas and whose name ended in "ski" to ask if they wanted to move to the east stand upper tier, which was given over to Polish fans along with the usual South Stand block.

It'd be nice to recreate that sort of atmosphere in England, but – as son Tom pointed out – it was almost exclusively an adult male gathering. It didn't stop them keeping quiet during the nice old-film tribute to Malcolm Allison put together just before the start.

After that, it was almost constant chanting, singing, jumping, a weird backs-to-the-pitch set piece (later taken up by City fans) and a mock mosh-pit battle that really baffled one steward.

Sean R: 4/11/2010 Lech P 3 City 1

We had been to Poznan before of course, playing the now disbanded/amalgamated Groclin just a few years earlier when Kevin Keegan was in charge; the shock of going out to an unknown team being nothing new to us of course.

Once again the day trip option was the only realistic one to most of us who were fortunate enough to be able to go. Our arrival there was greeted by the sight of the meanest, leanest police force you are ever likely to meet. The balaclavas and guns seemed excessive, but as it guaranteed our safety we didn't complain, in fact they became the target of City fans keen to have a photograph or two taken with them, and they seemed happy enough to oblige.

The route into the City was a familiar one to those of us who had done the trip last time around, except for the torrential rain, which was an unwelcome hassle, given we had around seven hours to kill and no where to go! But we soon found a bar in a quiet location, and after having heard of one or two incidents from the night before, we kept a careful eye on events during the afternoon. I am glad to say there was nothing to report, and we managed to board the buses out to the impressive looking stadium which was about 9km out of the City.

Our arrival was certainly interesting. The stadium looked remarkably similar to ours from the outside, and we noted there was a welcome party waiting for us located behind the Police Lines. We soon learned that the match programmes weren't in our section, and we had to blend in with the scary looking locals in our efforts to find the elusive bloody things. It was inevitably doomed to failure, but other Blues did track them down, and thanks to all those who helped those of us without, it was appreciated!

They had, not surprisingly, sold out all the home sections, and it was difficult to see how the home support could improve on the fabulous away following which had descended on Manchester. As we were soon to discover though, we hadn't seen anything yet………….

Basically, the whole stadium was bouncing, it was a real spectacle, and I am sure I am not the only who was thinking how much we could learn from how this constant backing could be used to our advantage, If only we could replicate it at Coms.

We thought we had ended our poor run of form when Adebayor lashed the ball home from close range to make it five goals in three starts for him, and we somehow managed to make ourselves heard above the din. The reaction of the Poznan fans at the other end of the ground was somewhat bizarre to say the least, as the masses of fans ranked on the bottom tier, started to retreat from the middle of the goal outwards in both directions, before charging each other battle of Waterloo style! It was the oddest thing I've seen , and along with their dance disco routine seen at Coms, was certainly an eye opener, and dare I say it, impressive to watch!

Just as we thought we might go on to win it, we pressed the self destruct button once again, and Boyota's clearance only managed to ricochet off their player and into the net. Their third goal in stoppage time was an absolute peach. Given had no chance, 3-1 was certainly harsh on us.

When the final whistle did go, Adam Johnson was politely reminded by Brian Kidd not to forget to thank the fans, whilst the rest of the players took the hint to say thanks. The Poznan team were given a standing ovation as they did their lap of honour. They were considerably surprised and delighted to note that City fans also joined in the praise . This certainly fostered good relations between both sets of supporters.

As for the odd one or two Poznan idiots with Man Utd merchandise, well they certainly got their comeuppance as the police waded in, confiscated the stuff, and unceremoniously dumped them out of the stadium! It gave us a good laugh! We were gutted by the result obviously, but I don't regret the opportunity for us to have played against Poland's most well supported club.

A few idiots will always try and spoil it for the majority, but this club has left a lasting memory for me, and I will definitely be looking out for them in the future.

Leeds City/United

Leeds City, founded in 1904, playing at The Old Peacock Ground, which became Elland Road, were wound up by the FA in October 1919, following allegations of illegal payments to players. Their fixtures were then taken over by Port Vale, and the ground utilised by Northern Nomads FC for a short time until Leeds United were formed.

Immediately after City's demise, a meeting was called by Leeds solicitor Mr. Alf Masser at which Leeds United were formed and they joined the Midlands League. Discussions were held with their near neighbours, the bankrupt

Huddersfield Town club regarding a possible amalgamation but Town survived and both clubs went their separate ways.

Leeds United were elected to Division Two in 1920, and have generally flirted between the top two divisions until meltdown in 2004 when they dropped out of the Premiership and eventually into League One.

In the late sixties and early seventies they were a major force, winning League titles, (won again in 1992) Cups and European trophies.

They finished season 2010/11 in the Championship, playing in all white, having memorably knocked United out of the Cup 1-0 at Old Trafford in 2010 as a League One club.

Pre-war: 26 meetings with 15 City wins, 3 draws and 8 defeats.

First meetings of the teams were in 1909/10 in Division Two when for the first and only season it was a tale of two Cities, the Blues winning both games, 3-0 home and 3-1 away. First encounters with United came in 1924/25 when City then reeled off another three doubles. In 1927/28 City won 1-0 at Leeds in front of their highest crowd of 47,780 to clinch the Second Division title with two games remaining. A 6-2 home win was clocked up in 1937/38.

Post-war: 56 league meetings with 23 City wins 10 draws and 23 defeats.

The next significant game was a 3-4 loss, after City were 3-2 up, in 1959/60 at Elland Road on record signing Denis Law's debut in March 1960 in which he scored, as Leeds faced relegation. On Leeds' return to the First Division in 1963 they became a potent force under Don Revie, winning trophies and always challenging until dropping back down in 1982, but not always having their own way against City.

The 1968 game at Leeds, 51,818, was the only time I've been locked out of a game. (Dave W)

It became a tricky place to visit in the seventies, off the field, as their fortunes declined. There was a tape recording at half time in a 70's game when a bloke with a Geordie accent claimed to be The Yorkshire Ripper which silenced the crowd.

Probably the most significant game after that was City's 4-0 win at Maine Road which didn't prevent Leeds' march to the title, thankfully, although Leeds fans did manage to demolish the Platt Lane seats at one point.

In The Premiership, 14 meetings with 4 City wins, 4 draws and 6 defeats.

Season	H	A	Pl	W	D	L
Pre 03/04			12	4	3	5
03/04	1-1	1-3	14	4	4	6

In the FA Cup, meetings in five rounds:
1928 3rd rd 1-0 home
1967 6th rd 0-1 away
1977 5th rd 0-1 away
1978 3rd rd 2-1 away
2003 3rd rd 2-5 home

The 1967 game was the one where City changed their tactics becoming an attacking force, and although losing 0-1 to a dubious Jack Charlton header, this paved the way for the title tilt the next season.

Dave W: 26/2/1977 Leeds 1 City 0 and 7/1/1978 Leeds 1 City 2

I watched the 1977 fifth round FA Cup tie from their Kop when at half time a big City fan and his mate ran across the pitch to the City end as the teams came out. Gordon McQueen made a playful gesture at him and then bottled out as the fan approached. Joe Corrigan made probably the save of his career from Allan Clarke but Cherry ended our Cup dreams with a late winner. The following season in the 3rd round Cup tie City won 2-1 when two Leeds players squared up to each other. One fan invaded the pitch causing Peter Barnes to sidestep him at the City end and the fan was followed by hundreds more. After a delay, the players going off the field for a while, it was announced that the game would continue whatever time it took and though City conceded a goal we hung on to win the tie.

In the League Cup: Just the one meeting, in 1963/64 in the fourth round which resulted in a 3-1 City home win.

In the Full Members Cup City won 6-1 at home in round one and lost 1-2 away in 1990/91 in round four.

In the Charity Shield City lost 1-2 in 1969 at Elland Road, probably the biggest game between the teams.

Tony P: 16/10/1971 Leeds 3 City 0

In October 1971 I was fifteen years old. City had made a great start to season 1971/72 and were lying third in the old First Division behind United and Sheffield United. Leeds were tucked behind us in 4th place, and having seen all our home fixtures bar one, I decided that I couldn't miss the vital top of the table clash at Elland Road.

Over the past two or three years though, we had begun to see and hear more and more stories on the news about football hooliganism, with home fans targeting away fans at railway stations, fighting between fans and bottles being thrown into the away section of the crowd. My dad didn't want me to go to an away game unattended, so I went without telling him!

I booked my ticket in advance for the Football Special, having first made sure that my dad wouldn't want me to help out in the café he ran on a Saturday. I told him I had to be at school until midday to revise for exams, which he grudgingly accepted.

I made my way to Victoria station where a chalk written sign on a blackboard directed passengers for the 12.03 Special to Leeds, 95p return, to a platform that I suspected was normally reserved for transporting prisoners from Strangeways. The British Rail authorities were making sure that football fans were kept well clear of 'normal' people.

The hour long journey to Leeds was one of the most frightening of my relatively short life. Once the train was underway some fans began to unscrew light bulbs and toss them out of the window. Many of them seemed the worse for wear regarding drink and seats were slashed and calling cards left in felt tip on the seats and windows. I moved to different compartments, but found it safer to stand in the corridor. When we arrived at Leeds station we were met by a group of police with alsatian dogs. They marched us to Elland Road, the dogs making sure that no one strayed from the lines we were in and the police belted out a warning to anyone thinking of breaking ranks to nip to the pub.

We were herded into the away end, and as for the match, City did what they usually do in these important games. They held their own for all of seven minutes, went one down and eventually lost 3-0, with Neil Young coming on as a substitute in his last appearance in a City shirt.

With quarter of an hour to go I decided to leave early, as all looked lost. Indeed Lorimer scored a third as I left the ground and I reasoned that I didn't fancy being marched back to the station or become involved in any possible fighting between rival fans. I deliberately didn't wear a scarf or City hat so I blended in as I made my way to the station.

It was now 5'o'clock, and having thought about the trouble coming, and that fans would not only have continued drinking during the game, but also be in a foul mood I decided to catch an early train and purchased a single ticket for a train back to Manchester. I didn't check the platform number properly though, boarded the train, panicked when I thought it was the wrong one, jumped off at the next stop, where I was told it was the right train! I then waited for an hour for the next train, and arrived back at Victoria at 7.30pm., about 40 minutes after the Special arrived! I walked down Deansgate to Piccadilly, got on the 88 bus and arrived home, in one piece, just ten minutes before my mum and dad got home from work!

I wasn't put off by the journey, the hooligans, or the score line, as two weeks later, I was back on the Football Special to Huddersfield!

Friendlies: 1917/18 a 3-0 (Leeds City, National War fund) ,

Some connections: Don Revie (below), Robbie Fowler, Derek Parlane, Peter Barnes

Ground: Elland Road, (shown 2010) R/A 57,892 v Sunderland FA Cup 5th round 1967.

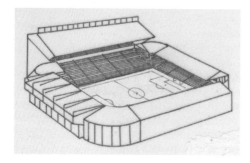

1973 Leeds 1 Wolves 0 at M/Rd

Leicester City

'The Foxes' were formed in 1884 when a group of young footballers met on the Roman Fosse Way and formed Leicester Fosse F.C. They moved from the temporary venue of Aylstone Road Cricket Ground in 1891 to Walnut Street, the ground later renamed as Filbert Street, where they stayed until the move to The Walkers Stadium in 2002. They joined Division Two in 1894/95, along with Burton Wanderers and Bury, taking the places of Middlesbrough Ironopolis and Northwich Victoria.

They were generally a First Division club, with stints in the Second Division, being six time winners, like City; were Division One runners up in 1929, reached four Cup finals from 1949 to 1969, all defeats, and were League Cup winners in 1964 and 2000. They were relegated in 2004, dropped to League One in 2008 but after promotion finished season 2010/11 playing in blue shirts and white shorts, in The Championship.

Pre-war: 34 league meetings with 19 City wins, 7 draws and 8 defeats. First meetings were in 1894/95 in the Second Division with City generally having the upper hand including a 6-3 home win in 1934/35.

Post-war: 48 league meetings with 19 City wins, 15 draws and 14 defeats. A 4-8 defeat was suffered in 1957/58 at Filbert Street but in the last game of the season in 1958/59 City won 3-1 whist Villa drew at West Brom to take the drop instead of the Blues.

In March 1975 Mike Doyle took over in goal (not for the first time) from the injured Keith Macrae, conceding a late goal as City lost 1-0.

In The Premiership: 6 meetings

Season	H	A	Pl	W	D	L
94/95	0-1	1-0	2	1	0	1
00/01	0-1	2-1	4	2	0	2
03/04	0-3	1-1	6	2	1	3

In the FA Cup, meetings in 9 rounds, plus a Final:

1920 2nd rd 0-3 away
1966 5th rd 2-2 home, replay 1-0 away
1967 3rd rd 2-1 home
1968 4th rd 0-0 home, replay 3-4 away
1969 Final1-0 Wembley
1989 3rd rd 1-0 home
1994 3rd rd 4-1 home
1996 3rd rd 0-0 away, replay 5-0 home
2004 3rd rd 2-2 home, replay 3-1 away
2011 3rd rd 2-2 away, replay 4-2 home

In the sixties there was a remarkable run of League Cup and FA Cup games with the teams meeting six times, culminating in the 1969 FA Cup Final which City won 1-0.

Dave W: 26/4/1969 Leicester 0 City 1

I attended the Final in my best suit with Sue, my wife, who was three months pregnant. We were living in Sheffield at the time and travelled down on the train. We obtained tickets from various sources including referee Roy Harper (who later that season sadly collapsed and died refereeing a game at York City) who was a friend of Cup Final referee George McCabe, both from Sheffield. We sat in the stand opposite the Royal Box and I'm afraid to say, I lost my temper with a kid who didn't support either team who was sitting behind me and who was calling Franny Lee for being fat. I was then told off by Sue, but I'd watched City being garbage for years and was proud we'd won the title and were at Wembley, so I was rightfully annoyed! They played Cliff Richard's Congratulations at the end, the game being over all too quickly. It was a cool but sunny day and we strolled in the park to let the crowds disperse before catching the train back to Sheffield in a compartment with an obnoxious insurance salesman who reckoned he knew the players.

Leicester were relegated after the final. A 5-0 League win in 1977 was registered with Brian Kidd notching four goals, and also a Geo Kinkladze inspired FA Cup third round replay 5-0 win in 1996, with City going down that season under Alan Ball, and remarkably Leicester gaining promotion with under fire manager Martin O'Neill.

John G: 26/4/1969 Leicester 0 City 1

I'd decided to hitch-hike down to London and was standing on the corner of Mauldeth Road/ Princess Parkway opposite the Princess Hotel, decked out with my blue and white scarf, bobble hat and of course, the blue rosette, thumbing every car which passed by, and hoping that I'd get at least as far as the M6 at Knutsford Services!

It was three days after my 24th birthday - yes, I was born on St George's Day, and I'm proud of it, and I had about £15 on me, equivalent of about £300 nowadays I guess. Not a fortune, but just about enough, I thought, to see me through. Trouble was that I had no ticket, so at least a fiver would have to be put aside for that.

I was a relatively naïve, young schoolteacher, not particularly well paid, and had liked a bet on the gee-gees since I was seventeen, so I had only what I had. £15!

It was around 8am when I left my Fallowfield home, and around 8.45 am when I was first picked up by a driver who said "I can take you as far as the motorway if you like", which was music to my ears! There was no if's about it, I was ecstatic…. Wembley here I come…

I was dropped off at junction 19 of the M6 and I hoped that City fans travelling by car would see me decked out, and if they had any room would pick me up.

I had to wait some little time on the motorway approach. Cars, from which sky-blue scarves were being proudly waved passed by, some of them full, and those which were not, getting an under-the–breath "you're not a proper City fan, otherwise you'd pick me up" expletive!

After about three quarters of an hour and just when I was starting to doubt my intentions, a sleek , polished, shiny Bentley-type vehicle (I was never much good at identifying cars) pulled over and through the open window a voice said "I can take you as far as Watford" I was chuffed, to say the least!

It transpired that the gentleman was an overseer – a kind of big time foreman I suppose

– of the construction of the M6 in Cumbria. He was obviously worth a bob or two, but it hadn't gone to his head and he even bought me a cup of tea and a snack at a service station. He dropped me off at Watford Junction, and from there I paid 1/3d and caught a train to Wembley.

It must have been about 1pm when I first glimpsed the twin towers, I had made it. Soon I was to arrive at the home of English football. Soon I would see my beloved Manchester City run out onto the hallowed turf. Today was going to be the greatest memory yet, I was sure; Wembley here I come.

There was, however, this little matter of getting a ticket, but with only a fiver to spare I soon realised I had little chance, even if I went to my absolute limit of £7 10s.

Six return journeys up a colourful, busy, noisy, Wembley way, and at 2.15pm I went back up to the stadium thinking that if I hadn't got a ticket by 2.15pm I'd set out to find a local hostelry.

The spivs were getting £10 for a ticket and it looked like the King's Head or The Rose and Crown for me, and with London beer being about 3s a pint I'd have to sup quite slowly. Unrelenting, I continued, calling "anyone got a spare ticket for a genuine City fan?" But as a gambler I knew it was a 33/1 shot. I gave one last desperate call "Anyone got a ticket for a fiver" and unbelievably an answer came back "you can have this one for a pound" heard by tens, if not hundreds of others. The bidding started and went up to £25, so my dream appeared shattered. But no "A pound I said and a pound it is" said the fan who insisted that this fresh-faced, young City fan, bedecked in blue and white should have the ticket. A friend of his couldn't make it, through illness, and he had insisted it should go to someone who was considered best qualified. Me! I placed the pound in his hand in return for the FA Cup Final passport. Twelve shillings and sixpence it was worth. The bloke had made a modest profit of 7/6d! I made my way to 'C' stand behind the goal, the very one where Neil Young hammered home Summerbee's cross.

I think I hitch-hiked to heaven that day!

In the League Cup, meetings in two rounds:
1965/66 2nd rd 3-1 home
1967/68 2nd rd 4-0 home

Some connections: Managers David Halliday, Sven Goran Erikson, Paul Dickov, Don Revie, David Oldfield, Darius Vassell, Ged Taggart, Neil Lennon, Martin O'Neill

Tony Book lifts the FA Cup after City's victory over Leicester City 1-0 in 1969

Ground: Filbert Street (shown 2002) R/A 47,298 v Spurs FA Cup 5th round 1928, moved to The Walkers Stadium in 2002, capacity: 32,500

relegated along with City. Since then they've been down to the Fourth but reached an FA Cup semi-final in 1978. They finished season 2010/11 in League One playing in red (blue in the sixties) shirts and white shorts.

Pre-war: Six league meetings all in Division Two, City winning all six including a 6-1 at home in 1926/27.

Post war: Eight league meetings in the 60's, City winning five, including a 6-0, in 1964/65 at home, drawing two and losing one.

In the FA Cup: Two meetings:
1919/20 1st rd 4-1 home
1925/26 6th rd 6-1 away

Connections: Frank Clark

Ground: Brisbane Road (shown 1960's) R/A 34,345 v W. Ham FA Cup 3 1987

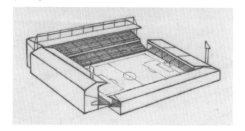

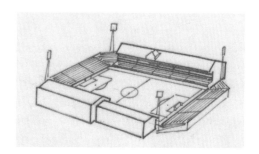

Leyton Orient

The 'O's' were formed by members of the Homerton Theological College who formed Blyn Cricket club in 1881 and carried on in the winter playing football. Eventually employees of the Orient Shipping Line became involved and the name Orient was chosen. Clapton Orient moved into Millfields Road in 1896, they joined Division Two in 1905, moved out to Lea Bridge Stadium in 1930, and in 1937 moved to Osborne Road, renamed Brisbane Road in 1946, as the name also changed to Leyton Orient. In 1967 they became just plain Orient, then added the Leyton again in 1987.

They spent many years in the Third Division South, moved up to Division Two in 1956, then Division One for one season in 1962/63 being

Lierse S.K.

Belgian club Lierse, full title Koninkijke Lierse Sporting were formed in 1908, based in Lier or 'Het Lisp' and nicknamed 'De Pallieters'.

They'd won the title three times in 1932, 1942 and 1960 by the time City played them. Lierse won the Belgian Cup in 1969 beating Racing White of Brussels 2-0 in the Heysel Stadium in front of 25,000 to gain entry to the Cup Winners' Cup. In the previous round (16th finals) they'd beaten Apoel Nicosia 10-1 home and 1-0 away. Their previous experience in Europe was the Champions Cup in 1961/62 when they lost 2-0 away and 3-0 at home to Barcelona.

They played in the Herman Vanderpoorten Stadium, capacity 14,538.

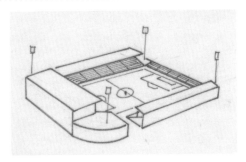

Second leg foregone conclusion, 5-0, goals from Summerbee, Lee (2), and Bell. Next match Academica De Coimbre in Portugal.

Friendly: 1978/79 a 2-2

In 1971/72 they lost 0-2 at home in the UEFA Cup to holders Leeds United but won at Elland Road in a shock 4-0 victory. They went on to win the title again in 1997, and the Cup in 1999, but dropped into the Second Division finishing seventh in 2007/08. They have now been taken over by Egyptian businessman Maged Samy who paid off their debts and also owns a club in Egypt with connections to Arsenal. Their colours are yellow and black stripes with black shorts but they played in white shirts and black shorts at City in the 1969/70 game.

The teams met in the second round (8th finals) of the Cup Winners' Cup in 1969/70 with City winning 3-0 away and 5-0 at home.

Steve P: 12/11/1969: Lierse 0 City 3

"I think that I shall never see a city lovelier than Lierre" (G.K Chesterton, who obviously saw more of it than I did!) The locals call it Lier anyway.

I probably went out via the Hook Of Holland on the Tuesday and overnight on the ferry, sleeping on boats and trains, the cheap way to spend the night. Bought tickets before I went and arrived at the ground early. Lots of Blues fans around, most spending the day in the Lierse supporters club. My first glimpse of a lager lout – not very loutish but too full of lager to see the match. He should have stuck to the wholesome food available at the bar - the menu included Filet Roll de Manchester.

Can't remember much of the match – it may have been here where we had loose tip up seats round the cinder track. We were behind the City bench and I seem to recall Mike Doyle on the bench shouting "come on Doris" to Ian Bowyer. It was an easy City win with goals from Bell and two from Lee. Travelled with the package tour fans on their coach back to Brussels. Day trip to Luxembourg next day then back via Ostend. Back home in good time to stuff United 4-0 on the Saturday.

Lincoln City

'The Imps were formed in 1883, and played at John O'Gaunt's. They were founder members of The Midland League in 1889, and in 1892 were founder members of Division Two as the first 'City', and moved to Sincil Bank in 1895.

Generally a lower league club they failed to gain re-election on a number of occasions but always managed to bounce back, eventually joining the newly formed Division Three North in 1921. In 1987 they were the first club to be automatically relegated to the Conference but again bounced back the next season taking Newport County's place.

They finished season 2010/11 in League Two being relegated to the Blue Square Premier league, playing in red and white striped shirts with black shorts.

Pre-war: 18 league meetings in the late 1890's early 1900's, City winning 12, including Lincoln's record defeat of 11-3 in 1894/95, losing 6, including a 0-6 in 1893/94 at Lincoln, obviously stinging City into that 11-3 win!

A scoreline of 11-3 cannot be ignored. The game was played on the 23rd March 1895, City's previous home game was a 7-1 win over Notts. County!

City opened the scoring on three minutes through Bob Milarvie. William McReddie then scored two quick goals, then Sandy Rowan made it four. Lees pulled one back for Lincoln, but from the restart an individual effort from Rowan made it 5-1 at half-time.

McReddie scored a sixth, just after the interval but Smallman for Lincoln made it 6-2. Billy Meredith then got in on the action, making it seven, then Rowan, McReddie, and Meredith again, made it ten. Lincoln gamely scored another when Smallman's cross was diverted in by Jack Walker, City's fullback, but Pat Finnerhan's deflected shot made it a final score of 11-3 (if you've kept up!)

Post–war There were two meetings in 1998/99, in Division Two, City losing 1-2 at Lincoln, but winning 4-0 at Maine Road.

In the FA Cup just the one meeting, in the first round of 1905, City winning 2-1 at Sincil Bank.

In the League Cup in the second round of season 1996/97 with City in the Division 1 and Lincoln in the Division 3. Lincoln won the first leg 4-1, and the second at Maine Road was an even more humiliating 1-0 Lincoln win.

Friendlies: 2003/04 a 2-2

Some connections: George Hannah/John McClelland

George Hannah

Ground: Sincil Bank (shown 1996) R/A 23,196 v Derby L/C 4 1967

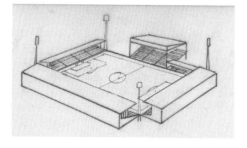

Linfield

'The Blues' were formed in 1886 in South Belfast, playing their home games at Windsor Park, also the home of the Northern Ireland International team.

When they played City in the first leg of the 16th finals of the European Cup Winners' Cup in 1970 they had won the Irish Cup 30 times and the League 27 times.

Their finest performance in Europe to that date was reaching the quarter final of the European Cup in 1967, losing to CSKA Sofia 2-3 on aggregate (2-2 home and 0-1 away).

In the first leg at Maine Road City managed a 1-0 win through Colin Bell. Their secretary, Harry Wallace, said it was their finest hour (and a half) in Europe.

In the second leg they beat City 2-1 with Francis Lee scoring. No doubt Harry W. was even more impressed! City went through against the part-timers managed by ex Luton, Sunderland and Everton manager Billy Bingham, on the away goals ruling. Not a very convincing start to the defence of the trophy.

Allan Wilson: 30/9/1970: Linfield 2 City 1

I am Belfast born and bred. In 1969 at the age of twelve I started following Manchester City. I was football daft and then when I picked a team I was City daft. I drove people in school crazy, in fact so much so that I remember nobody would tell me who had won the first ever Daily Mail 5 a-side competition because they knew I would go crackers about it. My school was in the south of Belfast and I lived in the north. Nobody I knew had heard of the school, I hadn't heard of it myself, but when I passed the eleven plus my dad had checked out the best available grammar school for me and told me where I was going. He was not, and to this day is not, a man you argue with. Another two lads from my primary school, who were finding it difficult to get places locally, also ended up in the same school. One, John, ended up in my class. We of course knew each other in primary school but we became good friends in grammar school catching two buses across the city every day to school and home again. My enthusiasm for City must have been infectious because two and eventually three other lads started to follow City, one of whom was my mate John. We had a circle of friends at school and one lad in particular, Colin, lived in the south of the city right beside Windsor Park, the home of Linfield and he was a Linfield fan.

In the 1970/71 season Manchester City drew Linfield in the European Cup Winners' Cup first round. City were coming to Belfast! I was fourteen, City mad, had only ever seen them on the TV but now, now, wow. I don't remember too many of the important details in fact I had to telephone Linfield to get some information. I think the game was played on 30th September 1970. It was definitely a Wednesday night. A nice chap called Ken told me Linfield made £7,000 from the game and there was a crowd of 25,000.

What I do remember is that Colin invited John and I to his house to have dinner on the day of the game. Colin was also in constant contact with Linfield about tickets and the kick off time. No tickets were needed, we could pay at the turnstiles, and the cheapest place to go would be the Kop. John and I knew the Kop, we had gone to watch Northern Ireland many times and always stood in the Kop but we knew this would be different. For instance, at Internationals, one half of the Kop would chant Liverpool and the other half would come back with United. John and I took great delight in shouting City in between. That was not going to happen tonight.

After school we headed for Colin's and his dad had a good dinner ready, Ulster hospitality. Colin got changed and John and I took our school ties off and we waited for years, well it seemed like years. Then off to the ground, paid at the turnstiles and into the Kop terracing. Then we waited a few more years for kick off. The teams came out and lined up in the area between the Kop and the main stand. There was terracing in front of the main stand and that is where the City fans were. How I wished I was in there, but I thought my accent might not be welcomed if I was in amongst them. The 'tunnel' where the teams came out was sectioned off by a high wire fence on both sides and the Kop was at a higher level than the terracing on the other side.

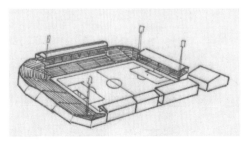

I ran over to the fence. There they were, Manchester City, my heroes. I was beside them with only a fence in between and then there he was, the great Colin Bell. I saw Colin Bell!! Then a City supporter, a skinhead with bovver boots, braces the whole bit, on the other side of the divide picked me out for some reason and started to give me a lot of verbal abuse. I wanted to tell him it was ok I supported City but I had thousands of Linfield supporters behind me and a lot of the guys who stood on the Kop would have been surprised to learn that there was a ball involved. So I just stood and took it but it was fine because Colin Bell was there.

Linfield played like men possessed. They were terrific. They scored first, through Billy Millen, so the tie was even. Then Franny Lee scored in front of the Kop and the floodgates were going to open. Of course they were, this was the invincible Manchester City. The Kop went crazy as Franny celebrated. I didn't see much of his celebration as the crowd flooded past me to vent their displeasure at him. Besides I was having my own private celebration. Then John and I looked at each other. You know that feeling when you know what each other is thinking? "Don't let your feelings loose just yet". The floodgates didn't open. Linfield continued to dominate and Billy Millen scored again, but we held on to win by the away goals rule. I also remember big Joe being hit by a whiskey bottle thrown from the Kop. He complained to the referee and was understandably reluctant to go back to the goal. At the end Colin bade us farewell and I had to admit that Linfield had done very well so I think we were all happy. Linfield had won and done Northern Ireland proud, but ultimately City had won through, and to be honest I would have been happier if Linfield had not done Northern Ireland proud and City had won by 5 or 6.

Then the journey home. Windsor Park is a fair distance from the city centre. It is walkable but tonight we had no choice. We were caught up in the Kop crowd. They liked to charge through the city and taunt the police. We were caught in a crowd chanting "SS RUC". At one point I met a friend of mine, not the sharpest knife in the drawer, and he was throwing bricks across a divide into a Catholic area. Linfield are a very Protestant team, think of Glasgow Rangers wee brother. We said hello and I quickly moved on. To be honest I didn't have much choice because people at the back of the crowd would start to chant "Hula" over and over again getting faster as their pace also picked up. These Hula charges were ongoing but the good news was that we got into the centre of Belfast pretty quickly and it felt effortless as we were swept along by the crowd. We jumped on a bus to take us to the north of the city which then left the centre and all of the Linfield fans behind, so John and I started to cheer our heads off. City were through. I remember sitting on the bus wishing City had won the game but thinking they were in the next round, and I had seen them. First time ever in real life I had seen them. I had watched Colin Bell my hero.

Friendlies: 1930/31 a 4-1, 1946/47 a 1-1, 2000/01 a 4-0

Liverpool

'The Reds' or 'Pool' were formed as Liverpool Association F.C. in 1892 when Everton vacated Anfield owing to a dispute between Everton and the Anfield landlord.

They were elected to Division Two in 1893, had ups and downs until 1905, went down in 1954, came up in 1962, and have won everything possible, but the Premiership title has eluded them so far. They finished season 2010/11 in the Premiership, playing in all red, but missing out on a Champions League place again.

Pre-war: 64 league meetings with 22 City wins 13 draws and 29 defeats.

First meetings were in 1893/94 and City didn't win any of the first 10 fixtures. In 1896, with 3 games to go, the teams drew 1-1 at Hyde Road. City won their last two games but finished as runners up to Liverpool on goal average, each with 46 points in Division Two.

City clocked up some nice doubles, in 1929/30 4-3 home, 6-1 away, 1935/36 6-0 home, 2-0 away and 1936/37 5-1 home and 5-0 away

In March 1920 King George V visited Hyde Road and watched the Blues beat 'Pool 2-1, which he applauded vigorously.

The March 1929 home fixture was Max Woosnam last game for City and he scored in the 5-0 win.

Post-war: 58 league meetings with 12 City wins 13 draws and 33 defeats.

Results were pretty even in the fifties until Liverpool's return to the First Division in 1962.

City's away win at Anfield on January 1st 1953 was their first away win since April 1952, also at Anfield!

In April 1971 Howard White made an all too short debut breaking his ankle and never playing for the Blues again.

City didn't manage another Anfield League win until 1981/82, after suffering 13 losses and 2 draws, with the reds often notching 4 or 5 goals. This rare Anfield win, 3-1 when Joe Corrigan was felled by a bottle thrown from the Kop.

Blue Moon was first aired at the opening game of the season in 1989, City's return to Division One.

Brian D: 26/2/1972 Liverpool 3 City 0

"Something happens to everyone who goes there!" warned my mate Steven Howe.

And it was true – those wackers would not only give you a good hiding, but pinch some of your clothes too! Well, City were top of the league and hot favourites to win the Title (Yes, really!) and we were going to go, Scousers or no Scousers. We decided to be sensible and not wear anything that would distinguish us as Blues, we would keep our mouths shut on the streets and hope to get away with it.

Towards the end of that season we were taken to a few matches by car, driven by Andy Cavanagh's Mum Madge and her friend, Anne. What an odd sight that must have been, two middle-aged women with three denim-clad youths in the back of the car! Anyway, on this occasion Terry (Cocking) couldn't come, so it was just Andy and me. We reckoned that the car would be the safest bet. We were seventeen by this time and much of the bravado of our younger days had diminished. At fourteen and fifteen we couldn't wait to be one of the 'big timers', in amongst it. By seventeen though, we were starting to realise how dangerous it all was, especially 'away'. Madge and Anne had arranged to meet some blokes they worked with in a pub and intended to watch the game from the Kop but we went in the Anfield Road end. It was packed (50,000+) and to my surprise there were loads of scousers behind the goal at 'our' end. The match was crap - we lost 3-0 – and as the third went in we decided to leave to get an early dash back to the car. In one of those 'happy' coincidences Everton were also at home, in the Cup, that day. In order to avoid congestion they had kicked off fifteen minutes early, our match fifteen minutes later. Yes, giving just enough time for all the Everton fans to get up to Anfield for a spot of 'Manc' bashing! As we left the stadium there was a gang of about a dozen blue scouse leaning on the wall across the road. We walked a few steps further before noticing some City fans getting kicked to bits by a wall further up the street, two local bobbies quite literally 'looking the other way'. We decided to go back into the stadium, and turned, but too late – the Everton fans had sussed us (not difficult really) and followed us up the street. They stood between us and the entrance. We ran through them – I would like to have said we gave as good as we got, but nowhere near and Andy got the worst of it – and up the steps back onto the crowded terracing, pushing and kicking our way through the mass, trying to get lost in the crowd. When we were well into the throng we stopped so as not to draw any more attention to ourselves. When the final whistle went we left with the masses and entered the stand on the side and walked along underneath that until we came out at the Kop exit. Trying to look happy (the home team had won 3-0) we hoped to blend in and make our way back to the car. Now, when you see a fight by a football ground it's most often a quick scuffle and people usually shout abuse or pretend not to notice. Not in Liverpool! We passed another couple of fights, loads of people of all ages stood around shouting encouragement as if they were ringside! One was taking place on a Zebra crossing with a crowd gathered around, even across the road and I can remember the belisha beacon post going 'ding' as someone crashed into it. We didn't stop and were so grateful to see the inside of that car.

As luck would have it City's next away game was at Goodison and I decided that discretion was the better part of valour (OK, so I bottled out!). Terry and Andy went and sure enough, Andy got done over again, this time quite badly. This was most unfortunate because Andy was a really nice lad, very funny and not at all interested in violence. He didn't dress as if he was looking for trouble or ever act tough – he just loved to watch City.

Sadly, Andy died, aged 44, some years ago, following a heart attack. Though I hadn't seen him for over 25 years I was still very sad to hear the news. So many memories...

In the Premiership: The worst defeat was a 0-6 at Anfield in 1995/96 which followed the 0-4 loss in the League Cup on the previous Wednesday. This was compounded by Rosler throwing his boots into the City end and manager Alan Ball saying on the radio that he'd enjoyed the game. In the return fixture on the last day of the season 'Pool went two up, City pulled back to 2-2 and the team were supposedly instructed by the management to play for time as they thought a draw might do, as advised by some clown in the crowd listening to a radio (but not an official from the club). There followed a bizarre scenario when Niall Quinn on the touchline told Steve Lomas to stop playing keepy-uppy as we needed to win. So ensued a frantic last few minutes where we couldn't produce a goal and down we went on 38 points same as Coventry and Southampton, but with an inferior goal difference. Manchester City, dontcha just love 'em?

It was not until 2002/03 that the next win came at Anfield with Nic Anelka's late goal costing Liverpool a Champions League spot, but the Blues came close in 2000/01 with a 2-3 loss when our two goals astoundingly both came from the penalty spot!. Since then at least the big defeats seem to have been eradicated.

Season	H	A	Pl	W	D	L
Pre 09/10			24	3	9	12
09/10	0-0	2-2	26	3	11	12
10/11	3-0	0-3	28	4	11	13

In the FA Cup, meetings in five rounds:
1956 5th rd 0-0 home, replay 2-1 away
1973 4th rd 0-0 away, replay 2-0 home
1988 6th rd 0-4 home
2001 5th rd 2-4 away
2003 3rd rd 0-1 home.

In the 1956 fifth round Cup replay game at Second Division Liverpool, Billy Liddell equalised just after the referee Mr Griffiths had blown for full time. Roy Paul immediately brought the City players off the pitch, and that was the last bit of luck City ever had at Anfield, with a 2-1 win.

In the League Cup, meetings in three rounds:
1969/70 3rd rd 3-2 home
1980/81 SF 1st leg 0-1 home, 2nd leg 1-1 away
1995/96 3rd rd 0-4 away
Biggest game was the League Cup semi-final in 1980/81 when Kevin Reeves' goal was

inexplicably ruled out by Referee Alf Grey and 'Pool won the tie 2-1 on aggregate despite a tremendous performance by City at Anfield to draw 1-1.

Friendlies: 1893/94 h 2-6, 1898/99 a 1-0, 1900/01 h 0-8, h 3-2, 1903/04 a 5-6, 1924/25 Everton/Liverpool X1 2-3 h, 1984/85 Everton/Liverpool X1 (Mark Higgins T/M) a, 1999/2000 2-1 h

Some connections: Didi Hamann, Steve McMannamann, Robbie Fowler, Nicolas Anelka, David Johnson, Mick Robinson, Joe Fagan

JOE FAGAN

Ground: Anfield (shown 2010) R/A 61,905 v Wolves FA Cup 4th round 1952.

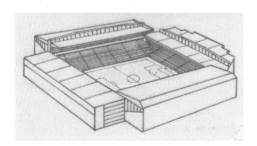

Sporting Lokeren SV

Lokeren is a small town located near to the historic Flanders city of Ghent close to Antwerp and Bruges.

Earlier in the year of 2003 they changed their name to Sporting Lokeren OV, the initials standing for Oost-Vlaanderen, Eastern Flanders the name of their province.

In 1970 it was the merge of Racing Lokeren and Standard Lokeren into Sporting, who made the Belgian First Division in 1974. They then played in the UEFA Cup for a number of seasons going out to, amongst others, Barcelona, Dundee United and Benfica.

After defeating TNS in the qualifying round City took on Lokeren who played in white shirts and black shorts, at COMS on September 24th 2003. After six games of the season they were bottom with two points, but in the qualifying round of the UEFA Cup they'd beaten Albanian Cup winners Dinamo Tirana 4-0 away and 3-1 at home..

In the first round first leg. City led through Sibierski in the 11th minute, Zoundi equalised in the 14th minute and Kristinsson put them ahead in the 40th minute. Fowler made it 2-2 after 70 minutes and an Anelka penalty in the 80th saved City's blushes before a crowd of 29,087 including 910 entertaining Belgian fans.

City fans looked forward to the first competitive fixture on mainland Europe, since March 1979 v Borussia M, on Wednesday 15th October, but were warned, in the home programme officially, that they would be sent home if found in the town, population only 36,000, prior to the game. This turned out to be total nonsense, (just for a change), and City fans enjoyed a good time there. 4,300 travelled by various modes of transport to swell the crowd up to 10,000. Entry to the ground wasn't via turnstiles, but an open gate, with hardly a ticket inspection, and a temporary stand had been erected behind the goal for the away fans. A slightly dubious penalty earned by Wanchope was converted by Anelka in the 18th minute which angered some home fans in the adjacent stand. This was further exasperated by the presence of their local rivals wearing City shirts and supporting the Blues, with scuffles ensuing. So City went through 4-2 on aggregate, thrashed Bolton 6-2 on the Saturday at COMS and looked forward with (mistaken) confidence to the draw for the second round.

Friendly: 1977/78 a 1-1

Connection: Jim Tolmie

Ground: The Daknam Stadium with a capacity of 12,000 but rarely filled.

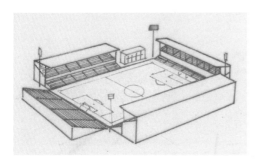

Loughborough

Were formed in 1886 when local teams Victoria and Athletic merged using the latter's Bromhead or Hubbard Cricket Ground. In 1887 they merged with the local Athletics club to form Loughborough Athletic and Football club, playing at The Athletic Ground. They entered Division Two in 1895 but struggled, also playing a couple of games at Filbert Street and The Vicarage owing to crowd trouble. In 1900 they finished bottom after a disastrous season, weren't re-elected, re-joined The Midland League but didn't turn up for the fixtures meeting and were declared defunct.

Pre-war there were 8 league meetings all in Division Two, between 1896 and 1899, City

winning 6, including a 5-0 and a 5-1 both at home, drawing 1, and losing 1

Ground: Athletic Ground R/A 6,000 v Leicester Fosse 1899

Luton Town

'The Hatters' were formed in 1885 when two local clubs, Excelsior and Wanderers met at Luton Town Hall. Wanderers had just changed their name to Luton Town Wanderers and had appeared in the FA Cup but were persuaded, at the meeting, to drop the Wanderers and become plain Luton Town.

They moved from Dallow Lane to Dunstable Park also known as Bury Park, then to Ivy Road, later re-named Kenilworth Road in 1905.

They were elected to Division Two in 1897, but failed re-election in 1900, eventually joining Division Three in 1920. They spent most of their time in the lower divisions, but made it to Division One in 1955 for five seasons, losing the 1959 Cup Final, dropped to the Fourth and made it back to Division One for one season in 1974/75 and again for seven seasons in 1982, winning the League Cup in 1988, before dropping back down, and out of the Football League in 2009.

They finished 2010/11 in the Blue Square Conference, having had 22 points deducted for going into administration, but failed to gain promotion in the play offs in 2010 at home to York City, amid, ironically, angry crowd scenes, and in 2011 against AFC Wimbledon at COMS. They played originally in white shirts and black shorts but in the seventies changed to orange shirts and black shorts.

They were one of the first to install a plastic pitch and after Millwall fans wrecked their ground in 1985 they banned away fans.

Pre-war: 6 league meetings between 1897 and 1939 with 3 City wins and 3 defeats.

Post-war: 30 league meetings with 10 City wins 12 draws and 8 defeats.

In the last game of the 1974/75 season City's 1-1 away draw sent Luton down to Division Two.

Luton gained revenge on the Blues in the last game of the 1982/83 season when Raddy Antic's late goal sent City into the bottom three for the first time that season and into Division Two. This was celebrated by Luton manager and renowned 'kerb crawler' David Pleat with a ridiculous touchline hop, skip and a jump in his 'loafers' before angry City fans caused him to leg it back into the dressing room.

Luton did well in the eighties, aided by their plastic pitch and away fans ban, though this was regularly breached by City and other clubs fans, but City never managed an away win at Kenilworth Road after the 2-1 win in 1960.

In the FA Cup, meetings in six rounds:
1936 4th rd 2-1 home
1938 5th rd 3-1 away
1953 4th rd 1-1 home, replay 1-5 away
1955 5th rd 2-0 away
1961 4th rd 6-2 abandoned, 1-3 away
1969 3rd rd 1-0 home

Dave W: 1/2/1961: Luton 2 City 6

We travelled down to Luton on the Football Special, and arrived in plenty of time for the kick off, City fans marching en masse down Kenilworth Road stopping the traffic as the rain came down. We spotted Sam Bartram, Charlton's legendary goalkeeper and then Luton manager going into the main entrance, before someone said there was some doubt about the game being on. The pitch was declared fit to play by referee Ken Tuck from Chesterfield and we took up our places on the open terrace behind the goal. After 16 and 18 minutes Ashworth put Luton two goals up and things looked ominous for the Blues. Denis Law had other ideas, completing his hat-trick in the 19th, 35th and 39th minutes, the latter two were stunning headers, prompting a fight between two drunken Luton fans rolling around full length on the sodden terrace, one of whom had applauded Denis's goals to the obvious annoyance of his 'mate'! If the referee had abandoned the game at half time no-one would have complained too much but he resumed the match after the interval. Denis scored two more headers, in the 51st and 56th minute, then made it six in the 67th after which the match was abandoned, with Bill Leivers furiously picking up and throwing down a lump of mud. Personally I was going mad and a Luton lady came up to me and said "don't worry son (I was 17) you'll win the re-arranged game easily!" Much discussions took place on the train journey back to Manchester on whether the result would stand, which of course it wouldn't and neither would Denis's goals count officially in the record books.

It was also the day I started smoking, aided by a lad called Nat who encouraged me to indulge in the Senior Service he offered. So a bad day all round. The re-arranged game was on the following Wednesday. I couldn't go and it was torture waiting for the result, the FA Cup being THE competition in those days. News came through that City were 2-1 down at half time, Denis, inevitably getting the goal, and then losing 3-1 at full time. Unbelievable. It turned out that Ken Barnes was injured early on and spent most of the game hobbling on the wing, but City were out of the Cup and I was gutted, vowing never to miss a cup tie again. It was to be another thirty years before I packed in smoking too!

In the League Cup, meetings in four rounds:
1962/63 4th rd 1-0 home
1977/78 2nd rd 1-1 away, replay 0-0 home, 2nd replay 3-2 at Old Trafford
1980/81 3rd rd 2-1 away
1988/89 4th rd 1-3 away

Some connections: Andy Dibble (shown), Brian Horton, Paul and Ron Futcher, David Oldfield

Ground: Kenilworth Road, (shown 2000) R/A 30,069 v Blackpool FA Cup 6th round in 1959

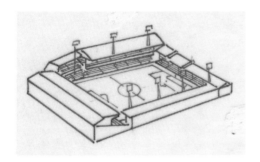

Friendlies:

Lancs Fusiliers 1904/05 h 2-1
Local Amateur X1 1909/10 h 5-1, 1914/15 h 2-0
Les Diables Rouges 1931/32 a 5-1
Lloret de Mar 1956/57 a 9-0
Lancaster City 1975/76 1-0, 1980/81 9-1,1998/99 a 2000/01 a
Lytham 1976/77
Legia Warsaw 1979/80 1-2 a, 1980/81 h 1-5
Leyland Motors 1981/82a 3-2
Lillestrom SK 1982/83 a 1-2
Los Angeles Heath 1985/86 a 1-1
Le Chaux de Fonds 1986/87 a 1-0
Lausanne Sports 1986/87 a 1-1
Lovangers 1987/88 a 12-0
Lervik 1989/90 n 10-0
Liasun 1990/91 a 1-1
Limerick City 1991/92 a 4-1, 3-1 a
League of Ireland 1992/93 a 3-0 @Bord Gais
Leek Town 1996/97 a
Leigh RMI 1997/98 a 2004/05 a
Livingston 1997/98 a 4-0
Lazio 2004/05 h 3-1(Thomas Cook Trophy)

MANCHESTER

INTERNATIONAL FRIENDLY

City

Tuesday, August 12th, 1980
at Maine Road
Manchester

KAZIU DEYNA . . . the Polish superstar who forged the link

V
**C.W.K.S.
LEGIA
WARSAW**

Polish First Division
and 1980 Cup Winners

KICK-OFF
7-30 p.m.

10p

M is for Macclesfield

The M's take us over to Cheshire, Stretford, Nottinghamshire, up to the North East, Denmark, Italy and London....

Macclesfield Town

'The Silkmen' were formed from a rugby club in 1874, having various names, Hallifield, Macclesfield, until taking their present title after WW2. They played at Rostrom Fields then Victoria Road until moving to The Moss Rose in 1891, and were a non-league club until 1997 when, after Sammy McIlroy became manager in 1993/94, were promoted to Division Three replacing Hereford United.

They finished season 2010/11 in League Two playing in blue shirts and white shorts.

The teams met in Division Two in 1998/99 with City winning 1-0 away and 2-0 at home

Dante F: 12/9/1998 Macclesfield 0 City 1

"Are you watching Macclesfield ?" that was the famous chant from the City end at Stoke when we were relegated in May 1998. As soon as relegation was confirmed the Macclesfield fixture stuck out like a sore thumb. However much of a low point, it was important to be there and I was lucky enough to be one of 1,500 or so Blues who got tickets.

I remember catching an early train, and arriving around 10am in Macclesfield, where the pubs were all hammered with Blues even at that hour. There was no police presence as the sleepy Cheshire town was invaded. This was our local derby for this season and defeat would be unthinkable - something almost impossible to live down.

On that day I met a fellow Blue, Carl Heald from Blackley, someone who I had disagreed with over the merits of the Francis Lee era, but that day he became a friend for life.

Onto the game and as someone who used to watch Altrincham now and again, in a ground resembling Moss Lane, it really hit me, how far we'd fallen.

The game kicked off and the Macc. fans were delirious. They were playing us off the park. I don't remember much about the game only we were under the cosh and Dickov was the only

one who was showing. Macc hit the bar and we were hanging on. I don't actually remember much about the goal only it was the Goat who put it away from about six yards and about a hundred City fans invaded the pitch - in honesty, more in relief than in celebration. The whistle went and we'd stolen the game 1-0. We were now seventh in Division Two - the real Division Three. Yes, it was just three points, but those points helped us to eventually scramble into the play offs and ultimately out of that Division. Those were dark days and in retrospect we deserve all the glory and money of recent times.

A red taxi driver mate of mine gave Michael Brown a lift back that day from the Moss Rose. Brown didn't play but commented on the players going over to the City end applauding the fans saying it was "embarrassing". I get annoyed when I remember people such as Brown. It was players like him, Nicky Summerbee and Kit Symons who had contributed to our all time low position.

The intention was to grab a few scoops on the way home but due to torrential rain we took shelter in the petrol station opposite the away end then we walked up to catch the train back to Piccadilly. We met up at The Waldorf and almost immediately heard that United were waiting for us at Wetherspoons. There was some handbags on Piccadilly Station approach but nothing more.

All I can say in summary is that it proves surely, that even at our lowest points, Manchester City mattered even to rival fans. But more importantly, our own fans felt Manchester City mattered and we never gave up on the club and that name.

Friendlies: 1897/98 a 2-1, 1901/02 a 7-1, 1975/76 a 1-1, 2005/06 a 1-1

Ground: Moss Rose (shown 2000s) R/A 9,003 v Winsford, Cheshire Cup 1948

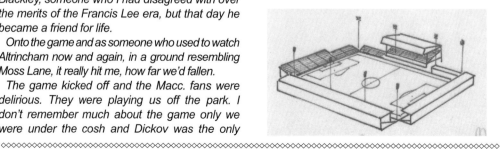

Some connections: Ian Brightwell, Brian Horton

Manchester United

Here we take an objective look at derby match encounters and the history of the local rivalry giving some insight as to why they're known by many as the 'Evil Empire', or 'The Dark Side' amongst less flattering terms and why everyone of my acquaintance, other than the 'manumafia' hates them.

Formed in 1878 when workers employed by the Lancashire and Yorkshire Railway Co. (so no Manchester connection!) company formed Newton Heath L&YR Cricket and Football Club which went bankrupt in 1902 when Manchester United came into being.

They played at North Road/Monsall Road from 1880 to 1893 then Bank Street and moved to the highly unoriginal ground name of Old Trafford in 1910.

They were elected to Division One in 1892, won the Cup once and the League twice but hovered between the top two Divisions up to the war nearly dropping to the Third in 1934.

Post war they were successful in each decade, winning cups and titles, though the team was rebuilt after it was decimated in the Munich Air Crash in 1958 (they wouldn't have won the title that year). It took years for United to recognise the plight of the victims and survivors of the disaster,

and when a charity match was organised in the 90's a huge chunk of the proceeds went to Eric Cantona, who had condescended to play. The disaster inadvertently propelled United to a new level of support through the wave of sympathy.

They then dominated after the cash cow for certain clubs, known as the Premiership, was formed in 1992/93 season, compounded by changes with respect to the European Champions Cup, becoming the Champions League, and worldwide TV coverage and subsequent revenue.

They finished season 2010/11 winning the Premiership title but losing in the FA Cup semi final and European Champions Cup final. playing in red shirts and white shorts.

Pre-war The teams first met in 1894/95 and up to WW1 United had the better of the 28 encounters with City winning 5 drawing 11 and losing 12.

In November 1894 Billy Meredith made his home debut for City in the very first derby, at Hyde Road, in a 2-5 loss. Also in that year goalkeeper William Douglas became the first transfer between the clubs going from City to United.

On Feb 26 1889 a friendly floodlit game was played between the teams in aid of the Hyde Colliery Disaster. Newton Heath defeating Ardwick 3-2.

December 1902 saw the first derby of Manchester City v Manchester United, a 1-1 draw at Bank Street.

In December 1906 City won 3-0 at Hyde Road and after the game in the club offices, bargaining began in earnest (!) for City's banned players, as the FA rules encouraged them to go to United, and the bans for some players were to be lifted in 1907.

United benefited from City's suspended players, which sounded very dodgy, and their then manager Ernest Mangall snapped up Meredith, Burgess, Bannister and Turnbull to help them win the League in 1908, the Cup in 1909, and the League again in 1911.

The first derby at Old Trafford in 1910 resulted in a 1-2 City loss.

In September 1912 City won 1-0 at Old Trafford and Mangall, the United manager then sensibly switched to City the following week.

In 1915 United stayed in Division One by the skin of their teeth, with a 2-0 home win over Liverpool, the match being fixed but the result being, strangely, allowed to stand

Between the wars it was the Blues who dominated the 16 meetings with 8 wins 4 draws and 4 defeats with City being losing Cup finalists twice and Cup winners once, plus winning the League in 1937.

City's main stand burned down at Hyde Road in 1920 and whilst never proven it was suspected that United fans were involved. The Blues turned down United's extortionate terms to share Old Trafford for a while, but rebuilt a terrace in a few weeks to replace the stand in time for the next derby. A record 6-1 City win was registered at Old Trafford in 1925/26, City scoring three times in each half, hitting the woodwork three times and United's goal coming just two minutes from time. United's record Old Trafford attendance came in a 1939 semi- final between Wolves and Grimsby – 76, 962,

Post-war: 72 league meetings with 19 City wins 28 draws and 25 defeats.

United engaged ex Blue Matt Busby as their manager after the war. He had been persuaded to join City as a player in the thirties and not

10. M. BUSBY.

to emigrate to the USA. He was also turned into a successful wing half after disappointing at inside forward, otherwise he could have been lost to the game. After Uwe Rosler's granddad reputedly bombed Old Trafford, United ground shared at Maine Road after the war for three seasons until 1949/50 (but never acknowledged in United's programmes) and finally won a trophy, after 37 years, the FA Cup in 1948.

The Fifties

Post war there seemed to be a switch in fortunes and United's gates generally increased (though they did record a gate of only 8,460 at one game) at their superior venue. There was also an increased media interest in the Reds' fortunes and any adverse publicity was actively discouraged, hence a 2-5 type defeat would be billed as "United involved in a seven goal thriller". Indeed, a mildly critical local journalist was once told he'd be banned from the team coach if he reported negatively!

83,260 watched the United v Arsenal game which Reds fans state as Maine Road's highest attendance, conveniently ignoring the 84,569 City v Stoke game. Anyway as previously stated there were probably 50,000 City fans there cheering for Arsenal. United by now had stolen Salford's 'Red Devils' nickname, later using the devil on their badge, and Salford strangely dropped it, later becoming plain Salford Reds.

City clocked up a 5-0 win at Old Trafford in 1955, and in 1957 after Peter MacParland's goals for Villa in that year's Cup Final the Villa man received death threats from United fans before an Old Trafford game. On the run up to the 1958 Cup Final Dennis Violett received poison pen letters from United fans who didn't think he should play at Wembley even though he had played in earlier rounds. After the Final which Bolton won 2-0 United fans bombarded the homecoming Bolton coach with stones and flour bombs.

The Sixties

After Dawson punched a goal in for United in 1961, in 1963, at 1-0, City had a good goal disallowed before Crerand whacked David Wagstaffe at half time. Then late on Denis Law kicked City goalie Dowd on the head and the referee gave a penalty to United which Quixall

David Wagstaffe

scored, and which virtually saved them from relegation. It is generally believed that 'modern' hooliganism was started at West Ham in 1967 when United fans tried to take the East End, and the Hammers vowed for it never to happen again. City played at West Ham a week later and the programme notes condemned some dubious refereeing decisions, and were quite damning of United fans' behaviour that day. This included missile throwing at West Ham players and hospitalisation of Hammers fans. It also concluded that if such conduct was carried into Europe it might bring more drastic measures. Very prophetic.

The Seventies

Francis Burns tried and failed to end Colin Bell's career with a tackle and City's title hopes in City's 3-1 win at O/T in 1968 but Colin and City recovered to take the title. George Best, though, did manage to virtually finish Glyn Pardoe's career in the 1970 derby at O/T. In 1971 United's 4-3 end of season win at injury hit City was their only win in 14 league derbies from Christmas 1967 to Easter 1976.

United's relegation in 1974, was confirmed by Denis Law's delightful backheel. The game was stopped with a few minutes to go (this was pre Fergie time) when United fans invaded the pitch disregarding their supposed respect for Matt Busby who appealed to them to "please leave the pitch". The first fences were then erected at O/T and honours were then even despite regular dubious refereeing decisions against the Blues.

Alan Oakes made his final appearance for League Cup holders City in the 1976 last game of the season, a 0-2 loss at O/T, his 561st (+3 subs) appearance for the Blues.

In the late 70's game at Old Trafford v West Brom., United fans heaped further disgrace on themselves by monkey chanting at the Albion black players, which was clearly heard on MOTD. Further crowd disturbances and hooliganism caused some of United's home games to be played away from Stretford at places like Liverpool, Stoke and the south coast.

The Eighties

After meltdown in 1982 City's only highspot was the 5-1 win at Maine Road in 1989, when United fans bravely infiltrated the women and kiddies' populated North stand, causing mayhem and the game to be stopped for a while, which didn't help their cause.

In the late 80's, Granada TV did a documentary on Ex-United Chairman and meat magnate, Louis Edwards on how he took over at United, and allegedly had bad meat delivered to local schools. This exposure accelerated his death, claimed son and then Chairman Martin Edwards, but no apology was forthcoming regarding the suspicious dealings and deliveries.

The Nineties

Moving on to the nineties, and when Eric Cantona was sent off at Selhurst Park for one of his dirty, sneaky, snidey kicks at a Palace player, as perfected by the Frenchman, he attacked a Palace fan in the crowd with an attempted kung-fu kick on his way back to the dressing room. This was excused as being a retaliation to racist comments. It was treated laughably by the FA, who banned Eric for months, to which he retaliated with his ridiculous 'Seagulls and Trawlers' speech.

Other disgraced United people were Kevin Moran (first player to be sent off in an FA Cup final), Lou Macari (allegedly involved in betting scandals), Mickey Thomas for counterfeiting, and even the great Sir Bobby Charlton was reportedly involved in some sort of ticketing scam. Alex Ferguson's 'brown envelope bung' was suitably hushed up by the authorities and his driving at speed down the hard shoulder of the motorway because he wanted a pooh was accepted as a plausible excuse

The Noughties and Reflections!

Chairman Martin Edwards was admonished for reportedly peering under the doors of ladies toilets whilst ladies were in action, and, not to be outdone, it was then Rio Ferdinand's turn to take a lengthy ban as he supposedly forgot that he should've been available for a drug test. Inexplicably he was later named as England's captain.

United had, by now, perfected the art of not only intimidating the media but now officials by disputing every decision given against them, virtually man-handling the referee on occasions (then hypocritically criticising others for copying this technique), and, when losing, insisting on extra time being added on. Indeed, this was most apparent when at 1-2 down to Sheffield Wednesday and with the O/T crowd in tears, in the first season of the Premiership, time was added on to the tune of 7 or 8 minutes until they'd scored two late goals, and they went on to win the title, the whole country guessing that it was a fix. This was also the period of their successful youth policy where they appeared to poach young players from wherever using whatever suspicious incentives they could think of.

Crowds went up from an average of under 40,000 in the late 80's to the current average of around 75,000 with approximately, therefore, 35,000 glory hunters, but with debts increasing to around £700 million under the Glazers.

In a game at Southampton, which United lost 6-3, the excuse of all time came out that it was due to the grey shirts United were wearing (they've never ever been beaten by the better team!)

Three of their personnel have been given knighthoods; Bobby Charlton, Matt Busby, even the surly and ungracious Alex Ferguson. This would have been fair enough if other players and managers, such as Bob Paisley, had had similar honours bestowed. Players in United shirts have always been favoured internationally, even when only reserves - goalie Ben Foster being a prime example. Outside O/T there are statues of three United players and a manager. Two of them are ex City, not a lot of United fans know this.

John B:

There has been no club in history, from its manager, to its ex-players, to its current players, to its supporters, more utterly consumed with spite than Manchester United in the Ferguson era. Success is never its own reward for this shower. No, victory must always be accompanied by a sneer, and defeat by a snarl; a gracelessness for every occasion. Referees who dare to give decisions against them are hounded, on and off the field, their reputations trashed, opponents that threaten their position are patronised and mocked in press conferences, journalists bold enough to take a critical stance are banned from the swamp sine die and even, as seen lately, liable to have their cars trashed by a balaclaved rent-a-mob. Score a big goal in a big game, and the first instinct of a Neville or a Rooney is to posture in front of the opposition fans, yet give them a taste of their own medicine and, as seen at Wembley in the semi-final, pompous displays of feigned outrage from the likes of Ferdinand, Anderson and that latest in a long, long line of fake hardmen, Rafael Da Silva, are the order of the day. For the fans of course, the same is true. A great number of them don't support united because the club means anything to them out of the ordinary, and I'm particularly talking about their legion of out-of-towners here, but because following the rags represents a chance to satisfy a character defect, the affording of an

opportunity to be what they perceive to be the biggest and the bestest. Nothing else could explain the regular presence of Singaporean and Bangladeshi reds on the MUEN site, attempting to belittle City for example. They don't go to games, they haven't ever had the experience of direct exposure to match going fans of other teams, so what possible authenticity can there be in their patronising sentiments. None is the answer. Just a desperate need to be a vicarious part of the manyoo gloating machine. Had Sky TV (and the marketing paradise that opened up in its wake), not come along beaming pictures of the only English side many had ever heard of - courtesy of Munich and Bobbeee Charlton and all that - into homes across the globe, and handing the rags a massive financial advantage that enabled them to buy the league title that had eluded them on a more level playing field for 26 years, then it's doubtful half of their support would even exist.

Brian D: 15/11/1969 City 4 United 0

I can still recall vividly my first derby match in November 1969 – I was fourteen. I travelled to the match on the 24 bus to Manchester, then by 'football special' to Maine Road. I went with David Porter, a Shaw lad who was in my class at Royton and Crompton. At 14 we were very much the 'wannabe' skinheads and were really up for it. I remember Dave announcing to the whole of the top deck of the bus, who were all United fans, that they had better not come into the Kippax! They were not impressed and we did the 100 metres from the bus stop to the stadium in well under ten seconds! Inside, the ground was packed with over 63,000. In those days 'segregation' consisted of a line of coppers between the rival fans, and the Reds were squeezed into about a quarter of the Kippax. I remember pushing our way through the City mob, looking for familiar faces, when I saw a red and white scarf. Puzzled, I looked up to see who was wearing it. A skinhead girl of about 17 had it hanging from a belt loop and on seeing my expression, without taking her gaze off me, she casually lifted it up and blew her nose on it!

The entire match was played with the sound of coins, stones and bottles hitting the roof and the girders. At one point the lad next to me suddenly jerked his head and as I turned I saw that a sharpened coin had cut right through his top lip. The match ended 4-0 to City but Francis Lee had scored a goal right on half time, which we had not realised hadn't counted. We thought it was 5-0! We walked back to the city centre feeling on top of the world, shouting up at the buses and banging on the windows of cars with Reds in them, spreading our fingers –"5-0" I remember feeling disappointed we had not seen some 'action' as this would have rounded the day off perfectly (emphasis on the word 'seen'!) When I got home it was straight round to all my mates houses to see how the day had gone for them. Derek Smalley had mistakenly gone into the United part of the terracing and had had his head cut open by a can thrown by a City fan! He said the United fans had been really good in helping him get medical attention – if only they had known!

In the Premiership: City wins included the last Maine Road derby 3 -1, and in the 2001 O/T 1-1 draw Roy Keane virtually finished Alfie Haaland's career with a disgraceful 'tackle'. The sporting O/T crowd giving Keane a standing ovation. The first COMS derby resulted in a 4-1 City win and City fans were impeccable for the minutes silence before the 2008 Old Trafford derby, a 2-1 City win, on the 50th anniversary of the Munich Air disaster. United's Paul Scholes' dirty play has always been excused by the media as "he can't tackle" and Gary Neville has been warned time and again, but without action, by the authorities for goading opposition fans aggressively (when they can't get at him!

Season	H	A	Pl	W	D	L
Pre 07/08			20	3	5	12
07/08	1-0	2-1	22	5	5	12
08/09	0-1	0-2	24	5	5	14
09/10	0-1	3-4	26	5	5	16
10/11	0-0	1-2	28	5	6	17
11/12		6-1				

In the FA Cup, meetings in seven rounds (+ a preliminary round)
1891/92 Qualifying rd a 1-5
1926 SF 3-0 Bramall Lane
1955 4th rd h 2-0
1970 4th rd a 0-3
1986 3rd rd a 0-1
1996 5th rd a 1-2 (Alan Wilkie giving United an outrageous penalty)
2004 5th rd a 2-4
2011 SF 1-0 at Wembley

The two biggest Cup games were the semi-finals of 1926 and 2011, City winning both games.

In 1926 City had stormed through to the semi-final, but were struggling in the league. The game was played at Sheffield United's Bramall Lane and both sets of fans were unhappy at having to cross the Pennines instead of playing at a more local ground such as Bolton.

City took the lead with a controversial goal which was adjudged to have just crossed the line from Tommy Browell in the 14th minute. He added another in the 76th minute and Frank Roberts made it three. The game was marred by a tackle by United's Barson on Sam Cowan, later known as the Barson Barge. He was later banned retrospectively until the end of the season.

In 2011 United were were firm favourites for a second treble with few pundits betting against them, and with their fans suggesting it was a waste of time City turning up! The match was played at the New Wembley on a hot April day. City fans were well up for it both outside and inside the stadium where they assembled well in advance of kick off singing the songs, whereas united fans only appeared in the ground a few minutes before the kick off after bricking, bottling and punching innocent stray City fans. When the United team was announced, the City fans turned their backs and performed 'The Poznan'.

United had the early play, Berbatov bringing out a fine one on one save from Joe Hart, then missing at point blank range. City though, slowly gained control, but went in at the break 0-0. Second half it was all City, and the goal came from Ya-ya Toure who took advantage of a misplaced Carrick pass, rounding the defence and stroking it through Edwin Van Der Sar's legs for 1-0 and ecstasy for City players and fans alike. Paul Scholes was sent off for a vicious lunge on Pablo Zabaleta, and the single goal proved to be the winner. City had upset the odds again and United's treble bid was in tatters.

In the League Cup, meetings in four rounds:
1969/70 sf h 1st leg 2-1 a 2nd leg 2-2
1974/75 a 0-1
1975/76 h 4-0 – in this game Martin Buchan virtually finished the career of Colin Bell with a horrendous tackle.
2009/10 SF H 2-1, A 1-3
Ferguson renaged on his decision to play his kids, so desperate was he to stop City winning a trophy, that he played a full strength team. With

City in control in the second leg at O/T United fans reverted to type, stopping City taking a corner by pelting Craig Bellamy with coins, missiles and bottles to stop the game. With City intimidated and concentration affected, United went upfield to score and went on to win the game 3-1 to go through to the Final but with the disgust of the football community and country hanging over them.

In the Charity Shield there's been just the one meeting prior to 2011, in September 1955 with United winning 1-0 at Maine Road, when 16-year-old United goalie David Gaskell, later famous for disgracefully showing his backside to the crowd, came on as a second half substitute and Bobby Johnstone had a back-heeled goal direct from a corner strangely disallowed. This should have indicated to all, the United mantra – disallowed goal and not even reported, anywhere except in the next City home programme v Sheff. Wednesday.

Friendlies: Pre-war there were many friendly games between the clubs, too numerous to mention.
Post war: 1951/52 a 2-4, 1953/54 h 3-2 (Henshaws), 1959/60 h 1-3, 1970/71 a 3-0 (Bill Foulkes T/M) 1971/72 h 1-3 (Alan Oakes T/M), 1973/74 a 2-1 (Tony Dunne T/M), 1975/76 h 3-4 (M.Summerbee T/M), 1976/77 h 4-2 (Glyn Pardoe T/M), 1987/88 h 1-3 (Manchester International Tournament /C Int Tournament), a 2-0 (A. Albiston T/M), 1988/89 a 2-5 (K. Moran T/M), 1989/90 a 2-0 (M.Duxbury T/M), 1991/92 h 1-2 (K. Barnes T/M), 1997/98 h 2-2 (P.Lake T/M), 2000/01 a 0-2 (D. Irwin T/M)

Some connections: Billy Meredith, Matt Busby, Denis Law, Wyn Davies, Peter Barnes, Sammy McIlroy, Terry Cooke, Andy Cole, John Gidman, Peter Schmeichel, Carlos Tevez, Brian Kidd, Peter Bodak....

United have played a number of semi-finals and replays at Maine Road:

1979 2-2 v Liverpool
1985 2-1 v Liverpool
1990 3-3 v Oldham, replay 2-1

Ground; Old Trafford (shown pre-war) R/A 76,962 Wolves v Grimsby FA Cup semi-final 1939, so Grimsby have, so far, been a bigger attraction at O/T than United!

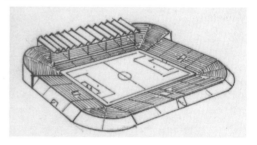

It was once ridiculed for its old fashioned perimeter fence, and is now similarly chastised for the silly brick wall behind the 'dug outs'. The ground has been extensively re-developed, but in an ugly way. There are no spirals to access the upper levels, only stairways. How quaint is that?! It's a far cry from the original aesthetically pleasing Old Trafford, which would now, surely, make Archibald Leitch turn in his grave.

They like to call it 'The Theatre Of Dreams' but its locality is close to the Liverpool Warehouse and terms such as the Cesspit, Leper Colony, Old Scaffold or Swamp seem more appropriate descriptions, affectionately adopted by away fans.

In summary, There is no doubt that United have produced great teams over the years, but the bias, hypocrisy, bullying, bitterness, and nastiness of the club is the reason that they're hated by many. It's not jealousy, it's the attitude. Sure, City, and other clubs have their problems but none of them profess to be the self appointed 'World's Greatest Club'. Does any other club in the country, Birmingham, London, Bristol, North East, Merseyside, Glasgow etc. have such undesirable neighbours? Surely not.

Mansfield Town

'The Stags' were formed either in 1905 but more probably 1910 when the Mansfield Wesleyans, formed in 1891, playing local football, spread their wings and joined the new Central Alliance in 1911. In 1919 they moved from The Prairie to Field Mill, and in 1931 they were elected to the Third Division South taking Newport County's place.

They were generally a lower league club but made it to the Second Division a couple of times and won the Freight Rover Trophy in 1987.

Athlete Daley Thomson was an unused sub in 1995, for a match v Cardiff, and Alvin Stardust is a supporter! After dropping down the Leagues and hitting financial problems they finished season 2010/11 in the Blue Square Premier League playing in amber shirts and shorts.

In the League Cup there have been two meetings. City lost the second round at home in 1964/65 3-5, Third Division Town going four goals up just after half time. Murray pulled one back then Mansfield made it five before Young and Kevan made the scoreline almost respectable. City, however, won the fifth round tie at Maine Road in 1975/76 4-2 (30,022) with Mansfield again in the Third Division..

Andrew H: 3/12/1975 City 4 Mansfield 2

Money was tight in those days, with my Mum as a single parent bringing up both myself and my younger sister, but still being good enough to pay for my Platt Lane season ticket and other visits to Maine Road for Cup matches. Whilst I was able to get junior reductions for the season ticket, for cash admission to Cup matches full price had to be paid for seats for all-ticket Cup matches in Platt Lane.

I remember being ecstatic when I heard the quarter final draw after the United game. Whilst the Stags had beaten First Division opposition in Coventry City and Wolves in previous rounds, they were bottom of the Third Division, and a home tie against lower League opposition at the quarter final stage was a deserved and fortunate reward for City. I recall little about an unremarkable game, other than Mansfield's tenacity in what wasn't an easy game for the Blues, and their distinctive amber and blue kit.

As I made my way home that evening along with the rest of the 30,000 Maine Road crowd

gleefully anticipating a two-legged semi-final, I would never have believed anybody that had told me that in the next thirty four years, City would reach the semi-final of a major cup competition on only three more occasions.

In the Auto Windscreens Shield game at Maine Road in 1998, City surpassed their 1964 embarrassment by losing at Maine Road 2-1 in front of a paltry 3007 crowd.

Friendlies: Mansfield 2003/04 a 7-1

Some connections: John McLelland, Nicky Weaver, Trevor Christie, Lee Peacock

Ground: Field Mill R/A 24,467 v Nottm. Forest F. A. Cup 3rd rd 1953.

Middlesbrough

'Boro' were formed in 1875 at a meeting of the Middlesbrough Cricket Club at the Albert Park Hotel. They first played at Linthorpe Road before moving to Ayresome Park in 1903, playing one game at Hartepool, then moved onto The Riverside Stadium in 1995.

They were elected to Division Two in 1899, promoted in 1902, and were generally a First Division club until the mid fifties after which they spent twenty years in the Second Division. After further spells in the Second in the eighties, they went down to the Third, fell into administration but were revitalised by Chairman Steve Gibson eventually winning their one and only major trophy to date, The League Cup in 2004.

They finished season 2010/11 in the Championship, playing in red shirts with white stripe and red shorts.

Pre-war: 52 league meetings with 21 City wins, including a 6-0 at M/Rd in 1935/36, 9 draws and 22 defeats, Boro going the first 17 games without a win at City, but winning at Boro 6-0 in 1903/04, and had a 6-1 win at Maine Road in 1937/38.

Post war: 44 league meetings with 22 City wins 11 draws and 11 losses, 'Boro winning only once at City until the arrival of the dreaded Premiership.

In the Premiership:
In August 1992 Niall Quinn became the first Premiership player to be sent off in the 0-2 loss at 'Boro, a game which also saw the end of Paul Lake's career.

In 2005, in the last game of the season at COMS, with the score at 1-1, Nicky Weaver came on in goal in the latter stages and David James moved upfield to no avail. Robbie Fowler saw his last minute penalty saved, the referee failed to give another blatant one and it was 'Boro, not City who went into the UEFA Cup for 2005/06

In the last game of the 2007/08 season, with manager Sven under threat from the sack by chairman Thaksin and the team demoralised, presumably, City suffered their worst defeat since 1962 when away at Wolves for the first game of that season they went down by the same score 1-8. It was a red hot day with many City fans in fancy dress, or shorts and T-shirts but within sight of the Riverside ground the weather changed to freezing smog. City went a goal down after 15 minutes Dunne giving away a penalty and getting himself sent off in the process. 'Boro scored again before half time, City then had a couple of chances but 'Boro smacked in six with just an Elano reply. No blame attached to goalie Isaakson. Off the field

the Cleveland police, for reasons of their own, digracefully laid into the City fans with batons.

Season	H	A	Pl	W	D	L
Pre 08/09			18	3	5	10
08/09	1-0	0-2	20	4	5	11

In the FA Cup, meetings in five rounds:
1904 3rd rd 0-0 home, replay 3-1 away
1972 3rd rd 1-1 home, replay 0-1 away
1992 3rd rd 1-2 away
1997 5th rd 0-1 home
2010 3rd rd 1-0 away

In the League Cup, meetings in two rounds:
1975/76 S/F 1st leg 0-1 away, 2nd leg 4-0 home
1991/92 4th rd 1-2 away
First meetings were in the two legged semi-finals in 1976, 'Boro winning 1-0 at Ayresome Park.

Dave W: 21/1/1976 City 4 M'Boro 0

For the return leg I was working in Knottingly and my boss, a West Ham fan, kindly agreed to drive me over to Maine Road and then stay the night at his home in South Yorkshire, despite me giving him merciless stick during working hours. I'd even dropped him from the office five-a-side team! (Brian, if you're reading this – hearfelt apologies) It was a foul night, strong wind with heavy rain and I worried whether the game would take place. The windscreen wipers packed up on his Hillman Minx on the M62 so we diverted to my folks home in Swinton for a squirt of WD 40 which did the trick. We parked up in Moss Side as the game kicked off and heard a couple of roars as we scurried to the ground. My boss suggesting that City could have scored a couple, which I pooh-poohed "City don't do things like that!" We arrived on the Kippax about a quarter of an hour after kick off. Standing on the right hand side of the Kippax a 'Boro fan in a sailor's uniform with a red and white scarf on was unperturbed when threatened by a City thug advising him in no uncertain terms that he was going to get a "bucketful of blood" at half time, which didn't materialise. Four nil, we're gonna win four nil chanted the Kippax (City had beaten them by that score earlier in the season) With a few minutes to go I was shouting at the Blues to be professional and keep the ball at all costs, thinking that we were only winning 2-0. "What's up with you mate, we're coasting at 4-0 up" I was told as I then realised that the two roars we'd heard were indeed for the two early City goals! When we arrived back at my boss's house we turned on the telly to see that City were two up, no action replays then, so we never ever go to see the first two goals.

Next meeting was in the fourth round in 91/92 season when City lost 1-2 to Second Division 'Boro when the fog miraculously lifted at half time allowing us to see the opposite end of the pitch.

Ged I.: 21/9/1974 M'Boro 3 City 0

People often ask me why I'm so negative about Middlesbrough, and my usual reply is "Have you ever been there?" I mean, what is there to like about a chemically-scarred, post-apocalyptic wasteland? What is there to like about a club where adult fans wear jester hats? What is there to like about a club that plays "goal music"? Absolutely nothing that's what. All they need is the foam hands to go with the jester hats and the goal music and they'll have the holy trinity of all that is bad about modern day football. OK, I confess to liking the couple of chuck wagons (to the east of the ground) that do excellent hot roast beef (or pork) butties, but that's the only thing I'll miss as we avoid playing them during their holiday in a lower division.

But is that all, or is there something more sinister? Well let me take you back to my first visit to 'Boro'.

It was the autumn of 1974 and Jack Charlton had guided Boro into the real First Division for the first time in ages. My mate Mick had passed his driving test and bought a cheap old car, so seven of us headed off in search of an entertaining day watching the Blues. We planned to arrive about an hour before kick-off as none of us had been to Ayresome Park previously, but a detour via a pub in Ripon put paid to that and we got there at about five to three.

The police wouldn't let us in the corner with the other City fans or in the paddock, and gave us the choice of the "Boys Pen" or the Holgate End. We'd heard of the Holgate End and chose the other option. Unfortunately the "boys" in the "Boys Pen" all seemed to be fully-grown men. Not only that but they all seemed to have weapon-shaped bulges in their pockets and took an instant dislike to the seven gobby Mancs that appeared in their midst.

The tension built for about half an hour then it became clear that a rethink was necessary.

Once again the police wouldn't let us in with the other Blues and dozens of Boro fans in the stands on either side of the Boys Pen were taking a keen interest in our position. So we ended up listening to the remainder of the game on the car radio. You may think that at least we'd enjoyed the benefit of a quick getaway, but Steve the Mickey Mouser had managed to find a safe vantage point and watched the remainder of the game thus delaying our departure.

My other contribution to this book covers a fraught trip to Newcastle, but at least we won that one. On our trip to Boro we lost three nil.

The interesting thing is that I went to Ayresome Park on another three occasions and I've been to their new home nine times and those dozen visits have passed without incident. But you know what they say about first impressions.

Friendlies: 1892/93 h 6-3, a 3-6

Some connections: Johnny Crossan, Alan Kernaghan, Adam Johnson (below)

Ground: Ayresome Park (shown 1990's) R/A 53,596 v Newcastle Div 1 1949/50. Riverside Stadium, capacity 35,100.

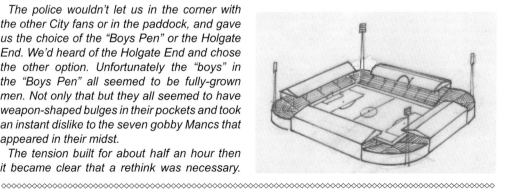

Middlesbrough Ironopolis

Formed in 1889 by some members of Middlesbrough, who were then an amateur club and Ironopolis became professional. They were elected into Division Two in 1893 replacing Accrington, and played for just one season before folding in 1894 replaced by Bury/Leicester Fosse/Burton Wanderers, (Division being increased by one). They played at Paradise Ground, R/A 14,000, adjacent to Ayresome Park and the North West corner was used for part of Ayresome Park which opened in 1903. They played in red and white stripes and white shorts.

Ardwick won the first encounter 6-1 at Hyde Road, but Ironopolis won the return, their first home game 2-0 also in September.

Friendlies: 1892/93 a 2-3, h 1-3

FC Midtjylland

'The Wolves' were formed in 1999 with the merger of two long standing clubs, Ikast FS (established in 1935) and Herning Fremad (established in 1918). They came into the UEFA Cup qualifying game with City on top of the Danish League, and had beaten Bangor City 10-1 on aggregate in the first qualifying round. The teams played each other in August 2008 with the Blues losing the first leg 0-1 at COMS, Joe Hart making a last ditch save to prevent them going two up.

Sean R: 28/8/2008: FCM 0 City 1

For the away leg, tickets were at a premium, and the kick off was brought forward to 4.25 pm in Herning which is some four to five hours drive from Copenhagen by car. Flights were made to Aarhus or Billunds in our case and we were coached to Herning giving us a couple of hours to enjoy the delights of the small port town. News came through which delighted us all, (of the return to City of SWP), so all we had to do now was to win through to the next stage. It was goalless until the very last minute when it looked like we were going out but Ched Evans rose and headed towards goal with the ball deflecting into the net off their defender. City

came close in extra time but it was then down to the penalty shoot out. Ched Evans scored, they equalized, Petrov scored, they equalized, Johnson missed (after also missing a one on one in extra time) Hart saved, Hamann scored and Hart again did the business and Corluka sealed it for City. We popped back into town, ignored the locals spoiling for a scrap, enjoyed time with their decent fans and made the journey home, relieved but happy.

Ground: SAS Arena, Herning, opened in 2004, on the Jutland peninsula, which has a capacity of 12,500

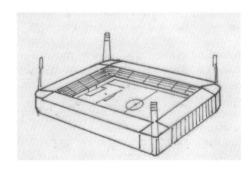

AC Milan

In 1899 an English resident of Milan, Albert Edwards, organised a game of football between English and Italian customers of neighbouring bars in the Via Berchet. This proved so popular that the rivals joined forces and formed 'Milan cricket and football club', retaining the English 'Milan' as opposed to the Italian 'Milano'.

They won the league in 1901, with four Britons in the team, and did so again in 1906 and 1907. In 1908 however some of their members defected to form Internazionale, who became more successful and AC didn't manage another title until 1951. This was followed by another five titles, four cup wins, two European cups and two Cup Winners' cups by the time they played City in 1978/79..

The teams first met in the UEFA Cup third round in season 1978/79. Milan had already beaten Lokomotiv Kosice (Czech), and Levski Spartak (Bulgaria) in the previous rounds. The first leg was in Milan, postponed by a day because of fog, City went two goals up but ended up drawing 2-2.The return leg at Maine Road saw City run out comfortable 3-0 winners in front of 38,026.

The Guvnor: 23/11/1978 Milan 2 City 2

We flew out on the Monday afternoon from Ringway (now Manchester Airport) on a scheduled BA flight for Milan. There was a Head Steward called Nigel who was wearing a City badge and had displayed a poster of our beloved Blues at the front of the plane.

There were about 150 City fans on the flight mixing with everyday passengers just flying out to Italy on business or on holiday. Nigel kept all of the lads well fuelled with alcoholic beverages and the flight was very pleasant. We arrived in Milan and headed straight to our hotel, unpacked, changed and decided to scour the City for our fellow fans to sing and let the Italians know we had arrived. It was about 16:00 hours and we had 24 hours to wait before our match.

We went round the city and joined up with about 50 lads who had also gone privately and not with organized trips. We saw Frank Horrocks and Helen Turner (with the bell) and Howard Yeats who was organising the Official Supporters Club. Frank, as he always did, said "Hi, behave yourself don't let the club down will you" I replied "you know me Frank, we will be good, very good" meaning of course that these Italians wouldn't get the better of us English City boys.

Four of us went along to a bar in the town just four of us. We were confronted with about six or seven of their boys in a bar, shouting abuse at us but hiding behind three burly doormen. They thought that we would be scared and just leave but we threw a few bottles at them, got thrown out and the Police came so we legged it and went to another bar. After about an hour we saw the same Italians who had tried to provoke us, passing the bar.

We slowly went outside and followed them to the square, where we let them have it. They were useless in a fight, begging for mercy, two ran and left the other four to get hammered and we hit and booted them all round the square, as it was easy when they had no police to protect them. We left the square when it started getting crowded with onlookers and we went back to the Hotel to lie low for a while.

Back out that night we were soon followed by the occasional spotter from their crew. But we were now twenty strong a match for any Italian crew. An equal mob of about twenty of their boys came at us, only to throw a few bottles and turn round and leg it. The night went on and a lot more City appeared in the town, Their lads did not reappear and so we all got drunk and went to bed, without having the fun we had hoped for.

The next morning we got up with the word from the locals that heavy fog was expected at about 2pm. Kick off was approaching, we had mobbed up and fought a few skirmishes in town and on the way to the match. We went into the ground only to find that the game had been called off.

City fans were kept inside for about half an hour whilst the locals went home and we were escorted back into town to the hotels. F*ck this I thought, I am not being told where and when I can go, by a group of coppers. So five of us escaped the escort and went down a narrow road away from the rest. We went about fifty yards and got ambushed by about a hundred of their boys, I thought that this was it; I got kicked to f*ck and stabbed in my back. The rest of the lads had been battered but somehow legged it. I couldn't but they did not finish me off as they heard sirens and disappeared. It seemed as if I was in London in the early 1900's with thick fog and nobody around to talk to or ask the way back. With blood coming out of every part of my body I got to a hotel front door and guess what? Frank Horrocks was there. His first words were "you just cannot behave yourself can you?" Not "what happened ?" or "are you alright?" I suppose I got what I deserved, but hey I am still around to fight another day. The Italians had nicked my holdall in which I had put the St George's flag - they had also nicked my wallet with all my cash. Bastards I thought, I am not finished yet though.

I went off to the hospital, got sorted and went back to the hotel. Upon arriving back there were about eight bodies sleeping, not only in my bed but all over the place, floor, bathroom and couch. I woke the kid in my bed cleared him out of it and went to sleep. The next morning the lads had a whip round and gave me some cash. Back in the land of living just feeling sore I looked like a battered and bruised alcoholic.

We were told that the game was back on that afternoon at 2pm. Great, a time to get organized and go for round two. We had to get out of the hotel though by10am. There was a police escort on to buses for those who had travelled separately, and we were to be joining up with the Official Supporters Club.

Whilst we were all waiting on the coaches to go to the ground, the hotel management came out with the police. Someone had nicked the small mini bar but one of the lads suddenly found it in the back of one of the coaches and it was handed over.

Back in the stadium, City were brilliant, we were 2-0 up but they did come back and get a draw out of the game in the last few minutes. This did put a damper on things but City, to their credit, did us proud - one of the few teams to get anything in the San Siro.

As we made our way down from the upper tier we noticed a skirmish on the lower tier where some of the City family members were being jostled by their boys. Brilliant, just what we needed, a last ditch effort to get our own back. A mob of us ran at them, got them in a corner and went to town. I did not recognize anyone from the night before, but hey ho! Revenge was sweet. The game ended in a draw but we won 4 – 1 in the battles. The Italians had been done on their own turf. I went home feeling sore but cocky, only to be told when I got home that my application to form a Supporters Club branch in Leicester, where I now lived, was being turned down and I had been banned for a year until I could prove I was a good boy! The Supporters Club did materialise and later I joined it, but I did manage to keep my activities away from the branch and away from other officials who wanted to curb my anti-social pursuits.

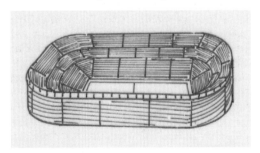

The San Siro was opened in 1926, being partly funded by a wealthy President, owner of the tyre company, Piero Pirelli, with a capacity of 35,000. Milan Commune took over in 1930, and the capacity was increased to 65,000. Inter moved in during 1947, then the capacity was increased to 82,000 in 1955. In the late seventies the ground was renamed after Guiseppe Meazza, a famous player for both clubs, but also retained the original name.

The clubs pay rent to Milan Commune (there's a novelty!) and the ground was revamped and upgraded for the 1990 World Cup.

Milan went on to win the title that year and followed up with further titles, European Champions Cup and Cup Winners' Cup wins, with wealthy Italian supremo Silvio Berlusconi as President.

City also played a friendly in 1981/82, a 1-0 loss, then in 2008 City won the Thomas Cook Trophy 1-0 at COMS. Surprisingly when we tried to sign Kaka later that season they claimed they'd never heard of us, but according to CEO Garry Cook, they 'bottled it'.

Friendlies: 1933/34 a 0-5; 1981/82 a 0-1

Connection: George Weah and the red and black strip adopeted by Malcolm Allison in 1968.

Millwall

'The Lions' were formed in 1885 as Millwall Rovers by employees of Morton and Company, a jam and marmalade factory in West Ferry Road. The founders were mainly Scotsmen and their first headquarters was The Islanders pub in Tooke Street, Millwall. They moved across the River Thames from the North Greenwich Ground to The Den in 1910. Crowd trouble caused closures by the F. A, in 1920, 1934, 1947, 1950 and 1978. They moved to The New Den in 1993. They were founder members of Division Three in 1920, spending most of their time in the lower divisions, but made the First Division in 1988 for a couple of seasons, and lost in the Cup Final of 2004, 0-3 to United.

They finished season 2010/11 in League One, gaining promotion via the play offs, playing in blue shirts and white shorts.

Pre-war: Just the two league meetings, in season 1938/39 Second Division, Millwall winning 6-1 at Maine Road when Frank Swift was dropped, being replaced by J. Robertson, and 3-1 at The Den to complete the double.

Post –war: 10 league meetings with 7 City wins and 3 draws. After the game at The New Den in 1998/99, City fans were kept in whilst Millwall fans enacted ugly scenes outside the ground. In the return at Maine Road they stopped off at Stockport and had a confrontation with United fans who were on their way to an away game and riot gear police were then utilised at the match at Maine Road with City. After the game City fans ran riot in the locality. This overall situation caused away fans to be banned for the 2001/02 fixtures and when City scored at the New Den the players amusingly celebrated in front of an empty stand, where the City support should normally have been.

Pete R: 26/9/1998 Millwall 1 City 1

A first season in the third tier of English football for the Blues and what better than a visit to the New Den on a pleasant September evening - although for those of us old enough to remember the Millwall neanderthals running amok in the 70's and 80's, a place to beware especially if you were brave enough to wear the shirt. I went with my son Tom (who was then 13) and we had decent seats in the front row of the upper tier behind the goal. So far so good, but there was a hint of what was to come when we went 1-0 down early in the second half and a number of their young fans invaded the pitch near the corner flag trying to goad us Blues. Now this is where I have a confession to make because shortly afterwards the ball ended up in the City net, again up the other end of the pitch, and cue pitch invasion number two. Tom and I, however, were so transfixed by the idiots on the pitch that we failed to notice the goal had been disallowed. So eyes back to the game and there are two Blues who think we are 2-0 down which meant that when Lee Bradbury grabbed a last minute equaliser, we were the only away fans who remained seated thinking it was a mere consolation goal. I've been to hundreds of games over the years but even when I've had a skinful beforehand I've never lost track of the score! By this time, however, mounted Police were in evidence with the locals, incensed by the late equaliser, ready for some fun and games. As a result we were kept in the ground for our own safety for getting on for an hour whilst the home fans took out their frustrations on the local constabulary. Eventually we were allowed out of the stand onto the area just outside the turnstiles where in the distance we could see the blue

flashing lights and hear the sirens of the Police vehicles trying to restore order. Dennis Tueart, who was then a director came over to explain that we were being kept back for our own safety, which I guess made us feel a little better. When we were eventually allowed to leave we were herded by the Police to Bermondsey tube station (where we didn't want to go) amidst streets littered with glass and bricks. Just a normal night in South London I suppose but were we glad to get away in one piece!

February 1999 and Millwall came to Maine Road. As was usual in those days we had stopped at The Swan at Bucklow Hill for a pint (Mary D's these days). That was until we spotted a Millwall minibus pull up outside. To be fair two of their fans actually started speaking to us in a fairly civilised manner but I sensed a menacing air and it was wise to drink up and leave. As for the game itself, City won 3-0, all the goals coming in the second half which predictably resulted in Millwall lobbing a number of seats and other missiles from their area in the North stand. Our seats were in the corner of the Kippax, separated from the away fans by the 'no man's land', but the bloke in the row in front somehow still managed to catch a £1 coin thrown our way. Must be true about there being more money 'darn sarf'! After the game pity the poor coach drivers as Blues bent on revenge ripped off windscreen wipers whilst a brick bounced back off the perspex rear window of another coach.

We made another visit to Millwall in December 2001 when Kevin Keegan's team played the home team off the park in a 3-2 win notable for a first senior goal for Shaun Wright-Phillips. Away fans were banned but Tom and I, living in Eastbourne, had no problem getting a ticket. How sweet it was to sit there with disguised grins on our faces as the goals went in, Darren Huckerby & Co. celebrating in front of the empty stand behind the goal where we Blues should have been.

John B: 29/9/1998 Millwall 1 City 1

Mercifully, by dint of their respective sizes and history, City and Millwall had met on only a handful of occasions, the last of which had been at the Old Den in the late 80's for a Cup replay (a 3-1 defeat), but this was our first visit to the new ground, built a stone's throw away from the original. Millwall's reputation for a thuggish, right wing following was well documented, and as any City fan present on the evening of the 29th September 1998 will tell you, well deserved.

There was no hint of what was to come when we set off straight from work for this Tuesday night fixture in South London, but on reflection perhaps trouble could have been anticipated. City had just fallen into the third tier of English football for the first time in their history, and with a regular 3,000 strong away following, were manna from heaven for every small town Johnny intent on testing their mettle against one of the big boys. The visit of Manchester City then, was always going to be a more attractive proposition to the Lewisham hooligan fraternity than say Northampton Town (two cars and a minibus) for example, and, duly motivated, it seemed that every semi retarded Ray Winstone wannabe, south of the Thames, had turned up at the New Den looking for blood.

The short train ride from London Bridge to South Bermondsey was punctuated by sloping headed morons wandering up and down the carriages, aggressively asking random passengers 'Are you Millwall? Are you Millwall?', with more of the same on the walk from South Bermondsey station to the ground. At the entrance to the away end, I asked a WPC why these people were not simply being arrested or even moved on, and received the following helpful piece of customer service advice – "well, you knew the risks when you came here, so tough".

The atmosphere inside the ground was no better. No-one in the lower tier of the West Stand bothered to face the pitch at any stage, preferring instead to pass the entire 90 minutes spitting poison at the away end, and when Neil Harris opened the scoring for the home team, other Millwall fans spilled out of the South Stand and on to the field, some running up to the halfway line to goad the City contingent. When they had another 'goal' disallowed they did the same thing. When City's Tony Vaughan and Millwall's Paul Shaw started a 20 man brawl near the touchline that saw both players sent off, several of the lunatics in the West Stand tried to join in. However, the ultimate catalyst for full scale violence was yet to come. In the 92nd minute, the Blues, attacking the end where their own supporters were located, won a corner, and when Lee Bradbury bundled the resultant cross gleefully into the back of the Millwall net to equalise, the City fans erupted in ecstasy. Simultaneously, the West Stand lower tier emptied with malice aforethought.

The final whistle blew at approximately 9.35pm. At 10.15pm, we were still locked inside the ground behind large steel doors at the back of the stand. Years later, watching the start of Saving Private Ryan, where the marines were waiting for the landing craft ramps to be lowered, and wondering apprehensively about what anarchy might lie beyond, I had an epiphany. "F*ck me", I cried out loud. "It's bloody Millwall!"

As it turned out, the steel doors led out only to an enclosed courtyard behind the stand, where we were duly corralled for a further half hour, before finally escaping altogether a full hour and 10 minutes after the game had finished.

The reason for the delay soon became apparent. Outside on Ilderton Road, from where we were given a huge police escort back to South Bermondsey station, it looked like downtown Gaza after an Israeli airstrike. There were Tactical Support Vehicles as far as the eye could see, police officers being treated in the backs of open doored ambulances, profusely bleeding police horses, stray riot shields, and bricks and glass, from walls and bottle banks that had been knocked down and overturned to act as sources of ammunition, strewn all over the streets. And then, even then, at a quarter to eleven at night, there were still odd groups of retards down the side roads, trying to get at us.

In his after match comments, City manager Joe Royle said "I cannot believe what I saw. It was a disgrace. If we had scored another goal in that atmosphere (and Lee Bradbury missed a late sitter), I don't think we would have got out alive", and although Theo Paphitis, the then Millwall Chairman, presumably anticipating his current role in light entertainment, countered by claiming (laughably) that if the City players were intimidated by a handful of youngsters running on to the pitch, they needed to "go back to kindergarten". Last word should go to someone with his head somewhat less of a distance up his own behind, Chief Inspector Chris Miles of the Metropolitan Police. "The violence was absolutely horrifying, the worst I have seen for a long time".

In the FA Cup meetings in four rounds:
1932 3rd rd 3-2 away
1937 6th rd 0-2 away
1938 3rd rd 2-2 away, replay 3-1 home
1990 3rd rd 0-0 home, replay 1-1 away, 2nd replay 1-3 away

Friendlies: 1894/95 a 1-0, 1954/55 a 1-0 (opening of floodlights)

Some connections: Jack Hillman (below)

Ground: The Den, (Shown 1990) R/A 48,672 v Derby F.A, Cup 5th round in 1937
"Why is that stand empty?" "It's the family stand!". The New Den Capacity: 20,146

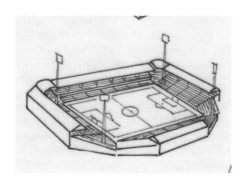

Friendlies:

Marseille 1933/34 a 4-4
F.C Mainz 1954/55 a 1-2
MTK Budapest/Red Banner 1956/57 h 2-3
Moscow Dynamos 1965/66 h 2-0
Mossley 1968/69 a
Morocco Nat X1 1974/75 a 2-3
Matlock 1976/77 a
Morecambe 1977/78 a Street testimonial
Memphis Rogues 1979/80 a 1-1
Man C. '69 team 1976/77 h 2-1 (T.Booth T/M), 1980/81 h 9-2
C D Malaga 1986/97 a 3-0
Mossley 1987/88 a
Matfors IF 1988/89 a 2-0
Mitsubishi Urawa 1992/93 a 2-0
Merseyside X1 1992/93 a (Graeme Sharp testimonial)
Munich 1860 1955/56 a 0-0, 2009/10 a 1-1
Munster Association 1908/09 a 4-2
P. Munster 1955/56 a 3-1

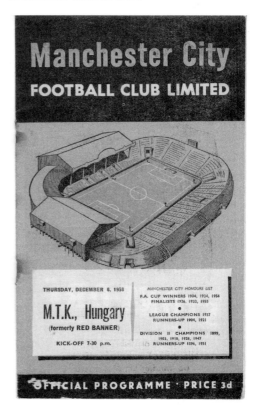

N is for New Brighton Tower

THE N's take us over to Lancashire, The Wirral, Tyneside, South Wales, Northamptonshire, then Cheshire, Norfolk and finally Nottingham, twice...

New Brighton Tower

'The Towerites' were formed in 1897 by the Tower company after the Tower Athletic Ground was built under the shadow of the Tower, being of oval shape with a cycling and running track, and an 80,000 capacity. Tower played there for three seasons in Division Two until 1901 when they were wound up, due to poor attendances. They averaged only around 1,000, despite commendable performances, being replaced by Doncaster Rovers. The 567ft (or 621ft) foot high Tower itself fell into disrepair and was dismantled in the 1920's. New Brighton F.C. moved into the ground in 1946.

City played them just twice in Division Two, in season 1898/99, drawing 1-1 at home and wining 1-0 away.

New Brompton

See Gillingham

Newcastle United

'The Magpies' or more commonly 'The Toon' were formed as a club called Stanley in 1881, becoming Newcastle East End in 1882 to avoid confusion with a club in County Durham of the same name. A club called Rosewood merged with them. Newcastle West End had been formed in 1882 and they played at St James' Park but went out of existence and Newcastle East End moved in becoming Newcastle United in 1892.

They were elected to Division Two in 1893, moved up to Division One in 1898 where they stayed until 1934 winning the title four times and the FA Cup three. After returning to the First in 1948 they won the FA Cup three times in the early fifties and the Inter City Fairs Cup in 1969 then yo-yoed between the First and Second Divisions, stabilising in the Premiership in 1993, but finished season 2010/11 in The Premiership after one season in The Championship, playing in black and white striped shirts with black shorts.

Pre-war: 66 league meetings with 19 City wins 16 draws and 31 losses.

First meetings were in Division Two in 1893/94. October 1894 saw the debut of Billy Meredith in a 4-5 loss at St James's. Newcastle had by far the better of the exchanges pre-war and City didn't register their first win at St James' Park until 1912/13, at the 17th attempt. However in the home game that season City missed three penalties. Newcastle went one up in the 7th minute, then City's Eli Fletcher's kick went straight at the keeper, who also turned aside Sid Hoad's follow up. Eli tried again half way through the second half but sent the ball wide of the left hand post. In the last minute Irvine Thornley had a go and Blake, the Toon goalie saved but George Wynn dashed up to net the rebound and give City a 1-1 draw. The 1923 game, a 0-0 draw was the last game at Hyde Road

In the final game of the 1925/26 season, one week after the Cup Final loss to Bolton, City lost 2-3 at Newcastle. With the scores at 2-1 Billy Austin's penalty was saved, Newcastle went 3-1 up and Browell made it 3-2 late on. Leeds and Burnley each won their home games 4-1 and City were relegated by one point, but with a slightly better goal average.

Post war: 60 league meetings with 21 City wins 13 draws and 26 losses.

Memorably, City clinched the league title 4-3 at St. James' Park in 1968. An estimated 20,000 Blues made the journey in a 46,492 crowd. Summerbee opened the scoring after Newcastle had hit the post twice, in the 30th minute, but they equalised two minutes later.

Neil Young restored the lead but the Geordies equalised again to make it 2-2 at half time with nerves jangling. Neil Young, then Francis Lee, who also had a goal disallowed, made it 4-2, but Newcastle scored a late goal to make it a sweat for the last few minutes but City were Champions, only five seasons after relegation and supposed oblivion to the Second Division. United lost at home to Sunderland on the same day, so City were two points clear at the top with 58 points. It is a myth, however, to say that the win didn't matter, City having a superior goal average, as Liverpool had a game in hand and could have finished with 57 points had they not lost it 1-2 at Stoke.

Dave W: 11/5/1968 Newcastle 3 City 4

On the way back from Newcastle we stopped off in Wakefield for a pint or two. It was a ghost town, the rugby team being at Wembley for the Cup final v Leeds, and on TV we saw Don Fox miss a last minute penalty right in front of the posts, which cost Wakefield the game in the pouring rain. "The poor lad" commentated Eddie Waring, and whilst we sympathised we still enjoyed our drinks!

At Christmas in 1977 City won an emotional game 4-0 at home when Colin Bell came back from injury at half time. Score was then 0-0 and in the second half the Geordies crumbled conceding four goals.

In The Premiership In May 1995, John Burridge, Newcastle's goalkeeping coach.   came on as sub for City aged 43 years 5 months, then played in the last three games of the season.

Season	H	A	Pl	W	D	L
Pre-08/09			20	8	5	7
08/09	2-1	2-2	22	9	6	7
10/11	2-1	3-1	24	11	6	7

In the FA Cup, meetings in seven rounds plus a Final:
1924 SF 0-2 St Andrews
1955 Final 1-3 Wembley
1957 3rd rd 1-1 away, replay 4-5 home
1969 4th rd 1-1 away, replay 2-0 home
1975 3rd rd away but played at M/Rd 0-2
1977 4th rd away 3-1
1995 5th rd away 1-3
2002 5th rd away 0-1

First meeting in the FA Cup was in the 1924 semi-final which Newcastle won 2-0 at St. Andrews, Billy Meredith's last appearance for City at the age of 49 years 8 months.

Then the teams met in the 1955 FA Cup final which Newcastle won 3-1 against a ten man City team, Jimmy Meadows going off inured after twenty minutes. In 1956/57 the FA Cup third round game was drawn 1-1 at St. James' Park and the replay won by Newcastle 5-4 in extra time at Maine Road after City were 3-0 up at half time. City finally ended the cup jinx with a 2-0 Maine Road replay win in the fourth round of 1969.

Ged I: 29/1/1977 Newcastle 1 City 3

City's fourth round FA Cup tie at Newcastle in January 1977 really captured the imagination. It was a repeat of the previous season's League Cup Final, both teams were doing well in the League and fixtures between the two sides usually produced a few goals. There was also the added factor that Newcastle's manager, Gordon Lee, was about to leave to manage Everton, and their fans weren't happy.
We arrived about ninety minutes before kick-off and elected to park in a town centre multi-storey about ten minutes walk from the ground. We'd heard the locals were slightly "enthusiastic" so didn't show any colours but we still stood out as all the Geordies (including cats and dogs) seemed to be wearing black and white scarves whether they were going to the match or not.
The police directed us to the corner of the Gallowgate End and everything seemed normal

until about ten minutes before kick-off, when we noticed a lot of pushing and shoving in the adjacent section. A lot of kids seemed to be crushed against the front and the police were pulling them out of their pen and into ours. Then the kids started getting bigger and bigger, and there was the added worry that there seemed to be a lot of people at the back of our section who didn't speak with Mancunian accents.

Those of you below a certain age won't recognise the situation I've described, in fact you'll have difficulty comprehending such non-existent crowd segregation policies. For those who do remember the fun and games we used to endure, will have a pretty good idea of what happened over the next forty-five minutes.

Soon after kick-off there was a bit of pushing and shoving and this gradually escalated throughout the first twenty minutes. We thought we'd scored midway through the half and although it was disallowed our celebrations upset the locals and complete mayhem broke out.

Scuffles erupted all over the terracing with some fans ending up on the pitch to escape the chaos. I was near an exit and was swept down the steps to the concourse as fans tried to avoid getting caught up in the mass brawl. My return was blocked by a steady stream of policemen chucking out those they thought were responsible. One enterprising Blue stood by the exit to the street and gave each departing Geordie a bit of a dig. Unfortunately the police soon cottoned on and he too was asked to vacate the premises.

The situation worsened to such an extent that the referee took the players off the pitch for a couple of minutes while things calmed down.

It was still a bit hairy as the players returned, and it threatened to get worse as an own goal gave City the lead. Newcastle's equaliser calmed things down slightly, but Joe Royle restored the lead just before half-time and it started to kick off again.

It was a lot calmer as the second half started and within ten minutes Gary Owen made it 3-1 to end the scoring despite several decent opportunities at each end. We'd reached the fifth round, but if you think our troubles were over, we still had to get back to the car.

We were kept in the ground for about fifteen minutes as the police tried to disperse the locals, and were then split into two groups; one for the coaches and one for the train. When we asked about getting to the car park we were given a three-man (and two-dog) escort to the top of an alleyway leading to the town centre and then told to "run like f*ck"!

We did as we were told and reached the front of the car park without incident, but had one further obstacle to hurdle before we were safe. We'd parked near the top of the multi-storey so decided to wait for the lift and while we were waiting, a group of City fans halfway up the car park decided to taunt a large gang of Geordies passing the car park at street level. They couldn't reach their tormentors so turned their attention to our group and we spent a couple of frantic minutes clambering through the car park level by level until we reached the car. We still weren't safe, but armed with an array of wheel braces, hammers and screwdrivers found in the boot, we felt a bit more secure.

The drive out to the A1 was uneventful and we pulled into Washington-Birtley Services to meet up with a couple of other car loads. We also bumped into two of my cousins who were enduring a rather draughty journey as the windows of their coach had been bricked.

You might think that such an experience would dampen our enthusiasm for trips to Tyneside, but eighteen days later we went back to see Dennis Tueart and Brian Kidd score in a 2-2 draw. Even that trip wasn't without incident as we broke down at the services and had to complete the journey by bus. After the game we had to navigate our way back to Washington before calling the RAC. The problem had been a broken fuel pipe and we stemmed the flow of petrol by trapping the pipe in a door while we went to the match. Even after the completion of the repair the car stank of petrol so this time it was our turn for a draughty trip as we returned to Manchester with the windows open.

To quote a Monty Python sketch: "Tell that to the kids of today, and they just won't believe it!"

In the League Cup, meetings in one round and a Final:
1976 Final 2-1
1994/95 4th rd 1-1 home, replay 2-0 away

In 1976 City won the League Cup Final 2-1 against a flu-ridden Newcastle squad, Peter Barnes opened the scoring, Newcastle equalised, then Dennis Tueart's overhead kick, just voted the best League Cup goal of all time won it for the Blues.

Friendlies: 1979/80 a 1-4 Ian McFaul testimonial.

Some connections: Peter Beardsley, Wyn Davies, Bobby Shinton, Shay Given

Ground: St. James' Park (shown 2010) R/A 68,386 v Chelsea Div. 1 1930/31

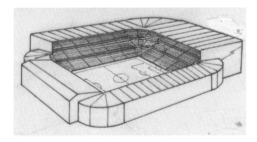

Newport County

'The Ironsides' were formed in 1912 when they moved into Somerton Park. They were elected to the newly formed Third Division in 1920, failed to gain re-election in 1931, but were elected to the Third Division South in 1932, moving back to Somerton Park, which also hosted greyhound racing. They made it to the Second Division playing one season in 1946/47, and reached the quarter finals of the European Cup Winners' Cup in 1981/82, going out to Carl Zeiss Jena of East Gerrmany, the eventual runners up, 0-0 away and 0-1 at home. They were relegated to the Football Conference in 1988 their place being taken by Lincoln City. They subsequently folded but reformed in 1989, becoming known as 'The Exiles', finally relinquishing Somerton Park in 1991.

They now play at The Newport Stadium and finished season 2010/11 in the Blue Square Premier League as Newport County, playing in amber shirts and black shorts.

Post war: The teams first met in 1946/47 in the Second Division, City winning 3-0 at Somerton Park and 5-1 at Maine Road on the 14th June 1947 the late end to the season due to the severe winter, with City having already clinched top spot a few games earlier. Roy Clarke, after signing from Third Division Cardiff City, made his debut against his home town team, going on, at the start of the next season to create the record of three games in three different Divisions!

In The League Cup: In the third round in 1962/63 City won 2-1 at Somerton Park in front of 9,898 but not many Blues there to witness it!

John L: 24/10/1962 Newport 1 City 2

If I had the chance to be transported back in time to attend any City game played during my lifetime, this is probably one of the ones I'd choose….

The new Football League Cup was still struggling to become established in 1962, this being its third year. Having overcome Blackpool (after two replays) in the second round, for the third we visited Somerton Park, home of Newport County in South Wales, on Wednesday 24th October…

The programme itself has a pale amber cover, but otherwise is a rather plain affair, and black and white throughout. An unusual feature is the team picture on the front – it's of City rather than the home team!! Inside, the brief editorial includes exhortations for County fans to get behind their team, who were having a rather average season in Division Four. Looking forward, plans were in hand for more steps on Somerton Bridge bank, although "the particular spare parts needed are proving difficult to obtain". Elsewhere, Mrs Prosser in the social club promised to "cater for all types of thirst", although I reckon that had our supporters club branch arranged a coach trip we could have fully tested that claim. Bingo tickets were popular, and with a large crowd expected for this game, there was to be a second prize of £5, with TWO first prizes of £10. Heady stuff.

The match was won by City 2-1, our first-ever away win in this competition, with Alex Harley and George Hannah notching – the

same George Hannah that had scored against City for Newcastle in the 1955 FA Cup Final. The attendance of around 10,000 was just less than double County's usual crowds. This proved to be our last ever competitive fixture in Monmouthshire, though we did send a first team for Len Ashurst's testimonial in 1982, when Newport included a certain John Aldridge.

We were just a few weeks before the famous "winter shutdown" of 1962-3, when City managed just one fixture between December 15th and March 2nd (thinking back, I got whooping cough that year….). Harry Dowd, and the youngsters Oakes and Young played, all three later collecting League and Cup winner's medals. One further point of interest (well, to me anyway) is that we used three goalkeepers in this League Cup campaign. Bert Trautmann started in goal in the second round v Blackpool, but was injured in late September, so Dowd assumed the green jersey. For some reason Steve Fleet, who hadn't played a first team game in eighteen months, was selected for the fifth round League Cup tie at Birmingham. Our campaign ended there with a disastrous 0-6 defeat, and Fleet never appeared again.

For programme collectors, these early League Cup matches can be amongst the hardest to obtain. The games were often poorly publicised – and usually quite poorly attended. You could expect to pay something over £150 for this programme now. Certain clubs (i.e. those with little or no regard for fellow members of the Football League), did not even bother to enter the League Cup until it began to establish itself with a Wembley Final and the prospect of entry into Europe.

Sadly, Somerton Park doesn't exist now, as it's been turned into a housing estate. Newport County went into liquidation in 1989, quite amazing when you think that they reached the European CWC quarter-finals in 1980/81. The club reformed within four months (as Newport County AFC), and after a traumatic five years settled at Newport Stadium, but still within the <u>English</u> FA's Pyramid system and are now in the Blue Square Premier League.

Some connections: Paul Sugrue, John McLelland, Andy Thackray

Friendly: 1982 away (Len Ashurst testimonial)

Ground: Somerton Park (shown 1960's) R/A 24,268 v Cardiff City D3 S 1937/38.

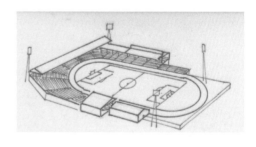

GOLDEN JUBILEE 1912-1962

Newport County a.f.c.

Vol. XII. No. 11   v. Manchester City, 24th October, 1962

DIRECTORS:
Chairman: Mr. John C. Bailey,
Vice-Chairman: Councillor Syd Jenkins,
Messrs. Horace Palmer, John Thraves, A.R.I.B.A., John Barefoot, John Harris.

Hon. Medical Adviser: W. J. Thompson, M.A., M.B., B.Ch., B.A.O.
Secretary: Mr. Keith Saunders, Assistant Secretary: Bryn Davies, Manager: W. Lucan,
Trainer: George Kitson, Assistant Trainer and Coach: Ray Wilcox.

Registered Office: SOMERTON PARK   Phone: 71542.

Official Souvenir Programme
Price – Sixpence

Northampton Town

'The Cobblers' were formed in 1897 by schoolteachers connected with the Northampton and District Elementary Schools' Association, and became original members of Division Three in 1920, playing at The County Ground, which was shared with Northamptonshire CCC.

They moved up from the Fourth Division in 1961 and made it to the First in 1965, going down after one season and finishing up back in the Fourth Division in 1969. Since then they've flitted between the lower divisions, moved to

Sixfields in 1994 (but the cricket club still play at The County Ground) and finished season 2010/11 in League Two playing in claret shirts with white shorts.

Post war: Six meetings, with four in Division Two in the early sixties, City winning only one and losing three. Then in 1998/99 in Division Two two meetings, both games being drawn, 0-0 home, 2-2 away (7,557 record).

Ex Blue defender Bill Leivers: 1/2/1964 Northampton 2 City 1

I played there in 1964 at The County Ground which was part of a cricket pitch so they had a temporary stand on one side. This bloke was abusing all the City players and in the second half when I retrieved the ball from the front of their temporary 'Kop' stand I glanced up and saw this loud mouthed idiot just as he shouted at me "You big headed bastard". So I thought it was time to shut him up, so I went up and punched him, not hard, on the nose!

At the end of the game a Police Inspector came into our dressing room. He asked "Who's the boxer then?" I said "I'm the boxer, and if you bring that same man in here and he repeats the same words, I'll hit him again whilst you're here".

His reply was "Well there are about 3/400 people out there who are saying they are sick of hearing him with his foul mouth at every game, it's about time someone shut him up."

The Police Officer said "He wants to prefer charges against you for assault". But I never heard anything more about it.

In the League Cup: Just the one meeting, in 1981/82 at Maine Road, City winning 3-1.

Some connections: Tony Adcock, Trevor Morley (below), Fred Tilson, Paul Sugrue

Ground: The County Ground (shown 1960s) R/A 24,523 v Fulham Div 1 April 1966. Sixfields capacity – 7,653

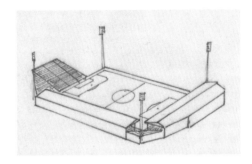

Northwich Victoria

The Vics, or The Trickies were formed around 1874 becoming a founder member of Division Two in 1892 but resigned in 1894, playing at non league level. They played at the Drill Field for 125 years before moving temporarily to Witton Albions's ground, then into the new Victoria Stadium in 2005/06. Struggles continued with ground ownership problems and they moved out to share Altrincham's Moss Lane ground.
They finished season 2010/11 in the Blue Square Conference North playing in green shirts and white shorts.

Pre-War: The teams met twice in season 1892/93, City winning 3-0 away on September 10th 1892, Vics first game, and drew 1-1 at home. In 1893/94 it was a 4-2 home win and a 4-1 away win for City.

They also played a couple of cup games at Maine Road, in 1976, beating Rochdale 2-1 in an FA Cup fourth round second replay and losing to Oldham 0-2 in the FA Cup fourth round in front of 29,000.

Some connections: Billy Meredith

Friendlies: 1892/93 H 1-0

Norwich City

'The Canaries' were formed in 1902 by two local schoolmasters, but when the FA declared the club professional and ejected them from the Amateur Cup in 1904 new officials were appointed and the club was re-established in 1905. They played at Newmarket Road until 1908, then The Nest and joined the newly formed Third Division in 1920. They moved to Carrow Road in 1935 and eventually made it to the First Division in 1972, but then hovered between the top two divisions. They won the League Cup in 1962 and 1985 and were runners up in 1973 and 1975.

Norwich finished season 2010/11 in The Championship and were promoted to the Premiership, achieving back to back promotions, having been promoted in 2010 from League One despite losing their first game 7-1 at home to Colchester (whose manager they then nicked!), playing in yellow shirts with green shorts.

Pre-war: Just the two league meetings, in Division Two in 1938/39, City winning 4-1 at home and drawing 0-0 away.

Post-war: Forty league meetings with 20 City wins 14 draws and 6 defeats.

Early sixties games were fairly even, but after that, Norwich wins were rare from the seventies onwards with City regularly winning at both home and away becoming a bogey team to the Norfolk boys.

Alan R: 30/12/1972 Norwich 1 City 1

Way back in the mists of time and in the days when British Rail would regularly run their 'Football Specials' to away games I, along with my two pals, Johnny Andrews and Allen Birkett, would occasionally use this service.

I boarded the number 169 bus to Gorton and then to Allen Birkett's front door. A quick knock and the door opened. I asked "do you fancy it?" Any doubts that I may have had about him 'fancying it' were immediately dispelled as he grabbed his coat and in no time at all we were boarding the 'special' to Norwich.

The journey was not much to write home about, it was the usual tatty British Rail carriages, an equally tatty buffet service. There was some concern when reaching the flat Cambridgeshire countryside as a heavy fog descended and the

train slowed down to almost a crawl. We had no idea how widespread the fog was but it seemed to go on for mile after mile with no end to it. Most of us had no idea of where we were, or how much farther we had to go. Eventually the train passed through a station and someone asked 'Where are we?' It's March said somebody else whilst another voice piped up, "Bleedin' 'ell, It was December when we set off!" Eventually the fog disappeared, the train picked up speed and we arrived in Norwich with loads of time to spare.

Our first move was to get to the ground to see if there were seat tickets available (you could do that in those days) and we were in luck. The next move was the pub, a few pints and a sandwich and then we were ready for the match. As we made our way to the turnstiles we had to pass a chap stood just outside the players entrance who, seeing our City colours, asked if we had tickets for the game. The gent concerned was City Director Ian Niven and we said yes we had. He then asked us if we would like to join him and other Directors for a drink after the match. We could hardly believe it as we said yes please. He then handed us two official passes and told us to meet him at the tunnel just before the end of the match. I have little memory of the match itself although the record shows that it ended all square at 1-1 with Tony Towers netting for the Blues. We made our way to the tunnel as requested and were just in time to see the Norwich centre forward receiving stitches to a head wound after coming off second best when tangling with our Tommy Booth. Ian Niven was there to meet us and he led us into the Norwich board room, asked us what we would like to drink (whiskey and Canada dry) and told us to help ourselves to the fine fare on display. We must have looked an odd pair with me in a donkey jacket and City scarf and Allen in normal match day clothes whilst all around us were the 'Suits.' Amongst those I remember being present were some of the City board members, the Bishop of Norwich, David Frost with his then girl friend the American actress Diahann Cannon (or Carroll) and Malcolm Allison. As Malcolm entered the room we smiled and nodded to him but there was not even a flicker of a smile off him in return. In fact it was as though he had never seen us. At least Ian Niven made sure that we were looked after until it was time for us to leave and make a run for the train home. That kind gesture by Ian has stayed with me for the best part of thirty seven years to remind me that Blues come from all walks of life, the common denominator being that blue shirt.

In the Premiership:
The 2005 Premiership game at Norwich was memorable for their Director Delia Smith's outburst at half time encouraging their fans to get behind their team, "Let's be 'avin' yer". It was 2-2 at half time after City pulled back from 0-2 down, and Robbie Fowler got a late winner for City, and Norwich went down that season.

Season	H	A	Pl	W	D	L
Pre- 04/05			6	2	3	1
04/05	1-1	3-2	8	3	4	1

In the FA Cup, meetings in three rounds:
1939 3rd rd 5-0 away
1963 5th rd 1-2 home City's third cup tie in ten days.
1981 4th rd 6-0 home

In the League Cup, meetings in four rounds:
1975/76 2nd rd 1-1 away, replay 2-2 home, 2nd replay 6-1 at Stamford Bridge
1978/79 4th rd 3-1 away
1989/90 3rd rd 3-1 home
2007/08 3rd rd 1-0 home

Friendlies: 1906/07 a 2-2

Some connections: Managers Ron Saunders and John Bond, Kevin Reeves (below), Darren Huckerby, Lee Croft, Justin Fashanu, Phil Boyer, Kevin Bond, Craig Bellamy…..

Ground: Carrow Road (shown 2005) R/A 43,984 v Leicester FA Cup 6th round 1963

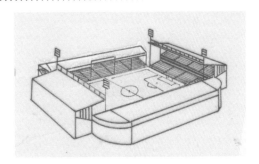

Nottingham Forest

The 'Reds' or 'Tricky Trees' were formed in 1865 in a meeting at the Clinton Arms, and were initially known as The Forest Football Club. They changed from playing 'shinney', a form of hockey, to football when they wore red caps.

They played at The Forest Racecourse, then The Meadows from 1879, Trent Bridge Cricket Ground from 1880, Parkside, Lenton from 1882, Gregory, Lenton from 1885, Town ground from 1890, then The City Ground from 1898. They also played games at Meadow Lane, including the 1946 November game v City when their pitch was waterlogged, (crowd 32,194), and in 1968 for a few games when their main stand was destroyed by fire during a match with Leeds United that August.

Forest were elected to Division One in 1892, won the FA Cup in 1898, flitted between the three divisions, won the Cup in 1959, League in 1978, European Cup in 1979 and 1980, League Cup in 1978,1979, and 1989, Simod Cup in 1989, Zenith D.S in 1992, dropped to the old Third and finished season 2010/11 in The Championship, playing in red shirts and white shorts.

Pre war: 30 league meetings with 16 City wins, including a 5-0 home win in 1905/06, and 5-4 away in 1927/28, 7 draws and 7 defeats. In 1924 a crowd of only 3,000 was recorded at Maine Road for the 1-3 loss.

Post war: 54 league meetings with 20 City wins, 16 draws and 18 defeats, one of the most notorious being the 1990 0-1 when Andy Dibble had the ball nodded out of his hand by Gary Crosby who followed up to score.

Tony P: 5/2/2000 Forest 1 City 3

City's promotion campaign (Febrary 5th 2000) under Joe Royle was well under way as City travelled to Nottingham to take on Forest. As usual, City took a massive following and we occupied the whole of one side and behind one goal. My mate Phil was working in Nottingham at the time and he booked rooms for four of us at the rough and ready hotel he was staying in. Forest got off to a great start and scored through a fantastic Bart-Williams strike, but City came back strongly and we ran out 3-1 winners. That night, the four of us celebrated the win in the pubs of central Nottingham and it seemed that many Blues had decided to do the same. Throughout the balmy evening, the occasional chants of "City" or "Blue Moon" could be heard drifting through the night air. At the end of the night we headed for the late bar at the hotel, where a group of lads from London were also having a drink. One by one we all went to bed and by the time I decided to call it a night at around 1.30am, it was getting boisterous in the bar. I thought nothing of it, bid goodnight to Phil, who decided to drink a little longer and went to bed only to be woken by banging on my bedroom door twenty minutes later. When I opened the door, Phil barged passed me and looked as if he'd seen a ghost. When I asked why he'd woken me at 2.00am, he said it had all kicked off in the bar when Chelsea supporting London lads started fighting with some other guys and he'd been caught in the middle. Still half asleep, I looked out of my bedroom window which faced the main road and could see nothing but a load of flashing blue lights. It seems as though I'd gone to bed just at the right time as ten minutes after I'd left all hell broke loose and when the police arrived they simply bundled everyone in the bar into a police van. Phil had just managed to get out in time, although not before being hit by a table; otherwise it wouldn't have just been a black eye he would have had to explain to his missus. The next morning the place looked like a battle zone, even worse than it normally did. Great result though!

In the Premiership:

Season	H	A	Pl	W	D	L
Pre-95/96			4	1	2	1
95/96	1-1	0-3	6	1	3	2

In the FA Cup, meetings in five rounds:

1902 2nd rd 0-2 home
1924 1st rd 2-0 home
1974 4th rd 1-4 away
1978 4th rd 1-2 away
2009 3rd rd 0-3 home

Forest have shocked the Blues twice in the FA Cup as a Second Division team, winning 4-1 in 1973/74, played at the City Ground on a Sunday, City's first Sunday game, owing to the power shortage, and also in 2009, winning 3-0 at COMS.

Roger R: 27/1/1974 Forest 4 City 1

Team: MacRae, Barrett, Donachie, Doyle, Booth, Towers, Summerbee, Bell, Lee, Carrodus, Marsh sub Leman.
FA Cup 4th Round.

I remember getting a lift from our next door neighbours – and they were kind enough to drop me off in Nottingham on this particular Sunday (a fairly unique occasion in those days!) so that I could visit a friend I had met on holiday. I then managed to get a lift off them to the match at the City ground - and because it was a complete "sell out" I remember having to stand on the gents toilet roof at the Trent end of the ground in the hope that I might see something. If truth be told, I hardly saw anything at all, but heard the huge roar of the home fans each time they scored! The main reason for me not seeing anything, apart form the fog that was lingering around Nottingham that day, was that there were two big blokes stood on the roof in front of me! Anyway, City famously lost the match 4-1. It was Duncan McKenzie's "special" day for Forest (then a Second Division club) and probably the first time that his name had come to the attention of the public in such a big way. It was also the time that Francis Lee famously said that City would never be a Sunday League team! Frank Carrodus scored City's consolation goal, but nobody really cared! I then had to walk through a dark and foggy Nottingham having hardly seen anything of the match to meet up with my next door neighbours once again for my lift home!

In the League Cup meetings in three rounds:

1975/76 3rd rd 2-1 home
1987/88 3rd rd 3-0 home
1993/94 4th rd 0-0 away, replay 1-2 home

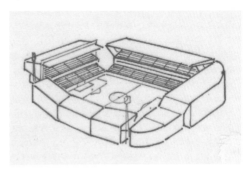

In the Zenith Data Systems Cup there's been one meeting, a 2-3 loss away in the 2nd round in 1989/90.

Friendlies: None

Some connections: Ian Bowyer, manager Frank Clark, Colin Barrett, Asa Hartford, Trevor Francis (below).

Ground: The City Ground (shown 2000's) R/A 49,946 v Man. Utd Div 1 October 1967

Notts County

'The Magpies' were formed in 1862 as the oldest club (the old joke is, "Who did they play?"), but the more likely date was 1864, being known as the Notts Football Club. They were founder members of the Football League, playing at various venues before moving to Meadow Lane from 1910.

They've been up and down the leagues making it to Division One from the Fourth in 1984 and again in 1991 for a few seasons. They won the FA Cup in 1894, and finished season 2010/11 in league One, playing in black and white striped shirts and black shorts (adopted by Juventus) with Sven as the surprising choice as Director of Football, but not for long!.

Pre-war: 46 league meetings with 24 City wins, 8 draws and 14 losses

First meetings were in 1893/94 in the Second Division, but pre-war the fixtures were mainly in the top flight with some big scores either way – 0-5 away in 1893/94, 7-1 home in 1894/95, 5-1 home in 1899/1900 and 1-5 away in 1908/09.

Post-war: 10 league meetings with 4 City wins 3 draws and 3 losses

From the 50's to the 90's league results were mixed in the ten encounters, though Jim Melrose scored a memorable goal in the 2-0 1984/85 Maine Road win, volleying home from virtually the half way line. In the penultimate game of that season City were 0-3 down at half time then Paul Simpson pulled two back to at least improve the goal difference, and give the

Blues a good chance of promotion, which was achieved in the last game v Charlton at home.

Simon C: 6/5/1985 Notts County 3 City 2

There were many signs on Saturday 6th May 1985 that all was not well, but me waking with a headache was not immediately the most obvious one. Students in Sheffield seldom survived a Friday night without a huge intake of alcohol of various colours and a massive and totally unnecessary Indian banquet to round it all off, and I was no exception.

Time to go to the match, then. By the end of this day, I would have squeezed myself into many heaving pubs and only got served in half of them, wandered around a strange and unknown city centre hearing the shouts of "Karma Karma Come On City" around every corner, seen grown men urinating in lines on the pavement, on grassy banks and all over the turnstiles, and watched in awe as chunky police horses galloped across the pitch, their riders wielding batons. I also saw City fans running across the terraces on all four sides of the stadium we were in. I watched as that hideous 80's creation perimeter fencing was removed before its time by our lads. I tried to listen to City's manager (Billy McNeill) and the opponents' manager (the late great Jimmy Sirrell) share a loud hailer to tell our end to calm down or we were out (all 13,000 of us). I saw City fans legging it down the tunnel to have a quiet word with some members of our playing staff. I watched promotion hover spectacularly into view and then be snuffed out in even more melodramatic circumstances. I felt my hangover disappear and then come thudding back three times worse just twenty minutes later and had morbid thoughts that I might never get out of Nottingham alive. This then was the promotion charabanc to Notts County, the Paul Simpson Show, the mass riot, the knees up to end all knees ups, the City comedy display to – we might have thought at the time – end all City comedy shows (subsequent games against Bournemouth, Bradford, Liverpool, Gillingham and Spurs have possibly since put this one in the shadow a little). This was the biggest invasion of an away town centre that I have ever been part of, the biggest comedy chaos carnival inside a ground that I have ever seen (and that includes Lokeren's double decker bus), both on the pitch and on the crumbling terraces, and the most unbelievable outnumbering of away fans to home fans until we later descended to the (old) Third Division in extremis (13,000 of an 18,000 crowd

wore light blue that day). In a nutshell, this, ladies and gentlemen, girls and boys, was Notts County versus Manchester City, Division Two, 1984/85 season. More fun with your clothes on you cannot have.

Tony P: 6/5/1985 Notts County 3 City 2

There was a good possibility that a City win would seal promotion and equally, County needed the points to avoid the drop. Nottingham is a hard place to drive to and my mate Jeff and I arrived just five minutes or so from kick off. The game was not all ticket and because we arrived so late, we made our way to the nearest stand and paid at the gate. It was only when we reached the top that we noticed that there seemed to be City fans in every stand, except in the one that we were in. The game was only a few minutes old when County stung us with the opening goal, midway through the half; they added a second and a third just before half time. It was the first time I'd ever been in the company of home fans and I can't say I enjoyed it. The County fans couldn't believe it and went crazier as each goal went in. I doubt that my polite applause at County's goals had anyone fooled, but the fans around me were too happy to notice. At half time, many of the City fans, who'd been drinking before and during the game began playfully running on the pitch to be chased by police and stewards, but as more fans joined in, things began to turn ugly and they began to take out their frustrations on Meadow Lane. Jimmy Sirrell made an appearance and pleaded through a megaphone for the fans to stop, but some Blues hoped that they could force an abandonment and continued until the referee announced that the game would go on, whatever. The locals around me were very unhappy, threatening to throw trouble makers into the nearby River Trent. I was a little worried that my Manchester accent would give me away, so I avoided speaking to anyone, until someone noticed that I had a radio with me and asked how Cardiff and Middlesbrough were getting on. I got away with my mock unknown accent and in a way; I was pleased to be with the home fans as it was the one stand that the police weren't going to target after the game.

In the FA Cup: Meetings in four rounds:
1962 3rd rd 1-0 away
1991 5th rd 0-1 away
1995 3rd rd 2-2 away, replay 5-2 home
2011 4th rd 1-1 away, replay 5-0 home

City crashed out of the cup in the fifth round at Meadow Lane in 1991 to a late goal after hitting the post and bar on numerous occasions (record receipts of £124,539), but gained revenge with a 5-2 third round replay win in 1995 after a 2-2 away draw. In 2011 a late goal from Edin Dzeko saved the Blues from an embarrassing defeat, then City won the replay 5-0 in the march to Cup Final victory.

In the League Cup: Meetings in four rounds:
1964/65 5th rd 1-0 away
1980/81 4th rd 5-1 home
1998/99 1st rd 1st leg 2-0 away, 2nd leg 7-1 home
2001/02 2nd rd 4-2 away aet

On September 11th 2001, the day of the World Trade Centre attacks in New York, City won 4-2 at Meadow Lane, after extra time in a game of subdued atmosphere which really shouldn't even have been played.

Friendlies: 1892/93 h 3-3, 1897/98 a 3-2, 1956/57 a 2-1, 1979/80 a 2-0,

Some connections: Dave Watson, Kasper Schmeichel, manager Sven G. Eriksson

Ground: Meadow Lane (shown 2011) R/A 47,310 v York City FA Cup 6th round 1955

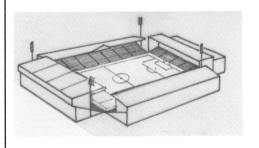

Friendlies:

Newton Heath see Man United.
Newtown 1895/96 h 2-3
Northern Nomads 1902/03 h 2-2, 1908/09 a 9-1,
Northwich District X1 1906/07 a 0-4,
Northwich and Witton X1 1913/14 a 5-3
Northern Premier League X1 1973/74 a 2-2
New South Wales 1969/70 a 2-1,4-1
Northern NSW 1969/70 a 4-1
Nigerian Forces 1974/75 a a 2-1
Napoli 1978/79 a 1-2
New York Cosmos 1979/80 a 2-3
NAC Brada 1980/81 a 3-2
Nuneaton Borough 1980/81 a 3-1
NIK Nykarleby IF 1987/88 a 5-0
New York Red Bulls 2010/11 a 1-2

COSMOS
VS.
MANCHESTER CITY

WEDNESDAY, MAY 21, 1980
GIANTS STADIUM/THE MEADOWLANDS

FIRST ANNUAL TRANS-ATLANTIC CUP

O is for Oldham

The **O's** take us over to Oldham, Cyprus, and down to Oxfordshire...

Oldham Athletic

'The Latics' were formed in 1895 as Pine Villa, but when Oldham County folded Villa took over their ground at Sheepfoot Lane and changed their name to Oldham Athletic. They moved to Hudson Fold after only one season but moved back to Boundary Park in 1906 and joined Division Two in 1907. They finished as runners up in 1915, but after relegation in 1923 remained in the lower leagues until the introduction of their plastic pitch and promotion to the top flight in 1991, after they lost the League Cup Final 1-0 to Forest in 1990. After relegation in 1994 they've struggled and finished season 2010/11 in League One playing in blue shirts and white shorts.

Pre-war: 24 league meetings with City winning 14 drawing 3 and losing 7, in the Second, but mainly the First Division.

Post-war: 14 league meetings with 6 City wins including a 5-2 at Oldham on the last day of the 1991/92 season, City finishing in 5th place for the second season running, 3 draws including 1984 when there were pitch invasions prior to the kick off by City fans, and 5 losses.

August 1987, City played at Oldham on a red hot day. City fans were generally dressed in T-shirts, jeans and trainers. Sadly the heavens opened and powerfully dropped freezing rain on us . It was the coldest I'd been at a footie match, certainly in August! City only managed a 1-1 draw at the aptly named Ice Station Zebra! It was also the day that Frank Newton's banana craze started with a single inflatable nicknamed 'Imre Banana' (after Imre Varadi)

Tony P: 20/4/1984 Oldham 2 City 2

As always, the local derby against Oldham at Boundary Park on Good Friday was well attended by travelling Blues, who, as you would expect in those pay-on-the-door days, infiltrated all four sides. The main body of City fans were behind the goal in the open end, but my mate Jeff and I were in the lower paddock alongside of the pitch. Across from us in the Main Stand, trouble was brewing as

Oldham fans objected to the City fans who were in there. Several fights broke out and from where I stood; I had a perfect view of an incident that could have ended up with a steward being killed. A lone steward had ventured into the seats to try to eject a group of City fans. He must have thought himself a bit of a hard man because instead of waiting for help from fellow stewards or police, he began fighting with a City fan and was either pushed off the stand or lost his footing. Either way he was clinging on to the edge of the top tier of the stand for dear life. Fortunately for him, help was on hand and he was pulled up to safety.

In the Premiership:

Season	H	A	Pl	W	D	L
92/93	3-3	1-0	2	1	1	0
93/94	1-1	0-0	4	1	3	0

In the FA Cup, meetings in two rounds:
1912 2nd rd 0-1 home
2005 3rd rd 0-1 away, when lowly placed Latics in League One won 1-0 at a cold and windy Boundary Park as City manager Kevin Keegan slumped lower and lower into his roll neck jumper.

Texaco Cup 1974/75 h 2-1

Some connections: Bobby Johnstone, Roger Palmer, Ricky Holden, Kenny Clements, Ken Branagan, Bert Lister, Joe Royle, Paul Dickov, Paul Moulden, Earl Barrett, Rickie Holden and managers Jimmy Frizzell and Les McDowall

Bobby Johnstone

Friendlies: 1896/97 a 0-2 (Oldham County) 1953/54 a 0-0, 1972/73 (Jimmy Frizzell T/M) 4-1, 1973/74, 2-2, 1974/75 RF, 1976/77 (Wood T/M) 1-3, 1983/84 (Dewhirst T/M) , 1985/86 h 3-1, 1986/87 a (Gary Hoolickin T/M) 3-3, 1989/90 a 0-2, 1990/91 (R. Palmer T/M) h 2-3, 1994/95 IOM 0-3, 2000/01 a 4-1, 2001/02 a * , 2003/04 a 6-0,

Ground: Boundary Park (Shown 2005) R/A 47,671 v Sheff. Wed. FA Cup 4 1930

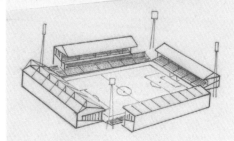

AC Omonoia

'The Greens' were formed in 1948 when players left Apoel F.C. due to political differences – common even today in Cypriot football. They entered the First Division in 1953. Since then they've won nineteen league titles, twelve Cypriot Cups and fourteen Super Cups, but recent struggles – Omonia finished only third in 2007/08 - had caused a change of Board and the introduction of new players.

After City had come safely through the qualifying rounds, the two teams met in the first round of the 2008/09 UEFA Cup, meaning a trip to Nicosia, the furthest that City have ever travelled to play a first team competitive fixture. Coming into the City game Omonia were joint top of their division. This was their thirty fourth season in Europe and they had only once previously met English opposition, in the first round of the Cup Winners' Cup in 1994/95 losing 6-1 on aggregate to Arsenal.

They progressed to this round by beating F.K. Miano 3-2 on aggregate and AEK Athens also 3-2 in the qualifying rounds. Colours were green shirts with white shorts alternatively all white with red and green stripe on the right.

The island of Cyprus only had one UEFA

standard stadium, the 23,000 capacity GSP Arena, and with Anorthosis claiming that for a Champions League game, the two clubs agreed to reverse the UEFA fixtures meaning that City were to play the away leg first. City won that 2-1 with around 900 Blues present, and then won the return leg, also 2-1 at COMS in front of 25,304 with 1560 very lively Omonia fans

Sean R: 13/9/2008 Omonia 1 City 2

This was a round trip of just under 4,600 miles and ten hours flying time for the trip from Manchester to Larnaca.

The decision was taken by UEFA to switch the ties around which made the journey, not to mention the cost, so much more difficult. The official trip only had thirty eight places up for grabs, and with no other options in the pipeline, I reluctantly booked for the three day package. It was a case of work most of the day on the day before the match, then travel over to Manchester Airport to join up with two hundred unsuspecting holiday passengers on the same flight. Familiar faces from past and present were clocked, and a couple of worried looking reds who'd not realised half the plane was going to be occupied mainly by City fans!

With the time difference of two hours, our arrival was around 1am local time, so we were grateful for the short transit time into the seaside town of Larnaca, and the Sun Hall Hotel. A few of the party went straight out to find the bars, but with a long three day stint facing me, I decided to grab some shuteye to re-charge the batteries! Twenty odd degrees in the middle of the night, what's all that about….??!!!

The day of the game was already upon us, and a leisurely time was spent beside the pool.

The coach turned up at 5.45pm to take us the thirty miles or so to the outskirts of Nicosia, where the game was to be played. The scorched earth and barren hills around us were a stark reminder that whilst we bemoan the rain back home, some countries don't see any for months.

As we approached the sports complex, it seemed like the locals had just abandoned their cars on the dirt tracks (their version of our B roads?!), and their dark green shirts, together with the Shamrock logo on the club crest made it look like a Celtic supporters club gathering.

Once again, the programmes were handed out free of charge (and having paid £33/45 euros for a match ticket it was the least they could do) Once inside the stadium, I was surprised to

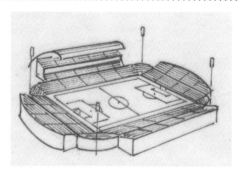

see that so many City fans had actually made the journey. The home support is noisy an hour and half before kick off, fair play to 'em, a reminder of how it used to be back at home before all seater stadiums etc.

Despite our numerous missed chances they went ahead direct from a free kick Our reaction was swift, and Jo was on hand to tap in the equaliser. We celebrated the goal and kept up the repertoire of City songs, new and old. Not long afterwards our Argentinian acquisition Zabaleta stormed down the right hand side before picking out Jo, who brought the ball under control before drilling home what would prove to be the match-winning goal.

After being held for a short while, City fans were allowed to disperse, and return to the various parts of the island where they had based themselves. Our return to Lanarca saw us hit the town, one particular highlight being a group of us in a techno/dance bar, bopping away to a remix of the Pigbag classic, and chanting the name of Martin Petrov in the chorus (we must have done this for four hours non stop), and if the locals weren't aware of him before tonight, they certainly were now……..! With two full days left to explore the island (well the bars to be more precise!), I have to say I was impressed.

Our official party of thirty eight had an absolutely cracking time, plenty of laughs, and banter.

Oswaldtwisle Rovers

City should have played the Lancashire Combination team at Hyde Road on 12th October 1895 in the FA Cup but withdrew and the fixture was deleted from the records

Oxford United

The 'U's' were formed in 1893 as Headington United who moved from The Paddock to the Manor Ground in 1925. Having changed its name to Oxford United the club was elected to Division Four in 1962 taking the place of Accrington Stanley. Oxford moved up the divisions, with chairman Robert Maxwell, even winning the League Cup in 1986, then went back down again and dropped to the Conference in 2006, after moving to the Kassam Stadium in 2001. Ironically a rejuvenated Stanley took their place! They finished season 2010/11 in the Blue Square Conference wearing gold shirts with blue shorts

Post war: Ten league meetings, City winning five drawing one losing four. First league meetings were in 1984/85 when both clubs gained promotion to the First Division.

Dave A: 29/4/1989 Oxford 2 City 4

April 1989: Promotion was still on the agenda with four games to go but we came into this match on the back of two defeats. We'd been thrashed by Blackburn at Ewood Park, 4-0, and had lost at home to Barnsley, 1-2, the previous week. But football was being played in the awful shadow and aftermath of the Hillsborough Disaster which had occurred only two weeks previously.

My mother was staying with us for the weekend and she and I drove down from Honley. We met up at the ground with some City friends, from Welwyn Garden City.

Oxford, of the dreaming spires, is very attractive, but industrial Oxford of the failing British motor manufacturing industry is not.

We lined up with Dibble, Lake, Hinchcliffe, Megson, Ian Brightwell, Redmond, White, Moulden, Morley, McNab, Gleghorn. No subs were used but David Oldfield was on the bench. We started well, went 1-0 up through Ian Brightwell but then fell away and were losing 2-1 by half-time.

My mother hadn't brought a flask and the half time queues for tea and/or toilets were lengthy so just after the start of the second half she went to the loo and said she could get us some tea or coffee on the way. She was gone about five minutes. By the time she came back to her seat we were 4-2 up with goals from Nigel Gleghorn, David White and an own goal from Colin Greenall. Greenall, a Lancastrian, was a bit of a journeyman footballer who had been signed by Oxford earlier that season to replace Tommy Caton who had been sold to Charlton. I still remember with great affection poor Tommy Caton. Four years and a day from the date of this game at Oxford Tommy died at 30 years of age from a heart attack.

But for years afterwards whenever City were losing at half time we used to ask my mother to do a Greenall and go to the loo or to buy some tea! It never really worked again and not to the same extent.

So we won comfortably in the end but one of my abiding memories of supporting City over 60 years is the scene as we left the ground. As we came out, presumably as part of some ill conceived security measure in reaction to the Hillsborough Disaster, there were well over 200 police dressed in riot gear, all holding batons and riot shields, waiting for us outside. There had been no trouble at the game, we were all happy but the impact of this sight nearly produced a nasty reaction in the collective mind of the few hundred City fans. Good sense prevailed but it was a seriously chilling moment and could have led to a serious confrontation.

Hillsborough, Maxwell, riot police, Tommy Caton were the tragic and odd threads of the memories of a successful season for City but overall it was a tragic one for football.

In the FA Cup the team's met in the third round of 1973/74 at Oxford, City winning 5-2

Some connections: Paul Simpson, Tommy

Caton (below), Imre Varadi, Bobby MacDonald
Friendlies: 1970/71 a 1-4, 1971/72 a John Shuker testimonial 3-2

Ground: Manor Ground (shown 1980's) R/A 22,730 v Preston FA Cup 6th Rd 1964.Kassam Stadium cap 12,500

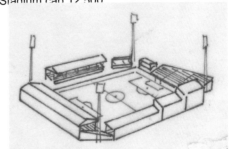

Friendlies:

Old Reptonians 1891/92 h 1-0
Oakland Clippers 1967/68 a 0-3
Olympiakos 1971/72 a 0-0, 1972/73 a 1-2, and a 0-0, 1982/83 0-2 a, 2005/06 T Cook h 3-1
Ope I.F a 1972/73 a 8-0
F.C. Osterode a 1983/84 4-0
Old Reds X1 Zebrugge 1986/87 ,
Obbola IK 1988/89 a 5-1
Off a 1988/89 a 7-1
Oslo Gret a 1989/90 3-3
Ornskoldsvikviks a 1990/91 4-1
Orgyte 2007/08 a 4-0
Orlando Pirates 2009/10 a 0-2

P is for Peterborough

The P's take us to Northamptonshire, the south coast, the Potteries and Lancashire...

Paris Saint Germain

Paris St. Germain were formed in 1970 when Paris FC merged with Stade St Germain. However Paris FC retained their name after promotion to the First Division in 1971, and PSG reformed to join the Third Division making it back to the First in 1974 whilst FC Paris were eventually relegated to the Second, then Third Division. They are owned by an American Investment Company, Colony Capital/Morgan Stanley (but now Qatar), and were founder members of G14.

PSG won the French Cup in 1982 and 1986, the title in 1986, the European Cup Winners' Cup in 1996 with George Weah, David Ginola and Youri Djorkaeff.

They qualified for the UEFA competition in 2008 after winning the French League Cup and in the first round beat Kayserispor from Turkey 2-1 on aggregate but lost at Schalke 1-3. They drew 2-2 at home to Real Racing club and went on to play Twente at home.

Connections are George Weah, Nicolas Anelka, Ali Benarbia, Alioune Tioure and Sylvain Distin, and they were managed by Paul Le Guen who had an unsuccessful stint at Rangers.

Ground is the Parc des Princes, which has a capacity of 46,480, and the club has a fan group called the Boulogne boys who are far right wing racist and anti Semitists. After a game v Hapoel Tel Aviv in 2006/07 season in the UEFA Cup which they lost 2-4 there were riots and Police informed them they must disband or face jail. At the recent Schalke game their fans were strip searched and relieved of all sorts of stuff – flares, knives, bottles etc. but our boys in blue sorted them out at COMS.

Season 2007/08 PSG finished 16th. Former players included Robert, Ochocha, Wilkins, Cisse, Heinze, Ardiles. At the time of playing City they were in 6th place with 26 points and home strip is blue with a red stripe.

The teams first met in the group stage of the UEFA Cup in December 2008 playing out a 0-0 draw at COMS.

Some connections: Nicolas Anelka, Ali Benarbia (shown)

Peterborough United

'The Posh' were formed in 1923 as Peterborough and Fletton, but suspended by the FA in 1932/33 and disbanded. In 1934.

The new club was formed by local enthusiasts, entering the Midland League a year later when they moved into London Road, but were not elected to the Football League until 1960 taking the place of Gateshead in Division Four.

They finished season 2010/11 in League One being promoted to The Championship, playing in royal blue shirts with white shorts.

Ground: London Road (shown 1981) R/A 30,096 V Swansea FA Cup 5th rd 1965

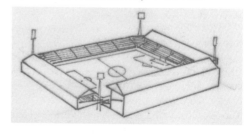

Dave W: 14/2/1981 Peterboro' 0 City 1

The one and only meeting of the two teams came in the FA Cup fifth round of 1980/81, which City won 1-0 with a Tommy Booth goal in front of 27,780 at London Road. There was much scuffling going on after the game and I myself was accosted by a (presumably) Gentleman farmer who was irate as he thought City were lucky. I was also able to obtain a newspaper photograph with Tommy Booth in action and me, my mate Eddie and Dave Ansbro, though I didn't know him then, could be clearly seen in the paddock in front of their main stand. I remember Dave giving their players merciless but amusing stick all through the game!

Plymouth Argyle

'The Pilgrims' were formed in 1886, as Argyle Athletic Club taking the name Argyle (or Argyll) which was a popular name throughout the land owing to Queen Victoria's interest in Scotland. They moved into Home Park in 1901; became Plymouth Argyle in 1903 and were a founder member of Division Three in 1920. They spent most of their time in the lower leagues and finished season 2010/11 in League One, being relegated to League Two, as well as going into administration, playing in green and black striped shirts and black shorts.

Pre-war there were just two meetings in 1938/39 in Division Two, City losing 1-3 at home and drawing 0-0 away.

Post War: Twelve meetings with six City wins, two draws and four defeats. City started off well with a double at Christmas 1946, 4-3 at home on the 25th, 24,532, then the teams headed to the station for the return game on the 26th which City won 3-2 in front of a slightly bigger attendance of 28,617. City then lost four on the bounce at Home Park, once, in 1987/88, after being 2-0 up only to lose 3-2, before the 1-0 triumph in 1988/89. Home games being generally won or drawn by each team.

In the FA Cup just the one meeting, in the fifth round of 1987/88 City winning 3-1 at Maine Road.

In the League Cup in 1973/74 City played a two legged semi-final, drawing 1-1 away (30,390) and winning 2-0 at Maine Road (40,117) Then

in the 1987/88 second round first leg it was a 1-0 home win and 6-3 away win in the second leg.

This game was postponed for a day and formed part of the longest travelling week in City's domestic history - Ipswich away on the Saturday, Plymouth away twice in the League Cup mid week, then away again on the Saturday to Plymouth.

Those that travelled with the supporters club were presented with a certificate!

Neil S: 15/10/1988 Plymouth 0 City 1

Miles upon miles of endless queues and concrete, occasionally interrupted by an overpriced sandwich at Hilton Park or its south west cousin. A game at Home Park has always been a tortuous expedition.

Like most City supporters, I associate Plymouth with a series of matches at the back end of the 1980s. I attempted the journey on three occasions, but only witnessed two fixtures.

When you travel to Plymouth you're not exactly ecstatic when City throw away a two goal lead and lose in the last minute. I was stood on the open terrace and the only thing I remember is that all the goals were scored at the other end. Nobody spoke for hours.

The following season, City played a midweek cup match at Plymouth and repeated the journey three days later. This was the week when the supporters' coaches got as far as Taunton before discovering that the cup game had been postponed.

My holiday entitlement didn't extend to the restaged game the following evening. I wasn't offered a refund and in typical City tradition they contrived to score six goals without my support.

For the third time, in 1988 I travelled on a supporters coach from Maine Road. Mick Chandley was an expert on motorway service stations and by the time we reached Plymouth I wasn't far behind. The Steward was also a Salford Rugby League fan and followed England all over Europe. Years later, I spotted him at Porto airport on the way home from Euro 2004.

We were gasping for a drink and made our way to the city centre. The locals were friendly and we had a stroke of luck in the shape of a pub landlord with two complimentary tickets. We bought him a pint and the tickets were ours.

We sat in the Main Stand with the City supporters to our right. This was the period when the inflatable craze was still taking everyone by surprise. It certainly amused the home supporters when the Alligator gave Scooby Doo a good kicking.

The game was drifting towards stalemate until a late City surge forced a number of corners. We were hardly set piece specialists and perhaps this lulled Plymouth into a sense of misguided complacency. Brian Gayle was unmarked at the far post and the away end was a sea of bananas.

We arrived back in Manchester at about 10pm and ended up supping with the local Hearts Supporters Club in the Brunswick. We compared notes on long coach journeys before catching the last train home.

In the Simod Cup in 1987/88 first round it was a 6-2 home win

Some connections: Tony Book, Malcolm Allison, Barry Silkman

T. Book *(Man. City)*

Friendlies: 1908/09 a 3-2, 1972/73 a (Bickle T/M), 2-2 ,1996/97 a 0-1,

Ground: Home Park (shown 1988) R/A 43,596 v Aston Villa D2 1936/37

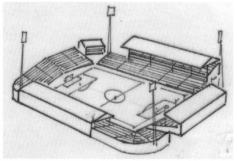

Portsmouth

'Pompey' were formed in 1898 playing at Fratton Park. They entered the Southern League in 1899, and joined Division Three in 1920. They made it to the First Division in 1927, pipping City on goal difference for the second spot, lost the Cup Final in 1934, won it in 1939 then again in 2008, plus were League Champions in 1949 and 1950. They also managed to drop down to the Fourth Division, coming back to The Premiership in 2003 where they finished season 2009/10 in administration, playing in blue shirts with white shorts, being relegated, losing in the Cup Final to Chelsea, then finished 2010/11 in The Championship.

Pre-war: 22 league meetings, all but two in Division One, with 9 City wins, 5 draws and 8 defeats.

Post war: 42 league meetings with 21 City wins 9 draws and 12 defeats. City didn't manage a win at Fratton until 1955/56 at the eighth attempt, after that losing only once in the next ten. In 2002 City, already Champions, won 3-1 at home, scoring their 108th goal of the campaign. If Stuart Pearce hadn't missed a late penalty a record 109 goals would have been registered.

Ian C: (Portsmouth fan) 5/3/1997 City 1 Portsmouth 1 - sometimes you wish you'd missed the ferry

I only went to Maine Road once, although I remember it well - some trips seem doomed from the start. Grandad always told me not to go to pubs before the sun went down. It was a rule he always observed - every day! A midweek evening kick off 'Up North', never a favourite for Pompey fans, especially those based 'offshore' on the Isle of Wight, but a complimentary ticket from a friend of a friend of that old City favourite Lee Bradbury was not to be sniffed at. We arrived at the assembly hostelry mid morning, plenty of time for the 12.30 coach departure, was the second mistake. Skipping breakfast was the first! Heading north through the steady drizzle with an increasingly queasy stomach and the steady throbbing at the temple, the ominous precursor of a migraine was temporarily fended off by a quick kip at the 5pm pub stop. As the wet weather and resulting heavy traffic had slowed the expedition, it occurred to me the two hours spent in the Newcombe Arms girding our loins would have been better spent pounding the A34. The wise heads consulted, calculated, estimated and decided. Time for a quick half and a pie. An hour later the usual miscreants were hauled protesting from the Snug, still clutching various pastry encased scoff. The increasing precipitation and decreasing speed of advance resulted in an unedifying scrummage of sundry waterproofs being hastily assembled and a rush for the turnstiles. Being complimentary, my companion Brent and I had to locate our own entrance, and, for the record, the Maine Road turnstiles were lower than 6'6" - I am higher than 6'6"- and could have done without the bash on the bonce! Entering at speed, missing the kick off and failing to locate a programme added to my increasing disillusionment about Manchester!

The Match - Pompey scraped a 1-1 draw, courtesy of a late Fitzroy Simpson equaliser. The retreat South was much of a semi-conscious blur, only to be rudely awakened by being deposited at Cosham, a northern suburb of Portsmouth, at some ungodly hour. We had blissfully assumed there would be a stop at the Harbour, but the coach driver, having dropped all his regulars, was off home and we were abandoned to the streets. An exorbitant taxi fare, despite Brent being ' in the trade' led to our only bit of good fortune of the trip. The ferry was late leaving (only a two hourly service at night). An hour crossing, twenty minute drive and hit the sheets about 4am.

I had set out with high hopes of a good look at one of the great traditional cathedrals of English football and the surrounding infrastructure but regrettably, the glory of Maine Road, Moss Side, the Curry Mile and all those atmospheric locations conjured up by the many great articles in KOTK was denied me and now it's gone forever. Not one of our best away days, but certainly one to remember

In The Premiership:
In 2003 it was the first league game at COMS a 1-1 draw and David Seaman's debut, in front of 46,287. A 6-0 win was clocked up at COMS in 2008/09.

Season	H	A	Pl	W	D	L
Pre-08/09			10	4	3	3
08/09	6-0	0-1	12	5	3	4
09/10	2-0	1-0	14	7	3	4

In the FA Cup, meetings in two rounds. City won the 1934 Cup Final 2-1, and the teams met again in the third round of 1936 which City won 3-1 at M/Rd, 53,340.

The 1934 Cup Final was memorable in many respects. City had returned to Wembley after captain Sam Cowan promised they would after losing the previous year's final to Everton 0-3. City, playing in maroon shirts and white shorts, went a goal down in the 26th minute from a terrific shot from Rutherford which Frank Swift thought he would have saved if he hadn't discarded his gloves pre-match. It looked like Pompey manager Jack Tinn's lucky white spats were doing the trick again. Freddie Tilson at half time told Swift not to worry as he'd "plonk in two in next 'arf". Brave talk, but when Pompey's Jimmy Allen went off for treatment Tilson did plonk one in, then three minutes from time, as promised, he scored his second and City's winner. Referee Stanley Rous eventually blew for time, nineteen year old Frank Swift then fainted and Sam went up to collect the Cup for the second time in City's history. The game was partly played in a thunderstorm.

In the League Cup the only meeting was in 1960/61 a 2-0 Pompey win at Fratton, the single sheet programme being the rarest City League Cup issue worth today about £300, if it can be found.

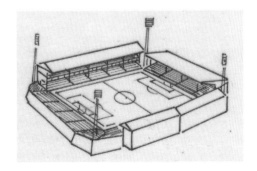

Some connections: Benjani, Fitzroy Simpson, David James, Sylvain Distin, Lee Bradbury, Kit Symons, managers Alan Ball and Ron Saunders

Friendlies: 1929/30 a 1-2, 1967/68 2-0 a; 1974/75 a 3-3, 1994/95 a 2-1

Ground: Fratton Park (Shown 1950's) R/A 51,385 v Derby FA Cup 6 1949

Port Vale

'The Valiants' were formed in 1876 playing at Moorland Road adopting the pre-fix Burslem in 1884 but dropping it in 1909 when they moved to Cobridge Athletic Ground. They entered Division Two in 1892 then it was ins and outs of the Division plus moving to the Old Recreation Ground in 1913. They were again elected to Division Two in 1919 taking over Leeds City's fixtures, then moved to Vale Park in 1950.

Generally a lower division club, Vale were in fact expelled from the League in 1968 for financial irregularities but were elected back into Division Four the following season.

They finished season 2010/11 in League Two playing in white shirts and black shorts.

Pre-war: 16 league meetings, all in the Second Division with City winning 14, drawing one and losing one.

There was an 8-1 win at home in 1893/94 and a 7-1 at home in 1902/03, when it was 5-0 at half time and the referee had to persuade Vale to come out for the second half! In 1918/19 season a 6-1 and 5-1 double was recorded.

Post-war: Just six league meetings in the 1990's; City winning three and losing three in Division One.

In one of these games, the night match in 1996 Levenshulme's Supporters Club Branch gave the first rendition of 'Lucky's' 'City 'til I Die' The anthem now adopted by the rest of football. He received no royalties for it.

In the FA Cup: Just the one meeting in the fourth round in 1991 City winning 2-1 at Vale Park.

Simon C: 26/1/1991 P.Vale 0 City 1

Burslem. January. Kilns as far as the eye can see. Smoke drifting across a grey pocked landscape. I felt like one of Blakes Seven, disembarking onto the mistrusting shifting sands of Alpha Potter. The FA Cup travels to all corners of our green and pleasant land and sets foot in some inglorious little nooks and crannies. This was one of those days. This part of my life was being carried out in various foreign countries in a vain attempt to get the exuberance of youth out of my system. It was proving hard to get rid of. I therefore descended on the Potteries direct from Venice or some fleshpot town on the continent

with a ticket that had come from my usual round the houses thank you ma'am routine. A female friend, a tour guide, whose parents lived in the Black Country, sufficiently close to Stoke to know someone who knew someone else, who had managed to smuggle a ticket out for me. I would be going to see my beloved City at Port Vale in the Cup. As usual I was in for a shock. This was the stadium that started out being called The Wembley of the North. When I got there it hardly merited rejoicing in the title Vale Park. The Main Stand was made of wood and less spacious than when the architect dreamt of Nat Lofthouse and Tom Finney, the Queen Mum and Abide with Me. My ticket seemed to be aiming me towards the middle of what was jokingly being referred to as the Main Stand. I took my seat surrounded by a set of people in bobble hats and flat caps and was immediately struck by my partner for the match. A round faced man tucking into the last dregs of a hot flask. I was more of a beer and vodka man in those days so the warm cloud of coffee gas coming over left me slightly non-plussed. Then he looked at me, apologised for taking up so much room, asked me if I could put his flask under my seat and began the match commentary. This was tone deaf, monotone, slow delivery Bert, the in-house club video commentator for Port Vale F.C. productions. Stardom by proximity faced me. I wasn't to know it, but, apart from getting my picture taken pointing smilingly at Kit Symons' black eye, after he had made an impressive clearance into his own face during a relegation battle with Bradford, this was to be the closest I ever got to football TV stardom. If you are one of the lucky few to own a copy of the official Port Vale video of this match (they sold at least eleven, so you might be), you can not only take pleasure from Bert's one tone, death-is-coming, dead-slow-stop commentary, but also the audible yelps and squeaks in the immediate background of a youthful City fan caught in the middle of a terrifyingly weird experience.

No League Cup or Premiership meetings.

Friendlies: 1899/1900 a 3-2, 1971/72 a 1-0 1981/82 (J.Miller T/M) 2000/01 (Foyle T/M) a Robbie Williams 'starred', 2006/07 a 3-0

Some connections: manager Brian Horton, Alex Williams

Ground: Vale Park (shown 1990's): R/A 49,768 v Aston Villa FA Cup 5 1960

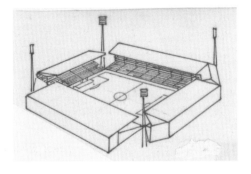

Preston North End

'The Lilywhites' were formed in 1881 and were founder members of the Football League in 1888, playing at Deepdale.

They won the First Division title in 1889 and 1890, nicknamed The Invincibles, and were runners up six times, last in 1958.

They won the Cup in 1889 and 1938, were runners up five times, but after 1961 sank down to the Fourth Division, recovered somewhat and finished season 2010/11 in the Championship being relegated, playing in white shirts and navy shorts.

Pre-war: 46 league meetings with 25 City wins including a 6-1 in 1904/05 at home, 10 draws and 11 losses. Frank Roberts made his debut at Preston in October 1922, a 2-0 win

Post war: 36 league meetings with 13 City wins 5 draws and 18 losses, including a 2-6 in 1952/53, 0-5 in 1954/55 – the introduction of 'the Revie Plan', Bill Leivers' debut, and 1-6 with The Marsden Plan' in 1957/58 but recorded a 5-1 in 1959/60 and a 5-2 in 1964/65, all at Deepdale.

Neil S: 10/2/2000 City 3 Preston 2

Pain, Plaster and Preston - On reflection, my reaction to the City equalizer was perhaps a trifle too aggressive. I was surrounded by a group of sneering United supporters and their mere presence had affected my judgement. Tempers were fraying and the neutrals were pleading for calm. Stepping Hill Hospital was a cauldron of hatred.

The previous Thursday my football career had ended rather painfully at New Mills Leisure centre. It was a typical reckless forward's tackle, but without Andy Gray making a ridiculous apology for Paul Scholes. Four days under a surgeon's knife with the Salvation Army offering soap on a rope as a consolation.

The morphine wore off approximately ten minutes before kick off. City were at home to Preston and the game was live on Granada. To add insult to injury, the lad who broke my ankle had also borrowed my season ticket.

I'd always admired Preston, but in 2002 they were one of our promotion rivals. Earlier in the season I'd travelled to Deepdale for the 2-1 defeat. Jon Macken had scored a spectacular winner from the half way line. Who could have predicted on such a depressing afternoon that Macken would later clinch the most dramatic comeback in the entire history of the FA Cup?

The bloke in the next bed was suffering from gout. He was friendly enough, but the Cantona pyjamas were always going to form a major obstacle.

My worst fears were confirmed when his family arrived, just in time for the Preston opener. All six of them cheered.

For the next ten minutes I sat and sulked in total silence as our Stretford cousins milked their obsession with ridiculing anything in a sky blue shirt. Thankfully, there was plenty of time remaining and City had talent in abundance.

Was it Goater or Wanchope? I don't recall, but as the equalizer hit the net, my crutch went flying across the ward. I pleaded innocence, but I was guilty on all counts. The nurse gave me a yellow card and threatened to turn the television off.

In time honoured tradition the United supporters left before the final whistle. City won 3-2 and my ankle was on the mend.

In the FA Cup, meetings in seven rounds from 1897 to 1948 then a gap of sixty years until 2007!

1897 1st rd 0-6 away

1902 1st rd 0-0 away abandoned in extra time, replay 4-2 away aet

1903 1st rd 1-3 away

1912 1st rd 1-0 away – Goalkeeper Walter Smith cried off just before kick off and Jimmy Goodchild played in goal, saving a penalty and Wynn scored a last minute winner!

1915 1st rd 0-0 away, replay 3-0 home

1925 1st rd 1-4 away

1948 5th rd 0-1 home
2007 5th rd 3-1 away

Friendlies: 1891/92 h 2-2, 1894/95 h 1-2, 1896/97 h 0-1, 1897/98 a 0-4, 1971/72 a (Alex Spavin T/M) 3-2, 1973/74 (Ross T/M) a * 1985/86 a 1-1,1998/99 a 3-2, (Shankly Tournament) 2002/03 (Ryan Kidd T/M) *

Some connections: Neil Young, Dave Connor, Jon Macken.

Ground: Deepdale (shown 2007) R/A 42,684 v Arsenal D1 1938

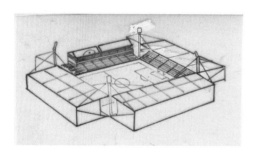

Friendlies:
P.Munster 1955/56 a 3-1
PSV Pforzheim a 1955/56 3-1
Pennsylvania UK 1957/58 6-1
Partick Thistle (In Sweden) 1972/73 5-0, 1976/77 (Tennent Caledonian Cup 3rd place) Ibrox Park 4-1, 1984/85 a 1-3
Panathanaikos 1973/74 a 2-0
Prestwich Heys 1974/75
F. C. Porto 1980/81 a 0-0, 2006/07 (T. Cook) 0-1 h
Penrith 1980/81 a 2-1
PSV Eindhoven 1981/82 a 1-1, 1987/88 h 3-1, 1993/94 a ? 6-5 on pens
Poole Town 1981/82 a 6-1
Piccadilly Attackers h 1983/84
F.C Pofungstadt 1983/84 a 4-2
Pitea/Hemingsmark 1990/91 a 4-0
Portadown 1991/92 a 1-0, 1992/93 a 1-1 Dublin
Port club of Jersey 1993/94 a 10-1?
Pontefract Colls a 1994/95 a, 1995/96 a
Portland Timbers a 2010/11 3-0 (in USA)

Q is for QPR

Just the one Q, which takes us down to West London...

Queens Park Rangers

The 'R's' were formed in 1885 or 1896 when Christchurch Rangers amalgamated with St Jude's Institute F. C then became Queens Park Rangers. They took over Loftus Road from Shepherds Bush F.C. in 1917 and were founder members of Division Three in 1920, but had two spells at White City, in the 1930's and the 1960's. Promoted to Division Two in 1948 they won the League Cup in 1967 the same year they were promoted again to the Second, They made the First in 1968 and were runners up in the League in 1976, and also the Cup in 1982 and the League Cup in 1986.

Ups and downs since then and they finished season 2010/11 in The Championship and with strong financial backing they were promoted to the Premiership playing in blue and white hooped shirts with white shorts.

Post war: 32 league meetings with 11 City wins, 11 draws and 10 losses. City managed a double in 1950/51 (Postponed game : December 30th 1950/51 at Maine Road, played on April 4th.) but didn't win at QPR again until 1989/90. 1992 saw the first live Sky TV Premiership game at City, a 1-1 draw. In 1993, at Maine Road, there was a sit down protest on the Kippax at the end of the game, a 3-0 win, in support of the 'Forward With Franny' campaign. In October 1994 at QPR it was 2-0 to City with half an hour to go when Rangers pulled a goal back and though Dibble and Edghill were sent off City hung on!

In the 2-2 draw in 1998 at Maine Road City witnessed the most extraordinary own goal ever when Jamie Pollock dribbled the bouncing ball back towards his own goal then headed it over Margetson in the City net.

Neil S: 28/2/1987 QPR 1 City 0

During the mid 1980s Robert Maxwell had a brainwave. Oxford and Reading would conceive a lovechild and call it Thames Valley Royals.

The reaction was predictably mixed. Financially, it made sense, but the fans were furious. Football without tradition was an alien concept.

Around the same period, QPR and Fulham began flirting in public. The hoops of Bowles and Marsh would merge with the club that gave us Johnny Haynes and George Cohen.

Ironically, Oxford and QPR had just contested the League Cup Final at Wembley. Both clubs were in the top flight, but their weaker neighbours enjoyed the greater potential.

Two decades later, Oxford are in the Conference and Fulham have reached the UEFA Cup Final. QPR have cash in abundance, but Reading are arguably the best run club in the Football League. Somewhere in the tale, lies the beauty of football.

Back in the spring of 1987, the QPR merge with Fulham was a realistic possibility. Loftus Road was a seething mass of indignation and a series of boycotts and demonstrations were planned for their next home game. The opponents were Manchester City.

Graeme Robinson was the fastest milkman in Chapel-en-le-Frith. He also boasted an imaginative attitude towards the concept of punctuality. Consequently, we set off for Loftus Road an hour late and arrived at about half past three.

Luckily, the game hadn't even kicked off. Hundreds of QPR supporters were engaged in a sit down protest. The stewards were clueless and nobody seemed quite sure what was going on. As soon as one fan was ejected, another would take his place.

Surprisingly, there was little sympathy from the travelling contingent, who chanted:

"BORING BORING FULHAM"

In 1987, the camaraderie between rival fans was virtually non existent. City had enough problems of their own to worry about the concerns of a team with a plastic pitch.

The game eventually started with City employing a clumsy defence and a lightweight attack. Was it ever thus?

We were sat on the back row of the upper tier and could only see half the pitch. Gary Bannister scored a late goal for QPR and City didn't mount a single attack.

159

Given a sense of majestic timing, the milkman broke down at Teddington Services. All we needed was Two Ton Ted to arrive in a bakers van.

After joining the AA for a ridiculous fee we arrived home at midnight.

In the Premiership :
QPR's win in 1994/95 was their first post war win at Maine Road at their 14th attempt! (they then won three, drew one, and lost one)

Season	H	A	Pl	W	D	L
Pre-95/96			6	2	3	1
95/96	2-0	0-1	8	3	3	2

In the FA Cup Fourth round in 1992/93 at QPR City won 2-1.

In the League Cup, meetings in four rounds:
1969/70 5th rd 3-0 home
1991/92 3rd rd 0-0 home, 3-1 away
1994/95 3rd rd 4-3 away
2003/04 3rd rd 3-0 away

Friendlies: 1908/09 postponed at kick off, 1972/73 a (Frank Sibley T/M) 1-0,

Some connections: Rodney Marsh, Stan Bowles, SWPhillips, Joey Barton

Ground: Loftus Road (Shown 2000's) R/A 35,353 v Leeds D1 1974 (Usually a decent place to visit with a good allocation for away fans in the tight double decker stand behind the goal)

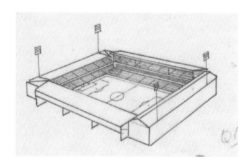

Friendlies:
Queens Park 1928/29 h 4-1
Queensland 1969/70 a 3-0
Queen Of The South 1984/85 a 5-1 (A. Ball T/M).

RODNEY MARSH

R is for Reading

The R's take us down to Berkshire, through Lancashire and over to Yorkshire...

Reading

'The Royals', or 'Biscuitmen', are the oldest club south of the Trent, and were formed in 1871. They amalgamated with the Reading Hornets in 1877 (in 1893 they lost 18-0 to Preston!) and were joined by Earley F.C. in 1899 after moving to Elm Park in 1896 when they vacated the Caversham Cricket Ground. They were founder members of Division Three in 1920, and were generally a lower division league club until reaching the Premiership in 2006 after winning the Simod Cup in 1988, and moving to The Madjeski Stadium in 1998.

They finished season 2010/11 in The Championship after being relegated from The Premiership in 2008. They lost 2-4 to Swansea in the 2011 play off final, playing in Royal Blue shirts and white hoops, with blue shorts

Pre-war: Four league meetings in Division Two in the late twenties with City wining two drawing one and losing one.

Post war: Eight league meetings with four City wins, one draw and three defeats. In the last match of 1996/97, in a First Division clash, City won 3-2 after being two goals down, with Blues fans urging Gio Kinkladze to stay, which he did.

Neil S: 27/3/1999 Reading 1 City 3

Some games remain buried in a shallow grave. All it needs is a word or a song and you find yourself transported to another football ground in a previous decade.

Any mention of Yugoslavia and I immediately think of Elm Park. City enjoyed a comfortable victory in 1987, just a few days after a vital win for England in Belgrade. A gang of City fans had travelled to both fixtures. Every single one of them looked pure evil.

This was the game when pal Andy Stoneley fell asleep at the wheel on the way home. Luckily, the rest of us were still awake.

Twelve years later I travelled to the Madjeski Stadium with pal Stewart Mackinnon, Mark Littlewood and my brother Alistair. To complete the Shaw gathering, my sister Rachel had caught the train from London. This was Reading's first big game at their new home, and the traffic was horrendous.

The City following for this match was astonishing. It was also the day when Kevin Keegan began his England managerial career with a 3-1 victory over Poland. Our paths would later cross, but I was more concerned with the location of my ticket.

City controlled the game, but sitting on the front row next to Moonchester, I found the whole experience quite disturbing. How can you concentrate when the City mascot is virtually sitting on your lap?

Throughout the game, the same thoughts circulated:

Was Moonchester a boy or a girl?

How had Moonchester travelled to the game?

How many loyalty points did Moonchester possess?

When Terry Cooke scored from a free kick, Moonchester lifted me off my feet. For the second half I swapped seats with Rachel.

City eventually achieved promotion, but Moonchester had scarred me for life.

In the Premiership:

Season	H	A	Pl	W	D	L
06/07	0-2	0-1	2	0	0	2
07/08	2-1	0-2	4	1	0	3

In the FA Cup, meetings in two rounds :
1968 3rd rd 0-0 home, replay 7-0 away
1993 3rd rd 1-1 home, replay 4-0 away

In the 1968 game with then Third Division Reading, a 0-0 draw at Maine Road, was endured, with Tony Coleman missing a late penalty.

In the replay at Elm Park, Reading must have wished that TC had scored instead of blasting over. It took City until the 26th minute to open the scoring, Heslop heading his first goal for City from TC's free kick.

Two minutes later Summerbee nodded in the second, then just after half time tapped in the third. After 63 minutes Bell made it four outpacing the defence to score emphatically from 20 yards. Number five came from Coleman, making amends for his penalty miss in the first game, after good work from Bell, ramming the ball home.

Summerbee grabbed his third in the 80th minute, and in the 84th minute Neil Young strode through the defence to make it seven, lashing in a twenty yarder. There followed the famous loudspeaker announcement to the 25,659 crowd "You have been privileged to see the finest side in the league tonight." It was City's record away win in the FA Cup.

In the League Cup, there's been just the one meeting in 1993/94 second round. First leg was 1-1 at home, second leg 2-1 away. The first leg attracted a crowd of only 9,967, some City supporters boycotting the game as part of The 'Forward With Franny' campaign.

Friendlies were played, both away in 1949/50 0-0 and 2004/05 4-1

Some connections: Dave Bacuzzi, Shaun Goater, manager Steve Coppell, Keith Curle, Ray Ranson

Ground: Elm Park, (shown 1980's) R/A 33,042 v Brentford F.A Cup 5 1927, prior to the move to The Madjeski capacity 24,200

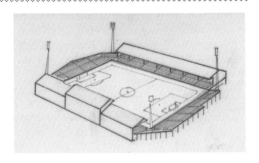

---◄►---

Real Racing Club Santander

Real Racing Club De Santander were formed in 1913, and eventually played at the El Sardinero stadium which holds 22,124, being built in 1988, and located near to a broad sandy beach on the Spanish coast.

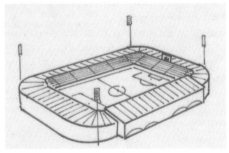

Ex players included Yossi Benayoun, Olof Melberg.

They qualified for UEFA in 2008 by finishing sixth the previous season, and when they played City were in 13th place in La Liga after 13 games with 15 points. They'd beaten F. C. Honka 2-0 on aggregate, lost 1-0 at F. C. Twente, drawn 1-1 at home to Schalke, and 2-2 at PSG.

The teams met in the group stage of UEFA in December 2008 with Racing club, playing in white shirts, winning 3-1 at home. City had already qualified and put on a poor show, but scored a late goal which in effect knocked Racing out of the competition owing to PSG gaining a result against Twente.

Sean R: 18/12/2008 RRC 3 City 1

Whilst it was nice to go into this fixture as group leaders, and qualification to the next round guaranteed, ticket prices of £41 and £66

respectively were a bit of a shock. The only day trip travel package available was Thomas Cook, who sub-contracted to Thomsons, which was a relief after the Schalke debacle (see 'S' chapter).

We landed at Bilbao a couple of hours after take off where it was damp, cold and miserable, just like in Manchester! We were immediately transferred by coach to Santander about 70 miles and an hour and a half away. We were dropped off an hour's walk away from the stadium and after visiting the ground and picking up the two free programmes we spent the next five hours strolling the sea front, eating at Pizza Hut, going back to the ground for the official programme, frequenting bars and swapping tales with fellow Blues!

The ground was not dissimilar to QPR's and the locals paid up to 100 euros for tickets. They were noisy and passionate as their team went three up but inconsolable when they heard that PSG's resounding win over Twente and Caicedo's late goal, (shaming the song "....he comes from Ecuador, he'll never f**king score!) meant they were out.

The trip was a pleasure to be involved in and it was heartening to know we could go abroad and act as ambassadors for our club and country. Long may it continue.

We arrived home, tired and weary, then went on to lose 2-1 at West Brom on the Sunday!

Some connections: Manager Paul Simpson, Neil Young, Mike Doyle (below), Steve Eyre

Ground: Spotland R/A 20,945 v Bradford City 1929

Rochdale

'The Dale' were formed in 1907 playing at Spotland when Rochdale Town went out of existence. They were elected to Division Three North on its formation in 1921. Their main claim to fame was reaching the second League Cup final in 1961/62 losing over two legs to Norwich City.

They finished season 2010/11 in League Two, finally, after over thirty years, gaining promotion in 2010, playing in all royal blue shirts and shorts.

The one and only meeting of the teams came in the League Cup of 1972/73 when City won 4-0 in the second round at Maine Road.

Friendlies: All away 02/03 6-0, 03/04 4-0, 06/07 3-2

Rotherham Town/United

'The Millers' were formed in 1870 before becoming Town in the late 1880's, playing at Clifton Grove, and were elected to Division Two in 1893 but failed to gain re-election in 1896.

Thornhill Town were formed in 1877 and became Rotherham County in 1905, playing at Millmoor, until the move to the Don Valley Stadium in 2008, entering Division Two in 1919. Town amalgamated with County to become Rotherham United in 1925.

They were generally a lower division club but had their moments in the Second Division, particularly when Tommy Docherty was in charge saying "I'll take them into Europe" and signing the likes of Dave Watson from Notts. County!

They also contested the very first League Cup final in 1961 losing over two legs to Aston Villa. They finished season 2010/11 in League Two, playing in red shirts with white sleeves and white shorts.

Pre-war: Six league meetings in the 1890's in Division Two (v Rotherham Town) City winning five and losing one.

Post war: Eight league meetings with six City wins including a 6-1 at Maine Road in 1963/64 and two draws.

The 1966 game at Millmoor was famous for City clinching promotion with Colin Bell's headed goal. Both Christmas games were postponed that year and played later in the season, Jan 12th at Maine Road, 3-1, and May 4th at Millmoor.

From the away programme : "A city like Manchester can support two First Division sides and, until this season, so much of the glory has laid on one side in recent years.

It is nice to see, and read of, success of 'coaching-minded' management members like Joe Mercer and Malcolm Allison who have worked so hard for the game wherever it has taken them".

Jackie H: 4/5/1966 Rotherham 0 City 1

I was working at ICI Blackley at the time. The game kicked off at 7.15pm and the train left at 4.45pm and I was working until 4.30pm so I had a dilemma : should I throw a sickie or ask for time off? My conscience got the better of me and I asked my boss if I could finish early and he agreed, so I skipped off to the station. The mood, as so often in the mid to late sixties for the youth of the day, was optimistic. We didn't have much time for a drink before the game as we wanted to get inside and soak up the atmosphere with the thousands of City fans. We stood behind the goal where Colin headed the winner, and at the final whistle someone grabbed the belt of my jeans and hoisted me over the high perimeter wall and onto the pitch where I had my picture taken next to Neil Young. It appeared in the Daily Express the next morning and my boss clocked it, of course, so I was relieved I hadn't taken a day off 'sick'! And we partied all the way home, in and out of the carriages on the train.

The teams next met in the League in 2001/02, City winning 2-1 at Maine Road, memorable only for a handball goal by Christian Negouai, and drew 1-1 at Millmoor.

In the FA Cup just the one meeting in the third round in 1979, City only drawing 0-0 at Maine Road but winning the replay at Millmoor 4-2, 3-0 up then having a scare at 3-2 before clinching it.

Friendlies: 1892/93 Town 2-2 h, 0-1 a

Some connections: Shaun Goater, Gerry Gow, Dave Watson, Nigel Johnson, Alan Kirkman.

Ground: Millmoor (Shown 2002) R/A 25,170 v Sheff United D2 1952 before the (unfinished) main stand development and the move to The Don Valley Stadium in 2008 cap: 25,000

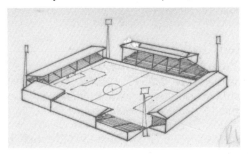

Friendlies:

Rossendale 1891/92 h 1-4, 1990/91, 1991/92, 1992/93
Renton 1891/92 h 5-1
Ripley 1904/05 a 3-0
Racing Club De Paris 1931/32 a 4-3, 1933/34 a 3-1
Red Star Olympique 1931/32 a 5-0 a
Rapid Vienna 1934/35 a 5-3
Randers 1948/49 a 4-1
Real Zaragoza 1951/52 a 3-1
River Plate 1951/52 h 3-4
RSD Strasbourg 1954/55 a 2-3
Rochester Lancers 1967/68 a 4-0
Real Betis 1976/77 a 1-1, 1980/81 a 1-3, 1986/87 a 0-0
A.C.Roma 1978/79 a 2-2, 1979/80 in New York 3 -2
Real Madrid 1979/80 a 2-5
Rhyl 1980/81, 1996/97, 2000/01 (City res)
Rosenburg 1981/82 a 3-0, 1991/92, 1994/95
Real Sociedad 1990/91 a1-1
Radcliffe Boro a 1991/92, 1994/95, 1996/97, 1997/98, 1998/99, 1999/2000, 00/01, 01/02
Raith Rovers 1995/96 a 2-2
Ross RF 1999/2000 a

S is for Salzburg

THE S's take us to Austria, Germany, Lincolnshire, Yorkshire, the Midlands, the South coast, Lancashire, the North East, Belgium, Cheshire, the Potteries, the Faroe Islands and South Wales...

Red Bull Salzburg

FC Red Bulls Salzburg nicknamed Die Bullens – The Bulls, were formed in 2005 from the Austria Salzburg club, after which breakaway fans formed SV Austria Salzburg who play in the lower leagues. The new owners alienated the fans by changing the kit to match the RB corporate colours and the badge to incorporate the RB logo. According to some sources the owners also declared that the club's history began in 2005 and have ignored everything before that time.

One story even claims that fans arriving at the ground wearing old colours were refused entry as it was seen as opposing the current owners. You'd think such mistreatment of fans would be frowned upon by the game's authorities but it goes without saying that Platini and company hadn't said a word.

Giovanni Trappattoni became their first manager with his assistant Walter Matthaus, but left to take over at ROI in 2008. The current Coach was Huub Stevens.

They'd won the title on three occasions, and been regulars in Europe. In season 2010/11 in the Champions League they beat HB Torshavn 5-1 on aggregate, AC Omonia 5-3 on aggregate but lost in the play off 3-4 on aggregate to Hapoel Tel Aviv to drop into the Europa Cup. Ridiculous, if you're out, you're out!

Home colours were white shirts with red shorts and away colours all black.

City did, of course, lose 2-1 to New York Red Bulls in the summer of 2010 in the USA, but this was not taken as an omen!

In the current season after four games they were in 8th place with one win, one draw and two defeats.

Salzburg is most famous for being Wolfgang Amadeus Mozart's birthplace and was the setting for the film 'The Sound Of Music' about the Nun Maria Von Trapp (obviously why they set on Trappattoni!) although the locals aren't too impressed with that film.

The city has a population of around 150,000 has three universities and hence a large student population.

The teams first met in the Group stage of the Europa Cup in 2010, City winning the first leg 2-0 in Salzburg, with goals from Silva and Jo in front of 25,100 (798 Blues). In the second leg it was 3-0 at home, with two goals from Balotelli and one from Adam Johnson in front of 37,552 with 207 Salzburgers. Much amusement was had when their substitute 'Alan' took to the field, prompting City fans to burst into appropriate songs.

In the group they went on to lose twice to Lech Poznan and draw twice with Juventus to finish bottom.

The first leg was played in the Red Bull Arena in Wals-Siezenheim, capacity 31,895, a neat, modern ground with double deck stands.

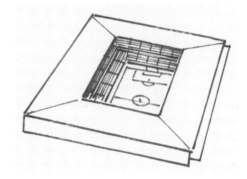

Sean (Von Trap) R: 16/9/2010 RBS 0 City 2

Not a bad place to kick off the Group stage games, and a healthy City following had plenty of options (including official club and independent trips) to reach the historic and very beautiful Salzburg. It's the birthplace of Mozart, and also some distance away from the mountain retreat (known as the Eagle's Nest) for the infamous Adolf Hitler.

City fans mingled freely and enjoyed the local hospitality, and showed that we do have a cultural side to our nature, as always with the help of a few beers to bring out the best in us!! (not forgetting some cracking places from which to hang the flags!). It was good, as always, to bump into so many familiar faces from Manchester.

Free transport was kindly supplied to move fans to the stadium which seemed to be a fair old hike if you fancied doing it by foot, most of us taking the easier option.

The stadium itself was very tidy and modern, and this game saw the attendance being almost double what they would expect for a league fixture. So with a noisy expectant home crowd, it was up to City to deal with it, and right from the kick off, that is exactly what we did. The game was still young when Silva calmly slotted home his first senior goal since joining the club. The Austrians very rarely threatened us throughout the 90 minutes, and we got a more than useful glimpse of how much Silva could influence proceedings out there on the pitch.

The strains of Blue Moon provided the appropriate backdrop to the Sound of Music tonight.......(followed closely by Wilky and co with their merry band's very own rendition of the Moston Arse Flute ,courtesy of copious amounts of the local brew....., sorry!).

It was a solid showing by the lads. Jo skilfully slotted home from a rebound save made by the busy Salzburg keeper. 2-0 in our favour certainly didn't flatter us, and the score then remained unchanged. With our free match programmes in our hands, City fans were duly whisked back to the airport in no time at all, and we managed to land back in Manchester just around midnight.

It was a cracking day all round (no doubt enjoyed by our author/editor who made it on the official trip, along with big Blue Roland Griffin!), and City fans were perfect ambassadors for the club once again.

⸻

Schalke 04

The club were formed on the 4th May 1904 as S.C. Westfalia 04, in the coalmining town, hence the nickname 'Die Knappen' (The Miners) of Gelsenkirchen, just a few short weeks after City became the first Manchester club to win a trophy, the FA Cup. The club changed it's name in 1924 to Schalke 04, changing its colours from red and yellow to blue and white, heralding another nickname 'Die Konisblauen' (The Royal Blues).

In the 1930's and 1940's Schalke was Germany's leading football team winning the Championship six times, and the German Cup, and were Hitler's favourite team, but their last title was in 1958. They were founder members of the Bundesliga in 1963 but generally struggled, though in 1969 they finished as runners up to Champions Bayern Munich in the German Cup Final and entered the European Cup Winners' Cup.

They played City in the semi-finals and won the first leg at home 1-0 but lost the second 5-1 in an unforgettable Maine Road night.

Steve P: 1/4/1970 Schalke 1 City 0

It was an Easter week jaunt to the Ruhr. My mate Alan had a pal Tony who worked for BEA in Dusseldorf and was going to be the translater for the English press and arranged for them to stay with a German colleague's girlfriend's parents.

So it was a Monday night berth on the Harwich – Hook ferry, followed by over three hours on the train to Dusseldorf, then off to find Tony and colleague at the BEA offices.

Tony took Alan and I to the German colleague's girlfriend's parents that night and next day it was a coach trip to Essen to pick up the press and then on to the ground in Gelsenkirchen, which was enclosed by a gate and a fence. They followed the team coach to the ground but weren't let in until a club official relented and in went the coach followed by two dozen City fans without tickets!

Reinhard 'Stan' Libuda scored late on for Schalke; it poured with rain; I got separated from Alan and Tony, and got the train back to Dusseldorf from Essen. It was past midnight and a kindly German couple I bumped into put me up for the night as there was a mix up as to where I should have stayed!

Imagine that, an English football supporter being put up by total strangers in a foreign country? I now wonder how we let the hooligans spoil it? How did we change from a time when football fans could trek three days across Europe by rail without spreading fear and vomit everywhere, and be welcome as visitors?

Dave A: 15/4/1970 City 5 Schalke 1

For the home leg I remember distinctly that we travelled over from Leeds in mate Ted's Fiat 500 and it took us all of two hours plus on a pleasant April evening. There was a crowd of 46,361 so parking was getting scarce by 7.15pm but we managed to get into an impossible space on Platt Lane by literally lifting the back end of the car up and swivelling it into the space on its front wheels!

City's team was Corrigan, Book, Pardoe, Doyle, Booth, Oakes, Towers, Bell, Lee, Young and Summerbee. George Heslop came on for Mick Doyle and Frank Carrodus for Mike Summerbee. The latter had been carrying an injury for some weeks and eventually missed out on the Final. City had lost the first leg 1-0 two weeks earlier. Derek Jeffries played in that match, so nervous tension abounded. I also remember the front cover of the programme; there was a picture of Tony Book, simply described as Captain alongside the Schalke 04 skipper Libuda but the caption said 'Mannschaftfuhrer'. I realised why I'd never fancied doing German! I have the programme in the loft. I must get it out sometime.

Nerves soon disappeared. City, with one of the best displays I've ever seen from them, overran the opposition with wonderful free flowing football led by Colin the King and won 5-1, a totemic scoreline. The goals came from Mike Doyle, Neil Young (2), Franny Lee and Colin Bell. The display was on a par with the 4-1 win over Spurs, the ballet on ice game, in December 1967.

We travelled back to Leeds very happily with the usual stop in Oldham and the week ended in great delight and with long celebrations after a 3-1 win at Elland Road over Leeds. No Lee, no Summerbee that day but goals from Bell, Towers and Young with Harry Dowd also playing. He made his last appearance for City four days later, the last League game of the season, in a 2-1 win at Sheffield Wednesday, with two goals from Ian Bowyer.

So Schalke were overcome. To be honest I don't think I had a clue or cared where they were from, there was no internet for quick research but I had a very pleasant trip there in 2008 and savoured something known as an away win!

Since 1970 they've been involved in a match fixing scandal in 1971, won the Cup a couple of times, have yo-yo-ed between the top two divisions and in 1997 they beat Inter Milan on penalties in the San Siro to lift the UEFA Cup.

The next time the teams met was in the group stage of the UEFA Cup in 2008 where City put on a great performance to win 2-0 in the Veltins Arena. A state of the art stadium having a sliding roof and retractable pitch. Capacity 62,000 for domestic fixtures with safe standing and 54,000 all seated for European games.

This was their third venue. They first played at the 35,000 capacity Gluckauf Kampfbahn from 1928, moved to The Parkstadion in 1973, capacity 70,298, then moved to The Veltins.

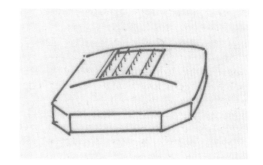

Dave W: 27/11/2008 Schalke 0 City 2

Thomas Cook ran a few different flights to this one and we opted for the two day overnight stay in Cologne, arriving at the hotel in the early afternoon. We took in the sights including the Chocolate museum, Cathedral, where City fans gathered on the steps and had photos taken, Christmas markets and the Nazi museum. The following afternoon we set off by coach to Gelsenkirchen in plenty of time. However the traffic was horrendous and the German Police were supposed to give the coaches an escort to the ground but after a twenty minute wait at a service station thirty miles away they failed to show up. We finally arrived at the Veltins Arena, after the coaches circumnavigated the ground before finding the coach park. We then faced a ten minute walk to the away end in the dark, and were searched at the turnstiles then eventually entered the away end, where it was utter chaos,, about twenty five minutes after the kick off but just in time to see Benjani put us a goal up.

Stevie Ireland wrapped it up in the 66th minute in what was City's best away performance of the season. On the Sunday, despite the Pilot's well wishes (to beat the dirty rags!) we lost 0-1at home to United, and Schalke went out at the group stage.

Scunthorpe United

'The Iron' were formed in 1899 when Brumby Hall F.C., playing at the Old Show Ground, consolidated their position by amalgamating with some other clubs, becoming Scunthorpe United F.C. In 1910 they amalgamated with North Lindsey United as Scunthorpe and Lindsey United, the link being Chairman Mr W.T. Lockwood. They were elected to Division Three North in 1950 when the division was increased in size, and were renamed as Scunthorpe United in 1958. They moved to Glanford Park in 1988. Cricket legend Ian Botham once played for them, but stuck to his day job

Always a lower division club but spent six seasons in Division Two from 1958 to 1964, and also finished season 2010/11 in The Championship being relegated, playing in sky blue shirts with three vertical claret stripes and sky blue shorts.

In the League the teams have met twice, at Christmas 1963 in Division Two, with City winning the first game 8-1 at Maine Road, with an attendance of 26,365 - which would have been one more had I not overslept and missed the 3pm kick off. City were one up at half time and scored seven in the second half! Two days later City won 4-2 at The Old Show Ground.

In the FA Cup, meetings in two rounds:
2005/06 3rd rd 3-1 home
2009/10 4th rd 4-2 away

In the League Cup, meetings in two rounds:
1974/75 2nd rd 6-0 home
2009/10 3rd rd 5-1 home

Andrew H: 10/9/1974 City 6 Scunthorpe 0

Having become a teenager just a few months earlier, this match represented, at the time, a significant milestone in my City supporting career. I had seen them score four or five goals on numerous occasions when they were at their formidable best at Maine Road, but until this evening, I had never seen them score six.

Under the illustrious management of Ron Bradley (yes, exactly!), this was only Fourth Division Scunthorpe's second ever visit to Maine Road, their previous visit having been an 8-1 thrashing by City in the league on Boxing Day 1963.

They didn't do much better on this occasion. I remember being tremendously excited when City scored their sixth goal to break my own personal record, and Colin Bell was in inspirational form on the night, scoring an impressive hat-trick.

I was one of only just under fifteen thousand at Maine Road that night, but "The Football Pink" the following Saturday published a piece with a photograph of every one of City's goals. I cut it out and had it on my bedroom wall for months afterwards. It was to be the early 1980's in the Second Division before I saw City again equal this six goal winning margin.

Friendlies: 2001/02 a 2-2

Some connections: Peter Beagrie (below), Alan Kirkman

Ground: Old Show Ground (sown 1960s - first English ground to have a cantilever stand) R/A 23,935 v Portsmouth FA Cup 4th rd 1954. Glandford Park R/A 8,775 v Rotherham Div 4 1989.

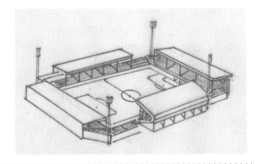

Sheffield United

'The Blades' were formed in 1889 after an FA Cup semi-final, played at Bramall Lane between Preston and West Brom convinced the Yorkshire County Cricket Club chairman that football could be successful at the venue.

They were elected to Division Two in 1892 and were generally a top flight club until the 1970's when they slipped down to the Fourth and back. They won the title in 1897/98 and were four times Cup winners up to 1925.

They finished season 2010/11 in The Championship being relegated, playing in red and white striped shirts and black shorts

Pre-war: 58 League meetings with 22 City wins, 14 draws and 22 defeats including a 3-8 at The Lane in 1925/26 a few days after City's 8-3 win over Burnley! This was sandwiched between three Blue doubles and a 5-0 away win in 1924/25. Sheffield United were City's first opponents at the new Maine Road ground in August 1923, a 2-1 City win in front of 56,993.

Post war: 46 League meetings, with City winning 21, including a 6-0 in 1999/2000 at Maine Rd., drawing 15 and losing 10. City's 5-2 home win in 1954 confirmed the arrival of 'The Revie Plan.' In 1991 at Maine Road, United's Vinnie Jones was booked after 5 seconds and sent off after 5 minutes!

Neil S: 15/11/1997: Sheff U 1 City 1

Using the dubious science of programme collecting I've probably seen City play at Bramall Lane more than any other ground. By hook or by crook we usually end up in the same division as the team with the best football song in England, 'A Greasy Cip Butty'.

Sheffield United were arguably the first major cub to hit the financial buffers after prioritizing ground improvements over strengthening the team. Indeed, on more than one occasion their spectacular plummet through the divisions was blamed on the curse of Yorkshire Cricket Club.

When Dennis Tueart repeated his overhead kick on the Saturday after the League Cup final victory, the Blades were already doomed for the Seond Division. By the time of our next encounter, City had also been relegated and Sheffield United were making the return journey from the Fourth Division.

When I first visited Bramall Lane I was still at school and Stockport County were the opponents. City were on the slide, but I didn't see them play in Sheffield until the autumn of 1984.

We turned left at the Leadmill and parked in the small cul- de- sac, opposite the Church. Curiously, we parked in exactly the same spot twenty four years later on the afternoon of the balloongate disaster.

By the autumn of 1997, City were peering nervously over the precipice. The team was a shambles and as Brian Deane converted an early chance, another thrashing looked highly likely. We were sat near the front of the lower tier and the atmosphere was turning ugly.

The stewards were attempting to eject a City supporter for foul and abusive language. As he attempted to resist, the situation deteriorated, with the fans around him observing a tearful small boy clinging to his arm.

The tug of war continued until a voice boomed from the back of the stand.

"JUST LEAVE US IN OUR MISERY! "

This was the game when Gerry Creaney made a belated comeback. I think he touched the ball twice. City didn't enjoy a shot on goal until the ninetieth minute, but as the seconds ticked away, the ball fell to Kinkladze on the right wing.

Time stood still as Kinky teased the full back into making a rash challenge. Inside and outside, he tormented until the covering central defender charged across too quickly.

Kinkladze surged between the two defenders and raced towards the near post. The goalkeeper was committed and Horlock side footed into the open goal. Cue bedlam.

The 1997-98 season was a series of tragedies obscured by a single miracle at Bramall Lane. There wasn't even enough time for the Blades to kick off.

We poured onto the streets in a state of utter euphoria. An old lady poured scorn on our rare moment of bliss as she waved her umbrella aggressively in my direction.

"YOU'RE GOING DOWN
YOU'RE GOING DOWN"

The Blades were blunted, but by gum she was right.

In the Premiership.

Season	H	A	Pl	W	D	L
92/93	2-0	1-1	2	1	1	0
93/94	0-0	1-0	4	2	2	0
06/07	0-0	1-0	6	3	3	0

In the FA Cup, meetings in four rounds:
1906 1st round 1-4 away
1914 4th rd 0-0 home, 1st replay 0-0 away, 2nd replay 0-1 Villa Park
1939 4th rd 0-2 away
2008 4th rd 1-2, nicknamed 'balloongate' as the first goal was scored after the ball, and City's defenders became confused with balloons on the pitch!

In the League Cup just the one meeting in the third round of 1988/89 City winning 4-2 at Maine Road.

In the Full Members Cup of 1985/86 Group three City won 2-1 at Bramall Lane and in 1990/91 Round two City won 2-0 also at The Lane.

In the Texaco Cup of 1974/75 City lost 2-4 at Bramall Lane. It was Denis Law's last ever game.

In the Anglo Scottish Cup of 1975/76 City won 3-1 at Maine Road.

Friendlies: 1893/94 h 0-2; 1896/97 h 1-3; 1918/19 h 1-0, a 2-3; 1982/83 a 2-2;

Some connections: Michael Brown, David White, Ched Evans, Brian Gayle (below)

Ground: Bramall Lane (shown 2008)
R/A 68,287 v Leeds FA Cup 5 1936

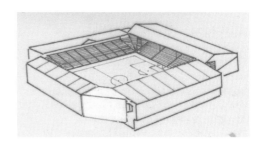

Sheffield Wednesday

'The Owls' were formed in 1867 by the Sheffield Wednesday Cricket Club (formed 1825). They played at Highfield, Myrtle Road, Sheaf House, and Olive Grove, before the move to Owlerton in 1899 which became Hillsborough in 1912. They also played at Endcliffe and even Bramall Lane for a while in the 1880's and 90's.

They were elected to Division One in 1892 and were generally a top flight team pre-war winning the title four times and the cup three times. Post war they were a yo-yo club, even spending time in the old Third Division but won the League Cup in 1991(beat united 1-0)

Indeed, they finished season 2010/11 in League One, playing in blue and white striped shirts and white shorts.

Pre-war: 48 league meetings with 10 City wins, but none at Hillsborough, 13 draws and 25 defeats.

In April 1937 City needed a win to clinch the title which was achieved to the tune of 4-1 against already relegated (with manu) Wednesday, which avenged the 1-5 loss at Hillsborough on December 19th. City then drew the last match 2-2 at Birmingham to complete a run of 22 games without defeat since the 3-5 loss at Grimsby on December 25th.

Post war: 40 league meetings with 17 City wins including a 6-2 at Hillsborough in 2001/02, 8 draws and 15 defeats.

Wins at Hillsborough were rare, but the 2-1 on the last day of the season in 1970 relegated Wednesday to Division Two. It was City's fourth away game on the trot and on a rainy night in front of 45,258 Mike Doyle rolled a weak penalty to the Wednesday keeper Peter Grummitt. Wednesday fans were pleased that Summerbee went off, being replaced by Bowyer, but aghast when I told them he'd be playing for his place in the European Cup Winners' Cup Final. Sadly for them Ian hadn't read the script and scored the two goals which won the game.

Roger R: 22/9/2001: Sheff. W 2 City 6

Team: Weaver, Edghill, Granville, Wiekens, Howey, Pearce, Benarbia, Etuhu, Wanchope, Goater, Tiatto Subs Dunne, Huckerby and Horlock.
Football League Division One (second tier)

This was possibly one of the best away performances I can recall from a City side. City had just signed a new player called Ali Benarbia, who had made a big impression in each of the two games he had played prior to this match, but little did we, as City fans, know how good he really was. This match proved it against a well organised Sheffield Wednesday side. City won the match at Hillsborough convincingly (and amazingly!) by 6-2. Benarbia himself was absolutely brilliant as City totally dominated the match from start to finish. I would love to know the "stats" from the game regarding the percentage of possession enjoyed by City that day. At a guess, I would say that it must have been about 75% to Wednesday's 25%? Shaun Goater scored two, as did Paulo Wanchope (one a penalty) Danny Granville and Benarbia scored the other two. This was the match when the balance of the team seemed to be right, and there was actually (for the first time for many years) an air of confidence amongst the City faithful, which proved to be well placed as City romped home to the First Division Championship and scored 108 league goals in the process! This equated to an average of well over two goals per match – and was some 32 goals more than the next highest scorers in the division that season (Wolves). It was, of course, in 1958 when City had last scored more than 100 goals in a season – so this really was a record-breaking campaign.

Dave W: 9/11/1968 City 0 Sheff. W 1

After the 1-0 home defeat by Sheffield Wednesday, in foggy November 1968, making a late return trip back to our current home in Millhouses, Sheffield, over the A57 Snake Pass, the head gasket on the Hillman Imp blew. After

being refused a room at the Snake Hotel as "the alarms had been set" the car was nursed back to Glossop by the AA, and Mr and Mrs W spent the night on a bench in the games room at Glossop Police Station!

In the Premiership 8 meetings with 3 City wins, 2 losses, both at Maine Road, and 3 draws.

Season	H	A	Pl	W	D	L
Pre-95/96			6	2	2	2
95/96	1-0	1-1	8	3	3	2

In the FA Cup, meetings in three rounds:
1904: 3-0 semi-final at Goodison with City beating the eventual League Champions.
1934: 5th round 2-2 away, where Wednesday's record attendance of 72,841 was achieved, though with some crowd casualties. City won the Maine Road replay 2-0 in front of 68,614.
2007: 3rd round 1-1 away, 2-1 replay home, 25,621 with 6,059 Wednesdayites.

In the League Cup second round in 1979/80 it was a 1-1 away draw and a 2-1 home win in the replay.

In the Full Members Cup Round 2 in 1991/92 it was a 2-3 loss at Hillsborough.

Friendlies: 1891/92 h 0-0; 1939/40 h 3-1; 1951/52 a 1-1; 1979/80 a 1-3;1998/99 h 0-0; 2005/06 a 1-1;

Some connections: Tony Coleman, Tony Cunningham, Andy Hinchcliffe, Imre Varadi (below), Nicky Weaver

Ground: Hillsborough (shown 2005) R/A 72,841 V City FA Cup 5 1934.

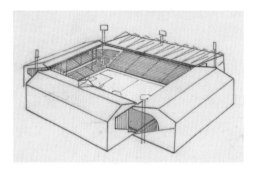

Shrewsbury Town

'The Shrews' were formed in 1876 after Shrewsbury Schools provided English and Welsh International players, but the present club came into being in 1886.

They were elected to Division Three North in 1950, flitting between the Third and Fourth Divisions but having a couple of decent stints in the Second in the 80's and 90's.

They played at The Old Shrewsbury Racecourse, then The Barracks, before moving to The Gay Meadow in 1891, then the New Meadow in 2007.

After a season in The Conference in 2003/04 they bounced back and finished season 2010/11 in League One playing in blue shirts and shorts.

Post–war: 8 league meetings, all in the Second Division in the 1980's, with City winning four, drawing two and losing two.

Neil S: 12/9/1987 Shrewsbury 0 City 0

Throughout the 1970's, the highlight of the football calendar was undoubtedly the draw for the early rounds of the FA Cup. It was a pompous, dark suited affair, but there was something about the serious tones of Ted Croker and the old bloke with the eye patch that gave the event an intangible glamour. This was English football enjoying its finest hour after the 1966 World Cup win.

My attitude towards the draw has never changed. I always want to visit a new ground or play at home against the worst team in the competition.

In 1979, an away game at Shrewsbury was a novelty fixture. Within a decade I was sick of the sight of Gay Meadow.

We hired a minibus for the 3-1 victory in 1983 and the 1-0 defeat the following season. In 1989 I travelled on the City Special from Stockport and squinted through the snow to witness Trevor Morley notching a late headed winner.

Sandwiched in the middle was a nondescript affair at the start of the 1987-88 season.

It was my turn to drive and Chris Girling moaned all the way. Mick Chandley was the navigator and Alan Kelsall spent the whole game trying to get Chris arrested. In short, we were a typical gang of travelling supporters.

In the archives of oblivion, the memories of the final minutes are buried in a shallow grave. City hadn't won an away fixture since about 1910 and as the referee allowed for injuries, we made our way to the exits. City were sliding down a slippery slope, but a goalless draw wasn't a total disaster.

Suddenly there was a fumble and a late challenge. Unbelievably, a Shrewsbury defender had gifted City a penalty. From boredom to ecstasy, the sight of the referee pointing to the spot was the answer to a thousand prayers.

The penalty was so late, the ball boys were taking down the corner flags. Jingle Bells was echoing around the 'Stadium'.

The rest is history. Neil McNab confidently sent the keeper the wrong way and charged deliriously towards the travelling hordes. The game was a major turning point and within three years Manchester City were Champions of Europe.

Either that or the penalty was saved. Sadly it was.

In the FA Cup, meetings in two fateful rounds. First, in the third round of 1965 a 1-1 draw at Maine Road with City losing the replay 1-3 (when it was announced on TV that City had won and I thought the bet I'd had with a red might be honoured for once!) Then in the fourth round in 1979 it was a 0-2 loss for the Blues on an icy pitch at Gay Meadow.

Friendlies: 2007/08 2-0 away (opening of the New Meadow)

Some connections: Ken Mulhearn, Joe Hart (overleaf), manager John Bond

Afterwards they fluctuated between the top two divisions, winning the Cup in 1976 as a Second Division team, beating the strong favourites United 1-0 (RIP Bobby Stokes). They went into administration in 2009 and finished season 2010/11 in League One being promoted to The Championship and playing in red and white stripes and black shorts.

Pre-war: 6 league meetings, all in Division Two with 3 City wins including a 6-1 in 1927/28 at home, 2 draws and one loss.

Post-war: 46 league meetings with 12 City wins, 14 draws, including a 0-0 at Maine Road in 1966 when they accompanied the Blues into the First Division, and 20 losses.
In 1987 the 2-4 home defeat saw the distribution of anti-Swales leaflets.

Ground: The Gay Meadow (shown 1980's) R/A 18,917 v Walsall, D3 1961. The New Meadow Capacity: 9,869

Lyndon D: 16/8/1980 Saints 2 City 0
1/11/2004 Saints 0 City 2

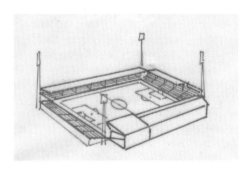

As a 16 year old this was my first serious away trip – I'd been to see City at Leeds a couple of years earlier and a family friend had taken me to see a League Cup tie against Blackpool the year before, but this was different. I'd managed to persuade my parents to let me go with a slightly older mate (Cyril) to the first game of the new season at Southampton. Looking back, as a parent myself now, this was quite a leap of faith on their part.

The media were excited about the return to English football of Kevin Keegan from his spell at Hamburg, but I was more interested to see how Tony Book & Malcolm Allison's Blues would fare in the new season. The previous couple of seasons had seen enormous turmoil and turnover of players as Allison had dismantled the old guard of Watson, Owen and Barnes and brought in the likes of Steve Daley, Kevin Reeves, and Steve McKenzie and brought through Nicky Reid and Tommy Caton. Little did I know that the season ahead would see the departure of Book and Allison, the arrival of John Bond, and the exciting run to the 1981 Cup Final.

Southampton

'The Saints' were formed basically from players of Deanery F.C. who were established by schoolteachers in 1880 and connected to St. Mary's Church. In 1885 the club was named as Southampton St. Mary's, the Church's curate becoming President. They moved from The Antelope ground in 1897 to The County Cricket Ground and then to The Dell in 1898, then to St. Mary's in 2001.
They were original members of Division Three in 1920 and spent 31 years in Division Two until 1953, when they dropped to the Third, but bounced back making Division One in 1966.

Cringingly for me, my mum couldn't help having to speak to Cyril to check out his suitability to "look after" her little boy. Having passed this interrogation Cyril and I were off bright and early from our homes in Morecambe to catch the Football Special from Piccadilly to the south coast. My memories of the game itself are hazy - funny what you remember after nearly thirty years. I recall glorious sunshine and the buzz of excitement around the ground. Inside the cramped little stadium we found ourselves literally caged in one corner of the ground – not only were there the usual railings separating us from the pitch and the home supporters, but I am pretty sure I remember there was also something above our heads too – a far cry from the luxury we all enjoy today. To this day I am still shocked at the conditions fans, particularly away fans, endured to follow their teams, including the route march under police escort from the railway station that was obligatory for fans on the Football Specials.

I can't remember much of the game – City didn't get started until the second half and were already two down courtesy of City old boy, Mick Channon. According to Tony Book's programme notes at the next home match he felt that had Tueart and Reeves taken second half chances we could have saved the match. I just remember the battering we took in the first half as Keegan and Charlie George opened us up at will.

The return journey to Lancashire proved far more eventful than the outward trip. We'd met up with three other Morecambe lads who had driven down in a small brown mini. I went along with Cyril's plan to hitch a lift back with these guys – seemed like a good idea to get a lift straight home – what could go wrong? First inklings that this might not be so straightforward came as we pulled up for "a pint" somewhere. As a naïve 16 year old this was alien to me and I waited in the car for what seemed an age. I remember phoning home to inform my mum of the new travelling plans. To her credit she didn't go off at the deep end as her youngest son calmly delivered the bombshell that he had no idea what time he'd be getting home or where exactly he was. We got under way again but we'd only been going a couple of hours when "Little Paul", the driver, (I never met Big Paul) declared that he couldn't drive any further and needed to sleep. A lay-by was found and five of us tried to get some sleep in a hot, sweaty, cramped mini. This was nigh on impossible and I remember giving up on this endeavour and clambering out of the car and sitting out in the crisp August evening. We did eventually get back to Morecambe the following morning and I slept most of the day – quite an adventure for a sixteen year old.

Many Morecambe Blues will remember "Little Paul" who was an active member in the early days of the Morecambe Bay branch of the Supporter's Club. Paul was a diabetic who passed away before his time. I remember a surreal experience as Paul was driving a minibus on the M6 back from a game. We became all too aware that he was in need of some sugar as he laughed outrageously as the bus headed towards the hard shoulder at an alarming angle. Fortunately someone grabbed the steering wheel and made him pull over. Nevertheless Paul was a great guy and avid Blue who is sadly missed.

Funnily enough my only other trip to Southampton came some twenty four years later (1st November 2004) with a certain Mr Keegan again involved, this time as our manager, and a similar 2-0 score line. I persuaded the current Mrs Day that she'd like a week-end on the South Coast with shopping thrown in, whilst I went to the City game to "tick off" Southampton's new St Mary's stadium. A little more comfort was involved in this trip with an overnight stay at a Holiday Inn and certainly more comfortable surroundings in the ground than the Dell. The football was very much the same, though, as City were battered in the first half, again conceding two easy goals – it should have been many more. This was a typical lacklustre end of Keegan era performance with City showing little fight and being outclassed by a mediocre Southampton attack led by Brett Ormerod. Let's hope that the days of City being rolled over by run-of-the-mill opponents away from home will become a little less frequent in the future!

City teams v Southampton: 16.8.1980
Corrigan, Ranson, Caton, Reid, Booth, Henry, Tueart, Daley, Sugrue, Power, Reeves (Sub Stepanovic)

1.11.2004
Seaman, Sun, Tarnat, Dunne, Distin, Sinclair, Barton, McManaman, Reyna, Fowler, Wanchope (Sub Sibierski)

In the Premiership: Saints spoiled the last game at Maine Road by winning 1-0. Crowd was 34,957.

Season	H	A	Pl	W	D	L
Pre-04/05			14	6	4	4
04/05	2-0	0-0	16	7	5	4

In the FA Cup: Meetings in two rounds: 1910 2nd round 5-0 away
1960 3rd round 1-5 astonishing home defeat, City going a goal up then conceding five to Third Division (and subsequent champions) Southampton.

In the League Cup, meetings in three rounds:
1978/79 5th rd 1-2 away
1982/83 3rd rd 1-1 home, replay 0-4 away.
1999/2000 2nd rd 0-0 1st leg, 3-4 2nd leg after extra time.

In the Tennents Caledonian Tournament of 1976/77 in Scotland 1-1 then eleven all in the penalty shoot out with Saints winning on the toss of a coin!

Friendlies: 1910/11 3-3 a.

Some connections: Mick Channon, Graham Baker, Dave Watson, B-W Phillips, Wayne Bridge, Matt Mills, Ivan Golac Phil Boyer, managers Alan Ball and Kevin Keegan

Ground: The Dell (shown 2000's) R/A 31,044 v Man U Div 1 1969/70. St. Mary's capacity 32,551

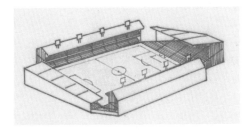

Southend United

'The Shrimpers' were formed in 1906 and joined Division Three in 1920. They played at Roots Hall until moving to The Kursaal in 1915, then The Southend Stadium in 1934 and back to Roots Hall in 1955.

Generally they were a lower division club but made the Championship in 2006, but finished season 2010/11 in League Two. playing in all royal blue.

The teams met twice in Division One in 1996/97 with City winning 3-0 at home and 3-2 away.

John B: 29/10/1996 Southend 2 City 3

Saturday afternoon on a sunny day in August or April would have been a good time to visit one of the most inaccessible grounds in the country, so at least the fans could have enjoyed a day out at the seaside. Alas, the fixture list computer churned out the very opposite of such a plum, in the form of a cold and rainy Tuesday night at the end of October, with everything shut bar the odd shabby pub and a couple of amusement arcades.

In the words of Morrissey, "This is the seaside town that they forgot to close down, oh come Armageddon come."

Thankfully then, reparation came in the shape of the football. This was City's first ever league game at Southend, but as it turned out, the journey, the weather, the inconvenience, were all worthwhile, for this was to be one of those occasions when the most naturally talented footballer of his age, had one of his very, very special nights.

When City had been relegated from the Premiership six months earlier, the big fear for many Blues was that Georgi Kinkladze, the club's little Georgian wizard, would leave for pastures new. That he then committed career suicide by opting to stay, in a division where he would be man-marked and kicked black and blue almost every single week, did not dissipate the thrill his continued presence gave the supporters. Kinkladze was a ray of light, a talisman, a diamond sparkling in a sea of shit, and at Southend, he was simply brilliant; a twisting, spinning, electrifying dervish, as out of place in the Stygian gloom of a wet and misty Roots Hall, as a Mozart concerto on a Jedward CD. By the time his befuddled Southend shadow was hauled off with 20 minutes left, after a night of utter torment, City were 3-0 up, with Kinky having scored two and made the other. First he teed up Uwe Rosler after one of his trademark 40 yard dribbles, then, after another mazy run and a slick one two, he rolled the ball into a twelve inch gap between keeper and post from an oblique angle, and finally after Paul Dickov had dived shamelessly in the box, he slotted home a nonchalant penalty.

There is however, an old adage. Give City a three goal lead, and they're just about level. Kinkladze departed injured after one of the opposition cloggers finally caught up with him, Southend pulled one back after 80 minutes, scrambled another after 85, and then laid siege to the City goal for the remaining 5 minutes, reducing the nerves of the travelling support to shreds. Shots off the line, acrobatic saves, open goals blazed wide, vociferous penalty appeals, we endured the lot…..and survived, just. Driving home afterwards, the match reporter on the radio was still drooling, exhorting listeners to get along to Maine Road to watch little Georgi whilst they still could, and although we took due advantage, the tragedy was that the old First Division soon took its toll, and we seldom got to see the little maestro play with such panache again.

In the FA Cup just the one meeting, with City winning 1-0 at Roots Hall in the fourth round of 1956, when to drain the pitch cockleshells were utilised in trenches and Bert had to play a blinder to keep the Third Division outfit at bay.

In the League Cup in 1986/87 the teams met in the second round. City drew 0-0 at Roots Hall in the first leg, the day after manager McNeill moved to Villa, and City won the second leg 2-1.

Some connections: Shaun Goater, Barry Conlon, Billy Lot Jones

Ground: Roots Hall (shown 1996) R/A 31,090 v Liverpool FA Cup 3 rd 1979

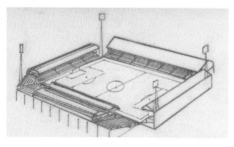

Southport

'The Sandgrounders' were formed in 1881 as Southport Central F.C. playing at Sussex Road Sportsground and Scarisbrook New Road moving to Ash Lane in 1905. They became Southport Vulcan F.C, in 1918, being owned by the motor company and the ground was re-named as Haig Avenue in 1921. Southport F.C were founder members of Division Three North in 1921, playing in the lower leagues, but were voted out of the Football League in 1978 replaced by Wigan Athletic.

They finished season 2010/11 being relegated from the Blue Square Conference but then were reistated owing to the expulsion of Rushden & Diamonds. They play in an all yellow strip.

The teams have met just the once, in the **League Cup** second round of 1969/70, City winning 3-0 at Haig Avenue.

Some connections: Jimmy Meadows (below)

Friendlies : 1900/01 a 1-3, 2009 RF

Ground: Haig Avenue (showm 1970) R/A 20,111 v Newcastle FA Cup 4 1932.

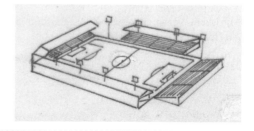

South Shields

'The Mariners' were first formed in 1897 but folded in 1902. South Shields Adelaide, 'The Laddies' came into being in 1899, dropping the Adelaide name in 1905. They moved from Stanhope Road in 1908 to The Horsley Hill Ground, R/A 24,348 v Swansea in 1926/27, joined the Second Division in 1919/20 but folded in 1930, the club being taken over in its entirety by Gateshead, in the move to Redheugh Park. They reformed again in 1936/37 playing at Simonside Hall but folded again in 1974. They re-formed yet again in 1951, moved to Filtrone Park in 1992 with links to the local Filtrone factory, manufacturers of cigarette filters and continue in non league football playing in claret shirts with sky blue sleeves and white shorts.

The teams met four times in the Second Division in 1926/27: 1-2 home, 3-0 away and 1927/28 2-2 home and 1-0 away so 2 wins 1 draw and 1 loss for City

Standard Liege

Formed in 1898 by students from a Catholic college, and moved to the Stade de Sclessin in 1909. They were Cup winners in 1954 and won six titles and two more cups between 1958 and 1971, Paul Henrard a local steel mill owner ploughed the money in.

They had a good pedigree in Europe reaching the semi-finals of the European Cup in 1961/62 losing to Real Madrid, and also lost to Leeds in the Q/F in 1969/70. They also lost to Leeds in the Fairs Cup of 1968/69 and went out of the Cup Winners' Cup semi-final in 1965/66 to Bayern Munich. In the UEFA Cup they'd reached the third round twice and before facing City had knocked out Dundee United. Och aye.

The teams first met in the second round of the UEFA Cup in 1978/79, City winning the first leg 4-0 at Maine Road, but losing the second leg 2-0 in Belgium.

Howard Y: 1/11/1997 S. Liege 2 City 0

As travel organiser for the supporters club, the actual game came as second priority to getting fans there and back safely.

My dad, Bob, worked in the travel club and organised the 24 hour flight with a one night stay in Brussels. At the last minute there were three cancellations and it was decided that Mary (my wife), my sister, and son Robert aged three, would use them. I knew nothing of this.

Supporters' club vice chairman, Ron McCoy, and took the two day, one night trip overland which was more economical than the flight.

On our arrival at the Liege ground where it was dark and foggy I saw our Robert sat on a fence, but thought it can't be? But it was, he was making his European debut at that age.

After a dismal result the players trudged off the pitch and Robert was upset that the team and Joe Corrigan, his hero, in particular, did not come over to the fans.

We got back to Brussels, tired and hungry, and found a bar we thought was selling food. A young blonde prostitute tapped me on the shoulder and asked me if I wanted sex! "No. I'm only here for the spaghetti bolognaise" I replied. On hearing this, Ron sent a mouthful of beer across the room and it was a story which followed me for years afterwards as you can imagine! The kitchen was closed anyway! There were no hitches on the trip, no trouble or hooliganism.

Friendly: 1966/67 a 1-0

Connection: Johnny Crossan.

Ground: Stade De Sclessin

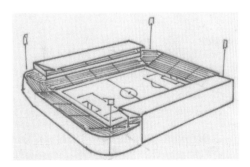

Stockport County

'The Hatters' were formed in 1883 by members of Wycliffe Congregational Chapel as Heaton Norris Rovers, changing their name to Stockport County in 1890. They entered Division Two in 1900, spending most of their time there. They moved from Green Lane to Edgeley Park, first occupied by the rugby club in 1902.

Post war seasons were spent mainly in the lower divisions before making it to Division One in 1996/97, staying there for five seasons until 2002.

They finished season 2010/11 in League Two, after going into administration, being relegated to the Blue Square Conference, playing in blue shirts and white shorts.

Pre-war: 4 league meetings all in Division Two, City winning all four. First in 1902/03 5-0 home and 2-0 away then in 1909/10 2-1 home and away.

Post war: 6 league meetings with one City win, 2 draws, and 3 losses.

Neil S: 2/5/1984 Stockport 0 City 4

The plot for Rocky V could have been loosely based on the relationship between Manchester City and Stockport County. Be nice to people on your way up because you might meet them on your way down.

During the 1981-82 season my sixth form budget extended to a season ticket at both Maine Road and Edgeley Park. I was stood on the Railway Terrace when Tommy Sword scored from a corner against Sheffield United and I also attended the return fixture at Bramall Lane

I always admired the camaraderie amongst the County faithful .They all appeared to live on the same street and enjoyed ridiculous nicknames from 'China' and 'Dicky Mint' to 'Hammerhead' and 'Captain Beefheart'.

At the end of the 1983-84 season Stockport celebrated their centenary with a friendly against City at Edgeley Park. The match was a one sided affair, but I was more concerned with getting home in one piece.

The game exposed the myth that hooligans are only interested in fighting with each other. Dozens of innocent City supporters were attacked in the streets as the Stockport low life vented their spleen. At one point two supporters were fighting on my car bonnet.

Despite the obvious warning signs I attended matches at Edgeley Park for almost another decade. To paraphrase Howard Kendall, I was married to Manchester City, but I was also sponsoring a little orphan child in Africa.

Unfortunately the little orphan child grew into a petulant spoilt brat. Maine Road was in turmoil and my two worlds collided on a dreadful November afternoon in 1997. City were hopeless, but there was something about the reaction of the County supporters that triggered a change in attitude. Never again would Stockport County benefit from my and many other City fans' financial assistance.

In the League Cup City won their first game in this competition 3-0 at Maine Road in 1960/61. Crowd was 21,005.

Friendlies: 1893/94 h 3-0 a 0-0; 1898/99 **h** 2-0 Healey Cup sf; 1901 H/Cup final 5-1; 1917/18 h 1-0 a 4-1; 1939/40 a 5-0 h 7-2; 1966/67 a 0-1; 1975/76 a 5-0; 1976/77 a 2-0; 1983/84 a 4-0; 1988/89 a 3-1 (Tommy Sword T/M); 1990/91 a 4-1 (Eric Webster T/M); 1991/92 a 2-2 (Andy Thorpe T/M): 1995/96 a ?1999/2000 a 2-1 (Roger Wylde T/M), 2000/01 1-4 a (Jim Gannon T/M), 2008/09 a 2-2.

Some connections: Ken Mulhearn (below), Alan Ogley, Bill Williams, Asa Hartford, Stuart Lee, Steve Fleet, managers Jimmy Meadows, Bert Trautmann, Mike Summerbee and Roy Clarke. Alec Herd played with son David, possibly the only time a father and son played together in the same team

Ground: Edgeley Park (shown 2010) R/A 27,833 v Liverpool FA Cup 5 1950

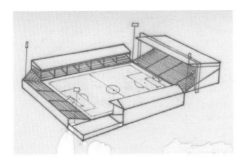

Stoke City

'The Potters' were formed either in 1863 or 1868 when a couple of Old Carthusians, apprentices at the North Staffordshire Railway Company, formed Stoke Ramblers. They played at Sweeting's Fields from 1875 moving to the Athletic Club Ground re-named the Victoria Ground in 1878 or 1883, then to The Britannia Stadium in 1997.

They were founder members of The Football League in 1888 but after relegation folded in 1908 due to financial reasons.

The new club was elected to Division Two in 1919 and changed its name to Stoke City in 1925.

They were a First or Second Division team winning the League Cup in 1972, before sinking to the third tier in 1998 with City but made it back to The Premiership in 2008 where they finished season 2010/11 reaching the FA Cup Final playing in red and white striped shirts with white shorts.

Pre-war: 28 League meetings with 11 City wins 7 draws and 10 defeats. In September 1900 local MP and future Prime Minister Arthur Balfour visited Hyde Road and kicked off the game which City won 2-0.

Post–war: 50 League meetings with 20 City wins 10 draws and 20 losses, including a 1-5 in 72/73 at Stoke. The 1-2 loss at home in 1972, inspired by a tremendous display by Gordon Banks started an end of season run of only 3 wins out of the last six games costing City the title. Trevor Francis made an impressive debut in 1981 at Stoke scoring two goals in the sunshine in a 3-1 win. Boxing Day at Stoke in 1988 saw approximately half the 24,056 crowd made up of City fans, the majority of them being in fancy dress as suggested by the *Blueprint* fanzine, and with the banana craze in full flow. Sadly, after going a goal up, City contrived to lose 1-3.

Barry C: 3/5/1988 Stoke 2 City 5

A trip across the Peak district from Sheffield; first visit to Stoke's new ground, the Britannia Stadium. It was one of my first visits to the new breed of stadium, ostensibly built to conform to modern standards after the Taylor Report on the Hillsborough disaster in 1989.

The sun was shining brightly as we arrived in the Potteries and, with the usual excellent directions from KK (courtesy of Steve Parish), we found the ground, went down the hill and parked up. Dedicated parking for wheelchair users, and right next to the ground! Brilliant! Things were looking good.

This was the final game of season 1997-98, and as things stood, City were 21st in Division One with 45 points, Stoke were 20th with 46 points, We needed to win, and would be safe provided Portsmouth 19th with 46 points didn't win at Bradford City and Port Vale, 18th with 46 points didn't win at Huddersfield.

We were ushered into the City end of the ground, all new facilities, through a tunnel and out on to a platform in the middle of the City fans. Brilliant! At last, after fifteen years' segregation since my accident, I'd be able to watch an away game among fellow Blues. And for once we could see the whole of the pitch, even the goal at the far end.

The view was great until the first time the ball came down the City end. As soon as it got to the edge of the box, everybody around stood up. The atmosphere was electric, but we couldn't see the pitch. I was shocked. The architects had managed to design, and had got permission from the planners for a brand new stadium with excellent access but, with a capacity away crowd, no view for wheelchair users as soon as the ball came within fifty yards.

The match had seven goals, but the only ones we saw were at the dim and distant far end. We actually had a better view of the Stoke fans fighting among themselves as their efforts to get to the City fans were thwarted by the constabulary. We watched, to the tune of "You're Stoke, you're a f**ing joke."

At the final whistle, we'd won 5-2 but then news came through that Portsmouth and Port Vale had won. As many had feared, we were down to Division Two for the first time ever. After Alan Ball and Frank Clark we'd begun to get used to hopes raised and dashed, players who weren't up to it, chronic underachievement and miserable relegation, but even so, the enormity of relegation to Division Three took some dealing with.

We left the stadium. Almost immediately we were brought to a halt; once outside, the police wouldn't allow City fans to go any further. It turned out they were keeping us back till the Stoke fans had dispersed. I remember thinking this would simply give the knuckle-draggers more time to prepare their ambush.

I needn't have worried. We were penned into the car park at the end of the stadium. The police lined up facing us, with their backs to the Stoke fans going home along a path above. All of a sudden small stones, then larger stones then chunks of bricks came flying through the air and landing among us. The police couldn't, or pretended they couldn't, see what was happening. I complained to a policewoman that someone was going to get hurt and as she turned to reply, a brick landed further up the line. There was a commotion, but even then the police did nothing. I pointed out to the WPC that, while able-bodied people might be able to dodge missiles, older people and wheelchair users weren't quite so nimble: we were a sitting target. However this failed to trouble her. We were left to dodge the missiles until her commanding officer deemed it 'safe' for us to move. It didn't feel safe!

It wasn't far to the car, but we'd been kept back that long that as we queued to leave, the players began to come out of the City dressing room on their way to the team coach. First out, looking hot, flustered and with a face like thunder, was Lee Bradbury. I was surprised, then began to feel sorry. He looked chastened, as if he was thinking "What more can I do? I've scored two goals, we've won handsomely, played these off the park in a sea of hostility, and despite all this we've got relegated. I'm totally hacked off, and where's my career going now?" Among his unhappiness there was anger. Hmm, not so different from what the rest of us were feeling then.

As we left the ground and headed for Sheffield, the road took us along a shallow valley. On the far side, among demolished buildings, was a brown

rectangle. It was the old Victoria Ground. It made a forlorn sight: a sepia past amid the dereliction. We decided to press on, and not to cross the valley to inspect more closely. £3.5 million Lee Bradbury, also by now on his way home, left City a few weeks later. Potential unfulfilled, he never played for a major club again. Next up for us, Blackpool at Maine Road in August.

In The Premiership:

Season	H	A	Pl	W	D	L
08/09	3-0	0-1	2	1	0	1
09/10	2-0	1-1	4	2	1	1
10/11	3-0	1-1	6	3	2	1

In the FA Cup, meetings in six rounds plus a final, with City wins including the 1-0 in the sixth round of 1934 R/A 84,569.
1911 1st rd 2-1 home
1921 5th rd 0-1 home
1934 6th rd 1-0 home
1973 3rd rd 3-2 home
1976 4th rd 0-1 away
2010 5th rd 1-1 home, replay 1-3 aet away
2011 Final 1-0

The teams played each other in the 2011 FA Cup final at the New Wembley. It was the first time that Premier league fixtures were played on the same day owing to the requirement for Wembley to be unused for two weeks prior to being available for the European Champions Cup final.

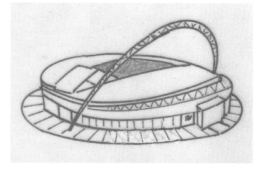

Stoke had beaten Bolton 5-0 in the semi-final and looked to be tough opponents with their physical approach, long ball and danger from long throw-ins by Rory Delap, and corner kicks. However, on the day, City manager Roberto Mancini got his game plan spot on. Stoke were restricted to just one clear cut chance with Joe Hart spreading himself to deny Jones a certain goal in the second half. City missed many chances but Ya-Ya Toure finally clinched it with a goal in the 75th minute at the same end as his semi-final winner against United. There were jubilant scenes at the end of the game with City lifting the Cup, ending the 35 year trophy drought.

In the League Cup, meetings in three rounds:
1963/64 semi-final 1st leg 0-2 away, 2nd leg 1-0 home to go out on aggregate 2-1.
1980/81 2nd round 1st leg 1-1 away, (Tommy Booth going in goal after Joe Corrigan was injured) 3-0 home in the second.
1981/82 2nd round 1st leg 2-0 home, 0-2 away in the second but a 9-8 penalty shoot out put City through. It was the first domestic match to be decided on penalties.
In the first leg of the semi-final, on Wednesday January 15th, at First Division Stoke, Second Division City were without their two main strikers Kevan and Murray. Stoke went ahead in the 43rd minute through a goal by John Ritchie. Five minutes from time Harry Dowd punched out a Bebbington corner and Asprey, previously given a hard time by Wagstaffe, smashed it home from 30 yards. Crowd was 21,019.

In the second leg, on Wednesday February 5th (Att 16,894) Derek Kevan returned to give City the lead after 29 minutes and it was 'game on' But whilst Stoke posed little threat City's finishing was poor and it was Stoke who progressed to the Final, losing to Leicester City 4-3 on aggregate.

Friendlies: 1891/92 h 5-2, h 5-1; 1892/93 h 3-3; 1893/94 a 0-4, h 6-3, 1894/95 a 1-5, h 1-4; 1899/00 a 1-0; 1956/57 a 1-4 ; 1964/65 IOM 1-2, h 3-0 ; 1973/74 h 3-1 (Johnny Hart; T/M) 1985/86 IOM 1-2; 2005/06 a 2-1

Some connections: Dennis Tueart, Mike Doyle, Peter Dobing, Nigel Gleghorn (below), Peter Beagrie

Ground: Victoria Ground R/A 51,380 v Arsenal Div 1 1937, Britannia Stadium (shown 2000's) capacity: 28,218

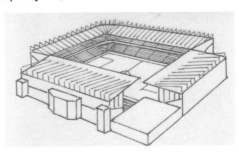

EB/Streymur

Founded in 1993 due to a merger between EB (Eiois Boltfelag), the older club by far, having been formed in 1913 (Streymur founded in 1976). This strengthened the club who rose from the lower leagues in the Faroe Isles making the top Division briefly then permanently in 2000, playing at the Vid Margair stadium, capacity 1,000. They had entered the UEFA Cup in season 2006/07 going out to a Finnish team Mypa in the first qualifying round. Season 2007/08 they'd won the Cup again in June to enter UEFA and were currently top of their league after 15 games 5 points clear, chasing their first title, half way through their season played in the summer and autumn months. Colours were dark blue and black stripes as per Inter Milan.

The teams first met in the first qualifying round of the UEFA Cup in 2008/09. with City winning the first leg away 2-0 in the Faroe Isles, the game being played at the larger venue of the Torsvollur Stadium with a female referee Nicole Petignat. City won the second leg 2-0 but played on Barnsley's ground (see page 32) as COMS was still recovering from the Bon Jovi concert.

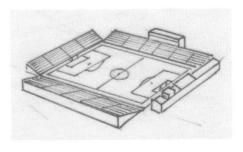

The Trawler Twelve: 17/9/2008
Streymur 0 City 2

Were a group of City fans who decided, during internet postings that it would be a wheeze to chance the trip of a lifetime by driving to Aberdeen, boarding the overnight ferry to the Shetlands, then chartering a fishing trawler to take them to the Faroes on the morning of the game. Leighton Gobbitt, was the 'big cheese' and brains behind the expedition. He was also the City fan pictured in tears at Stoke when City went down, photo being used as the Blues Mission Statement, something he had to live down, probably.

All went well until on arrival in the Shetlands the weather was found to be too severe to allow the trawler to embark on the last lap of the journey. By this time 4-4-2 magazine and the local and national media had picked up on the story. This publicity helped the boys to be taken by the Atlantic Airways plane, which had just dropped off the City team in the Faroes, to return and fly them over. Once in the Faroes they were told they'd be staying in a hotel paid for by Thomas Cook. After the game on the Thursday they were on the island until the Sunday. There was to be a further twist though when Dave Scally (ex Moonchester) was taken ill and rushed to the local hospital. He was operated on for appendicitis and it took him a week to recover. He was flown back to Manchester on the flight with the Streymur team and became a celebrity on the Island.

Connection: Gunnar Neilsen

Sunderland

'The Rokermen' or now 'The Black Cats', were formed in 1879 when a Scottish schoolmaster from Hendon Boarding School formed The Sunderland and District Teachers' Association F.C which then became Sunderland A.F.C. in 1880.

They played at Blue House Field, Groves Field, Horatio Street, Abbs Field, and Newcastle Road before the move to Roker Park in 1898 then The Stadium Of Light in 1997.

They were elected to Division One in 1890 staying there until relegation in 1958, winning the title six times and the FA Cup once. After

that it was all ups and downs but included winning the Cup as a Second Division team in 1973, but also a spell in the Third before making it to The Premiership in 1996 before further ups and downs.

They finished season 2010/11 in The Premiership, playing in red and white stripes and white/black shorts.

Pre-war: 62 meetings with 24 City wins, 13 draws and 25 defeats.

In April 1900 City goalkeeper Charlie Williams scored City's consolation goal in the 3-1 defeat at Roker Park. There are differing reports of the goal. One says it was direct from a goal kick, another that the full back flicked it up to Charlie who lofted it downfield, another says that a Sunderland penalty hit the bar, Charlie then caught it and booted the ball into the Sunderland net. Sunderland goalie, Doig, who touched it in, when asked why he let it go over his head into the goal was supposed to have said "well, as the blessed ball had already passed ten of you on the way, I hadn't the heart to stop it"

Four days after losing 1-6 at Middlesboro City won 5-1 at home to Sunderland, in April 1906.

In January 1932 City went 0-2 down at Roker, but won 5-2 with a Dave Halliday hat-trick.

Post-war: 44 league meetings with 21 City wins 6 draws and 17 defeats.

In April 1950 City went 2-0 up against then league leaders Sunderland, who reduced the arrears with a penalty. Bert then saved a further penalty which had to be retaken, and he showed his annoyance by kicking the ball into the crowd, but also saved the retake. With three games left City were relegated and Sunderland finished third, missing the title by one point.

City registered a 5-4 win at Roker in 1953/54 and a 3-2 end of the season Maine Road win in 1991 when Sunderland were relegated, their fans turning up in fancy dress in the 39,194 crowd,

Neil S: 15/8/1997: Sunderand 3 City 1

There was a period during the dark days of the mid nineties, when it was fashionable to blame all of Manchester City's misfortunes on the sacking of Peter Reid. The Club was a national joke and as the fans wallowed in apparent self inflicted misery, the resurrection of Sunderland was perceived as ample evidence for the prosecution.

An alternative argument suggested that the short term policy of Reid was part of the problem rather than the solution. His obsession with an ageing midfield, coupled with the disgraceful treatment of Clive Allen, Colin Hendry and Michael Hughes, was a major catalyst for the misery lurking on the horizon.

The arguments raged until the irony of Reid's demise at Sunderland in similar fashion. The long ball to Niall Quinn was fine, just as long as Plan B didn't involve a long ball to David White or Kevin Phillips.

On a Friday night, City visited Sunderland for the first competitive game at the Stadium of Light. The teams were heading in opposite directions and fearing the worst, we arrived at a surprisingly sun baked Wearside, in plenty of time for a good drink.

Our first dilemma was the choice of watering hole. How do you know which pubs are friendly when it's the first game at a new ground?

The taxi driver recommended a pub known locally as the Greyhound and dropped us off nearby. It was a scorching afternoon and the pavements were overflowing with a mass of red and white shirted Mackems.

Maybe the heat affected our concentration, but the first seeds of doubt were planted in the shape of two skinhead bouncers bowing theatrically in our direction as they opened the door. Something wasn't quite right.

There was a small queue at the bar, as a deaf and dumb local struggled to order a drink. Luckily the barman knew the appropriate sign language and I remember feeling impressed by his sympathetic reassurance.

It was only when Stewart ordered three pints and the barman offered a pencil, that the penny finally dropped. To paraphrase a well known City song, what on earth was going on?

The barman and bouncers were also deaf and dumb, and as a tap on the shoulder revealed a gorgeous looking blonde girl, dressed in a full Sunderland kit and matching hearing aids, my suspicions were confirmed... She was selling raffle tickets and as Stewart repeated his order in writing, Alistair uttered the understatement of 1997:

"We've walked through the wrong door!"

So the disastrous 1997-98 season began with three Manchester City supporters drinking in the Sunderland Deaf and Dumb Social Club and ended with seats on the pitch at the Britannia Stadium. Life is never boring.

We cut our losses and spent a couple of hours surrounded by deaf Sunderland fans. In all honesty it was the highlight of the day, as City succumbed weakly to the inevitable goal from Quinn and a catalogue of errors from the appalling Vaughan. You reap what you sow and Frank Clark had bought a one way ticket to the Second Division.

In The Premiership:

Season	H	A	Pl	W	D	L
Pre- 08/09			8	7	0	1
08/09	1-0	3-0	10	9	0	1
09/10	4-3	1-1	12	10	1	1
10/11	5-0	0-1	14	11	1	2

In April 2003 Mark Vivien Foe scored the last goal at Maine Road in a 3-0 win. Mark later collapsed and died of a heart attack whilst on International duty in the summer.

In the FA Cup, meetings in six rounds:

1904 1st rd 3-2 home
1913 2nd rd 0-0 home, abandoned after 58 minutes because of overcrowding. 41,709 officially, was a record attendance but City were fined £2,500, and lost the re-arranged game 0-2 away.
1928 4th rd 2-1 away
1955 S/F 1-0 Villa Park
1973 5th rd 2-2 home, replay 1-3 away
1983 3rd rd 0-0 away, replay 2-1 home
Roy Clarke scored the winning goal on a rain drenched pitch at Villa Park in 1955 to put the Blues into the Final v Newcastle, who took a replay to beat Third Division York City. The Blues played out a 2-2 home draw in 1973 against Second Division Sunderland who went 2-1 up after a poor goal kick from Joe Corrigan, City equalising in the last minute. The Wearsiders stormed through in the replay and went on to lift the Cup against Leeds. City later took Tueart, Horswill and Watson off their hands!

In the League Cup: Just the one meeting in 1979/80 3rd round 1-1 at home and 0-1 away.

In the Charity Shield of 1937/38 City won 2-0 at Maine Road, but were relegated at the end of the season!

In the Full Members Cup of 1985/86 it was a 0-0 draw at Maine Road with City going through on penalties, sparking a joyful pitch invasion!

Friendlies: 1891/92 h 2-1, h 0-0; 1896/97 h 2-1; 1897/98 h 0-0; 1998/99 h 0-0 (I. Brightwell T/M)

Some connections: Dave Watson, Dennis Tueart (below), Tony Towers, Peter Reid, Niall Quinn, Mick Horswill

Ground: Roker Park R/A 75,118 v Derby FA Cup 6 1933. Stadium Of Light (shown 2000's) Capacity: 48,300

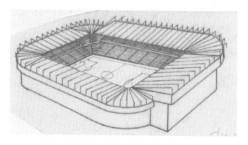

Swansea City

'The Swans were formed in 1912 and moved into The Old Ditch Field, although there was an earlier Swansea club with no connection, then to the Vetch Field. Swansea Town became Swansea City in 1970.

They were original members of Division Three in 1920 and flitted between the lower divisions until 1981 when they made it to Division One moving up from the Fourth Division in 1978 but then went all the way back down by 1988.

They moved to the new stadium in 2005 and finished season 2010/11 in The Championship being promoted to the Premiership and playing in white shirts and white shorts.

Pre-war: 6 League meetings all in Division Two with City winning four including a 7-4 in 1927/28 and a 5-0 in 1927/28 both at home, and losing two.

Post-war: 14 League meetings with 8 City wins, 2 draw and 4 losses.

Roger R: 2/11/1963: City 1 Swansea 0
Team: Dowd, Leivers, Sear, Kennedy, Cheetham, Oakes, Pardoe, Gray, Aimson, Kevan, Young.
Football League Division Two.

My first ever match (as a 7 year old!) the memorable date was November 1963 (oh what a night?!) This match was probably the single reason for me becoming so devoted to the Blues. I remember the day so well, it was bright and sunny with a sky blue sky and fluffy white clouds. The grass at Maine Road was a vivid green, City wore their traditional sky blue and white (and I've been "hooked" on the colours ever since, even the mints I keep in my car have to be sky blue and white!). If I remember correctly, Swansea (Town as they were then, they became Swansea City much later on when Swansea was awarded city status) wore orange shirts and white shorts, so it was quite a colourful occasion!

Alan Oakes scored the solitary goal of the game in front of a Maine Road crowd of only 16000+, and I had the run of the old Scoreboard end at half time as there was loads of empty space in there! It was my first experience of a "big crowd" and a passion for City that has endured through thick and thin ever since, to this day!

The teams have never met in either cup competition.

Friendlies: 1972/73 a 2-0

Some connections: Roy Paul (right), Vic Gomersall, Bobby Owen, Tommy Hutchison

Ground: Vetch Field (Shown 1980's) R/A 32,796 v Arsenal FA Cup 4 1968. The Liberty Stadium 20,500 capacity.

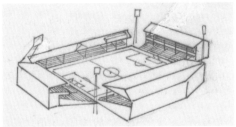

Swindon Town

'The Robins' were founded in 1881 by the Rev. William Pitt, captain of The Spartans, an offshoot of a cricket club who changed the club's name to Swindon Town before 1883 when The Spartans amalgamated with St. Mark's Young Men Friendly Society. They were original members of Division Three in 1920 and were generally a lower division club but made it to the Premiership. in 1993 for one season, after being involved in a Lou Macari betting scandal. They won the League Cup in 1969 and the Anglo Italian Cup in 1970.

They moved from a cricket ground, The Croft, to The County Ground in 1895, and finished season 2010/11 being relegated to League Two playing in all red.

Post–war: 14 league meetings from 1963/64 with 9 City wins including a 6-0, 1997/98 at home, 2 draws, and 3 losses, including the infamous 1-2 at Maine Road before the lowest post war attendance of 8,015, heavy snow being predicted for the day which was a few days after the FA Cup defeat at Shrewsbury.

Charlie H: 10/9/1963 Swindon 3 City 0

For the only time in my City watching career I hitch hiked to Swindon with my mate John. No special trains, no supporters club travel. Nothing!

City were at a low ebb after the relegation in May and I would estimate there were probably less than thirty travelling City fans.

The hitch-hiking adventure started on the A56 in Altrincham at Monday lunchtime. We were eventually dropped off near Ombersley just north of Worcester and were preparing to sleep the night in a country road bus shelter, when a half drunken rep offered to take us further on. He ended up allowing us to sleep in the car in his hotel car-park!

In Swindon we met a southern based businessman who treated us to a café meal, in return for the likelihood of complimentary tickets, which we sometimes obtained off Derek Kevan. John would ask "any spare tickets Mr Kevan" as he alighted from the team bus! I only had 2/9d left (14p) and luckily we did get comps. off the obliging Mr K.

On the return journey overnight after the game, we reached Gloucester, and were walking round the centre with a large bag containing our nick-nacks etc when we bumped into a copper on foot patrol. He gave us the once over, then realised that we were not fugitives from the August 1963 Great Train Robbery.

We then got a lift off a lorry driver who took us to Derby. From there we started walking the Matlock Road and a W.H Smith paper van gave us a lift to Matlock. Absolutely jiggered, John produced his secret ten bob note which he'd brought for emergency use only. It was enough for two singles to Didsbury on the old Manchester/ St Pancras line.

Swindon Town, top of the league at the time, had pasted us 3-0 and their team included Ernie Hunt (who became famous at Coventry) Don Rogers, and a certain 'gentleman' called Summerbee who was creating havoc! I think that at that time the attendance of 28,291 was their record, if not, certainly one of their highest.

In the Premiership two meeting in 1993/94 City winning 2-1 at home and 3-1 away

In the FA Cup, meetings in five rounds:
1910 4th rd 0-2 away
1930 4th rd 1-1 away, replay 10-1 home
1953 3rd rd 7-0 home
1964 3rd rd 1-2 away
2002 3rd rd 2-0 home

Some connections: Mike and Nicky Summerbee

MIKE SUMMERBEE
MANCHESTER CITY & ENGLAND

Ground: The County Ground (shown 1990's) R/A 32,000 v Arsenal FAC 3 1972.

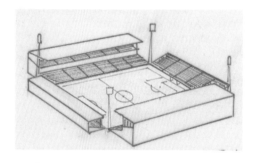

Stuttgart K 1953/54 a 2-2,
Saarbrucken 1954/55 a 4-4;
RSD Strasbourg 1954/55 a 2-3;
Sterk Dusseldorf 1955/56 a 6-1;
St Louis All Stars 1957/58 a 6-2;
St Francisco All Stars 1957/58 a 9-1;
St Mirren 1959/60 a 0-3, h 6-1; 1960/61 a 4-3;
Steirischer Graz 1960/61a 2-3
Sparta Prague 1967/68 h not played
South Australia 1969/70 h 4-0
Shooting Stars Nigeria 1974/75 a 1-0;
Stafford Rangers 1975/76 a 3-1;
South Korea B X1 19075/76 a 2-4;
South Korea Nat X1 1975/76 a 3-0 and a 3-0;
SC Heracles 1978/79 a 3-2
Sporting Club de Portugal 1980/81 a 2-1
FC Sinsheim 1983/84 a 4-1
Selanga State 1984/85 a 1-0
Seattle Storm 1985/86 a 1-0,
San Diego Sun 1985/86 a 3-1;
San Jose Earthquakes 1985/86 a 1-0
F.C Solothurn 1986/87 a 5-0;
F.C Sion 1986/87 a 0-1;
Sandefjord BK 1989/90 a 3-2;
S.F.Grei 1989/90 a 3-3
Skelleftea AIK 1990/91 a 11-1
Shelbourne 1990/91 a 4-1
Shamrock Rovers 1990/91 a 2-2, 4-2 on pens to win the Shamrock trophy!
Santos 1992/93 1-0 (Cape Town)
Sporting Lisbon 1993/94 a *, 2010/11 in USA 0-2
Stalybridge Celtic 1996/97 a;
Scarborough 1996/97 a 2-2; 1998/99 a 4-1 ;
Stirling Albion 1997/98 a 0-0
Silkeborg/F.C. in Aarhus 2002/03 a
Selkirk 2003/04 a 4-1

Friendlies:

South Shore 1892/93 h 5-1; 1896/97 h 6-0;
Sherton 1895/96 a 3-1;
Seedley 1898/99 a 4-0;
Stalybridge and Stockport 1922/23 h 1-0;
South African X1 1924/25 h 3-1
Slavic Sparta 1934/35 a 1-5, h 4-1;
Slovan Sparta 1935/36 h 4-1
St Johnstone 1935/36 a 4-3; 1973/74 a 1-0
Schivenfurt 1936/37 a 3-2;
Shelborne 1946/47 a 2-4; 1990/91 a 4-1;
St Helens Town 1949/50 a 2-0, 1950/51 a 6-0; 1996/97 a 3-0;
Sevilla 1951/52 a 1-5;

T is for Timisoara

The T's take us to, Romania, The South Coast, Wales, London, The Wirral and Holland

FC Timisoara

In 2000, the city's original club Politehnica 1921 Stiinta Timisoara were moved 347 miles to the east by Italian owner Claudio Zambon to Bucharest in order to boost their fanbase. The switch backfired, however, as the club now play in the fourth division of Romanian football.

AEK Bucharest then moved 347 miles west to fill the void in Timisoara when then owner Anton Dobos changed their name to Politehnica AEK Timisoara. They played in the same ground and the same kit as the old Poilitehnica club but were sued by Zambon and had to give up the history of Politehnica, club badge and kit, becoming F.C Timisoara. Marian Iancu replaced Dobos and is also President of the UK based oil company Balkan Petroleum (BKP) and has high ambitions for the club having invested £33M. In season 09/10 they eliminated Shakhtar Donetsk from the Champions League qualifying round before going out to Stuttgart in the next round. They finished second in the Romanian league in 2010 to enter the Europa cup.

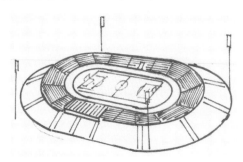

Home colours are all blue, away all white and third strip all yellow.

The teams first met in the Qualifying round of the Europa Cup in August 2010. City won the away leg 1-0 courtesy of a Balotelli goal. He was later booked and then suffered an injury which kept him out for weeks. Crowd was 24,000 with 244 Blues. In the second leg City secured a 2-0 win with goals from S W-Phillips and Boyata in front of 23,542 with 150 Romanians present.

The first leg was played in the Dan Paltinisanu Stadium, a multi purpose arena named after a Bucharest born centre-back who played for the Politehnica Timisoara from 1973 to 1983, and died just before his 44th birthday. The stadium's capacity is 32, 019 all seated and is the second largest in Romania.

Neil S: 26/8/2010 Timisoara 0 City 1

A hobby is something you enjoy, but an obsession rules your existence

For a small group of City fans the game in Romania was always going to be a lesson in logistics. Thomas Cook weren't interested so shopped around, but deep down I was always going to fly from Manchester to Munich and catch one of the three Timisoara connections. Four hundred pounds later, the flight was booked with two nights in Hotel Valentina, opposite the mysterious Banco Transylvania.

The connection at Munich was smooth and faultless. From leaving Whaley Bridge at 3:30am I was drinking in Romania at 2pm local time. Timisoara was two hours ahead so in real terms the whole journey had only taken around eight hours.

I travelled alone, but there were a few familiar faces on the 6:50 flight to Munich, most of them also appearing at the friendly in Dortmund. A mutual nod was the limit of our communication, given the fact that most of us had only managed a few hours sleep.

Lufthansa's cuisine amounted to the usual choice of a cheese or ham sandwich. It was too early for alcohol, but there's something about the English and free beer on a journey into the unknown.

Ordering currency had been a complete pain in the arse. The Listening Bank refused to listen and the Bank that likes to say yes said no. Nat West were the most helpful and kindly advised me to take Euros. All very well until the taxi driver frogmarched me to the ATM. Thankfully I hadn't forgotten my cash card as I paid him in Romanian notes.

The Home Office leaflet had warned of bandits, bushwhackers, dodgy plain clothes policemen and a Dickensian army of child pickpockets. Perhaps they thought we were playing Millwall.

Timisoara was trendier than most of us had expected. There was a relaxing student area within walking distance of the hotel and after bypassing the legendary Alan Potter I settled down for a few pints in Jacks Bar. Becks and Peroni served at only a pound a pint and the local Ursus beer was even cheaper.

The following afternoon I walked to the ground searching for a few souvenirs and a match programme. I found a tacky scarf and a beer garden next to the stadium.

The next couple of hours were as enjoyable as I've ever encountered watching City abroad. The locals had spotted my colours and welcomed me with open arms. A few Blues emerged from the shadows and despite the language barrier there was enough common ground for everyone to enjoy the camaraderie of football. A bit like Elland Road in the mid 1980s.

By the time of the kick off the word had spread amongst the travelling faithful. The atmosphere was friendly, but a combination of hot sunshine and a pound a pint was beginning to take its toll. I was completely bladdered, but some Blues had lost the ability to stand up.

It mustn't rain in Timisoara because the ground was a vast open bowl. The capacity was around thirty thousand, but the City support was minimal. The whole experience was a badge of honour and I wouldn't blame any City supporter who chose to keep his powder dry for another occasion.

In all honesty the game was a total blur. City adopted the Mancini style and gradually wore the opposition down with a mixture of possession football and clever interplay. Balotelli wanted to fight with everyone, but his last minute injury looked, and proved to be, far worse than Mancini wanted us to believe.

For some unfathomable reason the only song from City in the first half was a twenty minute (anti-gutter press?) rendition of the old classic, "Gonna Get Along Without You Now". The locals looked bemused, but not as much as the City fan who spent the entire game lay on the terrace in a drunken stupor.

I returned to my hotel for a few hours sleep, but some City supporters returned to the beer garden. By 6 am we were all at the airport along with a certain Shay Given, who assured

everyone that he was visiting a specialist in Munich.

As we waited in Munich for the return flight to Manchester we were joined by our old friend Mike Riley who had been a FIFA observer at the Juventus game at Sturm Graz. He was friendly enough, but looked slightly petrified at the sight of a City fan drinking from a bottle of brandy at 9am in a German airport. He wasn't alone, as the stewardess and pilot handed out a yellow card and final warning on the plane.

We landed at roughly 10:30 am UK time and by lunchtime I was back in the office after hopefully saving a day's holiday for the group stages.

Connection: Costel Pantiglimon

⧓

Torquay United

'The Gulls' were formed in 1898 and moved into Plainmoor in 1910 as Torquay Town merging with Ellacombe then with Babbacombe in 1921 to become United and joining the Third Division South in 1927 replacing Aberdare Athletic.

They've always been a lower league club; dropped into The Conference in 2007, but were promoted back into League Two where they finished season 2010/11 playing in all yellow shirts and shorts.

The teams first met in the League Cup second round in season 1983/84 (City in the Second Division, Torquay in the Fourth) The first leg was a 0-0 draw at Plainmoor, and the second a 6-0 City home win.

Next meetings were again in this competition, the second round in season 1990/91, City winning the first leg 4-0 at Plainmoor, but only drawing the return 0-0 at M/Road.

Dave W: 26/9/1990 Torquay 0 City 4

Our family had progressed from holidays in North Wales in the late 1950's to the south coast delights of Torquay, where the sea was clear, never went out far, there were no jellyfish, and Bruce Forsyth (I'm in charge) and Roy Hudd starred at the Babacombe Theatre! It took all day to get there, on Yelloways coaches, or we'd travel overnight and arrive the next day.

For the League Cup game in 1990 we did

it there and back on the night, due to work commitments the next day. A mate, Kevin, had sussed out which hotel the team were staying in and booked himself in there, so we visited before the game and chatted to the players and manager Howard Kendall, then followed the team coach to the ground.

The game itself was a coast and on the way home, doing the ton on the motorway (firms car!) we drove into the Services only to find them closed. On the way out we went past a police car which was lying in wait for speeding motorists, so a lucky escape!

Friendly: 1929/30 a 3-1

Connection: John Benson

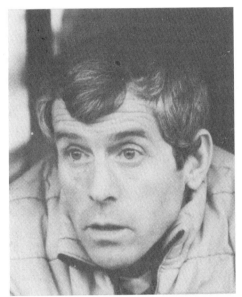

Ground: Plainmoor (shown 1990)   R/A
21,908 v Huddersfield T. FA Cup 4 1955

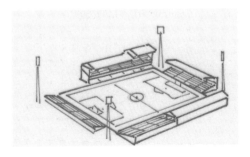

Total Network Solutions

LLansantffraid F.C were sponsored by TNS in 1997 and took on the sponsors name. They'd previously lost in Europe 1-6 on aggregate to Polish Cup winners Ruch Chorzow in 1996

The teams first met in the qualifying/preliminary round of the UEFA Cup in 2003/04.

The first leg was played at Eastlands (first competitive game) resulting in a comfortable 5-0 City win, though the crowd of 34,103 expected more (but Liverpool fared similarly – 3-0 home and away, when they played them a few years later)

The second leg was played at The Millennium Stadium, Cardiff, Wrexham's Racecourse Ground being unavailable. City fielded a virtual reserve team to win 2-0 in front of 10,123, most Blues taking advantage of an unusual visit to the Welsh National Stadium, though some struggled with the traffic.

When TNS were taken over by British Telecom in 2006, the sponsorship lapsed, there was a merger with Oswestry Town and they became The New Saints playing in the Welsh League in green and white hoped shirts with white shorts.

Friendly: 1998/99 rf

Ground: The Millennium Stadium (shown 2003)
Capacity: 74,500

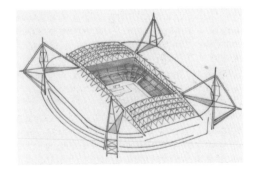

Tottenham Hotspur

'Spurs' were formed as The Hotspur F.C. from old boys of St John's Presbyterian School and Tottenham Grammar School, in 1882 from a cricket club. They played at Tottenham Marshes, then from 1885, after becoming Tottenham Hotspur, at Northumberland Park. They moved to The High Road ground in 1888, re-named White Hart Lane in 1920, though the ground isn't on WHL, and the nearest tube station is Seven Sisters, not Tottenham Court Road! The club were elected to Division Two in 1908, replacing Stoke or Lincoln, after winning the FA Cup in 1901 as a Southern League team.

Spurs spent most of their time in the First Division after their 1909 promotion, becoming Champions just twice, in 1951 and 1961, the first modern team to do 'the double' They are regular F. A Cup and League Cup winners, and were the first English team to win a European trophy, the Cup Winners' Cup in 1963, and have also won the UEFA cup on a couple of occasions.

They finished season 2010/11 in The Premiership playing in white shirts with navy blue shorts.

Pre-war: 28 league meetings with 13 City wins 7 draws and 8 defeats. Spurs never won a league game pre-war at City, and City won only two at WHL.

In November 1938, Bert Sproston was to play for Spurs but signed for City on the morning of the game and played in the 2-0 win.

In March 1939 at WHL City were 1-2 down with Sproston injured, but he scored two goals as City ran out 3-2 winners.

Post-war: 68 league meetings with 29 City wins, 19 draws and 20 losses

Between 1968 and 1979 City won 14 of the 22 league meetings with 6 draws and only 2 defeats.

There have been some big meetings between the clubs post war – the 5-1's at Maine Road in 1958 and 1959, the 1-5 at WHL in 1958, when the City players were affected by the Munich air crash, and the referee. The 1-0 City win at WHL in 1960 when a Spurs penalty was parried by Bert as the referee blew for half time, to deny Cliff Jones who netted the rebound. City later ended Spurs eleven match winning run with a 1-1 draw at The Lane in 1961. Then there were the 'ballet on ice' games of 1962, 6-2 and 4-1 in 1967 both at Maine Road, plus the 5-0 in 1977 which virtually sealed Spurs' relegation.

The Guvnor: 4/5/1968 Spurs 1 City 3

London, May 1968 this time it was the shelf at Tottenham about thirty of us went in and the Spurs boys were in good voice, "City, where are you" they were chanting at our crew behind

the goal. Little did they know, we were standing amongst them. The signal went up and in we went, we must have been in there for about three or four minutes, it seemed as if it was an hour. We did get battered but we had a go and hurt a few of them, One lad of ours was slashed with a Stanley knife and one guy had been hit with a steel truncheon. We did manage to get the kid who did that, and we used his own truncheon on him but got rid of it as the old Bill pulled us out. City fans were chanting "City here, City there, City every f*ckin where", and we earned a rapturous round of applause from the three thousand or so City behind the goal. After the game we ran the Tottenham bootboys off the tube station, our numbers were too great for them, they had not expected the amount we took.

In The Premiership: only four City wins, including the 5-2 at Maine Road in 94/95.

Season	H	A	Pl	W	D	L
Pre-08/09			22	3	4	15
08/09	1-2	1-2	24	3	4	17
09/10	0-1	0-3	26	3	4	19
10/11	1-0	0-0	28	4	5	19

In the F,A, Cup, meetings in a record ten rounds plus a Final

1909 1st rd 3-4 home
1914 2nd rd 2-1 home
1922 3rd rd 1-2 away
1930 3rd rd 2-2 away, replay 4-1 home
1935 3rd rd 0-1 away
1954 4th rd 0-1 home
1956 s/f 1-0 Villa Park
1969 6th rd 1-0 home
1981 F 1-1, replay 2-3
1993 6th rd 2-4 home
2003/04 4th rd 1-1 home, replay 4-3 away

Monumental games, full of incident, included the 1956 semi final 1-0 win at Villa Park. City started nervously and Bill Leivers kicked off the line early on, but City then took control with Bobby Johnstone scoring with a header just before half time. City had their chances in the second half but failed to increase their lead and suffered a stroke of luck when Bert appeared to hold Robb's leg five minutes from time, as the Spurs forward shaped to shoot into the open goal. No penalty was given, and City were through to their second successive final. In the 6th round of 1969 City overcame a surprisingly tough Spurs team 1-0, then the next meetings were the Centenary Cup Final and replay of 1981.

Up to the Final City had a tremendous record against Spurs and also boasted a higher average home attendance than the Londoners that season, so the media hype, Chas 'n Dave's 'Ossie's dream' and all that was a bit galling. Tommy Hutchison gave City the lead with a rare flying header, Steve McKenzie hit the post and Tommy Hutch deflected Hoddle's late free kick agonisingly past Joe's reach into the net. City were stronger in extra time but just couldn't make it count, and the game finished at 1-1 to Spurs' relief. City fans were well outnumbered on the Thursday night replay, with many Spurs fans infiltrating City areas at Wembley. Villa made it 1-0 after seven minutes, but City equalised with a Steve Mc stunning volley three minutes later, missed by many Blues who were battling with Spurs fans in the City end. Kevin Reeves made it 2-1 in the 50th minute with a penalty after David Bennett had been fouled, but Spurs equalised through Crooks in the 70th minute. Five minutes later Villa, sportingly applauded by City fans as he forlornly left the field when substituted on the Saturday, then scored THAT goal, and despite Tueart's late attempts the Cup was Spurs'. They went on to greater heights, becoming a bogey team for us as City went into decline. Oh what might have been?

Then there was the infamous 2-4 Maine Road loss in 1993, when the new Platt Lane/Umbro stand was opened, and City fans invaded the pitch, after Terry Phelan scored City's second. The club faced a suspended fine of £50,000 and one match to play behind closed doors. Some revenge was gained in the unforgettable win at the Lane in the 2004 replay. After being 0-3 down at half time, with Nicolas Anelka limping off and Joey Barton sent off, City produced the most famous come back in Cup history scoring four second half goals, despite being down to ten men, to win 4-3. Joy was relatively short lived as the Blues went out in the next round at Old Trafford.

In the League Cup, meetings in three rounds:
1992/93 3rd rd home 0-1
2003/04 4th rd away 1-3
2007/08 5th rd home 0-2

Some connections: Bert Sproston, Paul Stewart (below), Neil McNab, Clive Allen, Vedran Corluka

Friendly: 1982/83 h 0-2

Ground: White Hart Lane (shown 2000's) R/A 75,038 v Sunderland FA Cup 6 1938.

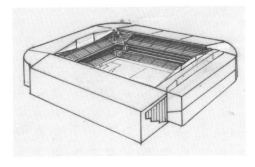

Tranmere Rovers

'The Rovers' were formed in 1884 as Belmont, adopting their present title the following year and joining the Third Division North in 1921.

They played at Prenton Park, but moved to a new ground, also Prenton Park in 1912 along with Northern Nomads who moved out in the early 1920's.

Again a lower division club, but having their moments including a League Cup Final appearance in 2000 losing 1-2 to Leicester.

They finished season 2010/11 in League One playing in all white shirts and shorts

Pre-War the teams first met in the Second Division in season 1938/39, City winning 5-2 at home and 9-3 away.

Post–war just the four meetings in the 1997/98 and 1998/99 seasons, City winning one and drawing three.

The teams have never met in either Cup Competition.

Brian D: 31/1/1998 Tranmere 0 City 0

My only trip to Prenton Park was memorable as it was the first time I took my son, Joe (named after you know who) then aged 7, to an away match. This was the season that culminated in our dreadful drop into the abyss of level three football. Bless him, in his first five years of supporting City we were either relegated or promoted at the end of each season – the poor lad thought that was the norm! Anyway, at this stage of the campaign I don't think I had really contemplated that this was likely. I decided that we would attend this match as it was the nearest away ground to us and, joy of joys, you could just turn up and pay at the turnstile. Almost as good as this was arriving at the stadium and being able to park on a field, right next to the ground. For someone used to parking on Hough End and having to walk/carry the lad the last 25 minutes to Maine Road this was decadent luxury!

Prenton Park is quite a tidy stadium with a decent capacity for a club that has always played in the lower divisions and consequently we had been given the whole of one end, which filled up as kick-off arrived. Joe still recalls two Blues carrying a life-sized cardboard cut-out of Alan Shearer on which they had placed a City shirt. This was paraded up and down in front of the stand whilst we all shouted "Shearer, Shearer". At the time, he was the absolute business and regularly scored for England. Typical of our self deprecation as, at the time, he was way, way beyond our means. (Sometimes it's useful just to remind ourselves of where we've been – it makes where we're going all the sweeter!). My memory of Tranmere fans, or "Plastic Scousers" as they are referred to locally (or "Skip Rats" as they are known to Wrexham fans) is that the other three sides of the Stadium were not much more than half full. We were entertained, however, by half a dozen or so kids in the near corner of the stand to our right doing their best impressions of hooligans. I certainly couldn't make out any of their chants, and I doubt that anyone else could so their posturing and gestures seemed all the more amusing, especially as there were

about four thousand of us! I have to say I felt we were made very welcome, chatty turnstile attendants and stewards, with young City fans being invited onto the pitch to take part in a Keepy-Uppy competition along with some local youngsters. So as ever, everything was great – until the football started! This was one of the worst matches I have ever witnessed in my life. We were poor, they were worse! I still contend that we had some good players at that time – Georgiou Kinkladze, "Mighty" Murtaz Shelia, Ian Brightwell and Uwe Rosler - but they looked like strangers to each other and what the system of play was supposed to be was anybody's guess. I had hoped that the mass of City fans would really raise the roof and give Joe a taste of 'real' atmosphere, away from the family stand. It was as much as we could do to stay awake, and the home fans were no better. Inevitably, due to the ineptitude of both teams, the score remained 0-0. At the final whistle I contented myself with the thought that at least Tranmere were yet another club who would finish below us (Doh!)

Friendlies: 1965/66 a 3-2, 1973/74rf, 1977/78 Tranmere/Everton, (Dave Russell T/M0 a 2-2, 1982/83 (Ed Robertson T/M) a 5-2, 1998/99 2-2 (Bill Shankly tournament at Preston), lost on pens, 2001/02 0-1 a, 2002/03 (Eric Nixon T/M) a 7-1, 2005/06 a 0-1

Some connections: Eric Nixon, Ged Brannan, Neil McNab

Ground: Prenton Park (shown 1998) R/A 24,424 v Stoke FA Cup 4 1972

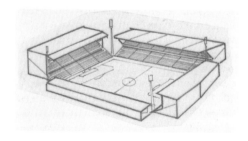

FC Twente Enschede

Twente were formed as recently as 1965 when Sportclub Enschede and the Enschedese Boys clubs merged playing at The Dickman Stadium (shown) until 1998 when they moved to the Grolsch Veste.

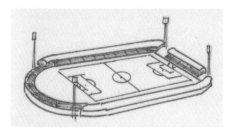

They'd never won the League when they played City, but finished as runners up in 1974, after which they went all the way in the UEFA Cup to the two legged final only to lose to Borrussia Monchengladbach. They won the Dutch Cup in 1977 and 2001.

The teams met in the first round of the 1978/79 UEFA Cup, with City drawing 1-1 away, thanks to Dave Watson and winning 3-2 at Maine Road with goals from Brian Kidd, Colin Bell and an own goal

Charlie H: 13/9/1978 Twente 2 City 0

This was my last European trip to watch City. After my experiences at Juventus, Widzew Lodz, and the gradual lowering of standards of English supporters in general, I'd reached the conclusion that I did not want to be anywhere near the English abroad. I did go to the 1998 World Cup Finals but made sure I avoided England games.

The Dutch football fans had a very bad reputation and this was reflected when we arrived at the Stadium having flown to Amsterdam, then coached to Enshede. I was staggered on arrival when we were surrounded and escorted to our part of the ground by dozens of alsatian-handling military-style police. That was probably the moment when I concluded "that's enough for me". My City European days were over. I was 33 at the time.

Roger R: 13/9/1978 Twente 2 City 0
Team Corrigan, Clements, Power, Viljoen, Watson, Futcher, Channon, Owen, Palmer, Hartford, Barnes
UEFA Cup First Round, First leg.

Now this was a great team having quality, experience, and talent. At this point in time, I can well recall City fans having high hopes for a great season ahead, and this result almost confirmed it. Against a well drilled Dutch outfit, City earned a great 1-1 draw with a rare goal from big Dave Watson. Dave was a real "tower of strength" at the heart of the City defence, and he often came up with the odd, usually important goal. I was working at City at the time and my mate Ian (in the office) and I both had the chance to go to the game with the official City party. Ian got the trip via the plane, and I got the "short straw" which was the trip via the Hook of Holland on the ferry, ending up in Amsterdam where we must have stayed for one or two nights, then travelled the short distance to the match. This trip was also memorable for me getting the chance to see the Anne Frank house, very moving, and also for a certain "liaison" with a beautiful and blonde member of the opposite sex, actually the most sexy and gorgeous woman you could hope to meet (!) but that secret will stay with me and the details are certainly not for printing here thank you very much!

In the summer of 2008 ex England boss Steve McClaren took over as manager. They lost in the Champions League 6-0 on aggregate to Arsenal and dropped into UEFA where they beat Rennes on away goals after a 2-2 aggregate draw. In the first group match they beat Real Racing Club 1-0 at home.

The teams met again in November 2008 in the Group stage of the UEFA Cup, City winning 3-2 at COMS.

They finished season 2009/10 as Champions of the Dutch League for the first time in their history, under manager Steve McClaren.

Connection: Paul Bosveldt

Friendlies: 1957/58 a 4-1, 1990/91 0-1 in Spain

Friendlies:

Third Lanark 1891/92 h 1-1
SC Tasmania 1959/60 a 2-1
AC Torino 1960/61 a 1-1 abandoned,
1961/62, h 4-3, 1992/93 a 0-0
Thor Akureyr1 1981/82 a 5-0
Trinidad 1981/82 a 2-1, a 4-0
Tampa Bay Rowdies 1982/83 1-0 a
Trenggana 1982/83 a 2-0
Timperley 1986/97 a rf
Tom Garner X1 1982/83 h, 1987/88, 1989/90
Tromso 1989/90 a 0-0
Truro City 1989/90 a 6-2
Tadcaster 1992/93 a rf, 1993/94 a rf,
1995/96 rf
Trafford 1995/96 a rf
Thailand Nat X1 youth game
Tianjin Samsing 1996/97 a 1-1
Torpoint 1998/99 a 2-1

U/V is for Valencia

Just the 'U' friendlies, and the one 'V' which take us over to Spain...

Valencia

'Le Che' (The Bats) were formed by students and foreign residents in 1902, after Citrus fruit merchants visited GB and also British sailors were spotted kicking a ball about at the port. They reformed in 1919 playing at a modest ground Algiros Park until moving in 1923 to Campo De Mestalla, eventually renamed, sexily, but briefly as Estadio Luis Casanova. The ground suffered damage in the Spanish Civil War, but was rebuilt impressively.

They've won the Spanish Championship and Cup on a number of occasions, particularly in the forties, and were the third biggest club in Spain behind Real and Barcelona. In the early sixties they won the Fairs Cup twice and were finalists once. They won La Liga again in 1971 under manager Alfredo Di Stefano, and entered the UEFA Cup as runners up in 1972.

Mario Kempes, who helped Argentina win the World Cup in 1978 was a future star for them, and they won the Cup Winners' Cup in 1980. After stagnating in the 80's and 90's they re-emerged in the 2000's to win La Liga twice, were European Champions League runners up twice and won the UEFA Cup in 2003/04 after which manager Rafa Benitez left for Liverpool. In 2009 they encountered financial problems, and work on the new stadium has now been halted, owing to the sale of the Mestalla falling through.

The first competitive meeting of the teams was in season 1972/73 and it was City's first entry into the UEFA Cup.

The first leg finished 2-2 at Maine Road in front of a crowd of only 21,698, Valencia playing in all white. In the return leg City underachieved again going down 2-1 in front of 54,000.

DI STEFANO—The Manager

Graham C: 27/9/1972 Valencia 2 City 1

Final details of our trip to Spain were being sorted out the Saturday before, on a train heading for Stoke-on-Trent, where City were playing at the Victoria ground. Our group consisted of Dave Leonard (alias Jack Le Feet), Dave Hanley, also a great Lancashire cricket fan, and myself, just a crazy football nut. During the short trip, travel details were discussed and a meeting point, Chorlton Street coach station was arranged for Tuesday at 11pm. I have to say the trip home from Stoke was a quiet affair as the home team demolished City 5-1.

So Tuesday evening arrived and we all secured ourselves on the 11.30pm overnight North Western service to London. (this service has served us very well over the years, getting us to the various London venues in the pursuit of following the super Blues)

After a bacon butty in our favourite cafe in Victoria, Heathrow was next on the agenda and off to Spain we went. I remember one of the topics we talked about at length on the flight was the absence of Joe Mercer this season.

Joe had been sent to Coventry and team affairs were in the hands of good old Malcolm Allison. Unfortunately for Malcolm the early results that season were not good.

Anyway, after getting a bus into the centre, we trampled around some back streets and eventually found our two star hotel. After a short rest and brush up we did the usual tour of the central bars and cafe's and eventually hopped on a tram to the ground.

We were quite impressed with Valencia's arena and to this day 37 years later I still do not know the official attendance. City's programme gave it as 35,000 but it was down as 54,000 in Rothmans annual. In the ground we joined a small but very loud band of City fans who cheered all through the match. I remember Valencia attacking from the off (as they did at Maine Road in the first leg where the result was 2-2) with the old Real Madrid legend Alfredo Di Stefano in charge. The home side came through 2-1 winners (aggregate 4-3) Rodney Marsh gave City hope but Valencia's pace up front caused too many problems.

City had Ronnie Healey in goal because of an injury to big Joe Corrigan. Ron came in for some stick for one of the goals, but overall I thought he did well enough. Anyway after supporting our team in a European country, it was back into the city to enjoy ourselves, which we did with a few other City fans.

For reference the team that lined up in Valencia was, Healey. Book. Barrett. Doyle. Booth. Oakes. Summerbee. Bell. Marsh. Lee. Towers. Only one substitute allowed in those days and it was Ian Mellor (the original Spider).

Coming home the same way we went, I remember hearing the sad news that the one time 'Mr Manchester City,' that grand old gentleman and Club President, Albert Alexander had passed away, on the day of the game.

Friendlies: 1986/87 a 0-2, 2007/08 h 0-1 Thos Cook Trophy, Sven's first home game in charge. 2009/10 h 2-0. 2010/11 h 2-0

Connections: David Silva

Ground: Estadia Mestalla cap. 55,000 moving to Nou Mestalla cap. 75,000

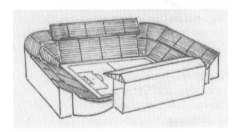

Friendlies:

Ulster United 1957/58 a 8-2

USA American soccer Stars 1957/58 a 7-2

US Fiave (Italy) a 5-0

Victoria 1969/70 a 3-0

Vancouver Whitecaps, 1979/80 a 0-5, 1980/81a 0-2, 2011/12 a 2-1

Vebo /Lovangers AIK 1987/88 a 12-0

BK-IFK Vaasan Pauloseur 1988/89 a 2-0

Vilhelmina 1990/91 a 7-0

Vicenza 1992/93 a 0-1

Verona 1992/93 a 2-2

Vitesse Arnhem 1977/78 a 2-1

Valerengen IF 1982/83 a 3-1

W is for Walsall

THE W's take us down to the Midlands, the South, London, Poland, Lancashire, and North Wales...

———⊷∗⊶———

Walsall

'The Saddlers' were formed with the amalgamation of Walsall Swifts (formed 1877) and Walsall Town (formed 1879), becoming Walsall Town Swifts in 1888, then plain Walsall in 1895.

They first played at The Chicory, then The Oval briefly in 1893, then West Bromwich Road, moving to Hillary Street in 1896, re-named Fellows Park in the 1930's and the Bescot Stadium in 1990.

They were elected to Division Two in 1892, failed re-election in 1895, were re-elected in 1896 until 1901 when they again failed re-election. Became original members of Division Three North from 1927 and flitted between North and South and Fourth, Third and Second divisions.

They reached the League Cup semi-final in 1984 and finished season 2010/11 in League One playing in red shirts and black shorts.

Pre-war: 12 league meetings, between 1892/93 and 1898/99, City winning all the homes (including a 6-1 in 1894/95) two aways, two draws and two defeats.

Post-war: 8 league meetings, with 3 City wins and 5 draws, the most notable being the 3-3 away draw in 1988/89.

They also pipped us to automatic promotion from Division Two in 1999.

Neil S: 25/3/1989 Walsall 3 City 3

Considering that our paths have rarely crossed, the memories of encounters with Walsall are remarkably large and varied.

We've played the Saddlers in both the old Second Division and the new Second Division. We also beat them in the League Cup at Old Trafford and the FA Cup at Fellows Park. Our

last engagement was at the Bescot Stadium. We've played with white balls and orange balls and even witnessed Steve Daley playing for the opposition.

Mick Chandley's cousin Stewart lived near Walsall. He supported Glasgow Rangers, but more importantly he was friendly with the landlord of the Royal Oak. The pub was within walking distance of Fellows Park and we'd supped there before games at Villa and Birmingham. When City played at St Andrews in 1989, the landlord had promised to arrange a football quiz before the Easter fixture at Walsall.

By the time of the match, a number of City supporting friends had asked if they could also attend the quiz. We entered four teams and the locals were just as keen. It was an enjoyable occasion and the landlord organised a buffet for the travelling supporters.

This was the game when all hell broke loose. Walsall raced into an early 2-0 lead, and as Andy Dibble collapsed in agony, our chances of salvation looked pretty slim as he was replaced by outfield player Nigel Gleghorn.

The goalkeeping jersey looked two sizes too big for Gleggers, but within twenty minutes City were level. Incredibly, we took the lead and with the game ready for the taking we were awarded a late penalty.

Not for the first time, the light at the end of the tunnel was the sound of an oncoming train. Neil McNab missed the penalty and after a suicidal David Oldfield backpass, Walsall were level. City hung on for grim life, but we left the ground with mixed feelings. In true City style we'd managed to draw a game that we should have won, but could easily have lost 5-0.

In the F . A. Cup, meetings in three rounds:
1933 4th rd home 2-0;
1963 3rd (much postponed) rd away 1-0; 1986 3rd rd away 3-1.

In the League Cup just the one meeting in 1973/74 second round resulting in a 0-0 away draw, 0-0 home draw in the replay and finally a 4-0 second replay win at Old Trafford.

Friendlies: 1965/66 a 1-1 ;1966/67 a 1-2; 1977/78 a 4-1;

Connection: Steve Daley.

Ground: Fellows Park R/A 25,453 v Newcastle Div. 2 1961. Bescot (now Banks')
Stadium capacity: 11,300, located adjacent to, and visible from the M6, one of the busiest motorways in Europe which they've finally recognised by erecting an advertising hoarding for the club, but which for some reason, has been up and down!

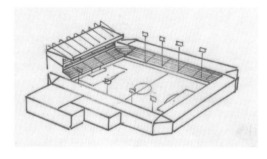

Watford

The Hornets' were formed as Watford Rovers in 1891, though another version of events says that Rovers were not forerunners of the present club whose history began in 1898 with the amalgamation of West Herts. snd Watford St. Mary's.

They played at Cassio Road until 1922 when they moved to Vicarage Road.

They were original members of Division Three in 1920, and were always a lower division club until reaching the First Division with Elton John as chairman in 1982 for six successful seasons, including a Cup final defeat to Everton in 1984. Since then they've had further seasons in Division One and the Premiership but finished season 2010/11 in the Championship playing in yellow shirts with black shorts.

Post-war:10 league meetings with 4 City wins, 1 draw and 5 defeats'
In August 1982 at Maine Road Joe Corrigan went off injured and Bobby McDonald took over in goal at 0-0. Tueart scored and City hung on to win 1-0, winning the first three games of the season to go top but contriving to get relegated the following May.

Colin S: 21/4/2007 Watford 1 City 1

It was my first visit here and I was lucky as I'd left it too late to get tickets and they'd sold out. However my luck was in as a friend rang to say he had his company's box at the game and would I like to join him. I was heavily involved in the Supporters' Trust at the time and was meeting one of the other members when I got the phone call so the two of us went on the train.

We finally arrived at the right place (which was bizarrely accessed via the adjoining hospital) just as our host did, so we were with someone who knew where they were going. The corporate facilities were actually Portakabins in one corner of the ground, opposite the end where all the City fans were but what they lacked in opulence, they more than made up for in the quality of the catering. One of the amusing parts of the afternoon was seeing Noel Gallagher and Bez arrive late into the away fans' stand being greeted with "Who are yer…"

The background to the game was that Watford had been promoted to the Premiership the previous season and looked like they were going straight back down. They'd been in the bottom three for most of the season and anything but a win against us would confirm their return to the Championship. City were in that dreadful final season under Pearce and were on 41 points with 4 games left and still not mathematically safe, with Charlton 9 points behind. We'd had that good run of three away wins at Newcastle, Boro and Fulham that had effectively saved us from the drop and despite losing to Arsenal, were reasonably confident against a team that wasn't good enough for the top flight.

Needless to say it wasn't great football but Watford had the better of the first half, missing a few decent chances. The second half was only 7 or 8 minutes old when Watford keeper Ben Foster took a back-pass and made a calamitous mistake when he played the ball out to the feet of Darius Vassell. Even the decidedly un-deadly Darius couldn't spurn such an opportunity and put us one up.

To give credit to Watford, they upped their effort, and on 75 minutes got one back. This left them 15 minutes to attempt to save their Premiership status but they couldn't do it and it was an interesting and slightly emotional experience being at the home ground of a club that had just been relegated. Charlton had also gained a point so, barring a complete disaster, we were safe. However, the drama wasn't over as phone calls came in telling us about Joey Barton's infamous interview with Ian Cheeseman, which finally sealed Pearce's fate (as was the intention I believe). A few days later, Barton sealed his own, with his physical attack on Ousmane Dabo.

In the Premiership: Two meetings in 2006/07 with a 0-0 home draw and 1-1 away draw.

In the FA Cup, meetings in two rounds:
1986 4th rd: 1-1 home. 0-0 replay away, 1-3 home 2nd replay
1997 4th rd 3-1 home.

In the League Cup just the one meeting in the 4th round of 1987/88, a 3-1 City win at home.

In the Full Members Cup 3rd round of 1986/87 it was a 1-0 City win at home.

Friendlies: None

Some connections: David James, Tony Coton

TONY COTON.

Ground: Vicarage Road (shown 2007) R/A 34,099 v Man U. FA Cup 4th round replay 1969.

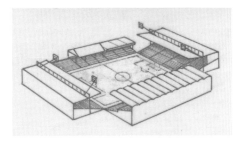

West Bromwich Albion

'The Baggies' or 'The Throstles' were formed when employees of Salter's Spring Works formed a football club in 1878 as West Bromwich Strollers, becoming West Bromwich Albion in 1891. They played at Stoney Lane, moving there from Four Acres in 1885 and moved to The Hawthorns in 1900.

They were founder members of the Football League in 1888, spent most of their time in the top flight, winning the League in 1920, the Cup five times and the League Cup once, but have yo-yo'd recently between the top two divisions but finished season 2010/11 in the Premiership, playing in blue and white striped shirts and white shorts.

Pre-war: 48 league meetings with 17 City wins, 13 draws and 18 defeats.

After the 6-1 home win in November 1921 Max Woosnam, who scored one of the goals, took the whole team out for a meal at the Midland Hotel after the game! There was a 2-7 loss in 1933/34, City's heaviest home league defeat. 2-0 up at half time, goalie and fullback then went off injured. The full back then returned but was limping on the wing, and 7 goals were conceded in the second half. Revenge came with a 7-1 win in 1936/37 at home, - but the Blues were without an away win from 1915 to the war!

Two test matches took place in 1896, a 1-1 draw at home when prices were increased keeping the crowd down to 8,000 and a 1-6 loss away consigning City to another season in the Second Division.

Post-war: 70 league meetings with 32 City wins, 11 draws, 27 losses.

City suffered a 2-9 loss in 1957/58, 4-2 down at one point and a penalty missed. City's 4-0 win in 1955/56 was the first at West Brom since 1914/15 season. City's 2-1 win at Albion in 1973, virtually sealed their relegation with one match to play. City's 2-1 home win on the first day of the season in 1981 was the first for three points. The game at The Hawthorns in 1988/89 was notable for the array of battling inflatables on the City terraces, deflecting somewhat from the 0-1 loss.

John B: 28/11/1987 WBA 1 City 1

Aside from our 1970 League Cup Final triumph at Wembley, on a pitch so rutted, muddy and gouged that it was only a couple of empty canisters of mustard gas shy of qualifying as No-Man's Land, City vs West Brom is a fixture remarkable for its lack of occasion down the years, and probably no contest was less memorable than this routine, mid season, 1-1 draw. Indeed the game has stuck in my mind not for Tony Adcock's late equaliser for City which cancelled out Don Goodman's opener for the Albion, nor for the fact that all 22 players wore shorts so obscenely small and tight that the whole spectacle should have been rated PG and young children barred from attending, but instead for the antics on the away end terrace. Speak to any seasoned football traveller and they'll tell you that the country's regional police forces have, down the years, approached the handling of the beautiful game with differing degrees of zeal and officiousness, ranging from the reasonably helpful (the Met), to the complete and utter bastards (West Yorkshire) to the absolute constables (West Midlands). West Midlands police in the 1980's virtually invented the concept of zero tolerance at English football grounds, to the point that there were Victorian temperance groups run by Mennonites that allowed more fun, and at the Hawthorns on this day in 1987, they were at their tyrannical worst. The attendance numbered barely 16,000, but 5,000 plus of these were City fans. I had driven down from the Wirral with my mate Neil and when the game kicked off the away end was heaving. There being not so much as a hint of trouble, or even come to that, any real badinage between the two sets of supporters. The West Midlands' finest decided, with shades of Constable Savage in the famous Not The

Nine O'Clock News sketch, to invent reasons (or so it seemed) to arrest people, and although we never quite reached the belligerent "looking at me in a funny way" proportions of Griff Rhys-Jones alter ego, the first half of the game was punctuated by the deployment of two and three man snatch squads, who would bulldoze their way through the throng to grab unsuspecting Blues by the collar and eject them from the ground for 'offences' no more sinister or apparent than swearing, shouting aggressively at the referee or looking like they might have had half a shandy on the way in. One minute you'd be talking to the bloke next to you, the next you'd be looking around in bewilderment, like Trigger when Del Boy fell through the serving hatch, wondering where he'd gone! By the time the game finished, the City end was half empty, and not because we'd been crap for once. In all the years I've been going to football before and since, I've never seen such an astonishing number of evictions, and especially not in the face of a complete absence of violence or antagonism.

In the Premiership:

Season	H	A	Pl	W	D	L
Pre-08/09			6	1	2	3
08/09	4-2	1-2	8	2	2	4
10/11	3-0	2-0	10	4	2	4

In the FA Cup, meetings in three rounds:
 1901 1st rd:0-1 away
 1958 3rd rd 1-5 away
 1977 3rd rd 1-1 home, replay 1-0 away

Roger R: 11/1/1997 WBA 0 City 1
Team Corrigan, Clements, Donachie, Doyle, Watson, Power, Owen, Kidd, Royle, Hartford, Tueart.
FA Cup Third Round Replay at the Hawthorns

City had drawn at home in the first match and as was the norm for replays, the home side were expected to win and to progress into the next round. Not so! City fielded an experienced side which fought hard in what was a "snowy wasteland" of a pitch at the Hawthorns. I can remember this match as I was working for City at the time and secretary Bernard Halford had entrusted me to drive down the M6 to meet Albion secretary Alan Everiss (what a nice bloke he was too by the way!) with the replay tickets prior to the first match. So I had a personal interest in the replay when it happened! Anyway, I was there to view the replay and like all true City fans "I kept the faith" in going to a match that could have been a lost cause. I was witness to City dominating the game and deservedly winning 1-0 thanks to a goal from Joe Royle. Expectations were high on the way home that this year might be a good one to win the Cup, but not so, as City crashed out in the 5th round at Leeds!

In the League Cup, meetings in three rounds:
!966/67 3rd rd 2-4 away
1969/70 Final 2-1
1980/81 5th rd 2-1 home

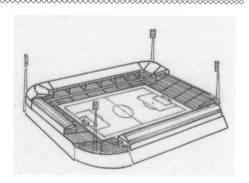

Dave W: 7/3/1970 City 2 WBA 1

Having beaten United in the two legged semi-final, and returning from Portugal after a tough European game with A.C. Coimbre, City faced Albion in the 1970 League Cup Final. The day dawned, it had snowed, and, living down a hill in Doncaster, I started to frantically try and dig my way out as the car wouldn't make it up the slippery slope. As I was about to give up a friendly neighbour, a Policeman, came down to help and after ten minutes of manic digging, I jumped in the car (Riley Kestral 1100) and made it to the station with minutes to spare for the last train to get me to London in time for the kick off. I met some pals outside Wembley who had a ticket for me and swapped with others so that we were all in the same pen. City were soon a goal down, Jeff Astle outjumping big Joe, but Mike Doyle equalised and Glyn Pardoe scored the winner in extra time. We had a few hairy moments with Albion fans on the way back to the station, but went home as happy as can be!

In the 1968 Charity Shield game at Maine Road Champions City beat Cup holders Albion, 6-1, new signing Bobby Owen scoring with his fist touch!

Friendlies: 1891/92 h 4-2;

Some connections: Derek Kevan, Peter Barnes, Gary Owen, Steve Mackenzie.

Ground: The Hawthorns (shown late 50's) R/A 64,815 v Arsenal FA Cup 1937. Highest ground in England!

West Ham United

'The Hammers' came about in 1900 when Thames Ironworks F.C., formed by employees of the shipbuilding yards in 1885 folded in 1900. They played at The Memorial Ground until the move to The Boleyn Ground or Upton Park in 1904.

They were elected to Division Two in 1919 which was increased from 20 to 22 clubs (though Glossop dropped out), spent most of the pre-war years in Division Two, but after promotion in 1958, have generally been a top flight club, winning the F. A Cup three times, and the European Cup Winners' Cup once. England won the World Cup in 1966 including three of their players, captain Bobby Moore, Martin Peters, and hat-trick hero Geoff Hurst. They finished season 2010/11 in the Premiership but were relegated, playing in claret shirts with light blue sleeves and white shorts

Pre-war: 16 league meetings with 6 City wins, none at Upton Park, 2 draws and 8 defeats.

Post-war: 48 League meetings with 23 City wins, 7 draws and 18 losses.

The 3-1 home win in 1947, with three games to go virtually clinched promotion for the Blues.

In March 1960 on Denis Law's (first) home debut, City, losing 1-0, were awarded a penalty in the 38th minute. Ken Barnes jumped over the ball and Billy Mac stepped up to slot home. After vociferous protests from, in particular, John Bond, the referee ordered the kick to be retaken. Inevitably goalie Peter Rhodes saved it! City, though, with three goals in six minutes went on to win 3-1.

In season 1961/62 City were 3-1 up at half time but lost 3-5, then won 4-0 at Upton Park. Season 1962/63 West Ham beat City 6-1 home and away, the home game being significant for Bert Trautmann's sending off for kicking the ball at the ref after the fifth goal with twenty minutes to go, Alan Oakes taking over in goal! The trouncing at West Ham came in the last game of that season when a win may have kept City up but after that result it was almost a relief to be relegated. The 1969/70 home game ended the Hammers high scoring at Maine Road when Jimmy Greaves, on his debut, scored two and Ronnie Boyce returned big Joe's clearance straight back over him into the net from way out in their 5-1 win!

Dave W: 7/11/1959 West Ham 4 City 1

In November 1959, as a 15 year old, I decided to sacrifice local away games at Blackpool (3-1) Preston (5-1) and Burnley (3-4) in order to save up for a visit to West Ham. London by train was advertised at thirty shillings (I went half price), leaving from London Road station, now Piccadilly, at either 11.55 pm on the Friday night or 8.10 am on the Saturday morning.

So it was the Friday night train for me. Met up with the usual crowd - Alan Galley and Co from the other side of town - Hyde, Dukinfield etc. and arrived in London in the early hours in dense fog. Typical. I'd missed three tasty away games for this one which looked like being postponed. The supporters club had arranged for a match with their West Ham counterparts, and as the fog miraculously started to lift we trekked off to the venue, West Ham's training pitch at Wanstead. City supporters were hammered about 11-1, it may have been more, I lost count. We set off disappointedly to Upton Park, where the older fans had a pint in a frightening looking pub whilst us youngsters waited outside. By half time City were two down to an early penalty and a John McTavish own goal, the first of his three in the next four games! Then the announcer gave out the morning's score and the whole crowd roared with laughter. Indignantly I shouted "yes, but you lot didn't have to travel down from Manchester overnight" "You're dead right son" responded a chirpy cockney fella. It could have been Reggie Kray, or maybe Ronnie, I couldn't be sure, but I did appreciate his gesture! Final score was 1-4!

The last game of season 1986/87 at Upton Park saw City second bottom with 39 points, and having to win to get a place in the play offs.

At that time it was a scary place to visit, and the main bulk of City fans travelled by train and tube with a police escort from the station to the ground.

The Blues were up against it, and at 0-1 I caught the ball in the crowd and threw it to Mark Ward from whose corner West Ham scored to make it 0-2. At the end of the game the Hammers' fans invaded the pitch and came over to the City fans behind the goal. Despite Blues chanting "where's your famous ICF" the Londoners, recognising the despondency, having been there themselves, applauded the City fans which was reciprocated. The Police escort was uneventful, with again, the Londoners showing Blues respect and despite batterings off the field either way in the past, this day gave rise to a 'whole new ball game'

Neil S: 11/11/2000: West Ham 4 City 1

"Like most City supporters, I've always admired the close knit support that follow West Ham. The Irons boast a fierce reputation, but their fans have always made City welcome. Somehow I doubt that United are offered the same hand of friendship.

According to his autobiography, Tony Adams launched into an epic drinking spree after the Semi Final defeat at Euro 96. Eventually, he surfaced in the Greyhound at Bethnal Green. The pub has always been a magnet for late drinking City fans.

At this point I should also pay homage to the Kings Arms in Bow and the Black Lion in Plaistow. Treat people as you find them and West Ham will always give you respect.

When Spencer Prior opened the scoring in 2000, a City supporter aimed a volley of abuse at his neighbour on the other side of the segregation barrier. Apart from being ill advised, he was also oblivious to the notion that some City supporters, myself included, were keeping quiet on the other side of the barrier. An hour later we were losing 4-1.

I knew that City were going to be relegated from the moment that Paulo Di Canio humiliated Nicky Weaver from the penalty spot. There was something about the goal that epitomized the gulf in class between City and the rest of the division.

From Mark Ward and Steve Lomas, to Ian Bishop and Trevor Morley, the similarities between City and West Ham are endless. Both clubs have enjoyed a colourful history with self destruction always lurking around the corner.

A Premier League without West Ham isn't a proper competition. They haven't won a trophy since 1980, but their place in history is set in stone.

I remember the ICF controlling the block between the Main Stand and the Platt Lane in 1982. The following season they bought all the seats in H Block. In terms of organised hooliganism, West Ham were light years ahead of the opposition.

I've seen City win, lose and draw at Upton Park. I've witnessed a Bianchi goal in the opening minutes and a Colin Hendry winner in the last minute. Some things never change, but the relationship between City and West Ham is surprisingly warm for English football.

In the Premiership: City wins, included the 2-0 at Upton Park, first game of the Sven era.

Season	H	A	Pl	W	D	L
Pre-08/09			14	5	3	6
08/09	3-0	0-1	16	6	3	7
09/10	3-1	1-1	18	7	4	7
10/11	2-1	3-1	20	9	4	7

In the FA Cup, meetings in three rounds:
1997/98 4th rd 1-2 home
2005/06 6th rd 1-2 home
2007/08 0-0 away, replay 1-0 home

In the League Cup: Just the one meeting in 1984/85, a 0-0 draw at Maine Road and a 2-1 win at West Ham.

Friendlies: 1912/13 a **4-2;**

Some connections: Ian Bishop, Trevor Morley, David James, Steve Lomas (below), Paulo Wanchope, Craig Bellamy, manager John Bond, Carlos Tevez, Eyal Berkovic

Ground: Upton Park/Boleyn Ground (shown early 2000's) R/A: 42,322 v Spurs Div 1 1970/71

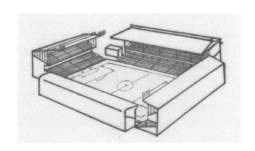

Widzew Lodz

Founded in 1911 as the soccer section of the 'Workers Sports Association' - Widzew Lodz' being the textile centre of Poland.

The club were never prominent, spending time in the lower divisions before finally eclipsing local rivals L.K.S Lodz finishing runners up in 1975/76 to top placed Slask Wroclaw and gained entry to the UEFA Cup, aided by Internationals, goalie Burzynski, centre back Junas, and midfielder Boniek. However, by the time they faced City they'd sacked their coach and 'were unsettled internally and in wretched uncertain form and wouldn't be facing the Blues with any degree of confidence' Some hope!

The first round first leg was played at Maine Road and resulted in a 2-2 draw. City went two goals up, Donachie was sent off, and after their equaliser a City fan invaded the pitch. The club were fined and forced to erect fences for future European games. The second leg was played at the LKS stadium which had a larger capacity than that of Lodz, and was filled with a crowd of 40,000. The scoreline finished 0-0 so the Poles went through on away goals.

Charlie H: 28/9/1977 Lodz 0 City 0

After drawing 2-2 at Maine Road where a micky-taking Boniek riled City fans (one invaded the pitch to have a go at him) the trip to Poland proved to be a nightmare. (Boniek went on to be a great player and had a good career in Italy with Juventus and Roma, even though, as the picture shows, he looked nothing like a footballer!)

ZBIGNIEW BONIEK

The outward journey was from Heathrow, coach first, then flight to Gdansk (Warsaw airport was closed) We then had a chilling journey from Gdansk to Warsaw. Poland was still in the communist grip and we saw military watchtowers at frequent intervals which made me feel as though I was in a World War Two film. Polish farmers were ploughing fields with horse drawn equipment, guided by gaslights at dusk!

The following day we travelled from Warsaw to Lodz and arrived at lunchtime. The game was not played at the 25,000 capacity Widzew ground but at the nearby 40,000 seater stadium (actually benches) of the more famous, at the time, L.K.S. club.

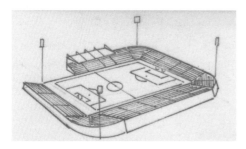

I don't remember too much about the game, but we were mixed in with the Polish fans in good seats on the popular side (the Kippax with benches) We were pestered by Polish people who wanted to accompany us to the toilets – not for sexual favours, before you ask, but for wanting to stake illegal currency exchange deals for pounds or dollars, at several times the normal rate, because that was the only way to obtain medical supplies and other commodities which they needed. Suffice to say that most of us went home with Polish money in excess of what we started off with. This money proved useless in the UK as it was not a currency traded in the usual way!

After the 0-0 draw which eliminated us we were coached back to Warsaw where, prior to a kip in our hotel, most of us went to the only western type nightclub, housed in the cellar or 'The Palace of Culture.' This was a 'crazy horse' type of venue and prostitutes were doing the rounds. One of our group of 35 went off with one for the night and it proved to be of benefit to him at a later stage.

After going to this club, and most of us retiring to bed late, we were due to be up at 6 am to go to the now re-opened Warsaw Airport. I was up on time but plenty weren't and I realised that they would have to be literally dragged out of bed onto the coach. We got away late, hit a massive traffic jam in the rush hour, arriving late at the Airport, where we found our seats had been sold to businessmen desperate to fly out of the Airport which had been closed for a couple of days.

After marching the stranded 35 round Warsaw whistling Colonel Bogey, Howard Yeats (Supporters club travel club organiser) managed to strike a deal with B. A. to fly us back to Manchester via Copenhagen. Unfortunately we all had to sign a document saying that we would refund the cost of an extra Hotel night and flight when we got home. The lad who had gone with the prostitute went straight to the airport in good time and refused to pay the extra costs to get home.

We eventually got back on the Friday and next day set off for Goodison Park for the league match with Everton.

Wigan Athletic

'The Latics' were formed after the demise of Wigan Borough. After years of non-league football they were elected to Division Four in 1978 replacing Southport, and, after Chairman Dave Whelan took over and invested, they went up the leagues and re-located to the JJB Stadium in 1999. They finally made it to the Premiership in 2005, but lost the League Cup Final in 2006 4-0 to United.

They finished season 2010/11 in The Premiership playing in blue and white striped shirts and dark blue shorts.

In the League the teams first met in season 1998/99, City winning both games 1-0.

Later that season in the Division Two play off semi-finals, City drew the first leg at Springfield Park 1-1, going bizarrely a goal down after 20 seconds, from a Wiekens/Weaver cock-up. Dickov equalised after 76 minutes, and Goater scored a disputed goal to win the second leg 1-0 at Maine Road to go through to the formality (!) of a Wembley Final against Gillingham.

In The Premiership:

Season	H	A	Pl	W	D	L
Pre-08/09			6	0	2	4
08/09	1-0	1-2	8	1	2	5
09/10	3-0	1-1	10	2	3	5
10/11	1-0	2-0	12	4	3	5

In the FA Cup, meetings in two rounds, both City wins.
1971 3rd rd 1-0 home,
2006 4th rd 1-0 home
City scraped through the 1971 Cup game 1-0 against non-league Wigan, in front of 46,212 whilst playing in the famous red and black striped away kit at Maine Road, which was a rarity.

Roger R: 2/1/1971 City 1 Wigan 0

City were having a comparatively indifferent season having won the League Cup and European Cup Winners' Cup the previous season but even so this tie against the then non-league Wigan Athletic was expected to be no more than a formality. Played at a foggy Maine Road with the "Match of the Day" cameras there (hoping for a giant killing act no doubt!) when the ground was undergoing renovation (the new North Stand was being erected where the old scoreboard end had once been). City were made to fight all the way against a well-organised Wigan side who had clearly done their homework on City and managed to frustrate the Blues for most of the match. In fact, it was only a single goal from my all time hero Colin Bell, latching onto a through ball and scoring the only goal of the game that ensured City went through to the next round (where they faced and also beat Chelsea at Stamford Bridge)

In the League Cup: Meetings in two rounds:
1982/83: 2nd rd 1st leg 1-1 away, 2nd leg 2-0 home.
2002/03 3rd rd 0-1 away

Friendlies: 1966/67 a 4-0; 1977/78 a 2-1.

Some connections: Fred Eyre, Manager John Benson

Ground: Springfield Park (shown 1999) R/A 27,500 v Hereford 1953/54. JJB/DW capacity: 25,000

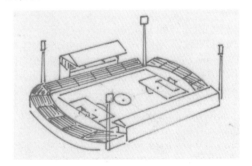

Wigan County

'County' were formed in 1897 playing in the Lancashire League at Springfield Park, but folded in 1900. They would be followed by Wigan Town, Wigan United, Wigan Borough, and Wigan Athletic.

They played City (then Ardwick) in the first round of the FA Cup in 1898 at Hyde Road losing 1-0 to a goal scored by Gillespie from a goalkeeping error.

Wimbledon

'The Dons' were formed as Wimbledon Old Centrals in 1899 by old boys from Central School, becoming Wimbledon in 1905. As a non-league club they won the Amateur Cup in 1963 and turned professional in 1964.

They moved into Plough Lane in 1912, and ground shared with Crystal Palace at Selhurst Park from 1993 to 2003.

In 1977 they were elected to Division Four replacing Workington and rose through the leagues to Division One in 1986 and the Premiership in 1992, after winning the F. A. Cup in 1988 as underdogs against Liverpool. They dropped out of the Premiership in 2000, into Division Two in 2004, becoming M. K. Dons who moved to Milton Keynes.

A new club was then formed as AFC Wimbledon who finished season 2010/11 in the Blue Square Premiership and were promoted to the Football League, playing in Royal blue shirts and shorts.

Post war: 12 league meetings with 2 City wins, 6 draws and 4 defeats.

Neil S: 25/8/1984 Wimbledon 2 City 2

In 2009 I travelled to Stamford Bridge in a Mercedes with Dee Brocklehurst and Derek Price. Twenty five years previously, we'd shared the back of a butcher's van from Whaley Bridge to Plough Lane. Our mode of transport had improved, but our love for Manchester City had never diminished.

Chris Girling was the driver and the usual Whaley suspects were sardined into the cheap seats.

On the opening day of the 1984-85 season, Wimbledon were still viewed as plucky underdogs. Dave Bassett was relatively unknown and the culture of the Crazy Gang was three years on the horizon. Any mention of Wimbledon in 1984 and your thoughts would immediately drift towards their legendary cup run in 1975, when they took mighty Leeds to a Third Round replay.

Plough Lane was a non-league ground, hosting Second Division football. The Social Club was completely overrun by drunken City supporters and this probably contributed to our overall sense of complacency.

In time honoured style, the season kicked off with City 2-0 down after ten minutes. Eventually we rallied, but our dreams of a comfortable

stroll in the park had been crushed. The season progressed in a similar manner.

This was also the game when Clive Wilson emerged as a genuine prospect for the future. He still remains one of my favourite City players of all time.

The previous season had ended with the Chelsea Headhunters causing havoc on the streets of Moss Side. City had retaliated and rumours were rife of unfinished business. Chelsea had drawn at Highbury earlier in the day and the word on the street suggested that their boys were on the way to Plough Lane.

In the days before mobile phones, most fans relied on the hooligan grapevine for information. City were no different and at half time, a barrage of bottle and cans were hurled at a gang of teenagers minding their own business outside the ground. They might have been Chelsea, but for all we knew they could have been locals taking their dogs for a walk.

...English football was only ten months away from its lowest point.

In the FA Cup there's been just the one meeting in round three in 1998/99 a 1-0 defeat for City at Selhurst Park

In the League Cup there have been no meetings

In the Full Members Cup there was one meeting at home in round two of 1986/87, a 3-1 City win.

Friendlies: None

Some connections: Keith Curle, Terry Phelan (below), Brian Gayle

Ground: Plough Lane (shown 1985) R/A 18,000 v HMS Victory FA Cup 3 1935

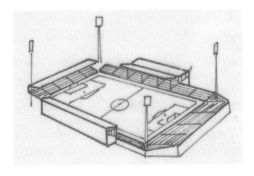

Wolverhampton Wanderers

'The Wolves' were formed in 1879 when players from St. Luke's (founded 1877) and Goldthorn (founded 1876) broke away to form Wolverhampton Wanderers A.F.C. They moved from Dudley Road to Molineux in 1889 as founder members of the Football League in 1888.

They won the FA Cup four times and became a powerful force in the League in the fifties, playing prestige friendlies, against the likes of Moscow Dynamos, Real Madrid etc., winning the league in 1954, 1958 and 1959 and narrowly missing the double in 1960. League Cup success came in 1974 and 1980, plus a UEFA Cup final appearance in 1972, losing over two legs to Spurs. In the eighties they went into decline, dropping to the Fourth, then yo-yo-ing, but finished season 2010/11 back in the Premiership, in their familiar colours of old gold with black shorts.

They have a few impressive celebrity fans including Robert Plant, Noddy Holder, and Kevin Rowlands (though he isn't very impressive).

Pre-war: 30 league meetings with 17 City wins, 4 draws and 9 losses. Wins included a 4-1 home and 6-1 away double in 1903/04, the first of three consecutive doubles. Losses included a 2-3 in the last match of season 1909/10 away (City won 6-0 at home!) which didn't stop City finishing top and gaining promotion. There was a 0-8 in 1933/34 at Molineux, and a 5-0 home win and 0-5 away loss the season after. Wolves first win at City was in 1937/38 at the 15th attempt!

Post-war: 70 league meetings with 21 City wins 18 draws and 31 defeats.

From 1955 until the 1965 games in the Second Division when City recorded a rare double, the Blues failed to beat Wolves in 16 attempts. We suffered some heavy defeats at Molineux, including a 3-7 in 1952/53, 2-7 in 1955/56 and a 1-8 opening game of the season thrashing in 1962 at Molineux, plus a 4-6 at Maine Road in 1959/60. Since then City have pulled it round somewhat. In the 1965 August away game Roy Cheetham became City's first substitute replacing Mike Summerbee.

The December 1956 game at Maine Road saw Bert's return in a 2-3 loss and it was the first Maine Road televised game on BBC TV's Sport Special programme.

In The Premiership:

Season	H	A	Pl	W	D	L
03/04	3-3	0-1	2	0	1	1
09/10	1-0	3-0	4	2	1	1
10/11	4-3	1-2	6	3	1	2

In the FA Cup, meetings in two rounds:
1911 2nd rd 1-0 away
1952 3rd rd 2-2 home, replay 1-4 away

In the League Cup, meetings in two rounds and a Final:
1971/72 2nd rd 4-3 home, after being 3-1 down.
1973/74 Final 1-2
1987/88 2nd rd 1st leg 1-2 home, 2nd leg 2-0 away

Dave W: 3/3/1974 Wolves 2 City 1

The second League Cup meeting was in the Final in season 1973/74, City losing 1-2. I didn't have a ticket for this game and put a request in the local paper, Sheffield Star, to no avail. So I went down without a ticket, arriving at Wembley, wondering what I was doing there, and feeling very vulnerable. I had a chat with ex manager Malcolm Allison, on Wembley Way, then bought a restricted view seat ticket off a tout and watched the game sat behind a stanchion. Kenny Hibbitt opened the scoring for Wolves, Mike Bailey ran the show for them, Gary Pierce had a blinder in their goal. Ex Blue Waggy went off, Colin equalised and hit the post, then the ball deflected off Rodney's heel to John Richards who smacked it into the net with 5 minutes to go. There were plenty of Blues on my train back to Doncaster, who then went on to Hull and the referee was called Dave Wallace!

Most recent meeting was in 1987/88 season, City losing 2-1 at Maine Road, with Eric Nixon letting in a soft one and Wolves fans supposedly banned. In the second leg I attended with a work colleague and Wolves fan Paul Vaughan and sat in the stand with the Wolves fans. City won a little luckily 2-0 to go through to the next round, and Paul later became my boss, though he didn't bear any grudges (I don't think)!

John B: 3/3/1974 Wolves 2 City 1

I guess if you're going to see your team live for the first time, then there are worse places you could do it than at Wembley Stadium in a Cup Final. Manchester, being a whopping 240 miles away from the family home in the South West of England, made opportunities to watch City always to be few in number. Dad had tried to get tickets for the away leg of the semi-final of the 1974 League Cup against Plymouth Argyle, and having keyed myself up to go, I can still remember the sense of disappointment when he couldn't lay his hands on any. What I did not expect then, was that the old man should manage to come up trumps for the final itself. In those days, every club in the country would receive a small allocation of League Cup Final tickets, and via a contact at Exeter City, dad had managed to get his hands on no less than three, and so, on the morning of March 3rd, with my granddad in tow, we made the then four hour trip up to London in the old boy's Morris Minor. Being only nine years old at the time, only flashes of the day remain. I can remember wearing a huge sky blue rosette mum had made, with a mini tin foil trophy fixed to the middle of it, I can remember dad dropping us off close to the ground, before driving off to find somewhere to park, cos granddad had arthritis and couldn't walk far. Then my granddad shepherding me away to safety up by the ground when rival fans, with huge flares, and scarves tied to their wrists, started fighting and throwing bottles, as we waited for dad.

As to the game itself, City, boasting an embarrassment of attacking riches in the form of Lee, Bell, Summerbee, Marsh and Law, were hot favourites and, unsurprisingly, dominated the game from start to finish. However, as had happened the year before in the FA Cup Final, when Leeds United had spent 90 minutes peppering the Sunderland goal, only to then leave empty handed, so we were to endure similar disappointment. A stand-in goalkeeper by the name of Gary Pierce cast in the role of Jim Montgomery, saved anything and everything that came his way. For the record, Kenny Hibbitt put Wolves ahead just before half time, Colin the King equalised on the hour and after Pierce had virtually single handedly kept City out for the remainder of the game, John Richards sneaked a winner with five minutes left. When the final whistle went, I cried tears of rage at the injustice of the result, and working myself up into a fine old tantrum, demanded we leave the ground as the Wolves team went up the steps to receive the Cup, but dad would have none of it. The lifelong character building exercise that is part and parcel of following Manchester City Football Club had begun!

Friendlies: 1893/94 h 1-2; 1899/00 h 1-2; 1976/77 a 2-1, 1995/96 a 1-2; 2004//05 a 3-1, 2006/07 a 2-1

1973 Leeds 1 Wolves 0 FA Cup SF at M/Rd

Some connections: Jimmy Murray, Barry Stobart, Dave Wagstaffe, Steve Daley (below), Manager Mick McCarthy.

Ground: Molineux, (shown late 50's) R/A 61,315 v Liverpool FA Cup 5 1939

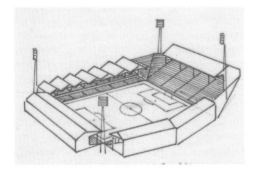

Workington

'The Reds' were formed originally in 1890, but folded in 1911. The new club came into being in 1921, they moved from Lonsdale Park to Borough Park in 1937, and joined the Third Division North in 1951 replacing New Brighton. Amongst others they were managed by Bill Shankly 1954/55, and ex Blues Bill Leivers 1966/67 and Bobby Johnstone 1978 (June to October). After struggling for some time they were voted out of the League in 1977 being replaced by Wimbledon, and joined the Conference.They finished season 2010/11 in the Blue Square Conference North playing in an all red strip.

There was just the one meeting between the teams, in the FA Cup first round in 1910 City winning 2-1 away.

Some connections: John Burridge, Paul Stewart

Friendlies: None

Ground: Borough Park (shown 1950's) R/A 18,628 v Carlisle Div 4 63/64 (promotion clash)

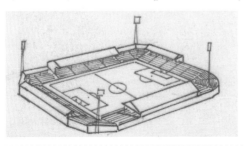

Wrexham

'The Robins' were formed in 1873 by a group of local businessmen, and are the oldest club still in existence in Wales, as in 1876 they were among the founders of the Welsh FA

In 1921 they became amongst the original members of Division Three North, and have generally been a lower league club although they competed in the European Cup Winners' Cup in the seventies to the nineties. Their home has always been the Racecourse Ground, which was developed from a cricket and cycle track area.

The club were relegated from the league in 2008 and finished season 2010/11 in the Blue Square Conference playing in red shirts and white shorts.

In the league the teams met twice in the Second Division in season 1998/99. The first meeting ended in a 0-0 draw at Maine Road and the second was the turning point of the season (NOT the Stoke home game as often reported), and City's fortunes, as a 1-0 win, courtesy of Gerard Wiekens was played out at a windswept and rain soaked Racecourse Ground on December 26th, Boxing Day. Ian Rush played for them that day and it was a rare occasion for him not to score against the Blues.

In the FA Cup third round of 1937 City won 3-1 at the Racecourse.

Friendlies: 1987/88 a 4-1, 1995/96 a (Cliff Sear T/M) 1-6, 2006/07 a 3-3

Some connections: Managers Les McDowall and Ken Barnes, Jeff Whitley, Andy Dibble, Wyn Davies

Wyn Davies

Ground: The Racecourse Ground (shown 2007) R/A: 34,445 v Man U. FA Cup 4 1957

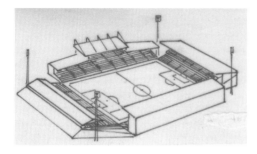

Wycombe Wanderers

'The Chairboys' were first formed in 1884 by a group of furniture trade workers as North Town Wanderers. After a meeting in the Steam Engine pub they became Wycombe Wanderers in 1887. They won the FA Amateur Cup in 1931 and were elected to Division Three in 1993 replacing Halifax Town (Maidstone United were also declared bankrupt) They played at Loakes Park until the move to Adams Park (now renamed The Causeway Stadium) in 1990.

They lost the 2001 FA Cup semi-final 2-1 against Liverpool and finished season 2010/11 in League One being promoted, playing in light and dark blue striped quarter shirts, light blue shorts.

The teams have met just twice in the League in the 1998/99 season in Division Two, Wycombe recording an unlikely double with a 1-0 home win and a 2-1 win at Maine Road, dashing City's hopes of automatic promotion.

Peter P: 10/11/1998 Wycombe 1 City 0 & 24/4/1999 City 1 Wycombe 2

"I was raised in High Wycombe, Buckinghamshire. This wasn't much help, football-wise, in 1969, when I was five and looking for a team. So, what was a boy to do? I wanted one of the glamour teams, one that was winning trophies and was on the telly. There they were: Wembley 1969 – City, in black and red stripes, so that was that.

It was all quite easy then: City were my "big" club and Wycombe Wanderers the team that

I went to watch much more often. They even occupied different footballing worlds – City in Division One and Wycombe in one of the big three amateur leagues, the Isthmian (the other two being the Southern and the Northern Premier in those simple times long before the Conference). In those days, Wycombe were very good, consistently winning or finishing close to the top of the league pulling in crowds of 1000+. In their Oxford Blue and Cambridge Blue kit (you couldn't make it up) my Wycombe heroes were all internationals (Amateur).

Apart from the league, which was regionally-based, the highlights of the season were the FA Amateur Cup with the final at Wembley and the FA Cup proper. Wycombe reached the semi-final of the former in 1972, losing to Enfield at Griffin Park, Brentford. We had regular runs into the main rounds of the FA Cup, the undoubted highlight being the 3rd round match v Middlesbrough (top of Division One under Jack Charlton) in 1975 when 18,000 packed into Loakes Park, with its sloping pitch as famous as Yeovil's. It is no lie to say that Boro were flattered by the 0-0 scoreline (a Boro fan offered to swap scarves with me out of respect for our performance – I declined!). We were the main game on the "Big Match" highlights show on the Sunday lunchtime.

So, life was simple: "big" club and home town club (incidentally, we all had a Scottish club: mine remains Hamilton as that was the name of my school) and never the twain shall meet.........or so I thought!

In season 1998/9 City and Wanderers ended up in the (old) Third Division, the SAME division for the only time in their histories. What happened, what did I do? Pinch myself, close my eyes and hope for the best.

Wycombe-City, Adams Park, Nov.10. Some City fans were panning the smaller clubs in this division on the pages of KotK. Well, we were both there on merit. Score: 1-0 Wycombe.

Return at Maine Road, April 24. City pushing for promotion and Wycombe playing their perennial yo-yo flirting with relegation. Score: 2-1 to Wycombe!

City went up after the great escape against Gillingham, and Wycombe did the double over us. Was I having my cake and eating it too? I'm not sure, but I don't think that I will ever have to work it out again.

Some connections: Martin O'Neill

Martin O'Neill

Western Australia 1969/70 a 1-1,
F.C. Wolfsburg 1983/84 a 6-0
FC Willem 11 1983/84 a 4-3
Waterford United 1984/85 a 4-1
Witton Albion 1987/88 a 3-3

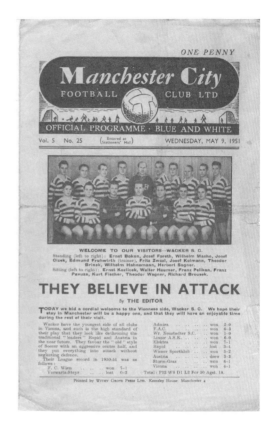

Ground: Adams Park (shown 1998)
R/A 9,250 v Reading 2001/02

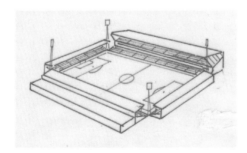

Friendlies:

West Manchester 1891/92 h 2-2; a 3-0; 1892/93
h 2-3; 1894/94 h 5-2; 1895/96 a 2-2; 1896/97 h
5-0 (M/C and Salford Cup semi)
Wellingborough 1900/01 h 10-1
Wuppertal S.V 1936/37 a 1-1
Western Command 1947/48 a 8-2
FC Wacker 1950/51 h 2-1
PSV Wernburg Frankfurt 1953/54 a 1-0
Wuppertal Combined X1 1953/54 a 2-0
S.V. Werder Bremen 1955/56 a 4-1 ; 1956/57 h
4-0, a 6-3; 1979/80 h 4-0, 1981/82 a 0-8
Wacker Insbruck 1960/61 a 4-1,

Y is for York

Just the one 'Y' which takes us over to the delights of the Cathedral City of York...

———◆———

York City

A York City club was formed in 1903 but had no connection with the modern 'Minstermen' who turned up in 1922 playing at Fulfordgate, joining Division Three North in 1929 and moving to Bootham Crescent in 1932.

They hovered between the lower divisions but as a third division club took Newcastle to a replay in the 1955 FA Cup semi-final which if they'd won, meant that they would have faced City at Wembley in the Final that year, with players such as A. Bottom. They've also knocked United out of the League Cup in recent years.

They never recovered from relegation in 1999, dropped out of the league in 2003/04, formed a trust, took on sponsorship from Nestle, renamed their ground Kit-Kat Crescent (really?!) and finished season 2010/11 in the Conference playing in maroon shirts and white shorts.

Post–war: First League meeting was in season 1998/99 when City were at their lowest ebb in the Second Division.

Dave W: 21/11/1973 York 0 City 0

The 1-2 loss in York in December saw the Blues drop to their lowest league position in their history, twelfth, For this game we had seats in the home stand along the side opposite the main stand. This meant having to make our way across the back of their covered 'Kop' and when we were half way across they scored an early goal so it was heads down as it erupted.

City equalised and it looked set for a draw. We came out early with five minutes to go, to sell a few zines at the City end and whilst making our way across the back of their 'Kop' again they inevitably scored again, and we abandoned our selling plan, City fans being disgruntled to say the least. However it all started to turn around, thankfully, in the next game at Wrexham.

Things had picked up by the time of the last game of the season when York were beaten 4-0 at Maine Road, a result which sent the Yorkies down, but confirmed our place in the play offs.

York supporters suffered further ignominy when their coaches were bricked, by City 'fans' as they left Moss Side.

In The League Cup The teams met in the fourth round in November 1974, playing out a dull 0-0 draw in front of 15,360 at Bootham Crescent. York's team included a couple of ex Blues, Phil Burrows and Chris Jones who hadn't made the first team at City.

Dave W: 19/12/1998 York 2 City 1

I took an afternoon off work, losing wages, in Barnsley for the afternoon/evening kick off, and went with a work colleague, a Leeds fan, who naturally took the piss as we struggled to get a result (Leeds won the title that year).

The Blues won the Maine Road replay 4-1 in front of 17,927, with a penalty from Lee and a hat-trick from Marsh who couldn't be bothered in the first game.

Connection: Paul Aimson

Ground : Bootham Crescent (shown 1998)
R/A 28,123 v Huddersfield FA Cup 6 1938

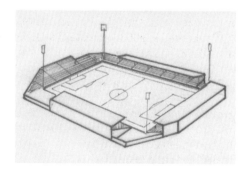

———◆———

Friendlies:
Zwolle 1977/78 a 1-1
Zurich 1933/34 a 3-2

Ex league and current league teams never played competitively

Aberdare Athletic – elected into Division Three South in 1921, failed re-election in 1927.

Aldershot – elected into Division Three South in 1932, folded in 1992, reformed as Alderhot Town, promoted to League Two in 2008, and finished 2010/11 in League Two.

Ashington F.C. – elected into Division Three North in 1921, failed re-election in 1929.

Boston United – promoted to Division Three in 2002, relegated in 2007.

Burton Albion – promoted into League Two in 2009, where they finished in 2011?

Cheltenham Town – promoted to Division Three in 1999, and finished 2011 in League Two.

Dagenham and Redbridge – were relegated back to League Two, where they finished in 2011.

Durham City – elected into Division Three North in 1920, failed re-election in 1928

Exeter City – elected to Division Three in 1920, relegated in 2003, promoted into League Two in 2008, and to League One in 2011. Away friendlies were played in 1990/91 (1-0) and 1996/7 (3-1).

Hereford United – elected into Division Four in 1972 promoted to League Two in 2006, where they finished in 2011. Away friendlies played in 1979/80 (2-1) and 1986 (8-0)

Kidderminster Harriers – promoted into League Two in 2000, relegated in 2005.

Maidstone United – promoted to Division Four in 1988, but folded in 1992. Away friendly played in 1982/83 (4-2)

Morecambe – promoted into League two in 2007, where they finished in 2011.

Merthyr Town – elected to Division Three in 1920, failed re-election in 1930.

M.K.Dons – formed in 2004 after Wimbledon moved to Milton Keynes, finished in League One in 2011.

Nelson – elected into Division Three North in 1921, failed re-election in 1931.

New Brighton – elected into Division Three North in 1923, failed re-election in1951.

Rushden and Diamonds – promoted into Division Three in 2001, relegated in 2006 and expelled from the Blue Square Premier in 2011.

Scarborough – promoted into Division Four in 1987, but were relegated in 1999. Away friendlies played in 1996/97 (2-2) and 1998/99 (4-1).

Stalybridge Celtic – elected into Division Three North in 1921, resigned in 1923. The teams have met in reserve friendly games.

Stevenage Borough – promoted into League One in 2011.

Thames Association – elected into Division Three South in 1930, but didn't seek re-election in 1932

Wigan Borough – founder members of Division Three North in 1921, but dissolved in 1931, when Wigan Athletic were formed.

Yeovil Town – promoted into Division Three in 2003, and finished in League One in 2011.

Contributor Profiles

Roughly In order of appearance!

1) Dave Ansbro: First game at home v Chelsea on 29th March 1948 to celebrate his third birthday (won 1-0). Frank Swift was in goal. Attended continuously ever since. Born Stepping Hill, brought up in Chorlton-cum-Hardy. Lived and worked in Yorkshire since 1963 doing missionary work on Tykes. Every game an 'away' game. The trip to the Faroe Islands an abiding memory. Married to Vron since 1967, now a passionate Blue having been a Stretford End Rag……….she was badly brought up suffering early child abuse! Daughters, Lucy, who lives in London, and Kate, who lives in Singapore, are also true Blues. One year old grandchild, Sophie, is a member of the Singapore branch of the MCFC Supporters Club, a great bunch of Blues who gather regularly on match days at Molly Malone's at all hours of the day and night.

2) Steve Parish: First City game March 1959 home to Newcastle (won 5-1). Born Prestbury (not posh, just a house used during and after the war after Manchester's main maternity hospital St Mary's was bombed). Married to Lynn with 3 grown-up children; son Tom is a regular KOTK seller and writer. A railwayman by trade but a clergyman since 1977, now in Warrington, hence The Blue Vicar. Recently put on again the red & black shirt worn at the European games described within, in honour of Neil Young, one of my favourite players.

3) John Burfield: First game was vs Wolves in the 1974 League Cup final at Wembley, aged 9. Cried so much as City slipped to a travesty of a 2-1 defeat, that parts of North West London became marshland. The exception to the rule that all City fans come from Manchester, grew up in Devon, before eventually winding up in London via Merseyside. Career civil servant, who has written for KOTK for the last 14 years. Married with 2 sons, both of whom were brainwashed at an early age and are season ticket holders at Eastlands as a result. City motto: Expect the worst and anything else is a bonus!

4) Rob Dunford: First game Blackpool home, May 1963 (lost 3-0) fine start! Family football network, Bury and City. Whole existence thenceforth – social contacts, studies, spending, courtship and marriage, wedded and single life, travel, employment and holidays - referred to and organised around City. Subsidiary blue shirt devotions:- Glasgow Rangers, Inter Milan, Swinton R.L., Best moment City v Blackpool August 1998 – seeing fans' loyalty mean that club would never fade. Worst moment leaving Maine Road. Finest fan fun 28 years on the Kippax; with the 'Blueprint' fanzine team and inflatables; City supporters club, Salford Branch 1970's. Defines self by City: Blue to the core

5) Neil Shaw: Lived in Whaley Bridge since 1980, but educated at Marple Ridge alongside the infamous pitch invader John Tague (Bury 1998). Dad attended the 1956 Cup Final so was never given a choice. First game v Chelsea 1-1 April 1971. Season Ticket holder since the halcyon days of Barry Silkman. Evening Manager of a Market Research company based in Hazel Grove. Divorced and once pawned his wedding ring to watch City play at Port Vale. Received nineteen pounds and City lost 2-1.

6) Dave Kelly (Guvnor): First game at home in 1957 aged 5 against Everton, lost 4-2. Went home sad, but that was it, was hooked. Had a season ticket for 30 years, moved to Leicester in 1973. Still goes but cannot get to a lot of games because of work, family ties and stupid KO times. Married to Deborah, three children, Lauren, Joseph & Josh. Josh is City till he dies. Dave is nearly 60 now, but still looks forward to meeting the Rags and beating them, forgive the pun. Proud of his City roots, and proud of all in this book.

7) Colin Savage:
First visit to Maine Road was for Bert Trautmann's testimonial in 1964 but first proper game he remembers was City v QPR in March 1969. Born and brought up in North Manchester, he was brainwashed into being a Blue by his (now sadly departed) mate Ray Chadfield. Got his first season ticket when the North Stand opened and sat just a few rows behind the late, great Helen Turner. Colin's son, who initially showed no signs of being a football fan, got hooked and got him more involved, culminating in his involvement with the Supporters Trust in 2006-7. Now he just watches from his seat in Block 109 but was delighted that his son has seen City win a trophy at Wembley after only 10 years of waiting! He's a freelance IT consultant, which usually means missing out on attending midweek games, but every cloud has a silver lining, which in this case is getting to know a top group of Blues in London.

8) Roger Reade: First game at Maine Road, at the age of 7, v Swansea Town (as they were then called) on November 2nd 1963, when City won 1-0 with an Alan Oakes goal. (Swansea wore tangerine shirts by the way). Born in Northenden, now living in Doncaster, South Yorkshire. Had two spells working for City at Maine Road (1975-1979 and then 1983-86) Was once Secretary and later Chairman of the Junior Blues club (as it was then called) during the 1970's. Previously worked at the PFA but is now at Blackpool F.C. but CTID.

9) Bryan Duffy: Native of Royton, now living in Mold, North Wales. First match City v. Burnley, November 1967, won 4-2. Pretty well lived a full life's experience through following the Blues, from the early heady days as a kid sitting on a barrier, to Skinhead adventures all over the country, right through to responsible father sat in the family stand and beyond. After twenty years in sports management, is now employed as a lecturer and works part time as a fitness instructor. He is a contributor to King of the Kippax and the Mad Hatter 'Internationals' web site.

10) Ted Knott: First Home game v Sunderland April 2nd 1956 (won 4-2). First away game v Blackpool October 19th 1957 (won 5-2).Born and Bred in Withington now living in Droylsden. Married to Margaret, with three grown up children and seven grandchildren. Occupation HGV Driver now retired

11) Steve Mingle: First game Sheff United at home, 16 Sept 1967, won 5-2. Brought up in Ashton-under-Lyne, moved down south after university, lived in Kent for 27 years, then Maidenhead for 5 and counting. Still a season ticket holder (as is partner Lindsey) Thrilled to have some more recent happy memories to go with the dim and distant ones. Rabid collector of City and Frank Sidebottom memorabilia. Author of *Lows, Highs and Balti Pies* and *Allison Wonderland*; hopefully more to come when time permits. Runs a small consultancy in the exciting world of company pensions and share schemes (along with a beleaguered and down-trodden rag, well aware that the times they are a changin'...)

12) Bernd Stefes: Born on September 27th, 1959 in Willich, Germany. City are his favourite club in England and Celtic in Scotland. A regular contributor to the Celtic history magazine 'The Celt' and occasionally to KOTK. Bayer Verdingen and Borussia Moenchengladbach are his teams in Germany. Was a season ticket holder at Verdingen for 29 years, but since they dropped down to the 6th division and B/M moved to a new ground only ever occasionally attends home games. Is also a member of the managing staff at German 5th division women's side SV Lurrip 1910. Was employed in his early years as a postman in the German Civil-Service, but after A levels studied and is now a Bachelor of Arts in pedagogics and politics.

13) John Leigh: From 1966 watched "A" and "B" team games, and the first team training at Cheadle as his school was next door. Graduated to a real home game v. Sheffield Wednesday in November 1968, a 10th birthday treat. Lost 0-1. His mother had to take him as his absent father was a r*d (fireside). Next game was away, a 2-1 win at O/T in 1970. Priority on starting work in 1977 was to find the £8 for a season ticket, just renewed for 35th year. Lives in Hazel Grove, married to Pauline, four kids, two grandchildren, all Blues of course. Author of Bobby Johnstone biography. Says he is privileged to support our unique club, and to know many seriously dedicated fellow-travellers.

14) Tony Petrie Born on Parkfield Street in Moss Side, just five minutes from Maine Road, but moved to Gatley when he discovered all City fans live in Stockport. His dad took Tony to his first game vs Preston in October 1963, lost 2-3. He was only 7 yrs old and too small to see over the crowd and relied on their cheers to tell him if a goal had been scored. He was convinced City had pulled back from 0-3 down to 3-3, but the goal must have been disallowed, and was very upset when Dad told him that City had lost. Dad had a café on Wilmslow Road and many of the players of the day would come into the shop for snacks and meals following training. Married to his first wife, Anna (a United fan) since 1981. Two kids, Charlie (20) and Andrea (16) Has worked as either a civil servant or local govt officer all his life except one year in the real world as a hairdresser.

15) Andrew Heydeman: First game the 1-0 FA Cup quarter final win v Spurs in 1969 with his dad, then they became season ticket holders in the main stand G block for the title chasing 1971/72 season. Moved to Block Y2 of the Platt Lane stand in 1974, still a s/t holder but watched Cup games from the hallowed terraces of the Kippax. His mum joined him as a s/t holder in Platt Lane in the early 80's, then they became s/t holders together on The Kippax from 1985/86, eventually in Block CC of the lower tier of the new Kippax stand. Daughter Zoe, mum Nena and Andrew all sat together as s/t holders in Block 202 of the East Stand at COMS until his mum's sudden and untimely death on February 15th 2011. City will always be an integral part of both Andrew's life and that of his family, encompassing virtually every emotional experience known to humanity. The City memories are endless and very precious to him.

16) Alan Menzies: Born on 2nd June 1935, making him the original grumpy old man. Sheila, his long suffering wife, made Alan a dad to two boys, Alan and Lee. Daughter sweet Lorraine, and husband Nick (an occasional corporate red) have made them proud grandparents to Amy and Emily. Blues all. First game, at Maine Road, was 1946, Frank Swift etc . when City were div 2 champs and until the mid seventies watched City from the Kippax. Met Alan Rowbotham there, and became a lifelong friend. Friends in love with City. In the mid seventies, after a heart attack Alan became a season ticket holder. Was a bus driver guard for MCTD from 1957 until 1977, when, after the heart attack had a year off work then resumed employment as a milkman for Express Dairies. Neil Young and Alan truly share a common bond.

17) Geoff Lord: Is ashamed to say that he can't recall his first match probably because all the family, dad, uncles and cousins were Blues so he knew that his turn would come as he 'grew up' and didn't mither too much. (Nan lived on Maine Rd, opposite the ground and Auntie made half-time butties for the boardroom on match days). When Geoff was at Old Moat Jnrs, the teacher, Mr McVeigh, took the class to an England schoolboys match v West Germany (he thinks); that would have been in 1952/3 and he'd certainly been to Maine Road before that. Born In Prestbury as a war babe and lived until 1965 in Fallowfield. Married to Liz, a life-long Blue who swung the deal by showing him a photo of her holding the 1956 FA Cup in Roy Clarke's garden. Two children and two grandchildren; son Tim never made it to Eastlands but is there in spirit as his name is on the 'Walk of Pride' wall in the players tunnel. Moved away to work in Leicestershire then Chesterfield, Derbyshire as a youth worker then teacher so missed a lot of games during the glory years. Graduated from the Kippax in 1990 and is now a season ticket holder in the peace and quiet of Level 3 , Colin Bell stand. Favourite player of all-time has to be Neil Young for all the obvious reasons plus he came down to Union Chapel on Wilbraham Rd, Fallowfield for a kick-about when Geoff and co were just starting a team but City came up with a better offer. In spite of living away from 'home' for so long Liz and Geoff have done their bit by signing up 14 kids over the years as Junior Blues; several are season card holders, all are long-suffering like the rest of us!

18) Jerry Dowlen: London-based supporter, born 1947, first game West Ham away 1963, (lost 1-6!). Favourite team: 1967-68 Book, Doyle, Oakes, Lee, Summerbee, Bell, Young, etc. Married to Nancy: four children (2 boys, 2 girls). Jerry works in the Lloyd's of London insurance market and he is a committee member of Cray Wanderers FC of the Ryman Premier League,

where the late Keith Riley (died 2005) was a fellow Cray and Man City fan.

19) Sean Riley: First City game, Law Back Heel Derby 1974, aged 9, season ticket holder ever since. Brought up in Failsworth, dad from Ancoats, mam from Collyhurst. Now living in Chadderton, married to City fanatic and New Moston lass,

Jane. Have had the honour and privilege to see every competitive game City have played since April 1989. (long may it continue!). Works in the chemicals and metals refining industry as a project co-ordinator.

20) Ged Isaacs, aged 53, first game Everton at Maine Road 67-68 – won 2-0, United lost 6-3 at West Brom on the same night and it set City up for the title. Current seat East Stand level 2. Lives in Bury and works in Technical support. First read KOTK in 88-89 at

Fratton Park, first contributed 1989, and has done so ever since. Saw an article in Private Eye that took the piss out of Martin Edwards and the rags following his aborted attempt to sell to Michael Knighton. This was published soon after we tonked them 5-1 and the article mentioned the result and also used the phrase "grotty canal-side location" when describing the swamp. I thought this needed a wider audience so I sent copies to all the City fanzines. Dave was the first editor I spoke to and I've been contributing ever since.

21) Rob Holmes: Aged 50. First game taken by his dad, a Scotsman who came down and married a Manchester lass, Spurs home 1969, drew 1-1. He was in the Platt Lane stand and remembers seeing the green grass of the pitch and Pat Jennings pulling the cross bar down to let the ball go over the bar! Lived in Moss Side, now Stockport, where else! Married twice, 3 kids, 22,12, 9, s/t holder in the family stand. A Bank manager, he also enjoys cycling, and holidays abroad.

22) Simon Curtis: First game at home v Arsenal in September 1980, drew 1-1. Born in Douglas, IOM, now living in Lisbon, Portugal with Paula, plus 2 mini citizens, Lucas (7) and Sam (4). Nervous wreck in sky blue since 1973. Contributor to KOTK, Back Page Football, Topical City, MCFC.co.uk, Man City magazine and blogger at Monument City, Down The Kippax Steps and Bifana Bifana. Seen City play through rose tinted spectacles and clenched fingers on too many occasions to remember clearly. From Carlisle to Gelsenkirchen and back. Has own business providing & designing training for companies in Greater Lisbon area.

23) Charlie Hadfield:- Brought up in Withington 1 mile from Maine Road First two games Good Friday and Easter Saturday 1955 both wins in front of 50,000 plus - and thought "this is good" ! Claim to fame:- Grandad was a friend of Horace Barnes (first ever goalscorer at Maine Road). Season Ticket since promotion in 1966 and active Supporters Club member from the same period.

24) John Gwynne: First game City v Pompey September 14th 1957, won 2-1, (Dave Ewing scoring from a wind assisted free-kick from the half way line). Born Shrewsbury, St George's day 1945. Moved north in 1957; lived in Fallowfield, Victoria Park, and, since 1975 Denton. Widowed in 1994, son Andrew is Member of Parliament for the Denton and Reddish constituency. Three grandchildren, two boys, one girl. Former schoolteacher. Sports broadcaster – cricket, darts, football, rugby league. Currently working for Sky Sports – Soccer Saturday. After dinner speaker/MC. Racehorse owner – Gulf Punch – trained by Milton Harris in Wiltshire.

25) Allan Wilson: First game Linfield at Windsor Park ECWC 1970, 2-1 loss. First home game v Spurs 1976, won 2-1 and was amazed to see so many City fans. Born in Belfast was football daft and when he had to pick a team decided if there was a team on the TV that he would stop playing football to watch, that would be his team. It was City, of course. Married with one daughter who was born in the Falklands, and his wife is Zimbabwean. Is a qualified accountant currently working in Nigeria and his family are in Northern Ireland. Has lived all over the World and has always managed to see City at least once a year. A frequent question he gets asked is "City with your accent?" or a variation on the theme. Was once asked this question by a City fan going to Hillsborough: "why not United with your accent?" "Because some of us can think for ourselves" Gave him a big smile and a handshake.

26) Dante Friend: Born St Mary's Manchester overlooking Maine Rd but now lives in Sale. First game home to Leeds, April 1985, lost 2-1. Third generation Blue and daughter is now a fourth generation Blue. Former fanzine editor & contributor and led the Lee-Out campaign "Free The Manchester 30,000". Contributed to local TV and radio on matters concerning City and has work published on City from books (including 'Catch A Falling Star' the Neil Young biography) to magazine articles.

27) Pete Roberts: First City match Plymouth Argyle away (League Cup Semi Final, 1-1 draw) in 1974 when living in the West country. Has lived in Eastbourne in East Sussex for the last twenty four years and been a season ticket holder along with son Tom for twelve. Wracked his brains trying to work out how to get a ticket for the Gillingham Play Off Final at Wembley in 1999 - phoned the ticket office who kindly sold him four tickets on the back of two season tickets. Drives up to every game but it seems a long way back when City lose. Worked at Lloyd's of London insurance market for the last nine years although as of eighteen months ago has been working in Chatham in Kent where Lloyd's have an office - just down the road from Gillingham's Priestfield stadium! Favourite player - Colin Bell.

28) Bill Leivers. Born Bolsover, 29/1/32, Bill signed for City from Chesterfield in November 1953 for £8,000, as a tall strapping defender who didn't stand any messing. He became a regular in 55/56, first as a centre half, then right full-

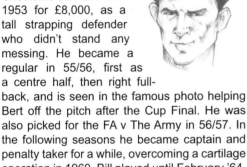

back, and is seen in the famous photo helping Bert off the pitch after the Cup Final. He was also picked for the FA v The Army in 56/57. In the following seasons he became captain and penalty taker for a while, overcoming a cartilage operation in 1960. Bill played until February '64, when he was sold for £1,000, to become player manager at Doncaster, then later Workington, and Cambridge United. After a break from football he went to Chelmsford, then Cambridge City, retiring in 1998, and now lives in St. Austell, Cornwall.

29) Alan Rowbotham: Was born a Blue, lived with his grandad in Droylsden, obviously a Blue, and taken to his first match by his uncle Joe in the 1946/47 season aged eight. Alan, a retired Mechanical Services Engineer, was married with four grown up children. His favourite p l a y e r was Bobby Johnstone, and favourite game was the title clincher at Newcastle in 1968. He was a loyal contributor to KOTK until his untimely death in January 2010.

30) Ian Cunningham: (Pompey fan) first game Pompey v Charlton, in 1953/54 aged eleven. First City game 1955 season v Newcastle FA Cup Final (lost 3-1). Long time KOTK

subscriber. Born Shanklin I.O.W, still there, married to Jean from Harrow, holiday romance turned into useful launch pad for away games. Four grown up girls, one boy died aged 17, 6 grandkids, all boys. 500 times + crossing the Solent and back – 1st Div to 4th and back to Prem. 2 +1 Cup Finals, many more relegations, still works full time for Dulux.

31) Jackie Heap: First match 1959 against Leicester, last match of the season. City had to win to stay up provided Villa didn't win on the same night. City won 3-1 and Villa drew at West Brom. Has been going ever since. First away match was in 60/61 against Blackpool. Biggest disappointment was not being able to go to the European Cup Winners' Cup Final, when pregnant with daughter Sharon. Highlights, to name but a few of many, were being at Rotherham when City gained promotion in 1966, winning the league at Newcastle, and Gillingham (now United and Stoke) at Wembley. Daughter Sharon has been a season ticket holder since she was three and her hubby Carl and two daughters are also season ticket holders.

32) Lyndon Day: First game v Leeds in 1976 – Brian Kidd double in a 2-0 win at Elland Rd. Born in Morecambe, third generation Blue from Cheadle. Twenty odd years as a teacher getting stick from too many ill-informed rag children. Looking forward to giving a load back. Married with one vaguely interested in City daughter who has been told she can marry anyone except a rag. Best City times – the football played by Keegan's men in Div 1 – Ali Benarbia – what a player!

33) Howard Yeats: Has supported City since 1954/55. Married with a grown up son, Robert, also a Blue. Worked mainly as an accounts controller. Did 42 games in the old second division in 65/66 promotion year - as a result of the difficulties encountered in doing that he joined the supporters club and became social secretary and eventually the travel club was formed. During the next 35 years he and Frank Horrocks together with other SC officials expanded the SC to the high level that it became (both membership and finances provided the foundations of the well supported organisation which is still well respected). Howard has a holiday home in Spain but always looks forward to his UK time for SC meetings and matches. He has many friends in the City family at all levels and is one of the most recognised City fans when walking round the stadium.

34) Barry Calder: First game Easter 1963 v Bolton Wanderers at Maine Road, won 2-1. Born St.Mary's Hospital Oxford Road, left M/cr at 18 months, grew up in Warwickshire and Cornwall. Married to Anne, also a Blue. Worked in South Yorkshire for 30+ years, living in Doncaster and Sheffield. Has followed City since watching the 1956 Cup Final on TV, unwittingly continuing the (male) family tradition of supporting City established in the early 1900s. Season ticket holder since 1985. Subscriber and avid reader of KOTK and other fanzines since Thatcher's government started demonising football fans in the 1980's. Now retired, loves spending winters on the new Kippax, and summers at Edgbaston.

35) Graham Corless: A football fan (and Salford Rugby League fan) who at one stage was the original Sean Riley – went to thousands of City games on the trot between the 60's and the 90's – has been to Wembley Stadium more than 250 times (mostly Internationals) and an estimated 1500 (probably more) plus of other games including non league and Scottish throughout the UK – at least four World Cup Finals and numerous club European games. A RECORD BEYOND BELIEF. Single and worked as a surveyor in the house building trade.

36) Peter Price: First game: Charity Shield, 1972, Villa Park (1-0 City, Lee 1 pen). Born in Birmingham (family of Villa fans), raised in High Wycombe, Buckinghamshire. Glory seeking 5 year old adopted City in 1969 – still waiting! Have the "Age 5" red and black shirt (badge in middle) to prove it. Married to Sandy, a Canadian Blue Jays and Maple Leafs fan; 2 children – Melissa (14) who has the shirt and Ben (12), whose allegiance was non-negotiable (see cover of KOTK 135). Very occasional contributor to KOTK, chiefly about the struggles to keep Ben out of the grip of more "glamorous" teams. Head of Geography at Charterhouse in Surrey (teaching far too many misguided boys who think that Chelsea have more history than City), a famous school in the history of football, and pop music.

37) Dave Wallace: First game at home v Preston North End in October 1955, (lost 2-0) aged eleven. Born in Swinton, now living in Leigh, via Sheffield, Doncaster, Hull and Astley. Married to Sue, 4 grown up kids 4 grandkids. Season ticket holder since the seventies. Editor of King Of The Kippax City fanzine from 1988. Seen City play on over 90 European and UK grounds in competitive games. Worked as a mechanical engineering draughtsman/Chief Draughtsman/Project engineer/manager now retired.

Bibliography

A to Z of Manchester Football
– Derek Brandon, Boondoggle Ltd,
London 1978

Big Book Of City – Gary James,
James Ward 2009

Champions – Manchester City 1967/68
– Phil Goldstone/David Saffer, Tempus
2005

Everything Under The Blue Moon -
David Clayton. Mainstream, Edinburgh,
2002

Engineering Archie - Simon Inglis
English Heritage, London, 2005

Farewell To Maine Road – Gary James,
Polar, Leicester, 2002

Football Grounds – Then and Now,
4th edition 2007, Ian Allen Publishing

Football League Tables 1888-2005 –
Michael Robinson, Soccer Books Ltd,
Cleethorpes, 2001

Football Through The Turnstiles
– Brian Tabner, Yore Publications 1992

Living The Dream – Dean Hayes,
90 Minutes Publications, 2004

Lost Football Grounds – Aerofilms
Ian Allen publishing, 2005

Manchester City A Complete Record –
Gary James, Breedon, Derby, 2006

**Manchester City A Complete Record
1887-1987** - Ray Goble, Breedon Books,
Derby, 1987

Manchester A Football History
– Gary James, James Ward 2010

Manchester The Greatest City
– Gary James, Polar, Leicester, 2003

Rothmans Football Yearbook 1996/97

**The Essential History of Manchester
City** – Ian Penney, Headline 2000

The Football Grounds Of Europe -
Simon Inglis, Willow Books 1990

The Football Grounds Of Great Britain
– Simon Inglis, Collins Willow, 1996

The Manchester City Story
– Andrew Ward, Breedon, Derby, 1984

The Pride Of Manchester
– Gary James/Steve Cawley, Polar,
Leicester, 1991

**The Ultimate Directory of English
and Scottish Football League Grounds
1888 to 2005** (2nd edition)
Paul and Shirley Smith. Yore Publications

Trautmann, The Biography
– Alan Rowlands, Breedon Derby 1990

**Wikipedia
Groundtastic
Soccer History
Programme Monthly
Backpass**

Subscribers

1 – 36 All contributors as listed in the profiles section.

Plus :

37) Gary James
38) Nigel Gregory
39) Steve Worthington
40) Howard Croft
41) John Schulman
42) Steve Rigby
43) Tony Ralls
44) David Bookbinder
45) Susan and Zac Bookbinder
46) Barbara Moreton
47) Roland Griffin
48) Sheila and Don Bradley
49) Andrea Griffin
50) Dave Miller
51) Ruth Thorne
52) Ben Kelly
53) Ross Bullock
54) Mark King
55) Roger and Maureen Hewlett
56) Frank Wallace
57) Chris Wallace
58) Chris Deary
59) Colin Brinkley
60) Frank Fariello
61) Carin Bowman
62) Mick Thompson
63) Kevin Bell
64) Ron Bellamy
65) Phil Bellamy
66) Steve and Cath Knott
67) Lee Walker (from Anne Lundy)
68) Mary Donsworth
69) Ellie Wallace
70) Joe Bamford
71) Heather Bamford
72) Chris Williams
73) Raymond Ashton
74) Alex Wallace
75) Steve Pearson
76) Mick Grayson
77) Mark Chidgey
78) Tom Casey
79) Terence Bailey
80) Susan, Jason, Ian Allcroft
81) Chris Howl
82) Mark Barton
83) Les McDonald
84) Phil Neale
85) Roland Foster
86) David Glyn Hall
87) Graham Antony Hall
88) Andrew Zuill
89) Mark Savage
90) Joan Horne
91) Ian Niven
92) Clive Robinson
93) Mark Freeman
94) Gary and Lisa Miller
95) Keith Richardson
96) Ashley Barras
97) Joe and Amy Gregory
98) Kevin Parker
99) Neil Ibbitson
100) Bill Dawson
101) Mark – le- Saint
102) James Whitworth
103) Paul Denny
104) Neil Bailey
105) Derek Price
106) Derek Hodgson
107) Dave Roberts
108) Wayne Norris
109) Gareth Jones
110) Robert Smith
111) Phil Banerjee
112) Louise Deeks
113) Nigel Goldsmith
114) Alun Jones
115) Clive H Foden
116) Eddie Humphrys
117) Glyn Ford
118) Alessandro Ford
119) Hannah Taylor (From Paul Taylor)
120) Isaac Price
121) Joe and Dolores O'Neill
122) Bernard Holland
123) Alex Bozman
124) Peter Thornton

Sportingold Ltd

Leading Auctioneers of Football Memorabilia

EIGHT AUCTIONS PER ANNUM

Forthcoming **Sportingold** Auctions

2011
November 4th (Fri)
December 15th (Thurs)

2012
February 2nd (Thurs)
March 23rd (Fri)
May 11th (Fri)
June 15th (Fri)
July 20th (Fri)
September 14th (Fri)
November 2nd (Fri)
December 13th (Thurs)

SHIRTS
CAPS
MEDALS
BADGES
PHOTOS
CONTRACTS
LETTERS
TICKETS
MENUS
PROGRAMMES AND
EPHEMERA
ACCEPTED FOR ENTRY

Special rates for ex-players

Contact:

Chris Williams
Sportingold Limited

Office: **01494 565921**
Mobile: **07785 290358**

E-mail: info@sportingold.co.uk

Web: www.sportingold.co.uk

Unit 7, Ministry Wharf
Wycombe Road
Saunderton
Bucks HP14 4HW